PUBLIC INSTITUTIONS IN INDIA

This volume presents an analytical appraisal of public
institutions in India. The purpose here is to give a history of
these institutions and to ask what explains their performance
and what might be learnt from their experience. It aims to
provide an account of the modalities through which state
power is exercised and policy enacted.

The study also contributes to debates on institutional change
and reform by bringing more analytical rigour and enlarging
the parameters of the debate. These debates are particularly
important given that Indian economy and society have
changed profoundly in the last decade and a half. Much of
the discussion is on how state institutions like the civil
service, the courts, the police, parliament, and regulatory
institutions will need to be reconfigured to better adapt
to changing circumstances.

W0234499

PUBLIC INSTITUTIONS IN INDIA
Performance and Design

Edited by
Devesh Kapur
and
Pratap Bhanu Mehta

OXFORD
UNIVERSITY PRESS

OXFORD

UNIVERSITY PRESS

Oxford University Press is a department of the University of Oxford.
It furthers the University's objective of excellence in research, scholarship,
and education by publishing worldwide. Oxford is a registered trademark of
Oxford University Press in the UK and in certain other countries

Published in India by
Oxford University Press
22 Workspace, 2nd Floor, 1/22 Asaf Ali Road, New Delhi 110002, India

© Oxford University Press 2005

The moral rights of the authors have been asserted

First Edition published in 2005
Oxford India Paperbacks 2007
27th impression 2025

ISBN-13: 978-0-19-568966-2
ISBN-10: 0-19-568966-6

Typeset in Garamond in 10.5/12
by Excellent Laser Typesetters, Pitampura, Delhi 110 034
Printed in India by Manipal Technologies Limited, Manipal

Contents

Tables and Figures

TABLES

viii • *Tables and Figures*

This is a list of tables/figures.

Introduction

DEVESH KAPUR AND PRATAP BHANU MEHTA

This volume is an analytical study of India's public institutions. It is a commonplace observation that societies are well governed and well organized to the extent that their public institutions can adequately manage the demands imposed upon them. States secure legitimacy and carry out tasks of development through a diverse range of institutions: executives, legislatures, courts, police, regulatory authorities, bureaucracies, commissions of inquiry, independent statutory bodies, development agencies, etc. Sometimes a broad based ideological vision may impart a degree of coherence to this myriad of interlocking institutions, laws, and agencies. But even under the most homogeneous of ideological constellations these institutions often compete with each other, set bounds on what other institutions can do, interpret directives in their own peculiar way and so on. Numerous studies of political and economic development have long recognized the important role the state plays as an autonomous actor—that is, its capacities to often act free from societal constraints and manipulate them and its capacities to set the agenda for society. In recent years, a considerable body of work, drawing from the insights of 'new' institutional economics (North 1990; March and Olsen 1984) and historical institutionalism (Hall 1986; Skocpol 1992), has developed that emphasizes the critical role of institutions and how and why they matter. Institutions perform a variety of functions: they structure incentives for actors within society and provide mechanisms for coordination, sometimes enabling and sometimes impeding it. As anthropologists have long argued, institutions have a considerable impact on processes of recognition and classification that go on in any society (Douglas 1986). In short, most aspects of our collective existence are unintelligible without taking the role institutions play seriously. Institutions can be a focus of study in two ways. Institutions can be used as an explanatory variable that accounts for certain outcomes of interest. For instance, there is a great deal of emphasis in recent literature on the ways in which institutional variation explains phenomenon such as variations in development (North 1990), the capacity of different capitalist systems to adapt to globalization (Hall and Soskice 2001) and so forth. The emphasis here is on delineating mechanisms by which institutions produce particular outcomes. On the other hand, rather than treating institutions as variables that explain other phenomenon, institutions can themselves be the object of explanatory attention. In treating institutions as the *objects* of explanation, the focus is primarily on the ways in which the micro incentives of actors within an institution explain certain features of the institution itself. Although we operate under the assumption that both kinds of interest in institutions have intellectual validity, the analytical focus of this volume is, as we explain later in this Introduction, more on the variables that have affected the performance of different institutions rather than the impact that performance has on broader outcomes.

The focus of this study is, however, *public* institutions in India. By public we mean simply the claim that these institutions represent some aspect of the exercise of state power. Our reasons for focusing on public institutions are simple. First, it is doubtful that anyone would argue that public institutions are unimportant in structuring the ways in which societies function. Second, despite the fact that different paradigms acknowledge the centrality of the state in their explanatory frameworks, there have been few analytical studies of the various institutions that go into the making of the state. With the exception of the literature on central banks and, more recently, on the judiciary, there is little systematic analytical work in developing countries that examine the myriad of institutions—both formal and informal, the commitments to procedures, the formal and informal incentives within state institutions, through which the state is both constituted and enabled to act on the one hand and constrained in its powers and capacities on the other. Third, in the context of the scholarly literature on India, there are almost no studies available of Indian public institutions. For in-stance the last significant analysis of Parliament in India was pub-lished in 1957;[1] the last of the Supreme Court as an institution in 1985 (see references in Mehta's chapter). Most institutions have not even solicited this much attention. This lack of empirical studies on India's public institutions has impeded the investigation of a whole series of important questions: How has the Indian state evolved over the years? What explains the variation in institutional performance of the Indian state? Does the Indian state have the capacity to adapt to a changing economic environment? It is our submission that many of the central questions of India's political economy are unintelligible without a clear grasp of the ways in which India's public institutions function.

Much of this neglect of the diversity of the institutions within the state and the problems specific to each institution has stemmed from certain methodological proclivities. In Marxist-inspired para-digms, the state was simply considered epiphenomenal to social forces. As such its own internal constitution, rules, incentives, and procedures had at best marginal bearing on outcomes. While there is a substantial body of literature that has recognized the state as an important autonomous actor, it treats the 'state' in aggregative and diffuse terms. And although it pays considerable attention to the policy choices that states make and demonstrates that the state can act autonomously from societal forces, the constituent institu-tions of the state itself receive little attention. Economic approaches to the 'state' emphasize the importance of incentive structures that result from over-extended and excessively *dirigiste* states but for the most part their focus has been to demonstrate how the state has been captured by interest groups. The constitutive institutions of the state—particularly in poorer countries—remain for the most part a 'black box'.

While it is by no means our contention that social forces, such as class structure and ethnicity, are not important variables in explaining state performance, a neglect of institutions in their own right seriously impedes a proper understanding of Indian society and politics. This is because it is manifestly the case that given the same background social conditions, and influences, there is consid-erable variation in the performance of different institutions. For

[1] Morris Jones, *Parliament in India*.

instance, some institutions better manage political pressures and societal demands than others. This wide variety in institutional performance itself needs explanation. Second, institutions and institutional capacity can themselves often shape the configuration of social forces. Thus, even if we acknowledge the importance of social forces, there is no intellectual justification for ignoring the study of institutions in their own right.

UNDERSTANDING THE EFFECTIVENESS OF INDIAN INSTITUTIONS

As with many developing countries, the performance of India's public institutions has become a matter of serious concern, both for the quality of the country's democracy and the well being of its people. Although an observer of contemporary India may be tempted to conclude that India's public institutions are severely stressed and weakening, in reality their performance has varied both across institutions and over time. While political mobilization has often exceeded institutionalization, with inimical consequences for governance, there is no simple relationship between the two. Indeed, as the chapter by Kapur in this volume argues, increasing political competition and concomitant political instability has strengthened some aspects of India's institutions while weakening others. For one, India's unhealthy trend at centralization has been reversed, critical for a country as large and heterogeneous as India. Second, the multiplicity of veto points has increased the need for consensus. Thus, as Manor's chapter illustrates, the selection of K. R. Narayanan (and later A. P. J. Abdul Kalam) as India's president, rejuvenated an institution that became moribund as a result of the overwhelming majority of a single party in the electoral college. Third, electoral uncertainty has given a new lease of life to 'referee institutions' like the Election Commission and the Supreme Court.

Despite the general dissatisfaction with India's public institutions, their successes should not be overlooked. When the former Prime Minister Atal Bihari Vajpayee argued in January 2001, 'Not once in the past five decades has the outcome of a single parliamentary election been questioned. Not once during the past thirteen elections has the transfer of power been anything but smooth,' he underscored an uncommon reality: the very fact that the Indian electorate takes this for granted is remarkable by comparison with other poor countries. And in turn, this feat, to a considerable extent, demonstrates the effectiveness of the Election Commission (EC) of India, an autonomous body whose powers are remarkable even by comparison with industrialized democracies. However, even the EC has had its failures—the conduct of deeply flawed elections over the decades in Jammu and Kashmir being the most notorious example. Although the EC was by no means the only constitutional body that failed in that troubled state, the human tragedy and the costs to India of this failure exemplify what is at stake when public institutions fail to discharge their functions.

Our purpose in this volume is to analytically assess the design, performance, and adaptability of the principal institutions of governance in India. The rationale is both simple and complex. Currently, there are three dominant explanations of the Indian state's poor development record. One view argues that the explanation lies in ideologically driven policy choices (Bhagwati 1995; Drèze and Sen 1998). Another strand of literature argues that the failure lies in the capture of state institutions by social forces (Bardhan 1998; Evans 1995; Waterbury 1993). A third view puts the onus on rapid rates of social mobilization which, it contends, have outpaced the capacities of institutions to manage that mobilization (Kohli 1990).

None of these explanations considers institutional design as an important variable. In contrast, this volume takes it to be the case that a critical factor explaining India's modest record in governance and development is the limited effectiveness of its public institutions. But we try and unpack some of the reasons why public institutions are effective or ineffective. We define effectiveness simply in terms of the institution's own stated goals. Our aim here is to improve our understanding of the factors that explain the variance in the effectiveness of public institutions in India through a far ranging assessment of the major institutions of the Indian state. We believe that the choice is particularly apposite for several reasons. First, the performance of public institutions in India has profound consequences for a sixth of humanity. Second, as one of the few non-Western democracies that has sustained itself since it became independent, the performance (or lack thereof) of India's public institutions may offer lessons for the many newly emerging democracies, particularly for lower income countries which, like India, face severe resource constraints. Third, as one of the most socially heterogeneous societies in the world, an analysis of the performance of India's public institutions also has implications for one of the most critical issues facing the global community: how to develop consensual forms of authority and manage competing claims in socially heterogeneous societies. Our aim here is threefold: First, an *analytic* appraisal of these institutions themselves. We stress the term analytic because the purpose is not (except by way of introduction) to give a history of these institutions but to ask what explains their performance and what might be learnt from their experience.

Second, the volume attempts to assess the manner in which these institutions assist, thwart, manipulate, and subvert each other. In this respect, our study will differ from the few recent studies of institutions in India which are largely stand-alone and do not analyse interactions among institutions (Potter 1996; Das 1998). The aim is to give a more complex account of the modalities through which state power is exercised and policy enacted.

In our view, a firmer grasp of this complexity is essential for understanding why policies are chosen, why they fail, and why they succeed. Focusing on just one aspect of government, the executive for example, or on an analytically diffuse category like the 'state' gives at best a partial and at worst a misleading view of the complexity of the policy process. For example almost all the studies of recent economic liberalization in India have focused on the executive and legislative branches of government. There is no study of how the judiciary has adapted to India's integration into the global system. How has the Indian legal system adapted to international norms and treaties? Are activist courts an impediment or a support to liberalization? Do India's legal regime and the manner in which courts interpret property rights deter investment? Or to take another example: it is widely argued in the literature on Indian politics that political conflict has increased. This proposition, while true, hides as much as it reveals. It doesn't quite explore the question—which institutions have been unsuccessful? Have some done relatively better in terms of maintaining their credibility than others? We hope that juxtaposing studies of different institutions in one volume will help us assemble a more nuanced picture.

Third, this study contributes to debates over institutional change and reform that are currently underway in India by bringing more analytical rigour and enlarging the parameters of the debate. These debates are particularly important in light of the fact that both the

Indian economy and Indian society have changed profoundly in the last decades. Much of the literature on India discusses the legislative underpinning of these changes. But there is relatively little discussion of how state institutions like the civil service, the courts, the police, Parliament, and regulatory institutions will need to be reconfigured to better adapt to changing circumstances.

Methodology and Scope

Institutions vary enormously in their forms, functions, and scope. They can be formal and informal, public and private. Our choice of institutions is governed by three criteria. One, to ensure that the scope of this inquiry is manageable, we have limited ourselves to federal institutions. Second, within the large set of federal institutions, the choice of institutions has been driven by their relative importance in the national context (the institutions are listed in the appendix to the Introduction). And third, the institutions have been chosen so as to ensure maximum variation on three dimensions: their goals and functions, their structures (statutory or non-statutory, relative independence) and their effectiveness. Each of the authors was given a set of questions to consider, although some were more relevant than others in particular cases. These questions set a broad framework within which to think the role and performance of key public institutions.

(1) *Initial institutional design*: What features of initial design and founding conditions have had an enduring influence in how these institutions have evolved.

(2) *The links between social and political change and institutional change*: State institutions are embedded in a wider political process. Their evolution and development is the outcome of distributional conflicts both in the society in which they are embedded as well as within and between the institutions themselves. Institutions like all organizations allocate resources and distribute power. And, like states, institutions are not homogeneous entities: they are composed of conflicting views and interests vying for the distribution of power and allocation of resources within institutions. In recent years, for instance, changes in the procedures for making appointments to high courts in India have involved not just a tussle between the executive and judiciary but also conflicts within the judiciary

itself over who had effective control. How do changes in the wider politics of society affect the functioning of institutions? In a democracy, institutions are the mechanisms through which the imperatives of governance and the demands of the governed are sought to be reconciled. How have Indian institutions coped with this interface?

(3) *The 'agency' problem*: An extensive literature on 'agency' has emphasized internal variables ranging from the structure of incentives, patterns of informational flows and mechanisms of information processing, allocation of authority, the differences between *de jure* and de facto authority (arising from lack of information in exercising authority or risk-averseness because of parallel or informal channels of authority), the nature of hierarchies and the degree of decentralization, as critical to understanding organizational performance. Are the internal incentive structures, informal norms, and acquired expertise of India's public institutions adequate to the tasks these institutions set themselves? Or do these procedures thwart the aims of the institution? For example, civil service rules were designed to give officials job security so that they could discharge their responsibilities without fear of retribution by capricious politicians. Over time, this argument was turned on its head; politicians learnt that they could use transfers as an instrument to 'control' individual civil servants. And civil servants found that they could engage in rent seeking behaviour and still not be fired. To take another example, in the case of India's courts, appeal procedures which were instituted to ensure judicial fairness may have ended up making the justice system less able to deliver the clear and decisive judgements that justice might require.

(4) *Rules versus discretion*: The internal constitution of each institution has, in the long run, a significant impact on its performance. An institution is constituted through rules and procedures. These rules govern the *raison d'etre* of institutions, they define their proper aims and functions and set incentives on how decisions within institutions are made. However, most institutions cannot have rules to cover all cases and contingencies; indeed, the discretion for action begins precisely where the rules are silent. This has profound consequences for how institutions are studied. First, institutions cannot be properly appraised only in terms of the formal structure that constitutes them. The ways in which discretionary power is exercised over time and the manner in which these

get congealed into precedents can also make the institutions path-dependent in certain ways.

Second, it is precisely because of the scope of discretion that individuals can matter within institutions. The point is not to have an abstract argument over whether individuals matter or structures dominate. The point is rather to identify precisely the manner in which individuals might matter, the points at which they do, and the institutional resources they can draw on and subvert rules.

Third, the incompleteness of rules means not only that discretionary power can be exercised; it often implies that the rules work at cross purposes. For example, most Indian institutions have elaborate recruitment procedures to ensure full oversight and fulfilment of procedural criteria. Yet the decision on when to make appointments is often left in the hands of the chief executive of the institution. While formally the chief may be constrained by the elaborate consultative mechanisms, he can exercise great power simply by the threat of not making appointments. Such mechanisms are common at all levels of government. What are the ways in which the allocations of powers within institutions work at cross purposes?

(5) *Compatibility of rules with incentives and goals, both within and among institutions*: The 'state' is not a unitary actor. This rather obvious proposition is understood in multiple ways. First, the state has a set of competing aims: growth, redistribution, securing legitimacy. These aims compete with and set limits on each other. Second, these aims are expressed through its various constituent institutions: Parliament for securing representation; executives for formulating policy; judiciary for superintending basic fundamental rights and constitutional values; bureaucracies for executing policy; special commissions for investigations and oversight, and so on. In part, sound policy outcomes depend not just on balancing different ideas but negotiating the competing interests and logic of these different institutions. This division of powers can have both benign and malign effects. On the one hand the multiplicity of institutional forms disperses power, provides a series of checks and balances, and allows for self-correcting mechanisms to come into play. On the other hand, this very complexity can often thwart effective implementation, innovation, and change. How have India's major public institutions negotiated with these competing demands? What are the coordination mechanisms between and among institutions?

(6) *Autonomy and accountability*: What incentive structures govern those who make appointments? What are the systems of evaluation, promotion, and transfers? Presumably the consequences for performance are likely to be different in systems with vertical accountability, wherein staff are evaluated by bureaucratic and political superiors, relative to one where the opinions of peers and clientele also matter. Rules that mandate a strict seniority-based hierarchy in the civil service can circumscribe the scope of politically driven discretion but at the cost of periodic screening for quality. Indeed, narrow 'rule based' appointment criteria are a preferred mechanism for particular bureaucratic groups to capture certain positions. For instance, rules that ensure that the chairman of India's National Human Rights Commission can only be a retired Supreme Court judge or that the members of the Central Vigilance Commission were to be drawn from the IAS, are transparent but nonetheless problematic. When even officials of so-called autonomous institutions seek appointments in a later period of time (especially post-retirement) in other branches of government, does inter-temporal incentive incompatibility effectively destroy the statutory autonomy of those institutions?

(7) *Self-restraint and exit*: Observers of public bureaucracies have long recognized that multiplicity of missions impairs bureaucratic incentives and erodes institutional autonomy. In particular, for 'institutions of restraint' such as the judiciary or statutory bodies like the Election Commission, which are designed to check behaviour that may have short-term payoffs but high long-term costs, their effectiveness has been critically dependent on an adherence to norms of self-restraint themselves. An expansionist agenda erodes self-restraint and resulting bureaucratic propensities tend to drive the institutions towards policy prescriptions designed to give themselves greater prominence, while undermining their effectiveness in their core functions. What explains this endemic feature in India's public institutions?

(8) *Capabilities*: To the extent that discretionary power matters within institutions, the quality of personnel becomes a significant variable in explaining institutional evolution and performance. How do patterns of recruitment impact institutional performance? Are the knowledge resources of institutions commensurate with the tasks entrusted to them? For instance, how do courts assess conflicting claims on environmental damage and legislation or how

does Parliament assess the complexities of financial sector liberalization?

(9) *Organizational culture*: Institutions have cognitive effects. They socialize new recruits; set up formal or informal structures that reward certain ways of seeing the world and doing things; and they allocate resources to producing certain forms of knowledge, privileging some issues over others. They shape views of the world—not only of their members but, through their transactions, those of others. How are world views within institutions constituted? How does the interaction between formal rules and informal norms (organizational culture) strengthen or subvert formal rules?

(10) *Time*: Time is a critically neglected variable in the analytics of institutions. A greater integration with the global economy has accelerated the pace of change that less developed countries (LDCs) are subject to, as impulses are transmitted much faster. Consequently, institutions, which are inherently backward looking, must adapt faster even while they are struggling to take root. But rapid change requires flexibility which in turn requires discretion. This, however, is particularly problematic for public institutions which, in general, are necessarily more rule-bound.

This has profound implications for India's institutions which are almost *sui generis* in their capacity to resist change. In part this is because time is a critical discretionary variable in the hands of both principals and agents in India's institutions. The Indian legal system takes more than a decade-and-a-half to render final verdicts on cases. Government initiatives designated as 'fast track' projects end up being anything but fast, in a system where 'undue haste' is one of the sharpest attacks to suggest gross impropriety. While rent seeking may partly explain the Indian system's legendary delays, multiple hierarchies and veto points, coordination problems, institutional overload (as in the legal system) and more recently, faster rates of political turnover and greater uncertainty about the likely winners in the general elections, also matter to varying extents.

WHAT HAVE WE LEARNT?

While the essays in this volume provide detailed and original insights into the working of the respective institutions they deal with, it might be appropriate at this juncture to indicate some of the results of these inquiries that are of general interest. These results not only shed new light on the Indian state, they open up further questions for study.*

The Central Paradox of the Indian State

One of the things that has struck the authors of this volume the most is the following paradox: those social scientists who study the state from the outside as it were, comment on the fact that the Indian state is captured by a particular configuration of social forces, be it a particular class configuration (Bardhan) or populist pressure (Kohli). Yet those studying public institutions from within are struck by the fact that the Indian state is not only excessively procedural and rule bound, but that these procedures and rules place tangible limits on the capacity of social forces to manipulate the state in their direction. Devesh Kapur's chapter, for instance, highlights the manner in which the labyrinthine character of the state—its complex architecture—makes it very difficult for social groups or particular interests to change its policies and its fundamental character. Bringing about change in the state is difficult, even when there are considerable populist pressures on the state. But the other side of the coin of the inertia of the Indian state is its systemic stability. Our key theoretical contention is that both features are characteristic of the Indian state and are a function of its complicated design. This does not allow for easy change, but it also prevents sudden reversals; it does not impede deterioration of particular institutions, but it always gives opportunities for self-correction. It makes the state less responsive to democratic pressure than we might expect it to be; on the other hand, it also prevents it from collapsing under the weight of the latest political fancy. Arguably, both the poor performance of the Indian state and its surprising resilience in the face of this poor performance are explained by the same factors: the internal institutional complexities of the state. To put it provocatively, what stands in the way of any ideology—be it socialism, communism, fascism, populism, liberalism—overrunning the Indian state, is the number of file notings that even an ideologue will have to wade through. The Indian state has no centre that can be taken over.

One concrete expression of this paradox is the fact that while citizens and social scientists judge the state by its outcomes, the

* The essays of this volume are drawn from the conference on India's Public Institutions at Harvard University, which took place in February 2001.

Indian state itself almost never takes outcomes seriously. Assessing the performance of public institutions requires clear yardsticks and criteria. Indeed, one measure of the performance of any institution is whether it has developed any criteria to assess its own performance. We can then ask both how well the institution has performed with respect to its performance yardsticks and whether these yardsticks are appropriate in the first place. A striking aspect of India's public institutions is the paucity of transparent performance criteria by which to gauge their performance. Indeed, the only criteria of performance seems be procedural fealty—an adherence to formal, incredibly detailed procedures leading to an obsessive focus on process rather than goals. The Indian state, despite so much social pressure, still has an extraordinary ability to inhabit its own virtual world; so long as its procedures are being followed, the consequences matter to it less. Why democratic pressure cannot break this logjam of procedure will require a fuller answer in its own right.

Formal Statutory Design is no Predictor of Performance, but does Predict the Possibility and Capacity for Rejuvenation

The recent literature on central banks and independent judiciaries emphasizes formal statutory independence from the executive and legislature to enable institutions to function more effectively, because they are then shielded from a good deal of political pressure. The studies here suggest that statutory independence is necessary, but certainly insufficient to ensure the real independence of institutions. If anything, as Pratap Bhanu Mehta's chapter on the judiciary demonstrates, the one axiom that is true for institutions is this: power flows to those who choose to exercise it. Judges and courts for example, have creatively reinterpreted their statutory authority and expanded their own power and enhanced their standing vis-à-vis the legislature and executive. On the other hand, Deena Khatkhate's analysis of the Reserve Bank of India shows that institutions abdicate their own power by choosing not to exercise it. A similar case could be made for the finance commissions which as Nirvikar Singh and Govind Rao argue, paid little heed to incentives that would encourage sound fiscal behaviour. However of late, with a fiscal crisis looming, this has begun to change.

*Institutional Trajectories show Strong Path
Dependence Despite Significant Changes
in their External Environment*

Arvind Verma's chapter on the police clearly highlights this reality. The Indian police was created in the late nineteenth century under the British as a police force to maintain law and order, where this was understood largely as preventing violence against the state, rather than crime prevention. Verma argues that from the start therefore, not only was the police deeply implicated in 'politics' but its entire institutional design—from the rules of recruitment, to the location of constabularies—was geared to this end. The net result is not only a deeply politicized police, but also one that is not professionally equipped to take crime prevention and control seriously. This is a historical legacy that has been very difficult to overcome despite massive changes in the external environment under which the police operate.

*Broad Multiple Goals Invariably Reduce Effectiveness;
Relatedly, Institutional Self-abdication is Important
for Long-term Effectiveness*

The weakness of some institutions leads others to expand their role. As Mehta's chapter demonstrates, this is apparent in the case of the Supreme Court stepping into the roles hitherto played by Parliament and the bureaucracy. This, however, leads to a widening agenda. Since the new objectives are additive, and not a substitution for previous objectives or institutional 'missions', it erodes institutional effectiveness. Observers of government bureaucracies have long recognized that multiplicity of missions impairs bureaucratic incentives as well as erodes institutional autonomy.[2] Furthermore, and this is especially the case with 'institutions of restraint', their effectiveness as institutions of restraint is critically dependent on their adhering to a norm of self-restraint themselves. As Arun Agarwal's chapter on the Indian Parliament demonstrates, when Parliament takes on the functions of the executive (such as through direct involvement in local development projects), it inevitably weakens its oversight function.

[2] See Wilson 1989. For a more formal analysis of these results see Dewatripont, Jewitt, and Tirole 1999.

In a similar vein, as the Krishnan and Somanathan chapter demonstrate, the reputational travails of the once-mighty IAS are to a considerable degree the result of that service's lack of self-restraint. As the state expanded, it placed its members in new positions of administrative power, from state-owned enterprises earlier to regulatory boards today. As a result its internal incentives changed from a focus on effective administration to the expansion of the state as an end in itself. In the process, however, it became increasingly exposed to manipulation from its political masters and criticism from civil society. The result has been a loss of its *esprit de corps* and the mystique which was critical to its effectiveness in exercising authority on behalf of the state.

Interlocking Relations among Institutions Means that the Whole may be Considerably Less than the Sum of the Parts

Most institutions depend for their effectiveness on the performance of other institutions. The Indian experience is replete with examples of institutions failing because one critical link in their ties with other institutions was found to be deficient. The deficiency of one institution cannot be removed by focusing only on that institution. One of the weaknesses of attempts at reforming institutions has been the lack of attention to the external links of these institutions (to other institutions). Indeed, this is the point at which the conflict between institutions is most palpable and institutional politics becomes a significant obstacle.

Analytically, there are three different approaches to this problem. One approach is analogous to a chain being as strong as its weakest link. For instance, even if the police force was extremely professional, its long run performance would deteriorate if the prosecutorial arm of the Government of India failed to prosecute criminals, or if delays in the criminal justice system effectively acquitted them. A different insight comes from multiple veto points inherent in multiple institutions. In the Indian case this takes the form less of formal vetoes than the veto inherent in delays. However, we want to emphasize that while delays often have high opportunity costs in economic decisions, they can sometimes have a salubrious effect in derailing controversial political decisions. For instance, the president is obliged to act in accordance with the reconsidered advice given by his council of ministers.[3] But merely returning an initial recommendation or simply not taking any action does make a difference. There is no time limit placed on the president, and as Manor's chapter shows, simply by not acting a president can put a brake, if not choke, constitutionally questionable actions by the government in power.[4] To take another example, more frequent elections have meant that the Election Commission's fiat to all ministries and departments against taking decisions and making announcements that could influence the election process (once elections have been announced), have predictably further squelched the pace of decision making.

Finally, systemic effects depend considerably on coordinating mechanisms. While in some cases, such as the Finance Commission, the statutory mechanisms have been reasonably effective in limiting damaging conflicts between the national and sub-national governments, other institutional coordinating mechanisms such as the civil service or the Cabinet, have deteriorated, although others such as the Inter-State Council are gradually becoming important.

External Oversight and Monitoring is no Substitute for Better Internal Incentives to Improve Performance

Given the long chain of delegation between the voter, elected officials, and public institutions, specialized institutions of accountability are essential monitoring and oversight mechanisms. Unfortunately, these institutions have amplified the focus on process over the achievement of goals. In any public organization, the principals (voters) delegate a task to it but have imperfect information about how the agent is going about the task. For voters, it is very costly to monitor a public institution to ensure that it is going about its

---

[3] As per Article 74 of the Constitution (after its amendment in 1978).

[4] Examples include President Zail Singh's not acting on the controversial Indian Post Office Amendment Bill of 1986; President Shankar Dayal Sharma returning the Representation of the People Ordinance, 1996 and the Constitution (Scheduled Caste) Amendment Ordinance, 1996 on the ground that promulgation of such Ordinances on the eve of elections would not pass the test of 'constitutional propriety'; President Shankar Dayal Sharma's returning of the recommendation of the Cabinet to impose President's Rule in Uttar Pradesh, requesting the Cabinet to reconsider its recommendation.

functions in the way they want, and the institution has better information than anyone else on how good a job it is doing. Given the limited incentives for institutions to monitor themselves, voters create independent monitoring and oversight mechanisms. As the chapters by Agarawal and Das chronicle, India has a variety of such institutions ranging from Parliament to the Comptroller and Auditor General (CAG) and the Central Vigilance Commission (CVC). Yet, judging by the widespread corruption and inefficiency in India's public institutions, the common assumption that increased public scrutiny would improve the performance of public agencies has been belied. There are several reasons that may explain this outcome. For one, the interlinkages among institutions means that the chain is often only as strong as the weakest link. Thus the consumer of the CAG is Parliament and as Agarawal and Kapur and Mehta (2002) argue, the decline of that institution has meant that the CAG reports have little effect. Indeed, as a result the quality of CAG reports itself has declined since its key consumer—Parliament—makes so few demands of it. Similarly, while the CVC has become more powerful as a result of the Supreme Court's interventions, it has to rely on the police to make its case. And, as Verma's chapter argues, the deep politicization of the police has made it one of the worst performing Indian institutions. And even if it has a good case, the long drawn out processes of India's legal system further limit the chances of successful prosecution.

This leads to the second reason why institutions of oversight have had little effect. If the probability of successful prosecution of erring public officials is low, then they are more likely to take risks that offer personal enrichment. Third, as Prendergast (2001) has argued, external monitoring may be no better because outside monitors (independent overseer departments, the Press, and so on) rely on complaints to initiate investigations. This means that the activities of the oversight institutions will be skewed towards cases where complaints are filed. This will invariably be in cases where actions were poorly conceived and/or executed (and even there they may not all be justified), *not the cases where actions promoting the public good were incorrectly not pursued.* In combination, these factors result in an incentive structure that leads to risk averse behaviour on the part of 'good' public officials while having little impact on those pursuing private enrichment opportunities.

Institutional Capabilities and not just Interests
alone are Important for Institutional Performance

One of the striking findings of many of the studies in this volume is that often institutions fail to deliver not because they are captured by particular interests but simply because they lack the capabilities to carry out their functions. Indeed, what is surprising is the extent to which lack of capability can obstruct even the legitimate interests of those who have 'captured' the institution. Many public agencies are notorious for not being able to spend even their budgetary allocations. We contend that such a phenomenon cannot be explained by resorting to 'interests' alone as an explanation. There is also clearly a great mismatch in the burdens a particular institution has to bear and its capacity to do so. Most of our studies find that India's public institutions are on the whole very weak in mobilizing all the available knowledge that is relevant to their functioning. Sometimes this incapacity is simply a result of the lack of resources, sometimes of a lack of self-awareness of what is achievable even within a constrained resource envelope. Most often, however, there is a clear mismatch between the complicated skills required by a particular institution and the skills its personnel actually possess. But often institutional rules themselves preclude capacity building. Some institutions, like the civil service and police, are notoriously incapable of drawing upon the expertise of a wider pool of specialists that are relevant to their functioning. Most Indian public institutions, in their patterns of recruitment and distribution of patronage and power, privilege career government officials. Lateral entry from other professions into significant positions of authority is still relatively rare, and this diminishes the government's capacity to carry out its functions.

Autonomy and Insulation are Necessary but not
Sufficient Conditions for Effective Public Institutions

An important feature of institutional design is autonomy and insulation. The Indian Constitution mandated the creation of an autonomous Union Public Service Commission to ensure that the appointment process was insulated from political pressures. Subsequently, the courts, in a series of rulings, virtually guaranteed public officials from dismissal, arguing that this was necessary to ensure that they could fearlessly discharge their official duties. Over time, both mechanisms became perversely twisted. The bureaucracy, now insulated from being dismissed for discharging its duties, was also insulated from being dismissed for not discharging its duties—indeed, even for egregious violation of the service rules of conduct. Rather than dismissal, the 'transfer raj' became the critical mechanism instrument to rent seeking behaviour (Wade 1985; Banik 2001). The strong statutory protection against dismissal has meant that incompetent officials can only be transferred, never dismissed. The absence of an independent administrative board to manage transfers and the posting of bureaucrats has led to the creation of a 'committed' bureaucracy, but the commitment is to politicians rather than the public good.

The politicians also learnt to pack the autonomous state (subnational) public service commissions with unscrupulous officials. The scandal in 2002 surrounding the Maharashtra and Punjab Public Service Commissions, where allegedly hundreds of government appointments were essentially sold, shows how poor appointments to autonomous institutions can destroy the institutions precisely because the insulation reduces scrutiny.[5] *Quis custodiet ipsos custodes?* Who guards the guardians? And how are they held accountable? And it is here, perhaps, that the Achilles' heel of India's public institutions lies.

Accountability and Corruption

Although corruption in India has been endemic, the scale, scope, and the contemptuous transgression of norms is one of the most severe challenges facing India's public institutions.[6] Corruption,

[5] Allegedly in the course of his tenure of six years, the Chairman of the Punjab Public Service Commission made nearly 3500 appointments 'earning' about Rs 100 crores in the process.

[6] The actions of a Sukh Ram (the Minister for Telecommunications in the Congress-led Rao government) who was caught with crores of rupees in cash in his house and claimed it could have come from anywhere (a new version of manna from heaven) or a Laloo Prasad Yadav (former chief minister of Bihar) whose party workers simply commandeered automobiles from show rooms for his daughter's wedding or Shiv Sena supremo Bal Thackeray's removal of the power minister in the NDA government (Suresh Prabhu) on the grounds that he was too clean, exemplify the brazenness of political corruption.

however, is simply one facet of the inability of India's public institutions to hold public officials accountable for their actions. From the school teachers who do not attend school to the apathy of public officials that results in dismal public health outcomes, from the Orwellian double speak that has led the term 'public servant' to mean that the public is the servant of public officials, the lack of accountability of public officials has inflicted a severe price on the country's citizens.

Even more egregious is the climate of immunity enjoyed by political actors responsible for even the most severe transgressions. This was exemplified by the actions of Indira Gandhi and many others during the Internal State of Emergency that was declared between June 1975 and January 1977. Indeed, it could be argued that this event was a critical juncture and marked a turning point in India's governance. Prior to the Emergency, opposition parties had resorted to extra-Constitutional means to force the government to step down. The Emergency in turn suspended civil liberties and, unsurprisingly, resulted in the sort of egregious acts that are common to authoritarian regimes. The elections of 1977 forced Indira Gandhi out of power and were seen as a vindication of India's democracy. However, neither Indira Gandhi nor most other officials (especially her son Sanjay Gandhi) were held accountable in any meaningful way. Her return to power a few years later established a precedent that the 'people's verdict' was the only legitimate means to hold political actors responsible for their action.

The lack of accountability created severe moral hazard. Any benefits accrued to the transgressor, while the costs, however severe, were faced by the country. Thus, precipitating ethnic violence became a pet option in electoral politics. If there were any upside gains they accrued to the particular political party; the downside costs were socialized. From the 1984 elections following the assassination of Indira Gandhi and the riots orchestrated by the ruling Congress party against the Sikhs, to the actions of the BJP in the demolition of the Babri Masjid in 1992 and more recently the Gujarat riots of 2002, political actors have shown a disdain for the rule of law, arguing that it is the people's verdict that is the final arbiter of accountability. Similarly, while it is widely acknowledged that the manipulation of the Kashmir elections in 1987 precipitated the crisis there and inflicted severe costs, none of the actors responsible for the manipulation of the election has been held accountable.

The causes of this deep malaise are manifold. The growth of corruption was driven in considerable part by the state's ubiquitous role in the economy and the changing contours of political mobilization which spawned patronage politics. Economic liberalization, entailing the state's withdrawal from direct economic activities and a curbing of its discretionary power, was expected to seek a reduction in the rent seeking activities of state officials. This does not seem to have happened for several reasons. For one, despite the state's withdrawal from economic activity, its role in a wide range of non-economic activities related to social, health, and environmental issues—from food safety to car inspections, worker safety or building regulations—has continued, if not actually increased. Second, economic liberalization has raised material expectations as a result of liberalization. These expectations of 'minimum needs' (especially in consumer durables) have risen much faster than commensurate increases in income in the public sector at large, adversely affecting the *demand* side of corruption. Third, there has been a marked shift in the norms not just in political life but in society (and voters) as well. Corruption is not simply a product of institutional incentives; it also reflects the ethos of society. The norms of both social and political tolerance of corruption have dramatically changed, and India's social heterogeneity, by providing fertile ground for political entrepreneurs, has exacerbated the problem.

Democratic societies normally have recourse to a range of accountability mechanisms. Elections are clearly one of the most important. These appear to have made little difference, in part because the basis of electoral politics has shifted to ethnic and caste politics where performance counts for little. At the micro-level, accountability is impeded by the lack of information, a result of the lack of the right to information. Knowledge is power and secrecy is the greatest bulwark against accountability. Some states have begun to pass legislation on the right to information that forces local officials to allow the public access to data about how public funds are being used. However, it is too early to judge the results.

The poor accountability of state public institutions extends to, and is amplified by, institutions of civil society. From sports bodies to the Bar Council of India, the Medical Council of India, business associations, or the Institution of Engineers, a whole range of meso-level institutions constituting civil society exhibit a pathology similar to that of public institutions. These institutions can have a significant effect on governance, by setting and enforcing standards and norms, resolving disputes and professional misconduct, etc. Their weakness spills over to state organs, which are already over-burdened and dysfunctional. Another important mechanism, the media, although ostensibly free, are compromised by their links to the very businesses and politicians they are supposed to monitor, and as a result have undermined their watchdog role. The problems of governance and poor accountability are not confined to state institutions and each reinforces the other.

Instead of enforcing accountability the Indian state has put in ever more intricate and suffocating rules that circumscribe operational autonomy and discretion of public officials. In the process, it appears to have the worst of both worlds. The few public officials with initiative have been stymied while the brazenly corrupt have prospered. And one implication, as Sanjay Reddy's chapter seems to suggest, is that trust in the Indian state has been the largest casualty. The resulting cynicism has meant that virtually all actions undertaken by public officials are deemed to be driven by venal private motives—and vague charges of corruption are hurled on any action. The credibility of state organs has suffered severely and these negative reputational externalities have made it much more difficult to attract capable individuals. The result—exemplified even in supposedly sacrosanct areas like defence purchases of major capital equipment—has paralysed decision-making.

Constitutions are necessarily operated by human beings and thus are no better than the men and the women who handle it. B. R. Ambedkar, the framer of the Indian Constitution had warned the Constituent Assembly: 'The working of the Constitution does not depend wholly upon the nature of the Constitution. The Constitution can provide only the organs of state such as the Legislature, the Executive and the Judiciary. The factors on which the working of those organs of the state depend are the people and the political parties they will set up as their instruments to carry out their wishes and their politics. Who can say how the people of India and their parties will behave?' He concluded: 'If the Constitution of India gets derailed, the reason will not be that we had a bad Constitution. What we will have to say is that man was vile.'

Ambedkar's sombre observations stand as a warning to those inclined to quick technical fixes for improving the effectiveness of India's public institutions. We hope the chapters in this volume will demonstrate, in careful analytical detail, the ways in which India's public institutions function. The general insights we have listed above are only indicative of the kind of results that the chapters contain. But if this volume convincingly demonstrates that the Indian state is not a black box, but a complex weave of overlapping and conflicting institutions, each with its own limitations of design and incentives, it will have served its purpose.

References

Banik, Dan (2001), 'The Transfer Raj: Indian Civil Servants on the Move', *European Journal of Development Research*, vol. 13, no. 1, pp. 104–32.

Bardhan, Pranab (1998), *The Political Economy of Development in India*, New Delhi: Oxford University Press.

Bhagwati, Jagdish (1995), *India in Transition*, Oxford: Clarendon Press.

Das, S. K. (1998), *Civil Service Reform and Structural Adjustment*, New Delhi: Oxford University Press.

Dewatripont, M., I. Jewitt, and J. Tirole (1999), 'The Economics of Career Concerns, Part II. Application to Missions and Accountability of Government Agencies', *The Review of Economic Studies*, vol. 66, no. 1, January, pp. 199–217.

Douglas, Mary (1986) *How Institutions Think*, Syracuse, NY: Syracuse University Press.

Drèze, Jean and Amartya Sen (1998), *India: Economic Development and Social Opportunity*, Delhi: Oxford University Press.

Evans, Peter (1995), *Embedded Autonomy: States and Industrial Transformation*, Princeton: Princeton University Press.

Hall, Peter (1986), *Governing the Economy: The Politics of State Intervention in Britain and France*, Cambridge: Polity Press.

Hall, Peter and David Soskice (eds) (2001), *Varieties of Capitalism*, New York: Oxford University Press.

Kapur, Devesh and Pratap Mehta (2002), 'India's Parliament as an Institution of Accountability', Report prepared for the Inter-Parliamentary Union, Geneva.

Kohli, Atul (1990), *Democracy and Discontent: India's Growing Crisis of Governability*, Cambridge: Cambridge University Press.

March, James and Johan Olsen (1984), 'The New Institutionalism: Organizational Factors in Political Life', *American Political Science Review*, vol. 78, pp. 734–49.

Morris-Jones, W. H. (1957), *Parliament in India:* Philadelphia: University of Pennsylvania.

North, Douglass (1990), *Institutions, Institutional Change and Economic Performance*, Cambridge: Cambridge University Press.

Potter, David (1996), *India's Political Administrators: From ICS to IAS*, Delhi: Oxford University Press.

Prendergast, Canice (2001), 'Selection and Oversight in the Public Sector', NBER Working Paper no. 8664, December.

Skocpol, Theda (1992), *Protecting Soldiers and Mothers: The Political Origins of Social Policy in the United States*, Cambridge: Harvard University Press.

Wade, Robert (1985), 'Why the Indian State is not better at Development', *World Development*, vol. 13, no. 4, pp. 467–97.

Waterbury, John (1993), *Exposed to Innumerable Delusions: Public Enterprise and State Power in Egypt, India, Mexico and Turkey*, New York: Cambridge University Press.

Weaver, Kent R., and Bert Rockman (eds) (1993), *Do Institutions matter? Government Capabilities in the United States and Abroad*, Washington D.C.: The Brookings Institution.

Wilson, James Q. (1989), *Bureaucracy: What Government Agencies do and Why They Do It*, New York: Basic Books.

APPENDIX I

Institutions Included in the Study

The following is a brief outline of the institutions we plan to examine in this project. For analytical purposes we have grouped them into three categories by their principal functions: institutions of oversight and restraint; coordination institutions; and economic institutions.

Institutions of Oversight and Restraint

1. *Parliament*: The evolution of parliamentary norms and practices and its performance as an institution is a vast subject. We propose, for the purposes of this study, to treat Parliament as an institution of oversight. How has the oversight function of Parliament coped with the greater turnover, increasing fractiousness, more fluid party affiliations and party alliances, even as the complexity of issues placed before it has increased? In particular, how the system of parliamentary committees has been subverted and the impact this has on oversight and appraisal of legislation.

2. *The Presidency*: In India's parliamentary system, the president while nominally the head of state, is a figurehead position. However, increasing governmental instability has increased the salience of this institution, and not surprisingly, controversies around it have grown as well.

3. *Comptroller and Auditor General (CAG) and the Central Bureau of Investigation (CBI)*: The CAG's independent audit function was designed to provide the necessary transparency essential to check acts of financial commission and commission by public entities and officials. Why, despite its statutory independence and countless reports, has it been so ineffective? The CBI was created to investigate corruption involving all state functionaries. As the principal investigative arm of the law its success or failures have had a profound influence in structuring the incentives for public officials. Its low rates of success (a conviction rate of about four per cent in recent years) in prosecuting corruption cases for example is not only an investigative failure, but has arguably contributed to undermining the legitimacy of the Indian state itself.

4. *Judiciary*: Arguably one of the most powerful branches of government, its role has been transformed considerably over time. Its interventions are having far reaching effects, not only in areas of constitutional protection of rights but also a wide range of policy issues like the environment, property rights, development initiatives, and so on. At the same time even as the scope of judicial activism and intervention has burgeoned, its effectiveness in the speed of dispensation of justice remains dismal and the quality of its rulings problematic. What are the conditions under which judiciaries become more active and are seen to usurp executive prerogative?

In what areas of the law has the judiciary been more effective? What are the ramifications of changes in the internal organization and procedure of the judiciary for a more efficient dispensation of justice?

5. *Police*: The most visible face of the state for an average citizen is perhaps also one of the most dysfunctional organs of the state. Why has democratic pressure not resulted in greater change?

Institutions of Coordination

6. *Civil Service*: Although most studies on India's civil service examine its developmental record, the crucial coordination role of the civil service in a federal system, both along vertical hierarchies as well as across different administrative hierarchies at different levels of government, has not received much attention.

Economic Institutions

7. *Reserve Bank of India (RBI)*: For a central bank with limited independence, the RBI has managed Indian monetary and exchange-rate policy with considerable success in recent years, especially given the excesses of India's fiscal policies. On the other hand its performance in the financial sector has been undermined by its multiple regulatory, oversight and supervisory, and ownership functions.

8. *Finance Commission*: Every five years, a constitutionally mandated Finance Commission is constituted to make recommendations with regard to the incidence of taxation and the sharing of tax revenues between the Centre and the states. Its recommendations are crucial to the health of India's fiscal federalism, as well as in accommodating growing pressures arising from increasing disparities between different states of the Indian federation.

9. *New Regulatory Institutions: Telecommunications Regulatory Authority of India (TRAI) and Securities and Exchange Board of India (SEBI)*: As a result of growing market liberalization, the Indian state has been moving from direct production to regulation. TRAI and SEBI are the vanguards of new regulatory institutions that are attempting to balance competing interests of private capital (both domestic and government), state-owned enterprises, the state, and consumers. Their performance has significant implications for the design of other regulatory institutions.

10. *Non-Statutory Institutions: Pay Commission*: The Indian state has a remarkable capacity to set up a large number of independent commissions to diffuse contentious issues, most of whose findings gather dust. In the case of the Pay Commission, however, its recommendations were partially accepted—with egregious fiscal consequences. This case study would help understand why some non-statutory commissions have a greater impact than others.

11. *Institutional Performance and the Public Imagination*: What is the relationship between the people and public institutions in a mass democracy? This question involves a variety of issues. First, how do the people view their institutions, how does public pressure come to be exercised upon institutions, given the vagueness of aggregate measures of public opinion? What are the criteria by which institutions are judged to be performing well? To what degree are institutions seen as amenable to public pressure and to what degree immune from it? What are the ways in which the people think of institutions as their own? How is the 'legitimacy' of institutions established?

1
Explaining Democratic Durability and Economic Performance
The Role of India's Institutions

DEVESH KAPUR

THE INDIAN PARADOX

Political Science has long been perplexed by India's exceptionalism in light of many of its conventional truisms. Indian democracy developed contrary to some of the key propositions on the prerequisites for successful democratic forms of government, presented by liberal political theorists as far back as John Stuart Mill—a society that was overwhelmingly rural, largely illiterate and exceedingly poor, lacked a bourgeoisie and a middle-class, and was extremely heterogenous. For long, India's majoritarian democracy was a significant 'deviant' case for consociational (power-sharing) theory (Lijphart 1997).[1] And Myron Weiner, in an elegant essay, shed light on 'The Indian Paradox'—a society racked by violent conflict even as its democratic politics endure (Weiner 1989). More recently, an extensive empirical analysis of the relationship between democracy and development in 135 countries again found that India was a major outlier, given its low levels of income and literacy and high

---

[1] Lijphart 'fits' India to his consociational model by an expansive view of consociationalism and a selective interpretation of India's realities (Wilkinson 2000).

levels of ethnic and religious unrest: 'India was predicted as dicta-
torship during the entire period...the odds against democracy in
India were extremely high' (Przeworski et. al. 2000: 83, 87).
India's democracy also confounds much of the received wisdom
on electoral politics in democracies. Voter participation in established Organization of Economic Cooperation and Development
(OECD) democracies has declined in recent years—and in part this
has been explained by the weakening of political parties. In India
parties as institutions have virtually collapsed (exemplified by the
severe organizational weakness of the Congress party), plagued by
intrigue, infighting, and factionalization. And while these have been
time-honoured traditions of Indian political parties, they have become particularly severe in recent years (Kapur 2000). Despite this
weakness of political parties, and contrary to trends in OECD
countries, voter turnout rates in India have increased from around
45 per cent in the first two general elections to 60 per cent in the
last two. And while voter turnout rates in OECD countries are
generally higher for higher income and more educated groups, there
is little difference in India. Furthermore, while incumbency in
OECD democracies confers an electoral advantage, the opposite is
the case in India where the probability of re-election is less than
half.

India also appears to be somewhat of an outlier in the burgeoning
new political economy literature. A number of studies find that
trade openness is positively and strongly correlated with the size
of the public sector (Cameron 1978; Rodrik 1998). For much of its
history India was a closed economy with a large public sector. In
the 1990s, it liberalized its trade regime even as it began to gradually
downsize the public sector. Another set of studies link the type of
political regime with the type of trade regime and predict that
democracies are more likely to support trade liberalization (Kubota
and Milner 1999). Again, for much of its history, the Indian experience belied this proposition.

This chapter examines another paradox posed by the Indian
experience: *more rapid and less volatile growth despite greater governmental instability* in recent years both temporally (relative to its
own past) and cross-sectionally (relative to other countries). Most
analysts have focused on the factors that explain the limited upside
in India's growth. But why has India not suffered severe political
and economic downsides similar to those experienced by other low

and middle-income countries? The paradox of India's higher growth rates and lower growth volatility relative both to its past record and countries in similar situations has emerged along with the deterioration of political stability. Political competition has intensified (more parties and greater frequency of elections), average tenure of governments at the Centre has declined, and political violence remains at high levels. How does one explain this paradox of substantially improved economic performance amidst a substantial decline in political stability?

This chapter argues that while economic reforms increased growth on the upside in India, the limited consequences of government instability are due to India's polymorphic institutions, which have provided a kind of institutional safety net that has limited the downside and given it a systemic resilience. India has found it hard to institutionalize the many organizational forms it creates, be it state institutions, non-profits and non-governmental organizations, think-tanks, and academic institutions or private firms. However, the country finds it easier to create new organizations which weave new strands even as earlier institutional strands fray. At the same time the process is not Schumpetarian. There are frequent gusts of the winds of creation, but the winds of destruction rarely blow. Thus entry is (relatively) easy, while exit seems well nigh impossible. What this means is that the very reasons why, despite India's greater political instabilities, the downside is limited, also gives rise to those very political instabilities in the first place, and in turn limits the upside as well.

In examining the Indian experience, this chapter confirms earlier work that economic agents are less risk averse or more tolerant about political instability in democracies than in authoritarian systems. The consequences of political instability depend critically on the reasons and the context in which it occurs. India, Italy, and Israel stand in contrast to seemingly stable China and Mexico (pre mid-1990s). A Falung Gong rally in China or the Chiapas uprising in the mid-1990s in Mexico were viewed as potentially serious concerns in the two countries. In contrast, the vast array of civil society groups in India means that the addition of yet another cult or religious organization would hardly be noticed in India. And for a country confronting a 'million mutinies', in Naipaul's evocative phrase, some much more virulent than Chiapas, a Chiapas uprising would be a storm in a tea cup. In the Indian case, there is at least some reason to believe that its greater political instability is a result of flowering of democracy as hitherto marginalized social groups begin to exercise a degree of the rights conferred to them by the democratic system.

But what causal mechanisms underlie the relationship between instability in a democratic context and its economic effects? This chapter argues that economic agents have greater confidence in the systemic stability of democracies despite overt manifestations of political instability, because democracies are more likely to develop a broad and deep matrix of relatively autonomous public institutions—institutions of restraint, regulation, coordination, and adjudication. There are councils, boards, tribunals, commissions, and a range of statutory and non-statutory institutions, and public and private institutions, that weave a 'thick' institutional web. The diversity of a country's institutional portfolio may reduce both risk (to systemic stability) and return (rates of economic growth). The presence of numerous autonomous public institutions, reduces the covariance risk across institutions, thereby minimizing systemic risk. At the same time multiple institutional veto points slow decision making and coordination failures are greater. I argue that these features of India's institutional landscape have given India a systemic resilience that weakens the downside risks of political instability—political volatility neither results in economic volatility nor amplifies into systemic collapse.

GROWTH AND INSTABILITY IN INDIA

Between 1951–89 (roughly four decades), India had nine general elections—roughly one every four-and-half years. Between 1989 and 2004, it had five—one approximately every three years. During this period, India has had seven prime ministers (Table 1.1). When a new government took over in October 1999, it was the fifth in four years. It was the first time since 1971 that an incumbent prime minister returned to power, and just the second time since then that the incumbent party returned to power.[2] No single party has won an overall majority since 1984, when the sympathy factor following Indira Gandhi's assassination returned the Congress party to power with a large majority. Since then the Congress party has

[2] In 1984 the Congress returned to power after the assassination of Indira Gandhi, with Rajiv Gandhi as prime minister.

been reduced from a long-time dominant position in Parliament to a minority. The National Democratic Alliance (NDA) government led by Atal Bihari Vajpayee has been the only non-Congress government (of seven) to serve out its full term. Paralleling the high frequency of government turnovers at both the Centre and in the states is the low incumbency rate of elected representatives more generally; roughly half of all incumbents lose in an election.

TABLE 1.1
Governmental turnover in India (1989–99)

Lok Sabha/General election	Duration	No. of governments
9th	15 months	2
10th	5 years	1
11th	18.5 months	3
12th	13 months	1
13th	Formed October 1999	1

The foremost reason for political instability is the collapse of the once dominant Congress. Congress spearheaded India's independence struggle and governed the country almost uninterrupted for most of its first 40 years of existence as a sovereign state. There are more than 40 parties in the Indian Parliament, most of which are quite weak. The current ruling coalition in India has twenty-four parties. With political parties serving as vehicles of individual ambition rather than ideological or programmatic goals, the resulting political promiscuity has led to a landscape in which Indian political parties form a constantly shifting kaleidoscope of fission and fusion. Although it has been argued that the system is moving towards a two-coalition system at the Centre (and two contenders at the state level), the composition of each is constantly changing due to party hopping by individual leaders and coalition hopping by parties. The result is endemic political instability in both the Centre and in states.

Other assessments that include broader criteria also raise questions about India's stability. An analysis of governance indices using the Polity IV Database and the Freedom House Surveys shows increasing volatility in India's governance indicators (Table 1.2), and in particular in the 1990s.

TABLE 1.2
India's comparative political stability[3]

Time period	India's rank by volatility of		
	Polity IV democracy index	Freedom House political rights index	Freedom House civil liberties index
1950–99	14 (36)		
1975–99	21 (52)	35 (95)*	52 (94)*
1991–9	43 (87)	82 (111)**	54 (111)**

* Time Period is from 1975–2001; ** Time Period is from 1991–2001.
Figures in ( ) are the number of countries on which data was available in the time period.

A recent analysis of 160 countries assessing their prospects classified India (along with 46 other countries including China, Russia, and Turkey) as facing moderate risk of instability. Of the 160 countries assessed, 33 were 'high risk' from a stability viewpoint (Gurr et. al. 2001).[4] The assessment was based on six criteria: avoidance of recent armed conflict; successful management of movements for self-determination; maintained stable and democratic institutions; access to substantial material resources; and free of serious threats from external environment. India's Kashmir imbroglio, ongoing self-determination conflicts (especially in the North-East), low levels of material resources, repeated changes in government, and a poor (both materially and conflict-prone) neighbourhood gave it low scores; it scored better, however, on the third criterion—durable, democratic political institutions.

Nonetheless, despite greater political volatility, economic growth has increased in recent years even as growth volatility has declined. India's per capita growth in the last two decades (1980s–90s) has been about three times its growth in its first three decades (1950s–70s), moving from 1.3 per cent to 4 per cent annually. India's average annual rate of growth of GDP during 1950–80 was anaemic at 3.5 per cent. During 1980–90, the rate of growth increased to 5.8 per cent and was exceeded by only eight out of 113 countries. In

[3] Political stability over a period of time is quantified by the standard deviation of the yearly values of the indices over a given period. The output is the rank of India over the total size of the sample pool.

[4] All but six of these are in Africa and the rest in Asia. Two of the six are in India's neighbourhood—Afghanistan and Pakistan.

the last decade (1990–9), India's rate of growth further increased to 6.1 per cent and was exceeded by only nine out of 131 countries.[5] In relative terms as well, it is only in the last two decades of the twentieth century that India's growth performance has been significantly above world averages (Table 1.3). Despite the downturn in the last three years (2000–2), India's growth rate continues to be above world average.

TABLE 1.3

Output growth: India and the world economy

(Annual average)

	1900–50	1950–60	1960–70	1970–80	1980–90	1990–9
World	2.1	4.2	5.3	3.6	3.2	2.5
India	0.5–1.0	3.7	3.6	2.8	5.8	6.1
India (population growth rate)	1.0	2.3	2.3	2.3	2.1	1.8

Source: Joshi and Little, Bradford De Long, Angus Maddison.

Furthermore, India's growth volatility has declined as well. Growth in the last two decades as well as the 1990s has been the least volatile in the twentieth century (Table 1.4). This decline in volatility cannot be explained simply by the underlying structural change in the economy whereby the share of the more volatile component of GDP (the primary sector) declined relative to the less volatile components (secondary and tertiary sectors). Each of the components of GDP exhibited either a decline in volatility or no change, with the primary sector showing the biggest decline. Independent India has seen only four years of negative growth of which one occurred in the first period (1950–1 to 1964–5), three in the second period (1965–6 to 1979–80) and none in the last two decades (Sivasubramonian 2000).[6] The last period is most interesting since it was in this period that LDCs, beset by a spate of debt and financial

[5] *World Development Report 2000–1*, Table 11. The comparator countries are those with a population greater than one million. Over the entire period (1980–99), India ranks seventh after China, South Korea, Singapore, Botswana, Vietnam, and Thailand.

[6] Even in the 1991 crisis, India's growth in 1991–2 was 0.8 per cent. It exceeded 5 per cent in both the previous year and the following year.

crisis, had the most volatile growth rates, and India itself faced greater political instability.

TABLE 1.4
India: coefficient of variation of mean GDP growth rates

1950–1 to 1964–5	1965–6 to 1979–80	1980–1 to 1999–2000	1991–2 to 1999–2000	1950–1 to 1999–2000
0.7	1.2	0.4	0.4	0.7

Source: Sivasubramonian, Table 9.4.

India's growth has been one of the least volatile among LDCs. Figure 1.1 compares India's growth volatility (as measured by the variances of GDP growth) with the average of the volatility of growth of low and middle-income countries (LMCs), as well as the average of all countries ('the world'). It is evident that India's growth volatility has been comparatively low.

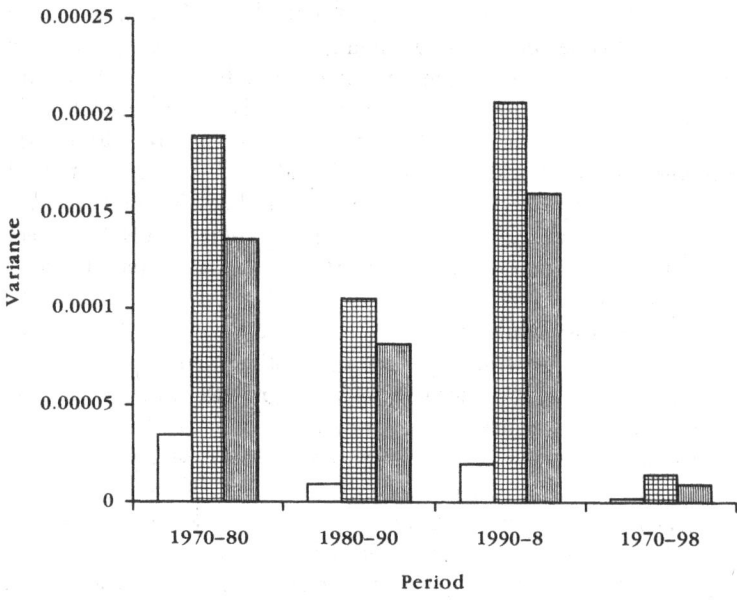

FIGURE 1.1: Comparative volatility of growth

At face value, this seems puzzling given the conventional wisdom on the relationship between growth and political stability (discussed in the next section). On the other hand, it could be argued that there really isn't any puzzle. There are many conventional factors that explain India's low growth volatility. Both its size and policy choices reduce its trade to GDP ratio and hence its exposure to external trade shocks. Its conservative policies on capital account openness and relatively high remittances from its diaspora reduce its exposure to capital flow volatility. Its political regime may also be a factor—democracies have more stable growth rates. Yet, as Table 1.2 indicates, India's political stability is more volatile relative to other countries in recent years.

As for India's higher growth rates there are many conventional factors here as well: a more market-friendly policy regime, greater openness of the external sector, a demographic bulge resulting in an increase in the working age population, better terms of trade (especially relative to the 1970s but not earlier periods), debt-driven growth, both internal and external (especially in the 1980s), and good luck (especially in the IT sector in the 1990s (Kapur 2002)). It could also be the case that India is simply harvesting with a lag the institutional investments of earlier decades. While the earlier languid growth masked the slow but steady establishment of its institutional base, the period of rapid growth could be masking the converse—a steady depreciation of India's institutional assets with foreboding lagged consequences down the line. It can be further argued that in the absence of instability, growth would have been substantially higher, approaching the levels of China, the most obvious benchmark.

Nonetheless, while there are several conventional factors that explain India's growth, there are many other elements in the burgeoning laundry list of factors explaining growth (more than eighty at last count) that are less favourable to India. India's economy continues to be less open than those of Latin America and East Asia, whether in trade, investment, or capital flows. It continues to be, in the words of the head of its central bank, 'one of the least globalized among the major countries'.[7] Corruption levels continue to be high (Transparency International 2000) and India's

[7] Bimal Jalan, Governor, Reserve Bank of India, 'Address at the Thirty-Sixth Convocation of the Indian Statistical Institute,' 15 January 2002.

administrative capabilities are only average relative to other big developing countries (World Bank 2000). It suffers from a poor neighbourhood effect—the political stability and economic performance of other South Asian countries has been considerably worse in recent years—which has shown to be costly for growth (Ades and Chua 1997). Its levels of illiteracy remain high and it languishes on human development indicator rankings (UNDP 2001). It ranks low on infrastructure development. All of these factors have been cited in other contexts as 'explaining' low growth. And finally, while, as noted above, India's terms of trade were relatively more favourable in the last two decades, it suffered from a host of other shocks, ranging from the plague to unprecedented (in post-independence India) religious riots, debilitating guerrilla wars in Kashmir and its north-east border, and international sanctions following its nuclear tests. Indeed, in 1998 and 1999, India had prolonged periods of political uncertainty and a conflict susceptible to escalation on its western border. For more than half of 1999, India was run by a caretaker government, and prospects of a prolonged spell of political uncertainty loomed large. It faced international sanctions amidst the international financial crisis raging at the time. Yet despite all this, India's economic growth remained quite robust—around six per cent, well above world average.

The disjuncture between India's economic growth and political stability consequently needs explanation. But before that we need to understand the possible links between political and economic instability.

Why and When does Political Instability Matter?

Political instability matters for a variety of reasons. Numerous studies have tried to examine the relationship between political instability and economic growth.[8] Mankiw (1995) in his review of the literature finds that 'political instability, as measured by the frequency of revolutions, coups, or wars is negatively associated with growth'. In their analysis of the relationship between political instability and growth, Alesina et al. (1996) define political instability as 'the propensity of government collapse' and find that in

---

[8] It may also matter for normative reasons as Huntington (1968) cautioned in his classic work: 'Men may, of course, have order without liberty, but they cannot have liberty, without order.'

countries and time periods with a high propensity of government collapse, growth is significantly lower. The period they examine, 1950–82, was, however, one where the propensity of government collapse in India was low (except for the late 1970s); yet so was growth. More recently, Persson and Tabellini (1999) find that 'political instability, as measured by more frequent regime changes, or political unrest and violence, is significantly and negatively correlated with growth'. Finally, Campos and Nugent (2000) find no evidence of a hypothesized negative and causal relationship between political instability and economic growth. Their emphasis on causality is important since it has been argued that the causal effects could run both ways. Rapid economic growth results in significant structural changes which could substantially reshape political bases and coalitions. Furthermore their results show that the drive· in the results between political instability and negative growth is Sub-Saharan Africa which is more than half the countries in many growth regressions.

One problem with these studies is measurement problems inherent in defining and measuring precisely what constitutes political instability, which ranges from executive turnover and regime change to riots, strikes, and political assassinations. There is an underlying problem in that both normalizing the data (for population size) as well as the absolute numbers are problematic in cross-sectional comparisons, when comparing a country of India's size to the majority of countries. Additionally it is not just the number of assassinations but who gets assassinated; not just the number of strikes but where they occur (a strike in a country's ports can bring economic life to a stand-still; but in its restaurants will have much less political salience even if the number of man-days lost in the latter is substantially greater); not just how many riots, but who is involved and where they occur (in the capital city or in the rural hinterland).

The mechanisms linking political instability with economic growth imply that the effects of political instability are amplified in countries at low levels of economic development for several reasons. First, the uncertainty engendered by political instability may lead to capital flight, increasing external debt with negative consequences for growth (Alesina and Tabellini 1989). Relatedly, economic uncertainty also increases a country's risk premium leading investors to opt out in favour of safer avenues. Financial markets in emerging economies lack the depth of their counterparts in more developed economies. Therefore, relatively small changes in financial activity from erratic retail investors or money managers (who sometimes reduce their allocation simply because they anticipate that their investors will pull money out) cause large swings, especially in equity and bond markets. These apprehensions are exemplified by the IMF's warnings to India about the dangers of political instability: 'We are in a new [global] political situation and political instability is not the best environment for bold reforms and stimulation for private investment and then growth.'[9]

Second, political instability shortens the time horizons of politicians, which are never that long to begin with for India (or indeed elsewhere). As a result, pressing long-term problems tend to be neglected. The day of reckoning is simply postponed, thereby ensuring that when it occurs it will be of much greater severity. India's large (and possibly unsustainable) fiscal deficits and poor stewardship of its natural resources (especially water) are two examples in this regard.

Third, political uncertainty extracts a price on the pace of reforms by stalling the necessary legislative changes that underpin policy reform. Bills introduced by one government languish when the government falls, forcing the next government to begin the process all over again. By law, the government's ability to make policy decisions is severely circumscribed once elections are announced.[10] Decision-making in India, never speedy to begin with, is further slowed.

Fourth, frequent elections have a high opportunity cost in the time politicians can devote to legislative and policy matters, given the claims of time and energy in campaigning (Kapur and Mehta 2002).

Fifth, elections and frequent changes of government have high direct and indirect resource costs. First, elections cost money. In addition to the direct costs to the exchequer, overall economic costs

---

[9] 'IMF warns India against political instability' *Times of India*, 24 April 2000.

[10] Once elections are announced, all policy decisions of the central or a state government need the concurrence of the autonomous Election Commission, which whets them for any short-term electoral pay-offs. This limitation matters more in unanticipated elections, which of course increase in times of political instability.

are substantially greater. Campaign costs are invariably more than the legal ceilings and, since election days are national holidays, the productivity losses are not insignificant. Estimates of the 1998 general elections placed overall economic costs at Rs 46 billion ($1 billion), with the total poll expenditures at about Rs 32 billion (including Rs 12 billion to the exchequer for conducting national elections) and the rest coming out of productivity loss due to lost working days.[11] Add in expenditures for elections to state assemblies and to local governments and functional bodies such as cooperatives and trade unions, and the costs of frequent elections (as a consequence of political instability) were probably around 0.5 per cent of GDP in the latter half of the 1990s.

But the indirect costs of frequent changes in government are probably higher. Politicians and small political parties extract a higher price for coalition loyalty—be it in indirect policy terms or simply in buying out through direct cash payments. In 1989, the minority government led by V. P. Singh suddenly resurrected the 'Mandal Commission Report' that had been gathering dust for more than a decade to boost political support. In 1993, in order to save the minority Congress government during a no-confidence vote mounted against it, payments were allegedly paid to several members of Parliament to persuade them to abstain.[12] In 1997, the Janata government headed by I. K. Gujral succumbed to pressure from its coalition partners and agreed to accept only certain parts of the Fifth Pay Commission Report; this proved to be a fiscal disaster for India, increasing the already precarious fiscal deficit by 1–1.5 per cent of GDP. Cash payments grease difficult seat adjustments between political parties. Local leaders who influence vote 'banks' command considerable resource payments. And there are deferred payments as well, the IOUs that are settled if electoral victory is forthcoming. It is argued that coalitions cannot implement coherent economic policies due to the pressures in appeasing disparate factions and partners. Energies are dissipated in managing the coalition itself rather than in governing more broadly and, as a result, both the pace and the quality of reforms suffer.

[11] Bhaskara Rao, Centre for Media Studies, New Delhi, 1998.

[12] This resulted in the indictment of former Prime Minister Rao for corruption in 2000 (subsequently overruled), the first such instance in India. Curiously the MPs who allegedly accepted payments could not be convicted due to loopholes in the People's Representation Act.

Political uncertainty has reputation costs as well, particularly among economic actors in times of rapidly changing markets. India has always been regarded as a ponderous polity, and frequent political uncertainty may, at a minimum, result in more 'noisy' signals to economic agents rendering decision-making more difficult. The only problem is that the evidence does not support the link between political instability and economic outcomes in India. Indeed the link between governmental instability and other manifestations of political instability are also not particularly strong. In the first three elections, between 1952 and 1962, the Congress was elected with comfortable majorities and other indicators of political stability were in conformity. However, the Congress also returned with comfortable majorities in 1971 and 1984 but in both cases the result was further political turmoil.

The correlation between political instability and economic outcomes is not only weak in India over time, but also across India's states, which have widely varying records of instability. Andhra Pradesh, seen as one of the most 'reform minded states', also has one of the highest incidences of political violence, manifest in the activities of the Maoist PWG. West Bengal's performance, where the CPI(M)-dominated coalition has ruled for nearly a quarter of a century, has been little better than the all-India average. Bihar has had one government in the 1990s, but the worst growth record. Punjab, which was wracked by a severe secessionist movement in the 1980s (and which had largely dissipated in the 1990s) grew faster in the former period relative to the more recent period.

An important reason why the links between instability and growth are weak is that stability itself can simply result in the persistence of poor policies. The former Soviet Union exemplified why stability is neither necessary nor sufficient for economic growth. Similarly the hegemony of the Congress party in running the national government in India led to the persistence of flawed economic policies, not because there was a lack of awareness of the negative consequences of the policies but because to do so would be to refute its own past. The problem was amplified because of the stability in the leadership of the party, which was vested in one family. Governmental turnover, within a constitutional framework, implies that the political landscape is competitive, and in both economic and political benefits of competition. But the converse is not true either: one can hardly infer that unstable governments are essential for economic growth or social stability implying that there is some optimal level of stability (or instability) which is conducive for economic development. The puzzle in India's case is why governmental instability does not amplify into systemic instability, in which case the negative economic consequences would surely be large. The usual answer is the country's democratic system but that in turn begs an answer to the paradox laid out at the beginning of this chapter. What explains the resilience of democracy in a low income, extremely ethnically heterogeneous, multinational state? The stability of the Indian political system had been a key concern of social scientists working on India and its policy makers. In recent years this pre-occupation has begun to be questioned on the grounds that the analytical concerns should be more focused on why India's democracy has delivered so little to the Indian masses. That is a fair point—one cannot eat stability. However, as the experience of Partition so starkly demonstrated in India's case, and the more recent experience in a range of contexts (be it Rwanda, Yugoslavia, Cambodia, Zaire, or Bangladesh (formerly East Pakistan)), the costs of systemic instability can be catastrophic. The maintenance of the institutions of democracy are critical for minimizing ethnic conflict (Easterly 2001). So, for a country with such extreme ethnic heterogeneity and endemic low level ethnic conflict, the importance of understanding systemic stability continues to be a matter of grave importance.

A Thick Institutional Web?

India's constitutional design lays out a set of statutory institutions whose effectiveness rests on critical *ceteris paribus* assumptions about norms, expectations, and social forces as well as a host of non-formal and non-statutory institutions that interact, subvert, and at times reinforce formal institutional structures. Many of India's institutions—bureaucracy, political parties, universities, investigative agencies, public enterprises—have markedly deteriorated and institutional decay, its causes and consequences for governance, has been an important subject of enquiry and concern.[13] The dominance

---

[13] See Bardhan 1998; Kohli 1990.

of one party (the Congress party), and the pre-eminence of a single individual in that party (Indira Gandhi) who, in stark contrast to her father, systematically undermined India's institutions (including the Congress party itself), were critical factors. However, there were three crucial facilitating factors: an institutional and ideological legacy that had led to a dominant role of the state in the economy and created large rent seeking opportunities for those with political power; India's extreme ethnic heterogeneity together with a vast historical baggage of deep social inequities; and first-past-the-post electoral system that created strong incentives to create and nurture narrow but committed ethnic vote banks. The result was that many of India's institutions were overwhelmed by excessive political mobilization or simply clogged up by interest groups.

Nonetheless, the system did not collapse (although in some parts of India, notably Bihar, it surely did). While most analysis of India asks why India has not done better, here I turn the argument on its head to ask why it did not do worse. An important reason why it has managed to survive politically (and indeed do better than its own past, by almost all economic indicators) is that the very reasons why certain institutions get weakened opens up space for both new institutions as well as other erstwhile moribund institutions. Additionally, the system's tendencies to create new institutions which may have a modest half-life of effectiveness, means that the simultaneous cycle of decay and rejuvenation gives the system a certain resilience. The result has been a wide array of institutional forms in India.

The tables in the Appendix lay out a framework to analyse key state institutions, their powers, and organizational design features that give them agency. There are several features of this institutional matrix that needs highlighting. First, there are elaborate criteria and rules of appointment for these institutions. The pool of candidates from which political authorities can choose is severely circumscribed by an empanelment list (a short-list) by another autonomous agency—the Union Public Service Commission (UPSC). This by no means implies that the process is not political—it undoubtedly is. Nonetheless, partisan politics is circumscribed relative to the alternative. The selected candidate may not be the best candidate but will invariably be above basic minimum standards.

Second, the periods of appointment to these institutions are non-discretionary either because of fixed periods of appointment or a mandatory retirement age. Thus despite political uncertainty manifest in weak coalition governments, the fact that life-cycles of key state institutions are out of phase with political cycles sharply reduces covariance risk, and in turn limits systemic instability. In the US or Mexico when a new government takes power, there is a substantial hiatus when new political appointees are being selected for hundreds of senior level positions. In a parliamentary system where executive turnover is higher, such a system could lead to a dangerous vacuum. Again, partisan packing of institutions owing allegiance to one party or group is limited both by high turnover and the exigencies of coalition politics. This provides both stability and limits the damage that could otherwise occur from the social and political polarization witnessed in India in recent years.

For instance when a government falls the Lok Sabha (lower house) stands dissolved. However, the Rajya Sabha (upper house) is a perennially standing body and its members are elected from state assemblies whose election cycles in turn are out of phase from federal elections. Consequently, governmental instability which results from no party having majority in the lower house, has also meant that the ruling coalition does not have a majority in the upper house. Although the upper house cannot exercise the kind of parliamentary control over the Cabinet that the Lok Sabha is constitutionally empowered to do, it has the power to block non-money bills. While this delays legislation (for instance, economic reforms) it ensures that the ruling party or coalition is forced to build consensus and cannot pass legislation that is socially contentious. It also ensures that significant institutional changes like constitutional amendments or appointments such as that of the president, cannot be undertaken without carrying at least some of the opposition parties. These institutional features mean that while the upside is limited (important legislation is delayed), so is the downside in that socially partisan legislation cannot be passed.

A theory of democratic stability with decaying institutions and institutional renewal

The effects of this phenomenon are schematically captured in Figures 1a, 1b, 1c.

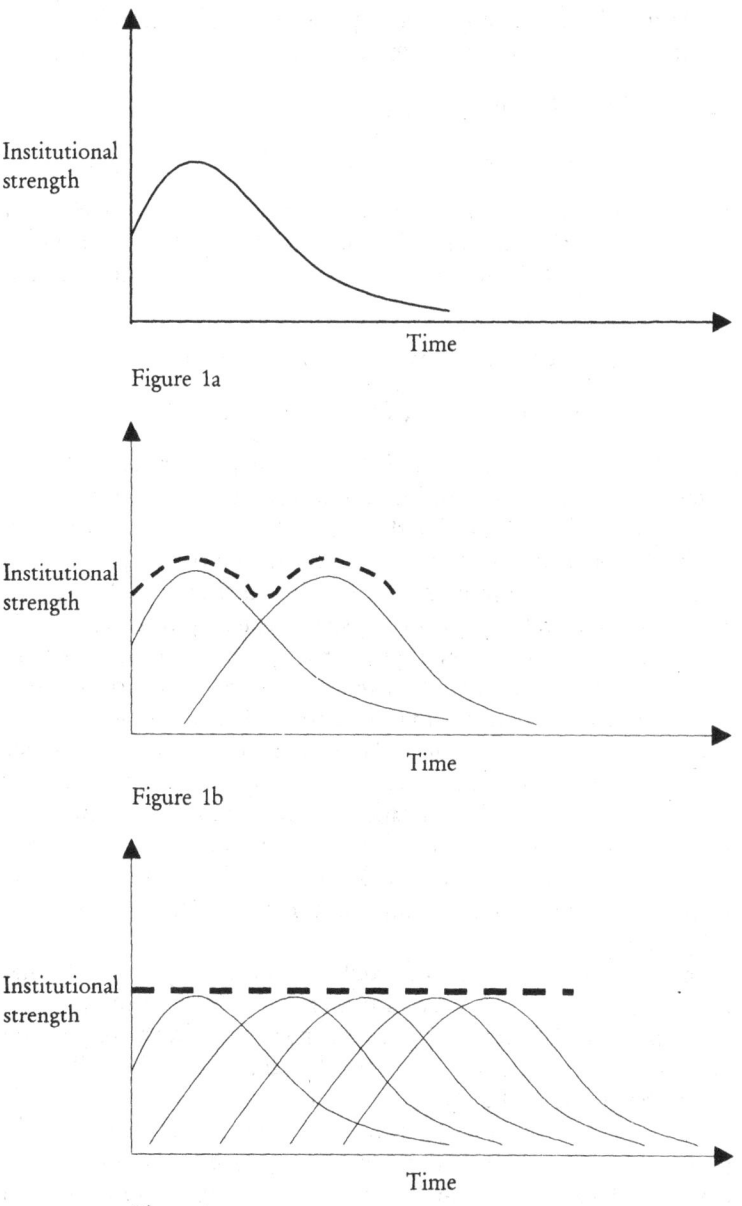

Figure 1a

Figure 1b

Figure 1c

Figure 1: Institutional decay and equilibrium

Assume that the supply of a quantity of public goods, Q, is a function of I_n institutions, where $(n = 1, 2...n)$

At $t = 0$, $Q = f(I_n)$, $n = 1, 2, ...n$

At $t = 1$, $Q^* = f(I_{n*})$,

Over time, many institutions decay and if no new ones come up, then $n^* < n$ and under reasonable assumptions we would expect $Q^* < Q$. Figure 1a is a schematic representation of such a situation.

If however, new institutions come up, such that,

At $t = 1$, $Q^* = f(I_{n*})$, $n^* > n$, $n^* = 1, 2, ...n, n+1, ...n+i$,

then the results are more ambiguous and depend critically on the extent to which new institutions are complements or substitutes for the ones that have fallen by the way side. If the new institutions are perfect substitutes, then as long as the number of new institutions is equal to the number of declining institutions, the equilibrium outcome could result in a systemic stability (Figures 1b, 1c).

Under more realistic assumptions the apparent robustness of this exercise could be questioned. In general the time and effort to build new institutions is greater than it is to weaken and destroy them. Second, in the Indian context (and often more generally) public institutions rarely die, however weakened they may become. As a result the institutional landscape gets increasingly congested, impeding policy coordination and implementation. I will come back to this issue later, but first make a case why there are several consequences of high governmental turnover that may paradoxically be benign.

An important outcome of rapid governmental turnover is that all political parties have been in power and in many cases, they are both in power (at one level of government) and in the opposition (at another level of government) at the same time. The BJP, Congress, the JD, the CPI (M) are all in power in some states and in opposition in some others. Most social groups are similarly in power in some states and at the receiving end in others; this churning has increased instability as witnessed in the low duration of governments in power. Given India's social heterogeneity, the instability inherent in coalitions has to be weighed against many other possible benefits. For one, coalition politics has considerably strengthened India's federalism. The serious misuse of Article 356 (which allows the federal government to dismiss state governments), has been severely curtailed. Second, since many critical economic reforms entail policy changes and implementation at the state level, coalitions have helped solve the hierarchical coordination problem between the Centre and the states. Third, turnover can be helpful in building consensus. It helps to loosen an 'opposition' mind-set, which is strong in parties that have never been in power—the very act of governing helps inject a healthy dose of pragmatism, especially in radical political parties. The dilution of the BJP's economic nationalism and social exclusion agenda is clearly due to the compromises inherent in coalition politics where it cannot form a government on its own. Fourth, the increasing number of elections—at the federal and state levels as well as at the local level (arising from the 73rd and 74th Amendments) have meant that the needs of election financing have increased the demand for campaign contributions. The need for more election funds has meant that with parties weak and the discretionary part of state spending declining, business—for better and worse—is playing a more important role.

Finally (and for the purposes of this chapter, more importantly), governmental instability has reinjected new vigour in a host of otherwise dormant institutions that remained in the shadows in the days of dominant single party governments. Given electoral uncertainties, politicians prefer, under a Rawlesian 'veil of ignorance' to strengthen 'referee' institutions, whether they be the presidency or the Election Commission. Even thieves prefer an honest person to another thief to organize the distribution of the spoils. For all these reasons the relative salience of India's institutions has shifted over time and this is particularly evident in the key institutions of coordination and restraint (Table 1.5).

The point is not that the counterpart institutions of the 1990s are perfect substitutes or more effective in discharging the role that was being performed by other institutions in the 1950s. In some cases, for instance the growth of market institutions to allocate scarce resources instead of the Planning Commission to perform the same task, the alternative is clearly more effective. In others, such as the corrosion of the police as an institution of restraint, new institutions like the National Human Rights Commission can at

TABLE 1.5
India's changing institutional web

	1950s	1990s
	Cabinet	Prime Minister's Office
	Planning Commission	Markets
Institutions of Coordination	Congress party	Inter-State Council/ National Development Council
	Bureaucracy	Bureaucracy and civil society actors like apex industry associations
	Norms of self-restraint (corruption)	Norms challenging social hierarchy
	Political parties	Election Commission
Institutions of Restraint	Constitution	Judiciary
	Comptroller and Auditor General	Central Vigilance Commission
	Police	National Human Rights Commission
	Finance Ministry	Reserve Bank
	Prime Minister	President

best only rectify egregious abuses by the latter. And monetary policy (the writ of the central bank) can only compensate to a limited extent profligate fiscal policies, which are the purview of the Finance Ministry. Nonetheless, an analysis of the key institutions of coordination, restraint and adjudication, and regulation, shows that the ability to create new institutions and in some cases resuscitate moribund institutions has limited the downside of the much lamented corrosion of Indian public institutions.

Institutions of Coordination

The 1950s were the heyday of the Congress party which ruled both at the federal and state levels. The party apparatus was a mechanism for vertical coordination of policies and programmes. At the federal level the Cabinet was critical for policy coordination across ministries. Resource allocation in a state-dominated economy was coordinated by the Planning Commission. And the bureaucracy, especially the elite Indian Administrative Service (IAS) provided a key coordinating mechanism, both vertically and horizontally at different levels of government. By the 1990s, the key coordinating institutions were substantially different. Large coalition cabinets meant that an ad hoc body created in earlier times, namely the Prime Minster's Office, became a relatively more important coordinating mechanism across ministries. Markets rather than the Planning Commission became much more important for coordinating resource allocation. The bureaucracy had weakened considerably, in terms of its reputation and capabilities. With the Congress party a shadow of itself, and no equivalent replacement in sight, the Inter-State Council (ISC), a formal constitutional federal forum set up under Article 263 in the late 1980s, and the National Development Council (NDC) a hitherto moribund non-statutory body, became more important. The latter had been set up to approve Five-Year Plans and provide feedback to the Planning Commission. Its meetings of India's chief ministers with the federal economic ministries rarely produced anything more than dreary rhetoric. Recently, however, this has changed, albeit modestly.

India's mounting fiscal problems and pressures on fiscal federalism forced a search for alternative institutional mechanisms. These institutional mechanisms have helped nudge 'fiscal federalism' into a less contentious issue by overcoming collective action and free rider problems among states and political parties. They have allowed greater cooperation between the Centre and the states and also between the states themselves on fiscal matters. In 1993, under the aegis of the NDC, a committee was formed which resulted in all chief ministers agreeing to the principle of a minimum agricultural power tariff—a major political issue. Since then implementation has been tardy, but the trend, however slow, is pretty clear. Tax harmonization efforts later expanded to sales tax reforms that resulted in uniform minimum sales tax rates in all the states. The states themselves agreed to monitor each other on implementation in late 1999. Here again progress has been extremely slow but just the simple fact of states agreeing to monitor each other was a step forward considering the political gridlock that existed. Furthermore, the committee of finance ministers was headed by the finance minister of West Bengal, a state headed by a political party which has been one of the strongest critics of economic liberalization, and included the finance ministers of states from a spectrum of political parties both in the governing coalition and the opposition.[14] Without any central intervention or any 'pressure' from the Centre a fiscally debilitating sales tax rate wars among states came to an end. As a result the undercutting of rates ceased and tax revenues are expected to improve with the higher sales tax rates and the fact that industries will not move from one state to another due to lower taxes elsewhere. Having successfully implemented its mandate on the sales tax issue, the monitoring committee has now been transformed into a body with greater powers. This committee has played an important role in building a consensus and coordinating the task of introducing the Value Added Tax (VAT) system in India.

Steps to rein-in India's stubbornly excessive fiscal deficit have been a singlular weakness of India's reforms. As we shall see later this is more a failure of institutions of restraint than of institutions of coordination. The institutional mechanism for the latter in this regard is the Inter-State Council (ISC). In the late 1990s, seven of the more reform-minded of India's chief ministers (representing six different political parties), formed a group under the finance minister. The group's recommendations were not unlike those of international financial institutions: if the states wanted the Centre to bail them out of their fiscal problems, they would have to undertake reforms. Again progress has been weak, in part because there are no enforcement mechanisms. However, the forum provided by the ISC has led to intensive and repeated interactions among the states, creating new networks and personal connections cutting across party lines. As a result there is also greater policy diffusion across states.

Earlier, decisions made at meetings of chief ministers or at the National Development Council rarely carried with them means by which they might be implemented. The recent reforms and activity provide an institutional mechanism for the ministry to nudge states to act on the decisions taken by their chief ministers. The states also know that decisions made at apex-level meetings should be implemented by everybody; this helps limit the populist

[14] The states include Uttar Pradesh, Punjab, Karnataka, Maharashtra, Gujarat, Delhi, and Meghalaya.

considerations that held back individual states from implementing harsh decisions in the past. The forum has also allowed states to collectively place their case with the Centre on fiscal matters. Other coordinating mechanisms that were dormant continue to remain so. The National Water Resources Council, for instance, has had little success in coordinating river basin planning and water use.[15] For over three decades, the states have opposed any moves by the Centre to play a role in inter-state river issues and the Centre has never been strong enough to overcome their objections. Even at the height of the Centre's dominance over states, from 1950 to 1970, with the Congress party controlling most of the states, the Centre could not enact laws relating to the development of any major river. The result has been that India has failed to develop its water resources through integrated river basin development, and internecine conflicts over rivers between states have become common and contentious. Even settlements of disputes by awards of inter-state tribunals (which under law are final and binding on the states), have proved ineffective with disputes over the implementation of the awards, leading to protracted legal proceedings in the Supreme Court. The high costs of the failure to resolve the dispute over the sharing of waters of the Cauvery river between Tamil Nadu and Karnataka, which has been politically contentious for more than half a century, is the most salient, but by no means exceptional example in this regard.

Institutions of Restraint

Many of the apprehensions surrounding the quality of India's institutions concern the declining probity (and often quality) of its public institutions, in particular the bureaucracy, legislative bodies, and the police. In earlier years, perhaps the most important institution of restraint was self-restraint arising from the norms and prevailing political culture. Over time, this norm of self-restraint

[15] The Constitution gives full control over waters of a river to a state (List II entry 17) but the states' rights are made subject to any law made by Parliament for the regulation and development of inter-state rivers to the extent the control of the Union is declared by Parliament by law to be expedient in the public interest (List I entry 56). This would prevent states from making conflicting claims to development in the sharing of the waters of a river. For example, Parliament has set up river valley authorities, like the Damodar Valley Authority.

eroded and formal institutional mechanisms set up to curb corruption, for instance the CBI, remained by and large ineffective (Das 2001). The Constitution had created the office of Comptroller and Auditor General (CAG) as an independent constitutional authority designed to scrutinize the accounts of the government and give reports to assist the legislatures in exercising their control over the executive. While arguing for the draft Articles up for consideration by the Constituent Assembly, Ambedkar (the chairman of the drafting committee of the Constitution) had argued that, 'that this dignitary (CAG) is the most important officer in the Constitution of India. He is the one man who is going to see that the expenses voted by Parliament are not exceeded or varied from what has been laid down by Parliament. If this functionary is to carry out his duties—his duties, I submit, are far more important than the duties even of the judiciary—he should be as independent as the judiciary.' When there was unsavoury criticism in the Lok Sabha in December 1952 about the functioning of the CAG, Jawaharlal Nehru chastised the members, saying, 'He is not responsible to Government and it is open for him to criticize Government in reports.... For him to be criticized on the floor of the House would tend to undermine the special position that has been granted to him and make it difficult for him to discharge his duties without fear or favour.' But the CAG proved to be an ineffective institution of restraint not because of fundamental flaws in institutional design but because of the weakening of the most important consumer of its products, namely Parliament and state legislatures. The latters' inability to use the CAG to press for greater accountability in the executive, proved in the end more insidious than overt political pressure on the institution (Kapur and Mehta 2002).

Nonetheless, there has been a rejuvenation in three institutions of restraint that were also part of the original constitutional design: the presidency, the judiciary, and the Election Commission. The increased salience of these institutions is due to the very reasons that have contributed to the problem in the first place: weak political parties with limited mandates. The decline of the Congress party and increase in the strength of regional parties has necessitated coalition governments and contributed to political instability. In turn this has created greater room for agency for institutions of restraint.

The institution of the presidency is a good example. In India's parliamentary system the president is nominally a figurehead but as with other countries where this is also the case (Israel, Italy, Ireland, Germany), the position's moral authority far exceeds its de jure power. Moreover, in critical political moments like hung parliaments, which signal political instability, the president's discretionary powers are amplified since the Constitution offers no clear guidance as to who to invite to form the government. It has also given the president greater cover in refusing to countenance misuse of Article 356, which allowed ruling governments at the Centre to dismiss state governments and subvert India's federal constitutional design. The powers of the institution of the presidency (and the institutional counterpart in the states, governors) that have been most effective in limiting the damage by an unchecked executive is the power of delay. For instance the president of India is also *ex officio* chancellor of Delhi University, one of India's premier universities. While the Education Ministry 'recommends' the choice of vice-chancellor (the equivalent of a university president in the US), the president must give his assent. In 2000, the president thrice rejected the names forwarded by the education ministry; ultimately, the hiatus and ensuing public uproar led to the appointment of a well known left-leaning economist.

One of India's most significant achievements has been the holding of free, fair, and credible elections in the face of tremendous odds. By any criteria the Election Commission (EC) has played a critical role in this process. The one case where it failed its mandate was elections in Jammu and Kashmir—a failure whose costs have been monumental. The statutory independence and powers of the EC stand out among election boards in developing and developed countries. It is noteworthy, however, that despite these statutory powers, the EC realized this in a substantive measure only in the 1990s, when there was no dominant political party. This has meant that in a polity where anything and everything can be politically contentious, electoral results (at least in the aggregate) are never contested by any party.

In turn this credibility has allowed the EC to make procedural changes to improve the electoral process without being stymied by a political backlash. For instance, modest changes in the Representation of the Peoples' Act considerably reduced the number of

Independent candidates campaigning for seats in the Lok Sabha in 1998 (Yadav and McMillan). Since 1952, when the first general election was held, the number of candidates for each constituency rose with every election. From 3.8 candidates per constituency in 1952, the figure rose to 4.5 in 1977. It touched double digits in 1984 and peaked at an average of over 25.7 per Lok Sabha constituency by 1996. Following the amendment to the Representation of the Peoples' Act in 1996, the average number of candidates per constituency fell to 8.6 in 1998.[16] It was 10.0 in the 2004 elections.

However, the EC's success is also in part due to another, less visible, institutional mechanism absorbing a potentially explosive issue. The Constitution says that Parliament shall make such arrangements as it sees fit for delimitation after each census. Given the possible political ramifications of a census in a heterogenous society such as India's, the relative political insulation of the conduct of India's census is remarkable.[17] There are two tasks of delimitation. The first is to demarcate the boundaries of parliamentary constituencies. The second is to increase or decrease the seat entitlement of a state on the basis of its population. In the 1970s, Parliament decided that it would not touch delimitation so as to avoid penalizing states that had done more to curb population growth rates. Since then, what could have become a polarized north-south cleavage has been put on the back burner until 2020.

The relationship between the judiciary and the executive has always an in-built tension. Post-independence India witnessed this

---

[16] The amendments raised the deposit that each candidate had to make from Rs 500 to Rs 10,000 (in reserved constituencies, it was increased from Rs 250 to Rs 5000). Candidates who failed to get more than one-sixth of the total number of votes polled forfeited their deposits. The number of those who had to propose an Independent candidate was increased from one to ten, and no candidate was allowed to contest from more than two seats in the same election. Also, all candidates had to file affidavits stating categorically that they had not been convicted on criminal charges. These measures primarily affected Independent candidates. While the average number of party-sponsored candidates came down only marginally (from six to five), the average number of independent candidates per constituency fell sharply from nearly 20 to less than four.

[17] Nigeria and Pakistan are two cases of censuses being cancelled due to political pressures. Even in the US the conduct of the census is not entirely free of political pressure as evident by Congressional pressure to scrap sampling techniques to count the homeless.

tension periodically in the 1950s and increasingly in the 1960s and early 1970s. The governments of the day repeatedly passed legislation and constitutional amendments to meet ostensibly radical (but usually populist) goals, and which tried to get around the courts by limiting judicial review. Finally, in a landmark judgement (popularly known as the *Kesavananda Bharati* case), the court ruled that Parliament could not amend the basic features of the Constitution and judicial review was held to be a basic feature of the Constitution.[18] The second critical judgement was in 1993 when a Supreme Court ruling virtually shut out the executive from appointments to the highest court—the power of appointment of judges was assumed by the Supreme Court itself.[19] Few courts in the world exercise this kind of power over their own selection process. At the time, a minority government meant that the executive was weak. But broader political processes, notably the upheavals following the demolition of the Babri mosque in December 1992 and the financial scandals surrounding the Harshad Mehta affair, considerably weakened the political and moral authority of both the executive and the legislative branches of government. This allowed the judiciary's ruling to go politically unchallenged.[20] Through a series of rulings, the judiciary further limited the executive's role in appointments to lower courts as well as an array of quasi-judicial bodies. Article 234 of the Indian Constitution provides for appointments to the judicial service of the state (excluding district judges) that are made by the governor of the state. These appointments are to be in accordance with the rules made by the governor in consultation with the state's public service commission and the high court of the state. Recently, the Supreme Court ruled that, in the appointment of judicial officers in a state,

[18] *Kesavananda Bharati* v. *State of Kerala* AIR 1973 SC 1461.

[19] *The Supreme Court Advocates-on-Record Association* v. the *Union of India* (1993) 4 SCC 441.

[20] An excellent example of the power of this ruling was the elevation of Justice Srikrishna from the position of chief justice of the Kerala High Court to the Supreme Court in 2002. He had headed an enquiry commission constituted to probe the bloody communal riots in Mumbai (between December 1992 and January 1993) that had strongly indicted the then BJP-Shiv Sena state government for its complicity. In 2002 the BJP and the Shiv Sena were part of the ruling NDA coalition at the Centre and while obviously discomforted could do little to block this appointment.

the consultation between the governor and the high court is mandatory and not a mere formality.[21] In 1994, the Supreme Court had directed the government to place all tribunals under the control of the department of legal affairs, so that their functioning might take a more integrated and coordinated approach.[22] Subsequently, the Court ruled that 'in the matter of appointment of chairman and vice-chairman and members of the tribunals which exercise even quasi-judicial functions, it is necessary to make appointments in consultation with the chief justice of India or his nominee and such consultation must be effective and meaningful.'[23] It further ruled (in a separate case) that the power of the government to establish special courts for specific purposes (such as administrative tribunals) could not exclude the jurisdiction of the high courts and consequently could only be established under the jurisdiction and supervision of the high courts.[24] Having ensured that the judiciary has a key role in appointments to tribunals, the Supreme Court enhanced the powers of tribunals in another significant ruling stating that the administrative tribunals are also vested with the power to declare contempt of court, for enforcing compliance of orders, and punishment for lapses in the matter of compliance. The Court argued that 'availability of jurisdiction for contempt provides efficacy to functioning of the judicial forum and enables the

[21] This observation came from the court in a judgement on a case pertaining to recruitment to Himachal judicial service. The Court ruled that 'The consultation contemplated by Article 234 of the Constitution is not a mere formality; it has to be meaningful and effective.' August 2000.

[22] Currently only the IT Appellate Tribunal, its 56 branches, and the FEMA Appellate Tribunal function under the Law Ministry. Other important tribunals like the Central Administrative Tribunal (CAT) and the Customs, Excise and Gold Control Appellate Tribunal are managed by different ministries. The CAT, with its 33 branches and 10 circuit benches, is under the administrative and budgetary control of Ministry of Personnel whereas the Customs, Excise and Gold Appellate Tribunal functions under the Ministry of Finance.

[23] Communication from Chief Justice of India to the Prime Minister, 14 June 2000. The dispute arose over the appointment of the Chairman of the Monopolies and Restrictive Trade Practices Commission (MRTP—India's equivalent of the FTC) by the Law Minister. The Chief Justice's admonition that 'Making appointment of the Chairman, MRTP Commission, without consultation with the Chief Justice of India is a serious matter which requires your kind attention,' eventually led to the resignation of the Law Minister.

[24] *L. Chandra Kumar* v. *Union of India* AIR 1997 SC 1125.

enforcement of the orders on account of its deterrent effect on avoidance.'[25]

It should be emphasized that the Supreme Court itself has been characterized by instability (frequent turnover of judges) and low accountability. Between 1987–99 the Supreme Court had twelve chief justices. In 2002 it had four! Moreover, while elections provide some (albeit not necessarily very meaningful) accountability of the executive and legislative branches of government, there is virtually no remedy for making an errant judge account for his actions other than impeachment, despite rules to investigate judicial impropriety. Impeachment is elaborate and cumbersome.[26] In the last fifty years, not a single high court or Supreme Court judge has been impeached.[27] However, as long as succession procedures are institutionalized and it enjoys high external legitimacy, these weaknesses are not especially debilitating.

As stated earlier, the failure to rein in fiscal deficits exceeding 10 per cent of GDP has been a singular failure of India's reforms in the 1990s. This is one area where the links between the underlying reasons for political instability (weak and multiple parties, coalition governments), and adverse economic outcomes are clear. However, it is interesting that while political instability and populism has manifested itself in fiscal populism in India, it did so through monetary expansion (resulting in high inflation) in Latin America. The usual explanation for (relatively) low inflation in India has been the exigencies of democratic politics. Since the poor are particularly hurt by inflation and also constitute a large fraction of voters, controlling inflation has been a high political priority. As a result even though India's central bank—the RBI—does not have statutory independence, it has enjoyed considerable latitude in this area. In the 1990s even as fiscal profligacy resulted in a rapid increase in India's debt burden in the 1990s to about 80 per cent of GDP

---

[25] Tribunals are amenable to high court jurisdiction (under Article 226/227 of the Constitution) but any order or decision of tribunals punishing for contempt is only appealable to the Supreme Court.

[26] The Judges (Inquiry) Act of 1968, framed under Article 124, and the Judges (Inquiry) Rules, 1969, framed under the Act. The procedures for impeachment are laid down in Article 124 of the Constitution.

[27] The Justice V. Ramaswami case in 1991 was perhaps the closest this came to happen.

in 2002 (70 per cent if external debt is excluded), inflation came down to around 3 per cent.

Part of the success is due to India's central bank the RBI which did a commendable job in managing the debt. It engineered a quiet turnaround in government borrowings, relying increasingly on transparent market borrowings instead of forced (and opaque) borrowings from the financial system. The (weighted) average cost of government borrowings fell from 12 per cent in 1997–8 to 9.4 per cent in 2000–1 even as the maturity structure of government debt increased from 6.6 years to 14.3 years in 2001–2. In 1996–7 the government could not raise any debt with maturity exceeding ten years; by 2002 nearly three-fourths of all new government debt had a maturity exceeding ten years, a result of the efforts of the central bank to develop a government securities market.[28] None of this could alone substitute for reining-in government deficits. But it did buy time to try and get a political handle on the situation.

India: An Emerging Political System of Weak Polycentrism?

In recent years, while India's politics has become more unstable, its growth rate has been higher and less volatile, both relative to the country's past and relative to other countries. This chapter has argued that India's systemic resilience arises from a multiplicity of institutions, whose capacity to exercise agency is enhanced by their administrative independence from political cycles. On the one hand these institutions provide a multiplicity of veto points that have made policy making and implementation Byzantine. As Arun Shourie, India's evocative former Minister for Disinvestment, put in, 'No enemy of India could devise a system better designed to paralyse decision making. Administration in India has degenerated into a system of endless correspondence and meetings as a substitute for action.'[29] The result, as the country's Chief Vigilance Commissioner put it, is a system with 'the engine of a bullock-cart and the brakes of a Rolls-Royce.'[30]

[28] The data is from the RBI Annual Report 2001–2.

[29] Quoted in A. V. Rajwade, 'Disinvestment: Clearing the Cobwebs,' *Business Standard*, 21 October 2000.

[30] N. Vittal, lecture at Lal Bahadur Shastri Institute of Public Administration, February 1996.

The effects of such a system are most manifest in India's poor governance—or the quality of government and its effectiveness in delivering material goods and social progress to a majority of its citizens. The most obvious effect is the legendary delays in decision-making in India which weakens the links between risk and reward in all aspects of public life, sharply distorting incentive structures. On the other hand their cumulative effect is to provide an institutional safety net underpinning democratic stability. The broader lesson of the Indian experience seems to be that weak governance and democratic stability can co-exist, and indeed the same causal mechanisms may give arise to both.

The story of India's public institutions is symptomatic of a broader characteristic of India. Whether it is public (state) institutions, think-tanks, NGOs, or firms, India has developed a great penchant and ability to form associations and organizations but much less of an ability to institutionalize them. The number of NGOs in India quadrupled in the 1980s and 1990s (from about 40,000 to nearly 200,000). New Delhi alone supports more than a hundred think-tanks. Yet it is unclear that this zest for associational life which Tocqueville found so important for the US, is serving a similar purpose in India. The proliferation of associations in all facets of Indian life reflects the difficulties of institutionalization in India—where fission rather than fusion is the more common experience. NGOs, think-tanks, firms, public institutions, and public enterprises all share a similar pathology—centred around individuals, poor institutionalization, a 'half-life' of good performance that lasts for just a few years, and rare exits or closures.

A theoretical construct that may help understand the role of India's multiple and complex institutional matrix in that country's underlying systemic stability is that of 'polycentrism' (Ostrom 1999; Ostrom et al., 1961). A polycentric political system has multiple coexisting centres of decision-making that are formally independent of one another. In practice, however, they may function independently or form interdependent links, and they may support or thwart each other. However, the interdependence follows some set of general norms and can thus be somewhat predicted. In such systems, this ordered set of relationships underlies and reinforces the fragmentation of central authority and overlapping of jurisdiction that would otherwise be deemed chaotic. The fragmentation of authority inherent in such a system is often seen to be inefficient (most notably in the case of metropolitan polities in the US where the theory was first applied) with the presence of various governmental bodies at different levels and overlapping jurisdiction leading to the phenomenon of too many governments but too little government.

It has been argued that polycentrism can be as, if not more, efficient than monocentric political systems, especially in the provision of public goods. Public agencies and officials (at different levels) can make alternative arrangements for providing and producing public goods for a given consumption unit (a constituency, in this case) at the level of aggregation that is most efficient (the government body can use other governmental bodies, NGOs, the members of the consumption unit). Polycentrism is further beneficial in maintaining constitutional rule. It resolves the paradox whereby the restraints imposed against the use of governmental prerogatives are enforced by those who enjoy the said prerogatives. Thus, the difficulties of self-regulation are resolved through a more mutual regulation shared among various bodies that are assigned limited but fairly autonomous powers. This is seen to be one of the defining characteristics of polycentric systems: that no single authority enjoys a monopoly on the legitimate use of power.

In recent years India has witnessed a weakening of many of its erstwhile strong institutions and as has been argued this has resulted in increased governmental instability. Concurrently, however, new institutions have appeared while some existing ones have taken on a new life. The result is an emerging Indian political system that represents a weak form of polycentrism. Clearly the reality of India's underprovision of public goods, be it primary health and education, sanitation and water services, belies any strong claims of a polycentric political system. Indeed it is only in the 1990s, with the resuscitation of India's federalism and local governments that it has been moving to a polycentric system, not just horizontally (that is, at the federal level) but also vertically. India's multiple institutions assist, thwart, manipulate, and subvert each other, but at the same time appear to have provided a system that undergirds apparent fragmentation and chaos. The very features that make governance more problematic also reduce covariance risk and thereby systemic threats to governability.

The chapter does not dispute the general sense that there is a crisis of governance in India; it does however, reject the claim that this implies a crisis of governability. Governance relates to the quality of government—its capacity to deliver services, regulate levels of public corruption, etc.... Governability, however, has more to do about the resilience of democratic stability. The multiplicity of India's institutional pluralism are both cause and consequence of its crisis of governance. The decline, decay, and corrosion of institutions need not be as serious a threat as the proponents of the importance of political order have argued. New institutional forms may (although need not) simply reflect the experimentation of a society in the throes of a revolutionary social change. We generally assume that markets are more efficient, the more the number of economic agents. In another context a denser network of associational life makes for greater social capital. The Indian experience raises the possibility that a greater variety of associational forms even if poorly institutionalized, may make for greater systemic resilience.

References

Ades, A. and H. Chua (1997), 'Thy Neighbor's Curse: Regional Instability and Economic Growth', *Journal of Economic Growth*, vol. 2, pp. 279–304.

Alesina, Alberto and G. Tabellini (1989), 'External Debt, Capital Flight and Political Risk', *Journal of International Economics*, vol. 27, pp. 199–220.

Alesina, Alberto, Sule Ozler, Nouriel Roubini, and Philip Swagel (1996), 'Political Instability and Economic Growth', *Journal of Economic Growth*, vol. 1, no. 2, pp. 189–211.

Bardhan, Pranab (1998), *The Political Economy of Development in India: Expanded Edition with an Epilogue on the Political Economy of Reform in India*, Delhi: Oxford University Press.

Bhagwati, Jagdish (1993), *India in Transition*, Oxford: Clarendon Press.

Blomstrom, M., R. Lipsey, and M. Zejan (1996), 'Is Fixed Investment the Key to Economic Growth', *Quarterly Journal of Economics*, vol. 111, pp. 269–76.

Brunetti, A. (1998), 'Policy Volatility and Economic Growth: A Comparative, Empirical Analysis', *European Journal of Political Economy*, vol. 14, pp. 35–52.

Cameron, David (1978), 'The Expansion of the Public Economy: A Comparative Analysis', *American Political Science Review*, 72, pp. 1243–61.

Campos, Nauro and Jeffrey Nugent (2000), 'Who is Afraid of Political

Instability?', William Davidson Institute Working Paper Series 326, William Davidson Institute at the University of Michigan Business School.

Das, S. K. (2001), *Public Office, Private Interest: Bureaucracy and Corruption in India*, New Delhi: Oxford University Press.

De Long, J. Bradford (2003), 'India Since Independence: An Analytic Growth Narrative', in Dani Rodrik (ed.), *In Search of Prosperity: Analytic Narratives on Economic Growth*, Princeton: Princeton University Press.

Drèze, Jean and Amartya Sen (1995), *India: Economic Development and Social Opportunity*, Delhi: Oxford University Press.

Easterly, Bill (2001), 'Can Institutions Resolve Ethnic Conflict', *Economic Development and Cultural Change*, vol. 49, no. 4, pp. 687–706, July.

Easterly, W., R. Islam, and J. Stiglitz (2000), 'Shaken and Stirred: Explaining Growth Volatility', Annual Bank Conference on Development Economics, Available from: http://www.worldbank.org/research/growth/paauthor.htm

Gurr, Ted Robert, Monty G. Marshall, and Deepa Khosla (2001), *Peace and Conflict 2001—A Global Survey of Armed Conflicts, Self Determination Movements and Democracy*, Integrated Network for Societal Conflict Research (INSCR), January.

Hausmann, R. and M. Gavin (1996), 'Securing Stability and Growth in a Shock Prone Region: The Policy Challenge for Latin America', Inter-American Development Bank WP-315, January. WP-315, http://www.iadb.org/oce/keyword_search.cfin.

Hopenhayn, H. and M. Muniagurria (1996), 'Policy Variability and Economic Growth', *Review of Economic Studies*, vol. 63, pp. 611–25.

Huntington, Samuel (1968), *Political Order in Changing Societies*, New Haven: Yale University Press.

Jenkins, Rob (1999), *Democratic Politics and Economic Reform in India*, Cambridge University Press.

Joshi, V. and I. M. D. Little (1994), *India: Macroeconomics and Political Economy, 1964–1991*, Washington DC: The World Bank.

Kapur, Devesh (2000), 'India—1999 Review', *Asia Survey*, vol. 40, no. 1, January–February, pp. 195–207.

————— (2002), 'The Causes and Consequences of India's IT Boom', *India Review*, vol. 1, no. 2. pp. 91–110.

Kapur, Devesh and Pratap Mehta (2002), 'India's Parliament as an Institution of Accountability', Report prepared for the Inter-Parliamentary Union.

Kohli, Atul (1990), *Democracy and Discontent: India's Growing Crisis of Governability*, Cambridge: Cambridge University Press.

Kubota, Keiko and Helen Milner (1999), 'Does more Democracy lead to more Open Trade Regimes?' Unpublished manuscript, Columbia University.

Lipjhart, Arend (1996), 'The Puzzle of Indian Democracy: A Consociational Interpretation', *American Political Science Review*, June, vol. 90,
no. 2, pp. 258–68.

Maddison, Angus (2001), *The World Economy: A Millennial Perspective*,
Paris: Organisation of Economic Cooperation and Development
(OECD).

Mankiw, G. (1995), 'The Growth of Nations,' *Brookings Papers on Economic Activity*, vol. 1, pp. 275–310.

Mitra, Subrata (1999), 'Effects of Institutional Arrangements on Political
Stability in South Asia', *Annual Review of Political Science*, vol. 2,
pp. 405–28.

Ostrom, Vincent (1999), 'Polycentricity (Part 1)', in Michael D. McGinnis
(ed.), *Polycentricity and Local Public Economies: Readings from the
Workshop in Political Theory and Policy Analysis*, Ann Arbor: University of Michigan Press, pp. 52–74.

Ostrom, Vincent, M. Charles Tiebout, and Robert Warren (1961), 'The
Organization of Government in Metropolitan Areas: A Theoretical
Inquiry', *American Political Science Review*, vol. 55, pp. 831–42,
December.

Persson, T. and G. Tabellini (1999), 'Political Economics and Macroeconomic Policy', in J. Taylor and M. Woodford (eds), *Handbook of
Macroeconomics*, North Holland: Amsterdam.

Przeworski, Adam, Michael Alvarez, Jose Cheibub, and Fernando Limong
(2000), *Democracy and Development*, New York: Cambridge University Press.

Pritchett, L. (1998), 'Patterns of Economic Growth: Hills, Pleateaus,
Mountains, and Plains', World Bank Policy Research Department
(February) Working Paper #1947.

Rao, Bhaskara (1998), New Delhi: Centre for Media Studies.

Rajwade, A. (2000), 'Disinvestment: Clearing the Cobwebs', *Business Standard*, 21 October.

Reserve Bank of India, *Annual Report 2001–2*, Mumbai.

Rodrik, Dani (1998), 'Why do more Open Economies have Bigger Governments?', *Journal of Political Economy*, 106(5), October.

Sachs, Jeffrey, Ashutosh Varshney, and Nirupam Bajpai (eds) (1999), *India
in the Era of Economic Reforms*, New Delhi: Oxford University Press.

Sivasubramonian, S. (2000), *The National Income of India in the Twentieth
Century*, New Delhi: Oxford University Press.

Transparency International (2000), Corruption Perceptions Index, http://
www.transparency.org

Times of India (2000), 'IMF warns India against political instability', 24
April.

UNDP (2001), *Human Development Report*, New York: Oxford University Press.

64 • *Public Institutions in India*

Weiner, Myron (1989), *The Indian Paradox*, New Delhi: Sage.
Wilkinson, Steve (2000), 'Consociational Theory and Ethnic Violence', *Asian Survey*, October, Vol. XL, no. 5, pp. 767–91.
World Bank (2000/2001), *World Development Report, 2000/2001*.
Yadav, Yogendra and Alistair McMillan (1998), 'Poll 98 Results: How India Voted', *India Today*, 16 March.

TABLE A1.1
Institutions of restraint

Institution	Responsibility	Membership criteria	Selection process	Sanctioning power
President (S)	Oversees the executive branch of the Union, as well as the Armed Forces.	Term: 5 years, can stand for re-election. Qualifications: Must be a citizen of India, at least 35 years of age, and must not have held a position for profit under the government of India (with the exception of president, vice-president, governor, or minister).	Elected by electoral college consisting of members of both houses of Parliament and state legislatures.	Delay signing off on bills and appointments. Moral suasion.
Supreme Court (S)	Acts as the guardian of the Constitution and ensures and enforces social justice.	Term: Until age of 65, further public appointment allowed. Size: chief justice and not more than 25 other judges. Qualifications: At least 5yrs as a high court judge or 10 yrs as an advocate of a HC, and/or is in the opinion of the president a distinguished jurist.	President appoints every judge but must consult with the chief justice of the SC, who is appointed on the basis of seniority. A committee of the SC recommends names to the president. Removal of a SC judge must be approved by a majority of 2/3 of the members of both houses.	It is empowered to issue directions, orders or writs, including writs in the nature of habeas corpus, mandamus, prohibition, quo warranto and certiorari to enforce them.
Armed forces (S)	Defends and protects the nation.	Term: On basis of seniority. Retire at age 58. Size: Qualifications:	Chiefs appointed by the president.	Apolitical. Most trusted institution in situations of internal conflict.

TABLE A1.1 *contd*

Institution	Responsibility	Membership criteria	Selection process	Sanctioning power
Election Commission (S)	Conduct of elections to Parliament and state legislatures, and to the offices of president and vice-president of India.	Term: 6 years Size: One Chief Election Commissioner and other commissioners as the president sees fit. Currently 3 members. Qualifications: No qualifications stated in the Constitution.	Appointed by the president. Removed in the same manner as a Supreme Court judge.	Reviews (and can reject) all orders (including transfers) by incumbent government once elections are announced. Controls entire administrative apparatus during elections.
Central Vigilance Commission (S)	Receives corruption complaints against government officials and gets them investigated, then makes recommendations as to whether to prosecute and punish, and if so, how.	Term: 4 years for the Central Vigilance Commissioner and 3 for the other 4 members, no further public appointment. Size: 5 members with a total staff of 279. Qualifications: 3 of the 5 members must have had or be in a position in the civil service and have experience in insurance and banking, law, and vigilance.	Appointed by the president after consuling with a committee of the PM, the home minister, and the leader of the opposition party in the House of People. Removed by the president after an inquiry by the Supreme Court.	Power to instigate investigations as it sees fit. Oversees functioning of Central Bureau of Investigation. Strictly an advice giving institution.
National Human Rights Commission (S)	Examines complaints of violations of human rights.	Term: 5 years, no further public appointment. Size: 5 members. Qualifications: chair must have been a chief justice of the Supreme	President appoints members based on recommendations of PM, home minister, and leaders of opposition parties and speakers of both houses. The president can order	Makes recommendations to the SC and central government to prosecute, fine, jail, etc. violators. Can make its inquiry public.

Table A1.1 contd

Institution	Responsibility	Membership criteria	Selection process	Sanctioning power
		Court, one member must have been or is a member of the SC, another a CJ of a high court, and two others human rights experts.	removal after a SC inquiry and recommendation.	
National Commission for Scheduled Castes and Scheduled Tribes (S)	Investigate and monitor all matters relating to the safeguards provided for the Scheduled Castes and Scheduled Tribes under the Constitution; conduct inquiries into specific complaints with respect to deprivation of rights of SC/ST.	Seven members.		Has the power of a civil court.
National Commission for Minorities (S)	Examines the insurance of the enforcement of safeguards for minorities.	Term: 3 years. Size: 6 members. Qualifications: Must be from the minority community of India.	Nominated and appointed by the central government. Removal by the central government.	Same powers as a civil court: summon anyone, receive evidence from affidavits, receive any document requested. Also, makes recommendations for action to be considered by the Parliament.

Table A1.1 contd

Institution	Responsibility	Membership criteria	Selection process	Sanctioning power
Governor (S)	Oversees the business, laws, and rights of the citizens of the state that he governs.	Term: 5 years, at the pleasure of the president. Qualifications: Must be a citizen of India and at least 35 years old.	Appointed by the president, upon the advice of the Cabinet. Increasingly, the chief minister of the state where a governor is being appointed is consulted. Can be removed by the president, after consulting with the PM and the home minister.	Similar to president but at the state level.
High Court (S)	The 'state Supreme Court'. Oversees all state tribunals and lower courts.	Term: Until age of 62, further public appointment allowed. Size: Qualifications: Must have for at least 10 years held a judicial office in India or been an advocate of a high court or 2 or more such courts in succession.	The president appoints every judge after consulting with the chief justice of the SC, the governor of the state, and the chief justice of the high court.	Has powers over all state tribunals and lower courts. Can issue writs, direction, or orders to any person or government within its territory.

Institution	Responsibility	Membership criteria	Selection process	Sanctioning power
Cabinet (S)	Collectively responsible to Parliament.	Member of Parliament.	Nominated by coalition members; proximity to PM.	Considerable but opaque.
Prime Minister's Office	To the prime minister.	Discretion of prime minister.		
Finance Commission (S)	Considers the taxes levied by the Union in order to assign and distribute them to states.	Term: 5 years unless the president and Parliament dissolve it earlier. Size: Qualifications: The Chair should be experienced in public affairs. Members should be qualified to be judges of a high court or have specialized in finance and economics.	Parliament determines the procedures for appointment.	
Planning Commission	Coordinates investment decisions and resource allocation to states (non-statutory).	Prime minster is ex-officio chairman.	Appointed by PMO.	Limited.
Inter-State Council (S)	To arbitrate disputes between states and between the central government and states (statutory).	Key Cabinet members and chief ministers of states.	Consensus.	Peer group pressure.

TABLE A1.2 contd

Institution	Responsibility	Membership criteria	Selection process	Sanctioning power
National Development Council	Approve Five Year Plans.	PM, finance minister and chief ministers of states.		
Delimitation Commission (S)	Reallocates parliamentary seats based on changing population across states (statutory body).	3 members of which 2 are high court or Supreme Court judges. Appointed by central government. 1-chief of Election Commission, ex officio.		Orders of the Delimitation Commission are consolidated by the Election Commission and has force of law.
University Grants Commission (S)	Determines and maintains standards of teaching, examination and research in universities, and allocates resources to them.	Term: chairman 5 years, vice-chair and members 3 years, further appointment for up to 1 more term possible. Size: Chairman and vice-chairman, 10 other members. Qualifications: Chair cannot have been or be an officer of the central or state government, 2 members chosen from central government, no less than 4 current university professors, the rest must have knowledge in specific fields, or are vice-chancellors of universities.	Selected by the central government. Removal by the central government.	Recognizes rights of university stature.
Agricultural Prices Commission	Sets floor prices for key crops.			

TABLE A1.2 *contd*

TABLE A1.2 *contd*

Institution	Responsibility	Membership criteria	Selection process	Sanctioning power
National Water Resources Council	River basin planning and water allocation decisions.			
Law Commission	Renew/repeal obsolete laws; review effectiveness of judicial administration.	Chairman, vice-chairman, member-secretary and members are appointed by central government for a 3-year term.		Can only make recommendations in report. Of its 175 reports, recommendations from 91 have been fully implemented, 33 reports have not been implemented and 51 are in various stages of consideration.

Note: (S) = Statutory Institution.

TABLE A1.3
Adjudicating institutions: Tribunals

Institution	Responsibility	Membership criteria	Selection process	Sanctioning power
Income Tax Appellate Tribunal		Term: Retire at age 60. Size: Qualifications: For judicial members: held judicial post for at least 10 years, been a member if the CLS for 3 years, or been an advocate for 10 years. For accountant members: practiced for at least 10 years as a chartered accountant or served as assistant commissioner of income tax for 3 years.	Appointed by a committee of a judge of the Supreme Court, the law secretary, and the president of the tribunal.	
Administrative Tribunals	Adjudicates disputes between the state and public officials.	Term: 5 years or until 65 (chair and vice-chair) or 62 (members) year of age, whichever comes first, further appointment possible. Size: Varies. Qualifications: Similar to a HC judge for judicial members. Administrative members must be or have been additional secretary or joint secretary, or any equivalent post.	The president appoints all members of the tribunal. The chair is appointed after consultation with the chief justice of India. All other members after consulting with the state government.	Same powers as courts: to issue writs, direction, or orders to any person or government within its territory. Can enforce compliance of orders and punish for lapses in the matter of compliance through power of contempt.

TABLE A1.3 contd

TABLE A1.3 contd

Institution	Responsibility	Membership criteria	Selection process	Sanctioning power
Foreign Exchange Regulation Appellate Board	Hears appeals from the orders of the Director of Enforcement.	Term: Size: 4 Qualifications: The additional secretary to the law minister is the full-time chairman and two joint-secretaries from the ministry of finance are part-time members.	The central government constitues the tribunal.	
Labour Tribunals	Rules on matters pertaining to dismissal of workers, application and interpretation of Standing Orders, legality of strike.	Term: Fixed, further reappointment possible. Size: 1 Qualifications: Must be or has been a high court or district court judge.	The central (for national tribunals) and state (for state tribunals) governments after receiving the recommendations of the Labour Department and high court.	
Monopolies and Restrictive Trade Practices Commission	Prevent concentration of economic power, control monopolies, and prohibit monopolistic trade practices. Investigates cases of abuse through reference of central government or from involved parties.	Term: 5 years, further appointment possible, but no more than 10 years total. Size: Qualifications: Chair must be, has been, or is qualified to be a Supreme Court or high court judge, and the other members must have specialized in relevant areas.	The central government appoints and removes, after consultation with the Supreme Court.	Empowered to hold investigations upon receipt of information from any trader, consumer or affected party; can place injunction against any party when evidence that the said party is about to engage in monopolistic trade practices.

Institution	Appointment and removal of commissioners	Funding	Consultative process	Appeal of decisions, relation to government policy
Reserve Bank of India	Appointed/nominated by the central government for a period of four years; governor and not more than four deputy governors as official directors.	Self.	Multiple relating to its main functions: monetary authority; exchange rate management; regulate and supervise the financial system.	The central bank is not statutorily independent of ministry of finance; however the relationship is more cooperative than confrontational.
Telecom Regulatory Authority of India	Appointment by central government. Removal: central government, following recommendation of dismissal by Supreme Court.	Presently funded through central government budget. Provision to charge fees, establish Telecom Regulatory Authority of India General Fund to meet expenses.	Art. 11: 'The Authority shall ensure transparency…'. Consultative Review on methodologies and proposals (e.g. recent tariff-setting exercise).	High court. Central government can issue policy directives, and can decide whether an issue constitutes policy.
Central Electricity Regulatory Commission	Selection committee established by central government.	Consolidated Fund.	Commission Advisory Committee. Public tariff hearings. Consultative paper on tariff approach.	High court for appeal on question of law. State government can issue policy directives.

TABLE A1.4 contd

Institution	Appointment and removal of commissioners	Funding	Consultative process	Appeal of decisions, relation to government policy
State Electricity Regulatory Commission	Selection committee appointed by state government. Removal: governor, following recommendation of dismissal by high court.	State Consolidated Fund.	State Advisory Committee. Art. 37: Commission shall ensure transparency.	High court. State government can issue policy directives, and can decide whether an issue constitutes policy. Central Electricity Authority resolves disputes between ERC and state government over what constitutes policy.
Stock Exchange Board of India	Fixed term appointments with ex officio membership of RBI.			Government can supersede SEBI in grave emergencies, if SEBI unable to discharge duties, if SEBI persistently fails to comply with government directives under Act.

TABLE A1.4 contd

TABLE A1.4 *contd*

Institution	Pricing	Licensing	Dispute resolution	Other
Telecom Regulatory Authority of India	Notify tariffs for all telecommunications services. Regulate revenue sharing between service providers, technical aspects of inter-connection.	Recommend need, timing, terms and conditions of new service providers. Recommend revocation of license. Ensure compliance of terms and conditions of license.	Settle disputes between service providers, and between them and consumers.	Ensure effective compliance with universal service obligations. Render advice to government on telecommunications. Protect consumers' interests. Facilitate competition and efficiency in the sector. Maintain register of interconnect agreements.
Central Electricity Regulatory Commission	Generation: plant owned or controlled by central government; or selling to more than one state. Inter-state transmission. Frame guidelines for tariff-setting by SERCs.	Inter-state transmission entities (under the amendment to the 1948 Electricity Supply Act passed in 1998).	Settle disputes between generators and/or transmitters which come under its tariff regulation purview.	Promote competition, efficiency, and economy. Associate with environmental agencies to develop environmental regulations for the sector.
Tariff Authority for Major Ports	Set tariffs at all major ports, including for private licensees at ports.	Central government, through ministry of Surface Transport.	Public tariff hearings, public consultations on tariff principles (although there are no specific legislative clauses relating to this).	Central government has right to require authority to charge certain rates. Central government can suspend authority on notification in Official Gazette.

2

The Indian Parliament[1]

ARUN AGRAWAL

INTRODUCTION

The bicameral Indian Parliament came into being with the first national elections in independent India in 1952. Its historical antecedents can be traced back to the Indian Councils Act of 1861. However, the post-Independence Parliament bore little resemblance to the colonial councils of the nineteenth century, or even the Legislative Councils that followed the Montagu-Chelmsford Reforms of 1919 which aimed gradually to develop self-governing institutions for the 'natives' (Hanson and Douglas 1972). The legislative leviathan (Cox and McCubbins 1993), that is the Indian parliament churns out more than 50 Acts every year. It represents the kind of democratic politics with which Lord Morley, the Secretary of State for India in 1908, wanted to have nothing to do (Thakur 1995: 136). The first elected Indian representatives, it is true, were inducted into the Legislative Councils on a significant scale after the Government of India Act of 1935. But as an experiment in transferring power to elected representatives, these councils were a short-lived failure. The Second World War was a signal for the imprisonment of most of the leadership of the Indian freedom struggle, and the end of legislative reforms aimed at self-rule.

[1] I would like to thank Geoffrey Garrett and Devesh Kapoor for their suggestive comments in the framing of this chapter. Most of the quantitative information on the parliament has been collected from website of the Indian parliament: < *http://www.alfa.nic.in* >.

It was only after the drawing up of the Constitution and the creation of the twin 'Representation of the People' Acts in 1950–1 that national elections led to the first parliament of an independent India (Kashyap 1992). Since its inception, the composition of the Indian Parliament, especially its lower house, the Lok Sabha, has been a reliable index of the changing political preferences of Indian voters.[2] The Parliament has been far less successful as a means to control the exercise of executive power. The most significant evidence in favour of this argument was the state of Emergency that Indira Gandhi declared in 1975, for reasons that most political analysts believe to be related to personal aggrandizement. Also symptomatic of this failure is the erosion of procedural norms that are the basis of parliamentary business, particularly after 1975. Institutional changes in parliamentary committees in the 1990s may help shift the political relationship between the Parliament and the government, but the outcomes of these changes is not yet clear. Finally and relatedly, members of parliament have often acted in ways suggesting that their re-election depends relatively little on the services they perform for their constituents. By examining these three propositions about (a) the degree to which the Parliament is an index to changing voter preferences, (b) its legislative performance and its success in ensuring the accountability of the government, and (c) the nature of the relationship between re-election prospects and constituent service, this chapter provides a brief introduction to the Indian Parliament. At this point, the chapter serves a primarily descriptive function.

Basic Information on the Indian Parliament

Between the two houses of the Parliament, the Lok Sabha or the House of the People, with its 543 elected members is by far the one with greater legislative powers.[3] It is led by the Speaker of the house who is usually nominated by the majority party. He votes only in case of a tie. Members of Parliament (MPs) are elected on the basis

[2] As Thakur remarks, 'no general election in India has produced an overall result that was not a fair reflection of voter preferences' (1995: 142).

[3] Two members of the Lok Sabha are nominated by the president from the Anglo-Indian community.

of universal adult suffrage (see Figure 2.1 for a quick statistical snapshot of elections to the Lok Sabha). With 18 as the qualifying age to vote, India has the largest electorate in the world, now numbering over 620 million voters. Members of the Lok Sabha are elected from single member constituencies, in first-past-the-post voting, where the candidate with the largest number of votes is the winner. Voter turnout has typically hovered between 50 and 65 per cent. Therefore, as one might expect, parties forming government, even when they have seemingly overwhelming majorities in the Parliament, often do so with a mandate from less than a third of the electorate.

Whereas the Lok Sabha is elected directly by the people every five years, the Rajya Sabha or the Council of States is a continuous body, its members elected by an electoral college. Each member is elected for a six-year term, and a third of the members retire every two years. The Rajya Sabha's 250 members are led by the vice-president of India who is the upper chamber's ex officio chair. The legislatures of the states elect 238 members, and 12 are nominated by the president upon the advice of the Cabinet. (See Table 2.1 for the state and region-wise distribution of the members of the Lok Sabha and Rajya Sabha). The regional distribution of parliamentary seats makes clear the preponderance of the Hindi-speaking north in elections and in Parliament.

The underlying logic for the Rajya Sabha is that it acts in defence of the interests of states. But in practice the capacity of the Rajya Sabha to do so has been limited. The first reason is the numerical superiority of the Lok Sabha. In any joint sitting, the Lok Sabha outnumbers the Rajya Sabha 2:1. The Rajya Sabha has neither the power to introduce money bills nor to refuse its assent. It does not even have the power to procrastinate for more than two weeks since at the end of that period a money bill pending before the Rajya Sabha is considered to have passed. A further reason for the lesser importance of the Rajya Sabha was the initial dominance of the Congress in national and state level elections. It was only after 1978, when Indira Gandhi lost national elections and the Congress no longer formed the national government that for the first time the party affiliation of Rajya Sabha members were significantly different from those of the majority party in the Lok Sabha. However, as regional parties come to control state governments more pervasively, party affiliations of Rajya Sabha and Lok Sabha members

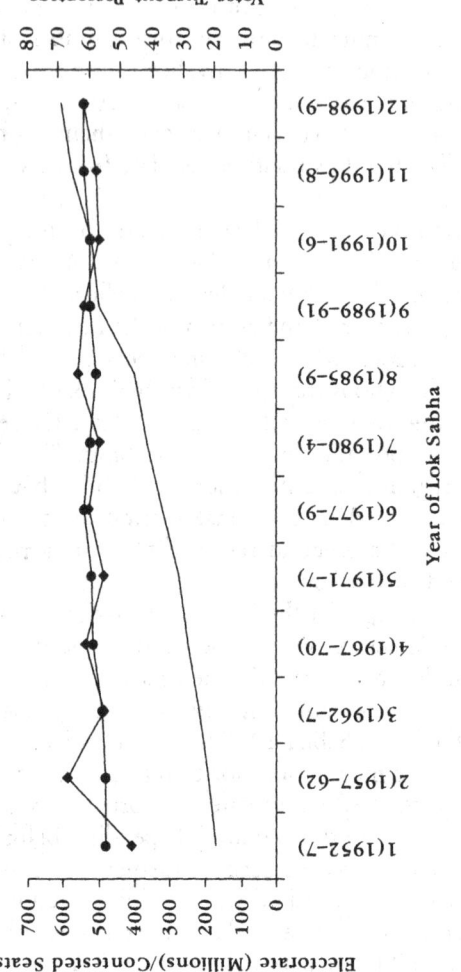

FIGURE 2.1: Statistical snapshot of Lok Sabha elections (1952–98)

TABLE 2.1
Distribution of parliamentary seats by region and state

North			South		
States	Lok Sabha	Rajya Sabha	States	Lok Sabha	Rajya Sabha
Bihar	54	22	Andhra Pradesh	42	18
Haryana	10	5	Karnataka	28	12
Himachal Pradesh	4	3	Kerala	20	9
Jammu and Kashmir	6	4	Tamil Nadu	39	18
Madhya Pradesh	40	16	Andaman and Nicobar Islands	1	
Punjab	13	7	Lakshadweep	1	
Rajasthan	25	10	Pondicherry	1	1
Uttar Pradesh	85	34			
Chandigarh	1				
Delhi	7	3			
Total	245	104	Total	132	57

TABLE 2.1 *contd*

TABLE 2.1 *contd*

East			West		
States	Lok Sabha	Rajya Sabha	States	Lok Sabha	Rajya Sabha
Arunachal Pradesh	2	1	Dadra and Nagar Haveli	1	
Assam	14	7	Daman and Diu	1	
Manipur	2	1	Goa	2	1
Meghalaya	2	1	Gujarat	26	11
Mizoram	1	1	Maharashtra	48	19
Nagaland	1	1			
Orissa	21	10			
Sikkim	1	1			
Tripura	2	1			
West Bengal	42	16			
Total	88	40	Total	78	31

Total for Lok Sabha = 543 (545 with 2 Anglo-Indian members nominated by the president).
Total for Rajya Sabha = 250 (Currently 245, with 12 members nominated by the president).

are likely to grow more heterogenous. On balance, the Rajya Sabha may have a formal status equal to that of the Lok Sabha in the electoral college that chooses the president, but its constitutional standing and legislative powers are vastly lower.

In both the houses, the quorum is 10 per cent of the membership. Decisions on most bills are made by a majority of the members actually present and voting. Legislation can in principle be enacted by a very small proportion of members in either of the two chambers. Indeed, the major business of Parliament is to enact legislation, although it also has constitutional, financial, and governmental powers. It is the sole body that can amend the Constitution, and has undertaken more than 90 amendments since Independence. It is also the only body with the power to raise taxes and spend money, including the authority to pass the annual budget. The failure of the government to ensure the passage of the budget is automatically a vote of no-confidence. Finally, the Cabinet is collectively responsible to the Parliament. A significant innovation in the relationship between the government and the Parliament was the creation of standing departmental committees in 1993 that now oversee each of the ministries. The impact of these committees as watchdogs on the actions of the government is not yet clear, however.

The Parliament as an Index to Changing Voter Preferences

The membership of the Indian Parliament and its composition have been a rough but reliable indicator of changing voter preferences. At one level, this is a tautological statement. But where developing countries and transitional political institutional arrangements are concerned, even this seemingly straightforward proposition, it can be claimed, is difficult to establish. And although it may seem self-evident in the Indian case now, it is all too easy to forget commonplace perceptions even as late as the 1980s that elections in India were no more than a means to rubber stamp the dominance of a single party, the Congress, or even, the dominance of a single family, the Nehrus.

Significant alterations in who represents a particular parliamentary constituency, and in the identity of the majority party in Parliament are sufficient (although not necessary) conditions for the proposition that the Indian Parliament is a reliable index to changing voter preferences. The history of the past half century of parliamentary elections suggest that there have been significant changes in the composition of the Lok Sabha, the only chamber of the house that depends upon direct election by voters (see Figure 2.2).

Even during the period of Congress hegemony in the first three national elections, and its somewhat more contested domination in the following two elections, there were substantial changes in the overall membership of the Lok Sabha. But after the resounding victory that Rajiv Gandhi wrested for Congress in the 8th Lok Sabha, the fortunes of different members of the Parliament have varied in a far less predictable manner. Table 2.2 provides information on new faces in the Lok Sabha following each election. The figures suggest that sitting members of the Lok Sabha cannot be too certain about being re-elected. It seems a reasonable inference that on an average, incumbents have a somewhat greater than even chance of re-election.[4]

The obvious argument against this evidence is of course that under parliamentary systems, where parties exercise significant control over who gets the party ticket and stands for election, it is not changes in individual constituency representation that are important, but changes in who the majority party turns out to be. On this score as well the Indian electorate has shown a convincing ability to register its assessment of the party in power. Even in purely quantitative terms, there have been five changes of government since Independence, all of them in the past quarter century. It is true that some of them have resulted from horse-trading of votes within the Parliament, rather than being a clear electoral verdict in favour of a particular party. Nonetheless, the mixed message from the electorate was foundational in determining who would have majority support in the Parliament, and form the government.

More importantly, electoral results have reflected government performance and broader socio-economic and political shifts. The unexpected ouster of Indira Gandhi in the wake of her decision to declare a state of emergency and assume close to dictatorial powers,

---

[4] Although it may seem that over the past three elections, the chances of re-election have increased, it should be kept in mind that the past three elections occurred within the space of just over three years.

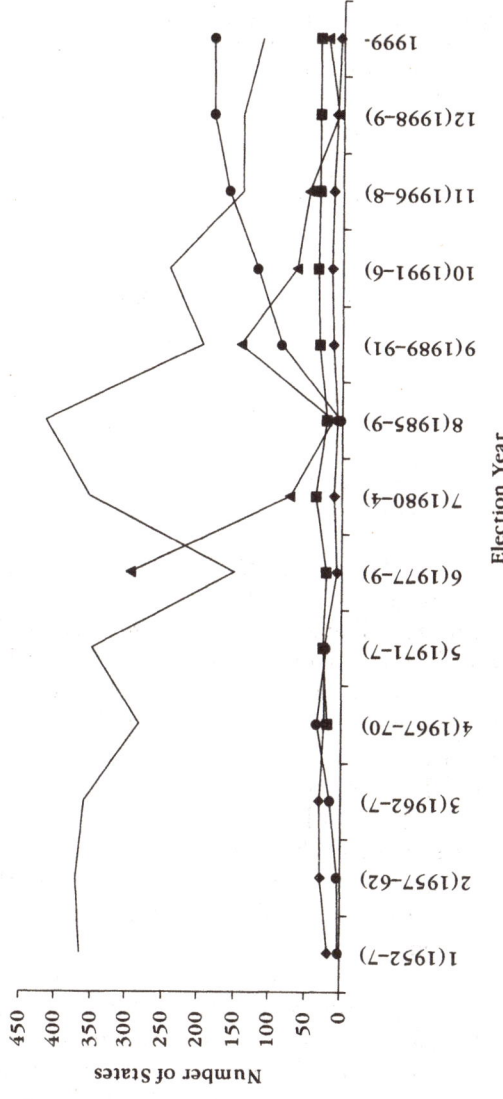

FIGURE 2.2: Changes in party strength in Lok Sabha (1952–99)

Election Year

Number of States

— Cong/Cong(I) — JanSangh/BJP — CPI — CPM — Janata/splinters

TABLE 2.2
Re-election prospects of sitting members of the Lok Sabha

Election year	Seats contested	New members in the Lok Sabha	Chance of re-election
1957	482	263	.46
1962	491		
1967	515		
1971	518	260	.50
1977	540	398	.27
1980	526	386	.27
1984	507	301	.41
1989	523	264	.50
1991	524	230	.56
1996	540		
1998	541		
1999	541	182	.66

the subsequent verdict against the Janata government, and the decline of the Congress in the 1990s are testimony to an electorate that might be mostly illiterate, but which is sensitive to government incompetence. The death of the old Congress that had led the country to Independence was signalled even before any change of government. The resounding victory of Indira Gandhi in 1971 occurred concurrently with the defeat of most of the older Congress stalwarts. The success of her populist slogans and military victories in the early 1970s have, however, demonstrably lost their appeal to the electorate of the 1990s. Neither the Bharatiya Janata Party's hope that military engagements would unite the country in its favour, nor the tired slogans and politics of the Congress have gained much ground for the two parties.

What Figure 2.2 does not reveal is of course the change in the fortunes of national parties in the 1990s. Table 2.3 shows the major gains that regional and state-level parties have made in the last four elections against the national parties. Over the past four elections, regional and state parties have increased the share of their votes in elections from 13 per cent to 27 per cent at the same time as their share of parliamentary seats has gone up from 51 to 158 (ECI 2001). Their gains, the table shows, have been almost precisely the losses of the national parties. The current inability of any of the national parties to win clear favour demonstrates the unwillingness of Indian voters to reward political calculations based mainly on populist, sectarian, or polarizing appeals.

TABLE 2.3
Performance of national and regional parties
in parliamentary elections (1991-9)

Election year	National parties	Regional parties
1991	478 (80)	51 (13)
1996	403 (69)	127 (21)
1998	387 (68)	101 (19)
1999	369 (67)	158 (27)

Note: Figures in parentheses are share of popular vote.

Legislation and Accountability

Legislation in the Indian Parliament involves three stages corresponding to the three readings of a bill in parliamentary systems in general. The first reading of the bill includes its introduction, and the explanation of its contents and aims. After the second reading, the bill can be taken into consideration and put to vote immediately, referred to a select committee or to a joint committee of both the houses, or circulated for eliciting public opinion. The first course of action is rare, and the last course of action is also relatively uncommon. Most bills are referred to committees. Select or joint committees report back on bills with their recommendations. Their recommendations may also contain minority notes of dissent. At this point, the minister in charge can either ask that the bill be recommitted to a committee, or be taken into consideration. Once the bill is placed before the house, members consider it clause by clause, and can move amendments. After all the clauses are dealt with, the bill is listed for its third and final reading at which point only tidying-up amendments are permitted and the bill is put up to vote. All amendments must be approved by the Cabinet, even if the approval comes ex-post facto owing to lack of time. After the speaker certifies the passage of the bill, the bill is sent to the second house, where the entire process is repeated. Once both houses have passed a bill, it is presented to the president. Upon receiving his assent, the bill becomes a law, and is published in the Gazette of

India. Bills do not lapse when parliamentary sessions are terminated; they carry over into the next session.

The Indian Parliament has produced a prodigious amount of legislation. The first twelve parliaments passed a cumulative total of nearly 2500 bills. Although legislation can be introduced either in the Rajya Sabha or the Lok Sabha, by either the governing party/ coalition or by the opposition and as private member's bills, the vast majority of legislation, including all money bills, is moved by the government. A flavour of the legislative business of Parliament is evident from the fate of bills that were passed by both the houses in three recent sessions of the Rajya Sabha (see Table 2.2). The table shows that bills introduced in Rajya Sabha take far longer on average to become Acts. It also shows that a greater proportion of bills originate in the Lok Sabha. It is interesting as well to note that in the three sessions of the Rajya Sabha for which Table 2.2 contains data, not a single bill that passed was a private member's bill.

Part of the reason that private members' bills do not get very far is simply that the time available to discuss them is limited. Only two-and-a-half hours on Fridays are set aside for private members' business, and the introduction of their bills alternates with the introduction of private members resolutions (Sanghvi 1972).[5] The number of bills pending before each house are for the most part private members' bills. Declines in the number of pending private bills occurs because the member either withdraws the bill, or has completed his/her term in the Parliament.

Parliamentary committees are the main venue where members of Parliament consider legislation introduced for the consideration of Parliament. Given the volume and complexity of legislation, and attention needed for matters brought up during Question Hour, in resolutions, through Call Attention Notices, and in Committee Reports, it would be impossible to conduct legislative business that requires detailed attention in plenary sessions of the Parliament.

Committees that assist in conducting legislative business can be classified into two groups on the basis of their form: ad hoc and standing committees. Ad hoc committees are appointed for specific purposes. Select and joint committees on bills constitute the largest proportion of ad hoc committees. Select committees are appointed

---

[5] For a discussion of the role minority groups can play in passing legislation, see Taylor-Robinson et al. (1999) who discusses the Honduran Parliament.

TABLE 2.4

Legislative business of the Parliament—188th to the 190th sessions of the Rajya Sabha

Session	Number of bills passed	House in which bill was introduced	Average time between introduction and passage by both houses	Number of bills pending
188	19	Lok Sabha: 9 Rajya Sabha: 10	Lok Sabha bills: 19 days Rajya Sabha bills: 23 days	Govt bills: 42 Private bills: 148
189	22 bills + 3 constitutional amendments	Lok Sabha: 16 Rajya Sabha: 6	Lok Sabha bills: 27 days Rajya Sabha bills:144 days	Govt bills: 48 Private bills: 84
190	21 bills + 2 constitutional amendments	Lok Sabha : 16 Rajya Sabha: 5	Lok Sabha bills : 46 days Rajya Sabha bills: 190 days	Govt bills: 40 Private bills: 101

in each house. Joint committees comprise members from both houses, and are appointed for legislation considered more important. Ad hoc committees can also be appointed to examine more general questions as for example those related to the efficient performance of the railways, the drafting of Five-Year Plans, or the adoption of Hindi.

Each house also has standing committees that are functionally specialized. Perhaps the most important functional committees are those that exercise control over the finances: the Public Accounts Committee, the Committee on Estimates, and the Committee on Public Undertakings. A second set of important standing committees were created in 1993. These Department Related Standing Committees (DRSCs) are supposed to act as watchdogs, and make the executive more accountable to the legislature. Three such committees were created in 1989, and on the basis of a report submitted by the Rules Committee, 17 departmental committees were created to cover all the ministries of the Union government (see Appendix 1 for a list of all the standing committees of the Lok Sabha and the Rajya Sabha). Departmental committees had been in existence prior to India's Independence and had enjoyed primarily advisory functions (Morris-Jones 1957: 308–15). But they were dissolved by the Nehru government on the grounds that such standing committees were not suited for a system that was modelled on the British Parliament. The recreation of these committees is potentially a major step toward greater parliamentary scrutiny of the government. Unlike select or joint committees on bills, that are created for considering specific bills and which are dissolved after the passage of the bill, the Department Standing Committees scrutinize the work of ministries and departments and their implementation of planned objectives on an ongoing basis, in addition to examining their demands for grants in the budget. Standing committees are reconstituted each year. Tables 2.5a and 2.5b provide information on the party affiliations of selected standing committees in the Parliament.

The most important standing committees in the Lok Sabha are the three financial committees: The Committee on Public Accounts, Committee on Estimates, and the Committee on Public Undertakings. The Committee on Public Accounts examines the accounts for the sums granted by the Parliament to the Government of India and the financial accounts of the government. It seeks

TABLE 2.5a
Party affiliation of chairmen of selected committees

Name of committee	Chairman's affiliation	
	Government	Opposition
Public Accounts Committee (1950–2000)	19	31
Committee on Estimates (1951–98)	45	3
Committee on Public Undertakings (1964–2000)	31	3

TABLE 2.5b
Party affiliation of members of selected committees

Name of committee	Chairman's party affiliation	
	Government	Opposition
Public Accounts Committee (2000–1) (Lok Sabha)	9	6
Committee on Estimates (2000–1)	22	9
Committee on Public Undertakings (1964–2000)	14	8
Business Advisory Committee (1999–2000)	11	4
Committee on Private Bills (1999–2000)	10	6
Committee on Subordinate Legislation (1999–2000)	8	8
Committee on Government Assurances (2001)	8	7
Committee on MPLADS (2001)	15	10

to ensure that appropriations have been utilized prudently and economically (Sanghvi 1970: 11). The Committee has 22 members, of whom 15 are selected from the Lok Sabha and 7 from the Rajya Sabha, on the basis of single transferable vote. The chairman is appointed by the speaker, and since Minoo Masani in the opposition was appointed chairman in 1967–8, the practice has usually been continued by the speakers of the house. Ministers cannot be members of the committee. The Committee appoints subcommittees and working groups to examine specific matters, and draws upon the services of the Comptroller and Auditor General in its examination of witnesses and financial statements. Since its reconstitution in 1950, the Committee has produced more than 1200 reports on the accounts of different ministries.

The Committee on Estimates, in contrast to the Committee on Public Accounts, examines whether appropriations requested by the government have been prepared with the greatest possible economy and in conformity with existing laws governing the raising of taxes and spending of monies. The Committee can also suggest alternative policies and the form in which estimates should be presented to the Parliament. Its 30 members are selected from the Lok Sabha (although no ministers can be members), also by means of the single transferable vote. In examining estimates, the Committee can gather evidence from government departments and ministries as well as from representatives from the general public. Since its formation, the Committee has prepared more than 900 reports, of which approximately half are reports on actions taken by the government in response to its earlier recommendations.

The Committee on Public Undertakings came into being in 1964, and was set up to examine the functioning of state-owned enterprises. It performs the functions of both the Public Accounts Committee and the Estimates Committee in relation to public enterprises, but does not examine matters of major policy or day-to-day functioning. Its 15 members are selected from the Lok Sabha (10) and the Rajya Sabha, also on the basis of single transferable vote.

In addition to the financial committees, at least three other standing committees of the Parliament also assist it in its relations with the government: the Committee on Government Assurances, the Committee on Subordinate Legislation, and the Committee on Petitions. The Committee on Assurances examines the extent to which promises made by ministers on the floor of the Parliament have been kept. The Committee on Subordinate Legislation is supposed to verify that the government does not use rule making to exceed the powers granted to it under parliamentary legislation. The Committee on Petitions examines specific grievances from citizens that have not been addressed through other channels.

Unlike committees in the United States Congress, the parliamentary committees in India that examine bills are for the most part ad hoc select committees that are dissolved after the business of the bill is concluded. As a result, most of the significant work on the writing of legislation is performed by the relevant departments as regards substance, and the ministry of law and justice as regards form. The legislative activity of select committees on bills is significant, but since they are in existence only for the duration of a bill they do not accumulate powers of political quid pro quo in quite the same manner as do standing committees. The activity of standing committees is focused more on ex post examination of bills (although they also at times consider bills before they have been passed), and scrutiny of government activities after the bills have been passed; a form of accountability more than direct control.[6] The impact of Department Related Standing Committees on government policies is also not yet clear because legislative processes and outcomes have simultaneously been influenced by changes in the support bases of different political parties and the emergence of coalition governments. But an additional important difference in the committees is that their composition is far more dependent on the majority party in the Parliament than is the case in the United States. As a result, although committees are significant actors in shaping legislation, their deliberations and recommendations are influenced to a far greater degree by the majority party and the government.

If the committees of Parliament, on the whole, serve only as an instrument with limited utility in ensuring the accountability of the government, a more informal and perhaps more useful avenue of accountability might be seen in the form of questions that MPs pose to the government during the first hour of each meeting. During these question hours, the government can be held to task for its programmes by any member of Parliament. The number of questions asked during the Question Hour has increased enormously over the past five decades. Less than 50,000 questions in oral and written form were allowed during the tenure of the first Parliament; this number climbed to more than 100,000 during the tenure of the 11th Parliament.

However, the increase in the sheer number of questions asked also means that there is significantly less time available to address any specific question. Further, the significance of informal forms of accountability depends considerably on the willingness of the Speaker of the house and of the Business Advisory Committee to admit matters that may prove to be uncomfortable to the government.

The greatest failure of the Indian Parliament to prevent abuse of executive powers occurred of course on 21 July 1975 when Indira Gandhi rammed resolutions approving the presidential proclamation of an internal Emergency through both the houses of

[6] See also Chinai (1970) who can be seen to argue for the strong position that there is only a limited or non-existent relationship between exercising control and ensuring accountability; this position would be hard to defend in light of game-theoretic arguments related to backward induction.

Parliament. Members of the Fifth Lok Sabha allowed the suspension of fundamental rights of Indian citizens, and raised scarcely a murmur against the government's position that in light of the subversive internal disturbances facing the country it was necessary to proceed with extraordinary measures to maintain peace and order. The Congress voted almost en masse to support the Emergency, and the resolutions passed the house by a margin of 336 votes to 59. A strong and unscrupulous leader with a large majority in the Parliament demonstrated the flimsiness of existing institutional safeguards against administrative excess.

Ultimately, of course, the extent to which the Parliament is a forum where the fact of executive accountability can be established depends upon the presence of a viable opposition, and the institutionalization of mechanisms through which accountability can be demanded (King 1976; Saalfeld 2000). In the last decade, both these developments have taken place, although in a manner that is not entirely free from differing interpretations.[7] India has witnessed the emergence of an opposition that is vocal and large, even if this has been at the expense of what some observers anticipated as a 'crisis of governability' (Kohli 1990). The result of the perennial disunity among the governing and opposition coalitions, it can be argued, has been less the establishment of accountability, more a pervasive concern for office among those who seek to represent the Indian people. The development of Department Related Standing Committees similarly has not been matched by powers to these committees to examine the bills introduced into Parliament. Only a small proportion of bills are referred even to select committees, and often they are passed in the form they were prepared by the minister's department. To give just one striking example, in the 9th Lok Sabha, 19 bills, including one on constitutional amendment, were passed by members on a single day in March, without referral to any committee or any discussion.

Representation of Constituents and Constituency Service by Members of the Indian Parliament

If the question of government accountability to Parliament is cause for some concern, the issue of whether the members of Parliament

---

[7] Manor (1988) examines some of the changes in state-society relations that affect how the parliament interacts with the executive as well.

are accountable to their constituents leads to an answer that might seem even more depressing. The most concrete data on the extent to which MPs have a strong interest in serving their constituents is to be found in the allocation and expenditure figures of the Local Area Development Scheme. This initiative was launched in 1993, and initially envisaged the allocation of Rs 10 million (approximately US$ 200,000) per year in each MP's constituency. The amount was to be spent through the district revenue administration, upon the advice and recommendation of a member of Parliament. Since 1998, on the ground that the Scheme was working especially well, the allocation for each constituency was doubled to Rs 20 million per year. This implies, that the total amount available to the MPs each year is about Rs 16 billion. To put this figure in perspective, consider that the total amount that the Indian government spent on holding elections in 1998 is just about Rs 6.6 billion (ECI 2001).

The guidelines for the operation of the Scheme were finalized in 1994, and a parliamentary committee prepared an assessment of the Scheme in 1999 (CMPLADS 1999). According to the committee report, the main reason for launching the initiative lay in the complaints of many MPs about the nature and pace of development projects in their constituencies. According to these complaints, in many constituencies, basic infrastructure related to development and poverty alleviation was lacking even after five decades of Independence. Although MPs, as 'true representatives' of the people in their constituencies recommended various urgent development projects to the administrative authorities, their recommendations did not receive sufficient attention and action, often owing to limited financial resources. By making available a reasonable fund to undertake constituency services, the Scheme sought to translate the developmental will of the MPs into concrete reality. One can safely assume that the Scheme, effectively implemented, would also provide incumbents an advantage in ensuing elections. At a minimum, the availability of funds should have allowed people's representatives to create political obligations and networks of alliances within their constituencies that could translate into gains at the polling booth on election day.

The guidelines for activities that can be undertaken as part of the Scheme specify few restrictions. Projects under the Scheme should be developmental, and funds for specific projects should be sanctioned within 45 days of an application by the MP. Funds available to the MPs do not lapse if they are not used: they can be utilized in the following year(s). Although MPs are advised not to undertake capital projects that cost more than a million rupees each, it is possible to request funds for larger projects when necessary. Funds from the Scheme can also be used to meet the costs of a large project. The implementing authorities are the usual welter of district administration officials, Panchayati Raj institutions, and nongovernment organizations.

From its very inception, the Scheme was criticized as diluting the legislative function of the members of Parliament, for the discretionary powers it gave them, for the incumbency advantages it confers on the MPs and their parties in a given constituency, for bypassing the stated emphasis of the government on involving local democratic bodies in implementing development. But over the period of its functioning, the implementation of the Scheme has drawn additional fire. The projects that MPs recommend for implementation are typically capital works, mostly undertaken through the existing system of contracts in Public Works Departments. Since by all accounts corruption is rampant in these context, the Scheme may have become simply another mechanism to siphon development funds to a select corrupt elite. According to A. Bardhan, the General Secretary of the CPI, 'MPs indulge in corrupt practices to siphon off money' (Iype 2000). There is little involvement of local communities in the recommendation or implementation of projects, and most works that have been initiated are of a routine nature. MPs have recommended temples, residential and office buildings, bought household items, and granted loans out of available funds (Iype 2000). MPs from Bihar, demonstrably the poorest state in India, have the distinction of using among the lowest proportion of available funds for development projects. Finally, although it is clear that members of Parliament have a strong interest in initiating development projects under this scheme, their interest in maintaining the initiated projects is far less certain or visible.

The most interesting and disturbing feature of the Scheme however must be that despite the advantages that it confers on a member of Parliament, the funds available under the Scheme have never been fully utilized. Unlike the Brazilian legislature which according to Ames (1995) is far more active in distribution of pork than on national issues, India's Parliament members seem far less willing to convert even available pork into votes. Under the Narasimha Rao government, when Rs 7.9 billion were available under the Scheme each year, 200 MPs did not use even a rupee. Even Prime Minister Atal Bihari Vajpayee, who is responsible for doubling the allocation to Rs 20 millions per year in 1998, had utilized only Rs 46 million of the 80 million he had been allocated since 1994. The level of utilization of funds available under the Scheme remains low across the board, as Table 2.6 shows. The figures seem to show the limited interest of the MPs in using even what might be characterized as free money as far as they are concerned, toward the development of their constituents.[8]

Interestingly enough, the pattern of partial use of the funds is widespread. Although more careful examination of the figures might reveal some unsuspected patterns, initial analysis on whether there were differences related to the presence of opposition ministries in the states, the level of development of the states, or whether the constituency was one reserved for SC/ST candidates do not reveal statistically significant variations. Thus, although a number of contextual factors might prevent MPs from ensuring the optimal use of available funds, and other proximate factors may be preventing even the utilization of available funds, it seems that MPs do not feel accountable to their constituents about how they use discretionary development funds, and they do not believe that fully using these funds is critical to their re-election.[9]

Despite significant media attention to the limited spending of funds in this scheme, it may be that only those MPs utilize it whose access to other sources of funds for their constituents is limited, and who believe that their re-election chances will be significantly improved if they use all available funds. One indication of this possibility is that if one examines the share of funds used by MPs elected from smaller states and union territories, it is significantly higher than those utilized by MPs from larger states. For union

[8] For a devastating literary criticism of the limited extent to which members of parliament attend to constituency interests, see Chatterjee 2000.

[9] The work of Miller and Stokes (1966) remains a classic on the issue of constituency influence. For some discussions that focus on responsiveness of state institutions, although in political contexts that are far different from those in India, see Bishin (2000), Maestas (2000), Berry et al. (2000), Judge and Ilonszki (1995), and Stokes (1998).

TABLE 2.6
Allocation and expenditure summary of the
MP Local Area Development Scheme (1993–2000)

No.	State	Allocation (in million Rs)	Amount spent (in million Rs)	Expenditures as proportion of allocation
1	Nominated	665.0	355.65	53.5
2	Andhra Pradesh	5479.5	3573.05	65.2
3	Arunachal Pradesh	256.5	166.79	65.0
4	Assam	1719.5	1121.85	65.2
5	Bihar	4808.0	3010.63	62.6
6	Goa	216.5	120.1	55.5
7	Gujarat	3137.5	1832.08	58.4
8	Haryana	1242.5	879.11	70.8
9	Himachal Pradesh	618.5	438.84	71.0
10	J & K	420.0	195.63	46.6
11	Karnataka	3425.0	2252.03	65.8
12	Kerala	2322.5	1270.3	54.7
13	Madhya Pradesh	3506.0	2365.57	67.5
14	Maharashtra	5551.5	2906.83	52.4
15	Manipur	271.5	204.95	75.5
16	Meghalaya	191.5	142.83	74.6
17	Mizoram	191.0	168.89	88.4
18	Nagaland	166.0	151.0	91.0
19	Orissa	2674.0	1396.47	52.2
20	Punjab	1540.5	695.85	45.2
21	Rajasthan	3136.5	1855.05	59.1
22	Sikkim	171.0	150.11	87.8
23	Tamil Nadu	5598.5	4373.47	78.1
24	Tripura	241.5	100.84	41.8
25	Uttar Pradesh	9545.0	6068.55	63.6
26	West Bengal	4405.5	2430.72	55.2
27	A & N Islands	50.5	32.71	64.8
28	Chandigarh	65.5	36.75	56.1
29	D & N Haveli	95.5	49.32	51.6
30	Daman & Diu	60.5	47.14	77.9
31	Delhi	919.5	564.14	61.4
32	Lakshadweep	75.5	71.64	94.9
33	Pondicherry	171.0	60.59	35.4
34	Chhattisgarh	1319.5	870.45	66.0
35	Uttaranchal	502.5	356.82	71.0
36	Jharkhand	1183.0	705.42	59.6
	Grand total	65944.0	41022.20	62.2

territories and states that send fewer than five MPs to the Lok Sabha, the utilization of allocated funds is just about 70 per cent in comparison to MPs from larger states who use less than 62 per cent of funds available to them. It is possible that even when MPs from union territories and the smaller states are from the ruling party, their access to other sources of funds for pork is limited in comparison to MPs from larger states. A more careful test of the proposition—that it is how re-election prospects are affected by access to funds from the Scheme that drives the use of available funds by MPs would take into account the margin of victory for a given MP.

CONCLUSION

This chapter has sketched the beginnings of an argument about the Indian Parliament that portrays it as an institution able to ensure executive accountability to only a limited extent in the post-Independence period. A significant difficulty in the emergence of a Parliament that could demand accountability from the executive was the absence of a meaningful opposition within the Parliament. What also assisted in making the Parliament impotent in the face of executive abuse was the absence of institutional mechanisms within the Parliament that could call the government to account, although perhaps no institutional mechanisms could have survived five successive majorities of the same party in a fledgling democracy. Examples of other experiments in democratic construction in Africa and Latin America scarcely provide any reason to expect the contrary outcome.

Although the late 1980s and 1990s have witnessed the creation of new institutions within the Parliament that can call government departments to account, the most important development is the evaporation of earlier social alliances that had given the Congress overwhelming majorities in the Parliament even when its share of the popular vote was always less than 50 per cent. The changed political landscape has been interpreted by some to be part of a larger dialectic of centralization/decentralization in Indian politics (Bose and Jalal 1997; Jalal 1995). But in any case, such a situation signifies at the least that no party in government can use its slim coalitional majority as a juggernaut to flatten the opposition and dispense with institutional process.

The changing reality of political representation has made the repetition of an authoritarian interlude less likely in India. But it has also simultaneously put the 'homogenizing, centralizing goals of the nation state under severe strain' (Bardhan 1997: 188) and seems to have made little difference in the extent to which political representatives take constituency service as being critical to their re-election. The most important evidence in this regard is present in data on the partial utilization of funds available to parliamentary representatives to undertake development projects in their constituencies.

References

Ames, Barry (1995), 'Electoral Rules, Constituency Pressures, and Pork Barrel: Bases of Voting in the Brazilian Congress', *The Journal of Politics*, vol. 57, no. 2, pp. 324–43.

Bardhan, Pranab (1997), 'The State Against Society: The Great Divide in Indian Social Science Discourse', in Sugata Bose and Ayesha Jalal (eds), *Nationalism, Democracy, and Development*, pp. 184–95. Delhi: Oxford University Press.

Berry, William D., Michael B. Berkman, and Stuart Schneiderman (2000), 'Legislative Professionalism and Incumbent Reelection: The Development of Institutional Boundaries', *American Political Science Review*, vol. 94, no. 4, pp. 859–74.

Bishin, Benjamin G. (2000), 'Constituency Influence in Congress: Does Subconstituency Matter?', *Legislative Studies Quarterly*, vol. 25, no. 3, pp. 389–415.

Bose, Sugata and Ayesha Jalal (1997), *Modern South Asia: History, Culture, Political Economy*, London: Routledge.

Chatterjee, Upamanyu (2000), *The Mammaries of the Welfare State*, New Delhi: Viking.

Chinai, Babubhai M. (1970), 'Parliament and Restraints over Executive Power', in L. M. Sanghvi (ed), *Parliament and Administration in India*, Delhi: Metropolitan Book Co., pp. 93–102.

Committee on Members of Parliament Local Area Development Scheme (CMPLADS) (1999), First Report of the CMPLADS presented to the Lok Sabha on 12 May 2000, New Delhi: Lok Sabha Secretariat, Government of India.

Cox, Gary W. and Mathew D. McCubbins (1993), *Legislative Leviathan: Party Government in the House*, Berkeley: University of California Press.

Election Commission of India (ECI) (2001), 'Statistical Report of General

Elections: 1991–99', *http://www.eci.gov.in/index_previous.htp.* 1/31 2001.

Epstein, David, David Brady, Sadafuni Kawato, and Sharyn O' Halloran (1977), 'A Comparative Approach to Legislative Organisation: Careerism and Seniority in the United States and Japan', *American Journal of Political Science* 41(3): 965–98.

Hanson, A. and Janet Douglas (1972), *India's Democracy.* New York: W. W. Norton, p. 95.

Iype, George (2000), 'Where has the money gone?' Parts I and II, www.rediff.com/news. Accessed on 12 December 2001.

Jalal, Ayesha (1995), *Democracy and Authoritarianism in South Asia: A Comparative and Historical Perspective*, Cambridge: Cambridge University Press.

Judge, David and Gabriella Ilonszki (1995), Member-constituency Linkages in the Hungarian Parliament, *Legislative Studies Quarterly*, vol. 20, no. 2, pp. 161–76.

Kashyap, C. Subhash (1992), *The Ten Lok Sabhas: From the First to the Tenth*, Delhi: Shipra, pp. 4–11.

King, A. (1976), 'Modes of Executive-Legislature Relations: Great Britain, France, and West Germany', *Legislative Studies Quarterly*, vol. 1, no. 1, pp. 11–36.

Kohli, Atul (1990), *Democracy and Discontent: India's Growing Crisis of Governability*, Cambridge: Cambridge University Press.

Krishna, Anirudh (2002), *Active Social Capital: Tracing the Roots of Development and Democracy*, New York: Columbia University Press.

Kumar, Sanjay (2001), 'Delimitation of Constitutencies', *Hindu*, www.hinduonnet.com. Accessed on 12 December 2001.

Maestas, Cherie (2000), 'Professional Legislatures and Ambitious Politicians: Policy Responsiveness of State Institutions', *Legislative Studies Quarterly*, vol. 25, no. 4, pp. 663–90.

Manor, James (1988), Parties and the Party System', in Atul Kohli (ed.), *India's Democracy: An Analysis of Changing State-Society Relations*, Princeton, NJ: Princeton University Press, pp. 62–98.

Miller, Warren E. and Donald Stokes (eds) (1966), *Elections and the Political Order*, New York: John Wiley and Sons.

Morris-Jones, W. H. (1957), *Parliament in India*, Philadelphia: University of Pennsylvania Press.

Przeworski, Adam (1991), *Democracy and the Market: Political and Economic Reforms in Eastern Europe and Latin America*, New York: Cambridge University Press.

Saalfeld, Thomas (2000), 'Members of Parliament and Governments in Western Europe: Agency Relations and Problems of Oversight', *European Journal of Political Research*, vol. 37, pp. 353–76.

Sanghvi, L. M. (ed.) (1972), *Parliament and Administration in India*, Delhi: Metropolitan Book Co.

Stein Robert M., and Kenneth Bickers (1994), 'Congressional Elections and the Pork Barrel', *The Journal of Politics* 56(2): 377–99.

Stokes, Susan (1998), 'Constituency Influence and Representation', *Electoral Studies*, vol. 17, no. 3, pp. 351–67.

Taylor-Robinson, Michelle, and Christopher Diaz (1999), 'Who Gets Legislation Passed in a Marginal Legislature and is the Label Marginal Legislature Still Appropriate?' *Comparative Political Studies*, vol. 32, no. 5, pp. 589–625.

Thakur, Ramesh (1995), *The Government and Politics of India*, New York: St Martin's Press, p. 136

Yadav, Yogendra (1999), 'Electoral Politics in the Time of Change: India's Third Electoral System, 1998–99', *Economic and Political Weekly*, 21–8 August, pp. 2393–9.

————— (2000), 'Second Democratic Upsurge: Patterns of Bahujan Participation in Electoral Politics in the 1990s', in Francine Frankel, Zoya Hasan, and Rajeev Bhargava (eds), *Transforming India: Social and Political Dynamics of Democracy*, Delhi: Oxford University Press.

Name	Lok Sabha	Rajya Sabha
Standing Committees	Committee on Public Accounts	Business Advisory Committee
	Committee on Estimates	Committee on Rules
	Committee on Public Undertakings	General Purpose Committee
	Business Advisory Committee	Committee on Government Assurances
	Committee on Private Members' Bills and Resolutions	Committee on Papers Laid on the Table
	Committee on Papers Laid on the Table	Committee on Petitions
	Committee on Petitions	Committee of Privileges
	Committee on Subordinate Legislation	Committee on Subordinate Legislation
	Committee on Government Assurances	House Committee
	Committee on Absence of Members from the Sittings of the House	Ethics Committee
	Committee on Privileges	Committee on Provision of Computers to Members
	Committee on Welfare of Scheduled Castes and Scheduled Tribes	Committee on MP Local Area Development Scheme
	Committee on Empowerment of Women	
	General Purposes Committee	
	Rules Committee	
	House Committee	
	Library Committee	
	Committee on MO Local Area Development Scheme	
	Committee on Provision of Computers for MPs	
	Railway Convention Committee	
	Joint Committee on Office of Profit	
	Joint Committee on Salaries and Allowances	

TABLE A2.1 contd

Table A2.1 *contd*

Department related standing committee	Committee on Commerce
	Committee on Home Affairs
	Committee on Human Resource Development
	Committee on Industry
	Committee on Science, Technology, Environment and Forests
	Committee on Transport and Tourism
	Committee on Agriculture
	Committee on Communications
	Committee on Defence
	Committee on Energy
	Committee on External Affairs
	Committee on Finance
	Committee on Food, Civil Supplies, and Public Distribution
	Committee on Labour and Welfare
	Committee on Petroleum and Chemicals
	Committee on Railways
	Committee on Urban and Rural Development

Committee on Commerce
Committee on Home Affairs
Committee on Human Resource Development
Committee on Industry
Committee on Science, Technology, Environment and Forests
Committee on Transport and Tourism
Committee on Agriculture
Committee on Communications
Committee on Defence
Committee on Energy
Committee on External Affairs
Committee on Finance
Committee on Food, Civil Supplies, and Public Distribution
Committee on Labour and Welfare
Committee on Petroleum and Chemicals
Committee on Railways
Committee on Urban and Rural Development

3

The Presidency

JAMES MANOR

Political analysts have devoted remarkably little attention to the presidency in India. This owes something to their (or rather 'our') habit of giving formal political institutions too little attention. But even if we focus only on analyses of institutions, more has been written both about the role of state *governors* within India's federal system, and about an executive presidency as a potential *alternative* to the present institution, than about that institution itself.

This writer has written three previous studies of the presidency.[1] But on each occasion, he had the feeling that he was examining a comparatively marginal institution—or at least an institution that achieves great political importance only very occasionally. In Westminster-style systems such as India's, that happens when no party commands a majority in the dominant lower house of a particular country's Parliament.[2] This occurred only twice in the first 38 years of the Republic of India's existence—after the 1969

[1] These studies are: J. Manor, 'Seeking Greater Power and Constitutional Change: India's President and the Constitutional Crisis of 1979' in D. A. Low (ed.) *Constitutional Heads and Political Crises: Commonwealth Episodes, 1945–1985*, pp. 126–41; J. Manor, 'India' in D. Butler and D. A. Low (eds) *Sovereigns and Surrogates: Constitutional Heads of State in the Commonwealth*, pp. 144–70; and J. Manor, 'The Prime Minister and the President' in J. Manor (ed.) *Nehru to the Nineties: The Changing Office of Prime Minister in India*, pp. 115–37.

[2] In India we have seen one exception to this generalization, in June 1975, when President Ahmed agreed, hastily, to sign a declaration of a state of

split in the Congress party, and in mid-1979. In both cases, presidents became hugely important players. During the latter episode, ferocious controversy arose, for reasons explained below. But since parliamentary majorities existed at all other times in those years, Indian presidents almost entirely avoided public controversy—although as we shall see, President Zail Singh (who held office from 1982 to 1987) courted it, and a few other ructions took place behind the scenes.

Since 1989, however, major changes have occurred that have increased the importance of the presidency—and both the *need for* and the *risks of* presidential interventions. The parliamentary elections of 1989, 1991, 1996, and 1998 all produced hung Parliaments (that is, no single party had a majority of seats in the Lok Sabha, India's lower house). In 1999, a coalition led by the Bharatiya Janata Party (BJP) obtained a majority. But for reasons discussed below, there are good reasons to expect hung Parliaments to become the norm once again at future elections—at least over the medium term.

The president has become more important since 1989 because he[3] is the referee in the game of government formation, and he decides whether to grant a prime minister's request for a dissolution of Parliament. In this era of hung parliaments, the former task has become more complex and difficult, and the latter is a potential problem. This makes it much more likely that the presidency will be engulfed in heated disputes which may occur even if presidents seek to avoid controversy—as they usually do.

It is also far more possible now for a president with an appetite for greater power than his office has traditionally possessed to pursue that goal. President Venkataraman *may* have attempted precisely that during the process of government formation in 1989. A president may also seek greater influence in 'normal' times as well—when a government is in place and when no dissolution has been requested. India's current President, K. R. Narayanan, has done so. He had at times disagreed (or *appeared* to disagree) with

---

Emergency at the request of Prime Minister Indira Gandhi. We still do not have a satisfactory analysis of that incident, and it will probably remain impossible to write one unless the Ahmed family opens the president's diaries which are reliably reported to exist.

[3] All Indian presidents have, thus far, been men.

governments. And in early 1999, he asked a sitting prime minister to prove his majority in the Lok Sabha when that was in doubt— a request which triggered the fall of the government and a fresh election.

Part of the explanation for such actions by presidents lies in the changed circumstances since 1989. The advent of hung parliaments has undermined somewhat the power of prime ministers and cabinets that hold office without majority support. And even when a government has a majority, its grip on power often seems rather precarious—because to remain in office, it must rely on a diversity of parties. The prospects of any government being re-elected also usually appear dubious—because since 1989, voters have persistently supported a plethora of smaller (often regional or caste-based) parties, and their continued backing for any party leading a ruling coalition is open to serious question.

All of these things have inspired the holders of some (though, importantly, not all) extra-parliamentary offices in India to seek, with some success, to assert themselves in ways that were largely unthinkable before 1989. In this chapter, we need to consider whether this trend—and the wider dispersal of power away from the prime minister and the Cabinet, and Parliament—has had much impact on the *presidency* as an institution and on the behaviour of individual presidents. It will become clear that it has indeed done so, but that other things were also at work. We shall see that presidents' actions are often influenced more by their personal proclivities than by this dispersal of power.

We must also consider whether greater assertiveness by presidents is *advisable*. This chapter argues that—beyond strict limits— it is not, because the changes which have occurred since 1989 present presidents with a curious paradox. Those changes provide them with many more opportunities to assert themselves, but they also make it more crucial than ever that presidents avoid controversy and the appearance of partisanship—things which nearly always come with greater assertiveness.

This chapter also argues that—since the post-1989 changes will inevitably require presidents to intervene more often—people in India must adjust their attitudes to what constitutes appropriate behaviour by presidents. They must begin to develop a somewhat higher tolerance for presidential activism during the process of government formation—a tolerance of the kind extended to heads of state in political systems where parliamentary majorities are seldom achieved, such as some of the systems in continental Europe.[4] If such an adjustment is not made, Indian presidents will often be unjustly accused of partisanship. To say this is to reiterate and not to de-emphasize the comment above about the need for presidents to seek to avoid the appearance of partisanship.

This chapter is divided into four parts. Part I briefly discusses occasions when presidents acted assertively in the period before 1989. Part II examines changes since then—the reasons for and the implications of the emergence of hung parliaments, and the tendency of some extra-parliamentary institutions to become more assertive. Part III analyses the records of India's three presidents since 1989, with special reference to presidential assertiveness. Part IV concludes by assessing the capacity of the office of the president to cope with the new challenges that have arisen.

I. Presidential Assertiveness before 1989

Since this chapter deals mainly with events since 1989, this discussion of the period before that year—when governments almost always had solid majorities in the Lok Sabha—can be rather brief. More detailed discussions of that era can be found elsewhere.[5]

The limitations on the powers of presidents when governments with solid parliamentary majorities were in place were established during the term of office (1950–62) of the first person to hold that office, Rajendra Prasad. He disagreed with Prime Minister Jawaharlal Nehru on many questions and twice sought privately to resist decisions by the Nehru government. On both occasions, it required threats of resignation from the Prime Minister to persuade Prasad to back down. But he did so, and this firmly established in practice what the Constitution made clear on paper—that while presidents can advise and warn governments and ask them to reconsider intended actions, they cannot defy the will of a government with a majority in the Lok Sabha.

Rajendra Prasad made occasional public statements which amounted to veiled criticisms of the government (as some of his

---

[4] For an introduction to some of these, see V. Bogdanor, 'European Constitutional Monarchs' in Butler and Low (eds) *Sovereigns and Surrogates*, pp. 274–97.

[5] See in particular, Manor, 'India'; and Manor, 'The Prime Minister and...'.

successors have also done). But these were largely tolerated, except on one occasion—when he said, in effect, that a president need not conform to the line laid down by the government. This was, understandably, sharply rebuffed. All of this left Prasad feeling powerless.[6] As a civil servant who had served as his secretary put it, 'There was no substance there...under the high dome of the presidential palace there was nothing but hollowness'.[7]

Most of the other six presidents who served between 1962 and 1987 were far more restrained than Rajendra Prasad had been. One of them, Fakhruddin Ali Ahmed has, with some justice, been criticized for being *too* restrained when presented around midnight on 25/26 June 1975 by Indira Gandhi and one minister with a request for the declaration of Emergency. He might have asked her to reconsider, which would have prevented the full Cabinet from facing a *fait accompli* at 6 a.m. the next morning. But Ahmed, who had been selected for his pliability, behaved as expected and gave way.

However, two later presidents in this period sought quite forcefully to assert themselves. The first, N. Sanjiva Reddy (who held office between 1977 and 1982), enjoyed some success, although less than he hoped for. On 15 July 1979, four days after losing his majority in the Lok Sabha, Prime Minister Morarji Desai of the Janata Party offered his resignation to President Reddy without requesting a dissolution. Reddy then invited the Leader of the Opposition, Y. B. Chavan, who headed the non-Indira Congress party to seek to form a government. When he failed to secure adequate support, the President turned to Charan Singh, who led a small breakaway group from the old Janata Party.

He initially appeared likely to obtain a majority thanks to support from Indira Gandhi's Congress party, but when this support was abruptly withdrawn, Charan Singh resigned and formally requested the President to dissolve the Lok Sabha and call an election. Since he had never obtained a vote of confidence, he had little justification for making such a request. His purpose in doing so was to prevent an invitation to the main body of the Janata Party, which was now led by Jagjivan Ram, a leader from the (ex-untouchable) Scheduled Castes who appeared likely to receive

---

[6] For more detail see Manor, 'The Prime Minister and...', pp. 119–21.
[7] P. Chopra, 'After Charisma' ch. 9, p. 15.

majority backing. President Reddy apparently preferred to deny Ram the premiership and acceded, very controversially, to Charan Singh's request. Many observers believed—rightly in this writer's view—that Reddy expected a fresh election to produce a hung Parliament in which he could exercise more influence than the Constitution intends. (See the discussion of this danger in Part III below.) In the event, the election which ensued yielded a solid majority for Indira Gandhi's Congress, so that whatever ambitions Reddy may have harboured were thwarted. But he was plainly far more assertive than any of his predecessors had been.[8]

The other example of presidential assertiveness in the pre-1989 period occurred when a prime minister had a solid—indeed, a four-fifths—majority in the Lok Sabha. Rajiv Gandhi had obtained this in a landslide election victory at the end of 1984, soon after the assassination of his mother and predecessor in office, Indira Gandhi. The President at the time, Giani Zail Singh, had been hand picked for that post by Indira Gandhi in 1982—in part because he appeared likely to do her bidding.[9] If Rajiv Gandhi had handled him sensitively, the President would probably have proved entirely amenable. But the Prime Minister, who came from a highly anglicized background, found Zail Singh's rough and ready ways distasteful. Rajiv Gandhi therefore set about ignoring him. He failed to meet his constitutional obligation 'to furnish such information...as the President may call for'.[10]

This caused Zail Singh intense irritation, and in 1987, he made his feelings plain—by threatening to withhold assent from a piece of legislation, and then by voicing his exasperation in press interviews. During the very public controversy that followed, it became clear that the Prime Minister (in cooperation with the very partisan Speaker of the Lok Sabha) had virtually ceased to visit or communicate with the President.

Zail Singh later stated that, out of the public eye, gravely serious actions were contemplated on both sides of this dispute. The President considered dismissing the government for 'irresponsibility and

---

[8] This is discussed in much greater detail in Manor, 'Seeking Greater Power...'.

[9] For an account of the curious logic that led to his selection, see Manor, 'India', p. 163.

[10] *Constitution of India*, Article 78.

corruption' over the Bofors arms purchasing scandal—something that would have triggered a full scale constitutional crisis and, probably, a general election. He also claimed that Rajiv Gandhi instructed an adviser to draw up documents to impeach him.[11] In the event, neither man followed through with these drastic actions, and the matter ended in 1987 when Zail Singh completed his term of office. But he came close to a spectacular act of presidential assertiveness.

The incidents involving presidents Prasad, Reddy, and Zail Singh were exceptions to the predominant trend in the pre-1989 period. In those years, presidents tended in the main to restrain themselves—as was only natural, given the prevalence of decisive election results and Lok Sabha majorities. Since 1989, however, things have changed and presidents have had to operate in very different circumstances. Let us now consider the implications of these changes.

II. Changes Since 1989: The Dispersal of Power and Assertiveness in Extra-Parliamentary Institutions

As we saw in the introduction to this chapter, the decade beginning in 1989 witnessed four parliamentary elections, none of which produced a Lok Sabha in which one party or alliance enjoyed majority support. There is more to say about all of that, but let us first note that presidential elections do not occur simultaneously with parliamentary elections.

Presidents are elected to five-year terms indirectly, by way of a complex formula giving varying weights to votes by members of both houses of Parliament, and of state legislatures. If a president dies in office (which has happened twice, in 1969 and 1977), a fresh election is held soon thereafter. But since all presidents since 1977 have served their full terms, this has meant that presidential elections have occurred in the second and seventh years of recent decades. Table 3.1, a timeline, provides readers with an overview of the staggered timings of presidential and parliamentary elections since 1989.

---

[11] See in this connection, M. Limaye, *Times of India,* 20 March 1987. On a dubious attempt by presiding officers in the two Houses of Parliament to bar discussions of this matter, see A. G. Noorani, *Indian Affairs: The Constitutional Dimension,* chs 8 and 9.

TABLE 3.1
Presidential and parliamentary elections in India

Presidential elections (name of winner)	Parliamentary elections
1952 (Prasad)[1]	1952 Jawaharlal Nehru
1957 (Prasad)	1957 Jawaharlal Nehru
1962 (Radhakrishnan)	1962 Jawaharlal Nehru
1967 (Hussain)	1967 Indira Gandhi
1969 (Giri)	
	1971 Indira Gandhi
1974 (Ahmed)	
1977 (Reddy)	1977 Morarji Desai/Charan Singh
	1980 Indira Gandhi
1982 (Zail Singh)	
	1984 Rajiv Gandhi
1987 (Venkataraman)	
	1989 V. P. Singh
	1991 Narasimha Rao*
1992 (Sharma)	
	1996 Deve Gowda/Gujral
1997 (Narayanan)	
	1998 A. B. Vajpayee
	1999 A. B. Vajpayee*
2002 (Kalam)	
	2004 Manmohan Singh

[1] Rajendra Prasad became India's first president at the creation of the Republic of India on 26 January 1950. But the first conventional election to that office, which he won, occurred in 1952.

The star next to the prime minister's name in Table 3.1 indicates that his party or alliance had a reliable majority—on its own—in the Lok Sabha. This has happened only twice since 1989. First, the Congress government of P. V. Narasimha Rao obtained a majority (in fact though not in name) in 1993 by bribing members of Parliament from the small Jharkand Mukti Morcha (a sub-regional party) to oppose a no-confidence vote against it. That assured the Narasimha Rao government of a majority throughout the rest of its five-year term, which ended in 1996. Second, the National Democratic Alliance government led by Atal Bihari Vajpayee obtained a majority (in name and in fact) at the parliamentary election of 1999 and at this writing, it retains it.

We should also note that in the hung parliaments between 1989 and 1999, some governments were much closer to majorities than others. This had a potent impact both on their capacity to govern authoritatively and on their prospects of long-term survival in office. (It also affected their relations with some presidents.) Narasimha Rao's Congress party won a large minority of the seats in the Lok Sabha at the 1991 election, and (unlike in the previous election in 1989) no other party had anything like its total tally of seats. This enabled it to make numerous difficult decisions—especially in the field of economic liberalization. It also meant that it had a reasonably good chance of seeing out its full five-year term (not least because the opposition to it was divided between parties that stood to its left and to its right).

By contrast, the three parties that took power after the parliamentary elections of 1989, 1996, and 1998 were less (usually *far* less) securely placed. In 1989, the party with the largest minority of seats (the Congress) preferred not to form a government, so Janata (the next largest party) assumed power thanks to the support from outside by the BJP and the Left. In mid-1990, however, Prime Minister V. P. Singh sought to appeal to India's disadvantaged section of voters by announcing his intention to implement the Mandal Commission report which recommended reservations in employment and education for such groups. This caused the BJP to withdraw support and Singh's government fell. It was replaced by another government with an extremely precarious hold on power, led by Chandra Shekhar, which lasted only a few months. The 1991 election duly followed.

In 1996, the largest single party (the BJP) was invited to form a government but lasted only 13 days because it failed to obtain majority support in the Lok Sabha. A minority government was then formed by H. D. Deve Gowda of the Janata Dal—that was dependent on the Congress party which did not join it. After just under a year, Congress refused to continue backing him, whereupon another Janata Dal leader (I. K. Gujral) became prime minister—with continued dependence on the Congress. His government lasted less than a year, and thus another parliamentary election occurred in 1998.

That election brought in a government led by the BJP, which depended for its very tenuous majority on an alliance with a large number of smaller, mainly regional parties. It was led by Atal Bihari

Vajpayee whose hold on power was precarious—mainly because of very public squabbling among his coalition partners. His government lasted into early 1999, but then collapsed when Congress' machinations with one coalition partner deprived it of a majority—an episode in which (as we shall see) presidential intervention played a part. After several months in which Vajpayee headed a caretaker government, the general election of 1999 gave his newly constituted and expanded alliance the first clear majority in a decade.

The point of all of this is that—except for the period between 1991 (or more accurately, 1993) and 1996—no government in the ten years after 1989 was securely placed in the Lok Sabha. This inspired people occupying senior posts in institutions that stood beyond the direct supervision of government ministries to begin asserting themselves to a degree that had been unthinkable before 1989 when parliamentary majorities were the rule.

It is, however, worth asking whether the advent of hung parliaments—and the dispersal of power away from prime ministers, their cabinets and parliaments which followed from it—fully explain this increased assertiveness. The evidence already available clearly indicates that it did not—other things mattered too.

It is important to recognize that not all of the institutions which were beyond the direct control of central government ministries became more assertive. The judiciary and the Election Commission plainly asserted themselves in this period, and so did state governments in the federal system. But some other such institutions did *not* do so. It appears that some of these variations are explained by the *personalities* of key figures within these institutions. Certain activist judges, certain chief ministers in state governments (whose number included both allies and opponents of ruling parties in New Delhi), and the irrepressible Chief Election Commissioner T. N. Seshan were plainly more inclined to act forcefully than were senior figures in some other institutions.

III. Have Presidents become more Assertive since 1989?

Let us now turn, in this context, to the actions of India's presidents since 1989. We must consider two questions. First, did those presidents become more assertive? Second, insofar as they did, was their assertiveness more adequately explained by (i) the advent of hung parliaments or (ii) personal proclivities?

India has had three presidents since 1989: R. Venkataraman (until 1992), Shankar Dayal Sharma (1992–97), and K. R. Narayanan (since 1997). Did they become more assertive? The answers vary. The available evidence yields a 'maybe' for Venkataraman, a 'no' for Sharma, and a 'yes' for Naryanan. This takes some explaining.

In his memoirs, President Venkataraman takes pains to show that he behaved with great restraint. It is clear that on many occasions, he was indeed restrained. But he largely fails to address one episode which has generated great controversy. It has been alleged that in 1989—either before the parliamentary election process had been completed, or just after it produced an inconclusive result—he made efforts to get himself selected as prime minister at the head of a government of national unity. This is said to have been inspired both by his own ambitions and by the widespread anxiety that no leader or party in that Lok Sabha could provide stable government. These allegations are mostly expressed verbally and few have appeared in print.[12] They come from a number of people who held prominent posts in various political parties at that time. This writer has stated previously that there is insufficient evidence available to substantiate these charges.[13] The only significant source of fresh evidence on this episode that has lately emerged is Venkataraman's memoirs and, not surprisingly, there is nothing in them to lend credence to the allegations.[14] But a recent discussion of this matter with leading political analysts in Delhi indicated that the allegations refuse to die down. Those analysts have heard stories of the then president's manouevres from too many politicians to disbelieve them. So we must leave the matter open by saying that *may be* Venkataraman made such an attempt.

The case of President Shankar Dayal Sharma is more straightforward. Press reports and other evidence on his presidency, including interviews with people who had frequent encounters with his staff, consistently indicate that he behaved with great restraint. The only suggestion that he might have sought to assert himself came from a knowledgeable Indian analyst who said that he occasionally

---

[12] But see M. Limaye, *Decline of a Political System*, p. 119. I do not regard Madhu Limaye as an unimpeachable source.

[13] J. Manor, 'The Prime Minister and…', p. 135.

[14] See chapters 21 and 22 of R. Venkataraman, *My Presidential Years*.

tried to influence events in a non-intrusive way—probably by way of 'advice' to prime minister which is routine practice.[15] Sharma thus appears to have acted in the tradition of his more cautious predecessors before 1989. He did so even though the government that held power during his last year in office was very precariously placed, so that he might have exerted considerable leverage. So in an era of hung parliaments, it is plainly not inevitable that presidents will become more assertive. But they *may* become so, if they are personally inclined that way—as the case of Sharma's successor vividly illustrates.

President K. R. Narayanan has held office since 1997. When he took up his post, he announced that he intended to be a 'working President'—a comment which suggested that he would be more proactive than many of his predecessors. His record since then has confirmed that initial impression. As we shall see, some observers believe that he has gone beyond the constitutional limitations of his office. We need to consider his actions in some detail.

The first clear sign that he intended to assert himself came in 1998. He was asked by the Janata government headed by I. K. Gujral (whose hold on power was rather tenuous) to endorse the imposition of President's Rule in the state of Uttar Pradesh. He sent the proposal back to the Cabinet with a request that they reconsider it, and they then chose not to pursue the matter. Narayanan won many plaudits for this action, since there was widespread disenchantment in India with the excessive use of President's Rule for partisan purposes. He was fully within his constitutional rights in asking the government to reconsider its decision. But he then said publicly that 'I am not a rubber stamp'. This statement was, if narrowly interpreted, an accurate description of his office. But it raised questions about his willingness to accept 'advice' from governments—which the Constitution plainly requires him to do.[16]

After the 1998 election brought in a coalition government led by the BJP—again without a firm grasp on power—President Narayanan provoked greater controversy on several occasions. The first occurred in August of 1998. Presidents traditionally give an

---

[15] Interview, New Delhi, 5 October 2000.

[16] During that 1998 episode, the test of this would have come had the Cabinet sent the request for President's Rule back to him a second time. But they declined to do so.

address to the nation on 14 August, the eve of Independence Day. By convention, a president sends the text of his speech to the government for vetting—and there have been occasions (notably in the time of President Zail Singh) when such texts were then altered on ministers' advice. In 1998, Narayanan chose not to make such an address, but to substitute an interview with a leading journalist. The content of the interview could not be vetted by ministers in advance. During the interview, the president subtly made clear his discomfort with the Hindu nationalist ideology of the ruling BJP. An eminent journalist, Kuldip Nayar (who is no supporter of the BJP) observed that—even though the government felt too weak to raise objections—Narayanan had been 'institutionally wrong' to take this action.[17]

The next day, at a meeting in the Central Hall of Parliament to mark the end of the 50th year of India's independent existence, the president gave an address that had not been vetted in advance by the government. Early in the speech, he noted that the BJP-led government had been in power for five months. Then later, he criticized people holding public office who saw it 'as an opportunity to strike gold'. The reference can of course be read to refer to politicians of all parties, but coming after the mention of the existing government in New Delhi, it was seen by some to be directed at that particular government. This provoked the same journalist to say that Narayanan had engaged in 'violation(s) of precedent...twice in two days'. He added that in earlier public statements, the President 'has challenged the entire direction of the new economic policy'[18] to which most major parties were largely sympathetic.

In early 1999, when one of the larger parties in the BJP's ruling coalition exited from it, the government appeared to have lost its majority. At that point, President Narayanan stepped in and requested Prime Minister Atal Bihari Vajpayee to establish—through a vote in the Lok Sabha—that he still had majority support.

The President was within his rights in making this request—the Indian Constitution lays down next to no detailed guidelines for presidents in such situations. But three objections might be raised nonetheless. First, Indian and Commonwealth precedents—for the

[17] *Deccan Herald*, 27 August 1998.
[18] Ibid.

most part—strongly suggest that inaction in such circumstances is the convention. (Note however, (i) that India's Constitution explicitly states that the president is not bound by precedents or conventions from other countries, and (ii) presidents have ignored *Indian* precedents established by their own predecessors often enough to make them, in practice, less than binding.[19] Indeed, the evidence suggests that the office of the president does not even keep a record of such precedents.[20]) Second, the President might have expected the opposition parties in Parliament to table an early vote of no-confidence—which provided a further reason for inaction. Third, BJP sympathizers could and did argue that the Prime Minister was entitled to continue in office until a vote of no-confidence succeeded. Until that happened, in their view, the President remained bound by advice from the government which obviously would rot have asked him to act as he did. This is to say that Narayanan was pushing his powers to the limit.

There is another dimension to all of this that cannot be ignored. The differences between President Narayanan and the two Vajpayee governments (before and after the 1999 general election—since as we shall see, differences did not end in 1998) have been greatly exaggerated. Many newspapers have overplayed them,[21] slightly or extravagantly, and opposition parties have gone about this very aggressively.

Clear differences emerged in January 2000 between the President and the Prime Minister over the government's decision to review the Constitution—differences which were set out by Narayanan in another un-vetted speech at the celebration of the fiftieth anniversary of the Constitution. Press reports indicated that he

[19] See for example, the discussion of precedents with regard to the dissolution of Lok Sabha's prior to election day, in Manor, 'The Prime Minister and...' pp. 133–4.

[20] See President Venkataraman's request during the election campaign of 1989 that a note be preapred on possible options—which appears to imply that no record of precedents (Indian or foreign) existed, in Venkataraman, *My Presidential Years*, pp. 314–15. It should be stressed that many other Commonwealth heads of state (including the British monarchy) also apparently lack such lists or records of precedents—though such matters are often, and in part understandably, shrouded in secrecy.

[21] See the criticism of other publications in an editorial in the *Hindustan Times*, 24 March 2000.

believed that since this was not a formal address such as he gives at the opening of a session of Parliament, he need not submit it for vetting. He was probably right, since there are no clear rules available for such occasions. But predictably, the speech triggered strong, positive reactions from the opposition parties. The Congress party hailed the President's 'wise words' as 'a lamp unto our feet and light unto our path'. A Communist Party of India-Marxist leader stated that he had adopted the 'correct position'.[22] The following month, after the ruling BJP's journal had accused the President of being 'partial' and of having 'descended into politics', a Congress party spokesman protested at what he regarded as a 'vituperative act of calumny' intended to 'besmirch' the President's reputation.[23]

The point here is that any president who is as assertive as Narayanan should expect such exaggeration—and he is plainly canny enough to understand this. (Presidents should also be aware of one other thing which compounds this problem—when so-called 'constitutional experts' provide instant commentaries to Indian newspapers on episodes involving the presidency, their views are usually intended to serve the interests of one or another party.) Are these inevitable exaggerations and political controversies good either for his office or for the polity? President Narayanan has obviously concluded that he can live with this, but numerous observers—including many who are not true believers of the Hindu right—have misgivings.[24]

One further incident needs to be noted. In March 2000, President Clinton of the US visited India. At a state banquet in Clinton's honour, President Narayanan departed from the text of a speech prepared by the Ministry of External Affairs—which, again, he is apparently free to do. After several positive references to the US, he said that (as one newspaper paraphrased him) 'globalisation was fast reducing the world to a global village but one that did not need a "headman"'. He alluded to the Cold War mentality that still influences American policy, and emphasized the continuing relevance of the Non-Aligned Movement, although

---

[22] *Hindu*, 28 January 2000.

[23] *Hindu*, 18 February 2000.

[24] See for example, the editorials in the *Times of India* and *Hindu*, both on 29 January 2000.

that went unmentioned in the government's National Agenda for Governance.[25]

This speech offended the Americans and caused intense anxiety in India's External Affairs Ministry. It provoked rebukes even from newspaper editors who have supported Narayanan's earlier outspokenness. The issue was not whether he was free to depart from the Ministry's text, but the things that he said when he did so. The *Hindustan Times* argued that 'Elementary courtesy dictates that when you are hosting a man for dinner in your house, you do not sternly lecture him or make vaguely insulting remarks'. It asked, 'should he be flying solo in the complex area of foreign relations?'.[26]

It is worth dwelling a little longer on the case of Narayanan, because—of the three presidents who have served since 1989—he has been the most patently assertive. Let us consider the *ideas* that appear to have inspired him to act in this way (which will tell us more about the implications of this era of hung parliaments for the actions of presidents), and then the *implications* of his actions for the presidency and the wider polity in an era of hung parliaments.

President Narayanan's assertiveness appears to be explained mainly by two or perhaps three ideas, each of which is probably more important than the changed character of the national party system since 1989 that is the main cause of hung parliaments.

First, like many others in Delhi these days, he appears to believe that the legitimacy of government in India is in some doubt, and that new approaches to development are needed to restore it. These questions about legitimacy do not arise because of changes in the party system and the tendency toward hung parliaments—those things are more symptoms of the problem, not causes of it. The problem is that government has come to be perceived as

[25] *Hindustan Times*, 24 March 2000. A subsequent attempt to play down differences between the president and the government on these issues (*Hindu*, 27 March 2000) is unpersuasive.

[26] 24 March 2000. It should in fairness be stressed that President Narayanan has not always been at odds with the BJP-led government. See for example the reference to echoes between his and the Prime Minister's major speeches in August 2000, in *Hindu*, 18 August 2000.

insufficiently responsive and inclusive. There is thus a need to find ways to open government up to previously excluded groups, to ensure that diversity is respected, and to seek greater synergy between state and society.

This writer should come clean and say that he agrees with these views, and thus that he regards this motive for acting more assertively as admirable. It is also worth stressing that presidents have not just the option but a responsibility to raise moral and constitutional concerns. But we shall see later in this discussion that even when such motives and concerns inspire presidential assertiveness, it can still do unintended damage.

The second thing which appears to lie behind the president's actions is closely linked to the first. He comes from a severely disadvantaged community, and feels—again understandably—that he therefore has a special responsibility to do all that he can to catalyse change that may help such excluded groups.

He *may* also be inspired by a third idea, which is more worrying. This is the notion that he has been elected by a wider constituency than that which supports not the present ruling coalition, the National Democratic Alliance, but the BJP which leads it. The BJP yielded so many seats at the last election to its allies that both the total number of seats that it won and its share of the popular vote were somewhat limited. It would not be entirely illogical for Narayanan to conclude that—despite the fact that he was *indirectly* elected—the large number of MPs and state legislators who supported him constitute a broader political base than the BJP now possesses. If that is in his mind, it might make him feel justified in acting more assertively.

This is worrying for reasons that were set forth, very perceptively—long before anyone imagined an era of hung parliaments—by Jagjivan Ram.[27] In an interview with Pran Chopra in the late 1960s, he expressed the following concern.

A president who chooses to play politics can in fact make himself a formidable power because the only restraint which Parliament can exercise upon him is impeachment which requires a three-fourths majority and a president who has

[27] Anxieties similar to those expressed by Jagjivan Ram appeared in the early 1950s in learned commentaries on India's Constitution, but it is unclear whether Ram had read them. It appears quite possible that he developed this insight independently.

played his political game with skill can never fail to obtain sufficient support in Parliament to [thwart this].[28]

Ram was mistaken about one detail—impeachment requires a *two-thirds* majority of the total members of both houses of Parliament (not just those present and voting). But his basic point has always been valid, and in an era of hung parliaments, it acquires still greater force. If no majority were easily obtainable in a Lok Sabha, an ambitious president might seek to assist someone to become prime minister on the understanding that the latter would then permit the head of state greater influence over the government than the Constitution intends. Such a president might even seize effective control of the government by issuing orders without taking the advice of ministers. An Indian president's orders do not need to be countersigned by the prime minister or others, as is the practice in some other systems.[29] This is not to suggest that President Narayanan intends any such thing—he clearly does not. But President Reddy appears to have attempted to acquire great leverage over a government in mid-1969 in just this way. So this is a concern that deserves greater attention in India.

Let us now turn to the implications, for the presidency and the polity more generally, of the kind of assertiveness which President Narayanan has engaged in. To grasp these, we need to recognize that future elections—at least over the medium term—are likely to produce either more hung parliaments or more of what we have today, coalition governments that may break up. This is likely because the conditions which produced four hung parliaments after 1989 still exist. Voting patterns at the 1999 general election, which gave the BJP-led alliance a parliamentary majority, differed little from those seen in the previous four elections. Huge numbers of citizens continued to support small regional or caste-based parties. The difference in 1999 was not that the BJP gained more seats or popular votes than before, but that it constructed an alliance in advance of the election that included a very large number of these smaller parties.

---

[28] Chopra interview with Jagjivan Ram, Part I, p. 4, in P. Chopra, 'After Charisma: A Study of the Evolution of the Office of Prime Minister in India', unpublished manuscript (1970-1). I am grateful to Pran Chopra for sharing this material with me.

[29] Ibid., ch. 9, p. 15.

There are good reasons to think that it may not be possible for any party to construct such broad alliances prior to the next few general elections. In 1999, when it set about constructing its huge alliance of 24 parties, the BJP found its way almost entirely open—because the Congress party unwisely declined to seek a broad coalition, and because the old Centre-Left 'third force' was in serious disarray. But now that coalition-building has earned it at least two and probably more years in power, the BJP is very likely to be challenged in the game of alliance-building at future elections—by one or both of the alternatives. That will probably ensure that smaller parties, which have consistently garnered substantial votes for a decade, will be sufficiently divided between rival alliances that no alliance gains a majority. On present form, it would not require the loss of many coalition partners to rival alliances for the BJP to lose its hope of a majority.

To say this is not to predict that an era of hung parliaments will continue indefinitely. Majorities in the Lok Sabha may well become obtainable again—probably in one of two ways. A wrenching event akin to the assassination of Indira Gandhi in 1984 might occur—and give one party or alliance a thumping victory. Or what the French call an 'issue of regime'—a dispute over fundamental principles of governance—may arise. We have seen examples of this on two occasions in India—and both times hefty parliamentary majorities resulted. In 1971, Indira Gandhi proposed to abolish poverty, and persuaded voters that their choice lay between reaction and reform. In 1977, the Janata alliance (or perhaps Indira Gandhi's Emergency regime) persuaded them that the choice lay between democracy and autocratic rule. It is conceivable that another 'issue of regime' might arise—even if none is visible at present.

But in the absence of such things, hung parliaments appear likely to persist for some time. And even if one alliance manages to scrape through with a majority, it is unlikely to be very secure. So we should expect continuing *uncertainty* and *instability* at the national level for some time yet. These things will require presidents to become more proactive and, if you like, assertive—*even if* they do not wish to do so—because there will be more occasions on which the refereeing that only presidents can do becomes necessary.

If that happens, it will be more important than ever that the ultimate referee (the president) is perceived to be non-partisan since without that, the legitimacy of the outcomes of his refereeing—that is, national governments—will be open to question. This is exceedingly important. There are thus more compelling reasons now than before 1989 for presidents to do their utmost to *avoid* perceptions (or misperceptions) that they are partisan. Such perceptions arose—unjustifiably—often enough *even before* the onset of the era of hung parliaments.[30]

So in sum: even though an era of hung parliaments creates greater opportunities—and often the necessity—for presidents to act assertively, it also generates strong new reasons for president *not* to do so, because assertiveness tends to generate suspicions of partisanship even when there is no such intention.

It is only fair to add that in an era of hung parliaments, people in India need to become more tolerant of legitimate presidential interventions—because the changed conditions will inevitably require more of these. They need to develop the kind of willingness to see that presidents seek to foster sustainable governments in fragmented parliaments that exists in, for example, Italy. But it is unrealistic to expect this change of view to happen swiftly—so over the medium term, presidents need to take great care to ensure that their interventions are indeed legitimate.

IV. The Shortfall—Some of the Time—in Staff Support for the President

Given the new burdens which presidents must bear, how well equipped is the office of the president to deal with them? This is a question that was never asked, so far as I can tell, before 1989 by any analyst—including me.

Over 400 people work on the president's staff, but nearly all of them attend to the maintenance and management of Rashtrapati Bhavan (the president's house)—tending its vast gardens, keeping the building ready for glittering state occasions and visits by foreign heads of state, etc. Only a tiny number of people provide support to the president in his dealings with the government of the day and other groups—not least the opposition parties—which seek to interact with him.

Such is the confidentiality (in many ways, rightly) that surrounds that side of his activities that it is very difficult to obtain information even on exactly how many people have served presidents on that

[30] See for example, Venkataraman, *My Presidential Years*, pp. 248–9 and 312–13.

front at various times. It is a matter of public record that a small number of officers from the Indian Administrative Service, other services, and the armed forces have worked under various presidents. But conversations with some who have done so indicate that nearly all of those people dealt with the running of Rashtrapati Bhavan and with state ceremonials. It appears that only a small handful have provided support to the president in his political role and that *only one* person is in a position to play a *substantial* role—the secretary to the president. And as we shall see, even this has not always happened in practice.

The secretary has a very difficult job at the best of times. And in an era when hung parliaments have become the norm, that job is—potentially at least—excruciating. Given all of that, what do we know of the people who have served as secretaries? Here again, information is difficult to come by. Indeed, all of the 17 well-informed civil servants (active and retired) who have spoken about this to the present writer have asked (understandably) for anonymity, and have requested that their comments be conveyed in somewhat vague terms. Nonetheless, even these comments provide us with one startling—and worrying—insight.

Senior officials who worked in powerful departments of the Government of India during the 1990s and who dealt with the office of the president found the quality of the people holding the post of secretary to be rather variable. They report that at least one and probably two of the three presidents who served in that period preferred to have secretaries who fell short of top quality. They adopted that approach because they wished to shoulder the political burdens of this great office almost entirely by themselves. Only one of the three presidents in that period is said to have sought out a secretary who was formidably equipped in his own right to provide substantial assistance on matters governmental and political.

These sources further state that, in the days when less able secretaries were in place, senior officials in key ministries of the Government of India made few attempts to develop dialogues of any substance with those secretaries. This was true even of the Prime Minister's Office. Those officials held back because they believed (i) that these secretaries were not capable of sophisticated exchanges, and (ii) that the presidents who had selected these secretaries preferred to handle serious political matters all by themselves. This meant that the only meaningful dialogues that occurred in those periods between important ministries and the office of the president involved ministers and presidents themselves. Only when a highly competent secretary held office did detailed discussions of immensely important political, governmental and strategic matters took place between senior officials in key ministries and the secretary in question.

This strongly suggests that during most of the 1990s, presidents were less fully informed on matters of state (and, necessarily, on politics) than they should have been and than they may have wished to be. It must be stressed that the presidents who selected less-than-formidable secretaries were themselves decidedly able men who were quite capable of dealing, on their own, with complex issues in a sophisticated manner. But despite that, their approaches clearly left them deprived of the full flow of information from key ministries that occurred when an outstanding person served as secretary. We also know that at times, both of those highly skilled presidents were not in the best of health. There were periods in which one of those presidents struggled visibly just to fulfil minimal ceremonial duties. (And, if we consider certain earlier periods, we know that not every man who has served as president has possessed the ability and sophistication to handle his political duties with any adequacy—even if he was served by a formidable secretary.)

All of this raises doubts about the capacity of the office of the president to cope with the political burdens that are placed upon it. The only occasion that we know about when a president sought to expand his team of advisers on governance was when President Rajendra Prasad asked Nehru to permit this in the early days of the Republic. The proposal was understandably rejected then, because the Prime Minister was rightly concerned about Prasad's desire for an expansion of presidential powers.[31] But now that the burdens of the presidency have clearly expanded because of changes in the national-level party system, an expansion of the president's staff appears in a very different light, as a matter of urgency. It is not for a foreign observer such as this writer to suggest solutions to this problem. Indian leaders are fully capable of tackling this matter. But it is important to recognize that, sometime in recent years, a genuine problem has existed.

[31] I am grateful to Granville Austin for this information.

References

Bogdanor, V. (1991), 'European Constitutional Monarchs' in D. Butler and D. A. Low (eds), *Sovereigns and Surrogates*, London: Macmillan, pp. 274-97.

Chopra, Pran (1970-1), 'After Charisma: A Study of the Evolution of the Office of Prime Minister in India', unpublished manuscript.

Deccan Herald (1998), 27 August.

Hindu (2000), 'Cong (I) hails President's "wise words",' 28 January.

———— (2000), 'A cautionary note', 29 January.

———— (2000), 'Cong (I) condemns "attack" on President', 18 February.

———— (2000), 27 March.

———— (2000), 18 August.

Hindustan Times (2000), 'Editorial', 24 March.

Manor, James (1988), 'Seeking Greater Power and Constitutional Change: India's, President and the Constitutional Crisis of 1979' in D. A. Low (ed.), *Constitutional Heads and Political Crises: Commonwealth Episodes*, 1945-85, London: Macmillan, pp. 126-41.

———— (1991), 'India', in D. Butler and D. A. Low (eds), *Sovereigns and Surrogates: Constitutional Heads of State in the Commonwealth*, London: Macmillan, pp. 144-70.

———— (1994), 'The Prime Minister and the President' in J. Manor (ed.), *Nehru to the Nineties: The Changing Office of Prime Minister in India*, London: Hurst & Co., pp. 115-37.

Limaye, M. (1987), *Times of India*, 20 March.

———— (1992), *Decline of a Political System*, Allahabad: Wheeler.

Noorani, A. G. (1990), *Indian Affairs: The Constitutional Dimension*, Delhi: Stosius Inc/Advent Books Division.

Times of India (2000), Editorial, 29 January.

———— (2000), 'The President and foreign policy', Chennai, 27 March.

Venkataraman, R. (1994), *My Presidential Years*, New Delhi: Indus.

4
Institutions of Internal Accountability

S. K. DAS

Institutions of internal accountability are arrangements to hold public entities and officials accountable for their actions. The Comptroller and Auditor General, Central Vigilance Commission, and Central Bureau of Investigation are three such institutions. While the Comptroller and Auditor General provides the transparency to check acts of financial omission and commission, the Central Vigilance Commission is an advisory body in matters of corruption and the Central Bureau of Investigation is the principal investigative agency of the Government of India in corruption cases.

COMPTROLLER AND AUDITOR GENERAL

The institution of audit goes back a long way. The Department of Audit was established in 1858, following a major administrative reorganization carried out by Lord Canning. Honourable Sir Edmund Drummond was the first Auditor General. In independent India, the designation was changed to Comptroller and Auditor General(CAG). The CAG derives his authority as the auditor of the government from Articles 149 to 151 of the Constitution. The duties, powers, and conditions of service of the CAG are laid down in a statute—the CAG's (Duties, Powers, and Conditions of Service) Act.

Audit takes place in two ways. One is the central audit: it involves examination of vouchers, accounts, and other records of the departments, and issuing of audit notes. The other is the local audit or inspection; it involves inspection by the Resident Audit Offices and peripatetic inspection teams, and issuing of inspection reports. The major findings of the audit notes and inspection reports are included in Audit Reports and sent to the concerned departments for being laid before Parliament. The Public Accounts Committee (PAC) and the Committee on Public Undertakings (COPU)—financial committees of the Parliament—select a few paragraphs from the Audit Reports, and after detailed examination and oral evidence, prepare their report and submit it to Parliament.

One feature of the initial design that has had an enduring influence on how the institution of audit has evolved over time, is its independence from the executive. The Montford Reforms of 1920-1 emphasized the independence of audit from the government. The independence was further strengthened in the Government of India Act of 1935 when the Auditor General was given the status of a judge of the Federal Court. In 1950, the independence of audit was written into the Constitution itself. The CAG is appointed by the president of India; he is given a term of office of six years and cannot be removed except by an impeachment process. His salary and other conditions of service are prescribed by a statute and cannot be varied to his disadvantage after his appointment.

The evolution of the institution has been shaped for the most part by changes in the political realm. When the institution was founded, it was a law and order state and audit was designed as expenditure audit—the accent was on individual transactions, checking them for financial regularity. When the nature of the state changed and development was sought to be achieved through large-scale public investment, the orientation of audit changed to value-for-money. In the welfare state, with improvement in the quality of life of its citizens as the state's objective, it was social audit as distinct from financial audit. When the state became increasingly involved in science and technology, science audit emerged—policy choices became more important for audit, with orientation towards results rather than procedure (Sathyamoorthy 1990).

Have such changes in orientation detracted from the goals of the institution? While some of the expanded functions like value-for-money and social audit remain within the bounds set by the goals of the institution, others such as policy audit certainly exceed the bounds (Iyer 1997). But, do such expanded functions undermine the institution's effectiveness in performing its core functions?

TABLE 4.1
Evolution of the institution of audit

Phase	Orientation
Law & order	Regularity, propriety
Developmental	Value for money
Welfare	Social audit, evaluation of performance and improvement in the quality of life
Science & technology	Policy audit, Study of assumptions, choices, policies, techniques, and processes

Source: Sathyamoorthy (1990).

They do; because, in the core function of expenditure audit, scrutiny by audit is selective due to constraints of manpower, and the expanded functions make it even more selective by placing further demands on the strained manpower.

Why, then, does the institution embark on such functions? There is a tendency in the institution to regard conventional audit as routine functions, and therefore, pedestrian. This is so, because other institutions in the state structure look down upon conventional audit functions; the functions are variously described as 'pettifogging', 'wooden', and 'unimaginative' (Iyer 1997). The institution is uneasy about how its conventional functions are viewed, and the result is a constant search for higher functions; the institution, understandably, is happier doing policy audit rather than commenting on financial irregularities.

The institution is big in size, and sprawling, too. Apart from the CAG's office, there are 105 field formations with 88 branch offices and 424 Resident Audit offices spread all over the country, with about 61,000 people working in it. For an institution of such size and spread, there is far too much centralization in the CAG himself. It is so, because, there is only one CAG for the central government as well as the state governments. India is perhaps the only federal country with a single CAG; even the Government of India Act of 1935 had envisaged separate and independent heads of audit for the states. Anecdotal evidence suggests that it was the career ambition of some audit officials, that resulted in an institutional structuring in which a wholly unacceptable level of concentration resides in a solitary CAG (Joseph 1994).

The centralization is evident from how authority is allocated within the institution. All important powers are concentrated in the CAG: he directs, monitors, and controls the activities of all the field formations, and is responsible for development of organizational objectives and policies, auditing standards and systems, laying down policies for management of manpower and material resources, and processing and approval of Audit Reports for being laid before Parliament (Activity Report 1998–9). Such a level of concentration means upward information flows of a substantial magnitude. In 1998–9, for example, the central audit audited 53,82,289 vouchers, accounts, and records, and issued 10,528 audit notes while the local audit inspected 33,054 units and issued 27,943 inspection reports (Activity Report 1998–9). The information in the various audit notes and inspection reports has to be processed for selecting a few paras to be finally included in the Audit Reports and laid before Parliament. Ironically, this also governs the internal incentive structure in the institution; the incentives are linked to whether the work done by the audit staff finally finds a place in the Audit Reports.

Meaningful audit work, however, is a difficult proposition because of the existing procedures in the institution. The procedures mandate that examination by audit can be with reference to the documents and replies provided by the departments; physical verification is not permitted. The procedures prohibit independent investigation beyond replies provided by the departments; external cross-check from sources other than the offices being audited is not allowed. Neither do the procedures encourage summoning a departmental official to appear in person and explain matters.

Why do the procedures prohibit so much? To answer that question, the procedures have to be put in perspective. The audit procedures are, in fact, a continuation of the processes borrowed from Victorian England where personal dishonesty was but rare. Audit, in those halcyon days, tended to privilege the word of the official and was happy to rely on records; it obviously felt no need for external corroboration.

The audit procedures have not changed with the times while the standards of integrity and probity have. Since the CAG has been given the power to decide on the nature and scope of audit to be conducted by him, it is difficult to understand why the audit procedures have not been modified to take care of the prevailing standards of personal integrity and probity.

Audit procedures also demand that the code which regulates how audit should be conducted, remain confidential. The Blue Book or the Memorandum of Secret Instructions, is a case in point. Other countries make a habit of making their audit codes public. In the United States, for example, the Auditing Standards of the General Accounting Office called the Yellow Book is a published document. Even in India, it was not always that the code was confidential; the story is still told of how a minister and a CAG feuded in public, and when the minister happened to quote a rule from the audit code which embarrassed the CAG, the code was made into a classified document overnight (Joseph 1994). The story may be apocryphal, but it has the merit of explaining how a single, whimsical action can have the effect of making institutional processes opaque. The result of such confidentiality is not particularly wholesome, either; the inaccessible manner of audit's operation has made the working of the institution a 'black box', and to that extent, repugnant to the departments whose transactions the CAG audits.

Discretion is occasionally exercised by audit staff either in omitting to audit the accounts of a department or failing to point out lapses when auditing them; such exercise of discretion is usually by way of connivance with the departments. The Fodder Scam is an example. In Bihar, the officials of the Department of Animal Husbandry embezzled funds running into 9500 million rupees through fraudulent drawals from the government treasury; the embezzlement took place over a period of several years. The Public Accounts Committee, in its report to the Bihar Assembly in November 2000, pointed out how the CAG's staff never got the accounts audited. The PAC went on to say that if the staff of the CAG had done their job, the scam could have been avoided (*Hindu* 2000).

Such exercise of discretion to subvert the goals of the institution has been rather rare; it is more common for the departments of the government to thwart audit by refusing to cooperate with it. Replies to observations of audit are often not provided or provided only after long delays and countless reminders. Replies, when provided, are either inadequate or evasive, and in any case, designed to obfuscate. Why does it happen? It has something to do with how the departments view audit. Audit is constituted as a negative institution intent on finding niggling faults and overstating them. Paul Appleby, an expert in public administration, had observed that auditing was a highly pedestrian function with a narrow perspective and very limited utility, and the institution of audit had induced a widespread and paralysing unwillingness in the government departments to decide and act (Appleby 1953). Appleby's observations are important if only for the reason that they reflect how departments view audit. Such a view translates into many ways in which departments thwart audit.

The Fifth Pay Commission had this to say:

Government departments have to develop a high degree of sensitivity to comments by the audit. The approach should not be to close ranks and rush to the defence of the delinquent official. The systemic defects should be removed at once and individual lapses punished with the utmost expedition (Pay Commission 1997).

The audit is powerless in the face of such recalcitrance; it has no power to impose a sanction—the best it can do is to put a paragraph in the Audit Report. Observation of audit carry no disagreeable consequence, either; the only way audit can pack some clout is when the PAC and COPU make adverse comments based on the observations of audit. But, then, the PAC and COPU are very selective in their scrutiny: they choose only a few paragraphs from the Audit Reports for examination and evidence. Following was the level of selectivity for 1997–8, and 1998–9.

TABLE 4.2
Level of selectivity of Audit Reports

Year	Total number of paras in the Audit Reports	Number of paras selected for review	Number of paras finally reviewed by PAC/COPU
1997–8	1209	76	16
1998–9	1478	87	32

Source: Activity Reports, CAG, 1997–8 and 1998–9.

For the year 1997–8, the number of paras selected for review was 6.28 per cent of the total number of paras in the Audit Reports, and the number of paras taken up for final scrutiny was 1.32 per cent. For the year 1998–9, the level was also low: the number of paras selected was 5.88 per cent while the number of paras finally reviewed was 2.18 per cent. The paras for some of the departments were not discussed at all—the scientific departments for the year 1997–8 and the Central Excise and Customs department, Autonomous Bodies and Scientific departments for 1998–9 (Activity Reports 1997–8 and 1998–9).

The Shakdher Committee which looked into the procedures in the context of examination of Audit Reports by the PAC and COPU, had recommended in 1993:

• Executive's response at all levels to audit's queries and inspection reports must be enhanced.

• Government must invariably respond, within the specified time frame, to CAG's references on material proposed to be included in Audit Reports.

• Government must take suo moto action on all issues raised in Audit Reports and should submit notes to PAC/COPU on such action.

• There must be better monitoring of follow-up action on Audit Reports (Kumar 1998).

There is now a vast accumulation of Audit Reports in the legislature and the committees have discussed only a fraction of the reports so far. Clearly, the effectiveness of the institution of audit is hampered by demand factor. Since the institution was designed to assist the Parliament in exercising financial control over the executive, the demand factor is endogenous to the institutional design. Can one think of a change of client to enhance the effectiveness of the institution? In most countries which have independent institutions of audit, the audit reports to the legislature. In the United States, the General Accounting Office is a part of the legislature, and in the UK, the CAG is an officer of the House of Commons. In making audit report to the legislature, the idea is to provide for a system of checks and balances in the functioning of the institution of audit which is otherwise autonomous.

It is true that the institution enjoys considerable autonomy from the executive. But, in one important respect, the autonomy is seriously threatened. Article 148 of the Constitution provides for the appointment of the CAG by the president of India; in other words, the appointment is done on the advice of the executive. It has so happened that the last four CAGs have been officers of the Indian Administrative Service (IAS) who were on the verge of retirement (Narsimhan 1997). By offering such a prestigious post-retirement job to its own officers, the government is in a position to assure itself of their continued loyalty. Arguably, such a practice enables the government to undermine the autonomy of the institution which is otherwise guaranteed by the Constitution.

Another way in which the autonomy of the institution has been undermined is by giving it a multiplicity of missions. When the institution of audit was founded, it was entrusted with both audit and accounting functions. In 1976, audit and accounting functions were separated; accounting is now done by the departments themselves in the central government. The accounts of the state governments, however, remain the responsibility of the CAG. This has important implications. Maintaining the accounts of the state government has meant diversion of much-needed manpower from audit function; out of the total number of 61,000 persons working in the institution, 25,290 persons do accounting work—more than 41 per cent of the total staff. The deployment of such large staff for the accounting function has undermined the effectiveness of the institution in its core functions of audit. What is even worse, there are long delays and appalling mistakes in the maintenance of accounts of the state governments. The financial transactions of the state governments as recorded by the CAG have not been reconciled with the accounts maintained by the departments of the state governments for years, providing, in the process, ample opportunities for fraud and embezzlement (Joseph 1994).

Maintaining accounts, obviously, is not the institution's forte, but, in respect of auditing, the institution has, over the years, built up knowledge resources which are commensurate with its auditing tasks. The accumulation of such knowledge resources has been made possible by the excellent quality of personnel. The executive cadre—numbering about 550—is, for the most part, recruited through the Union Public Service Commission by an open, competitive examination. The CAG has total autonomy in evaluating the performance of his staff, and also, in effecting their promotions and placements. The promotions and placements are linked to seniority and performance—totally free from non-merit considerations and ascriptive bias.

As a result, the institution has succeeded in creating, nurturing, and sustaining an organizational culture—insular, an unwavering belief in the virtues of independent audit, pride in performing constitutionally mandated functions, commitment to enforcing financial control over the government by exposures and sanctions—which is conducive to the realization of the goals of the institution.

The self-esteem of the institution has been undeniably high. A caveat is in order, though. The self-esteem seems to be sagging in recent years, and a spirit of cynicism is ascendant, at least in the higher echelons of the institution. This is so, because, the highest position in the institution—that of the CAG—has been filled up for the last twenty-two years by officers from the IAS in a manner that looks like the systematic exclusion of the audit personnel from ever making it to the top (Iyer 1997).

There is a vital flaw in the functioning of the institution, however: its delays are legendary. As is the common experience, the Audit Reports relate to transactions which took place several years ago. During the intervening years, it is very likely that government functionaries involved in irregular practices might have gone to other departments or retired from service or even died (Das 2001). The Fifth Pay Commission was driven to say,

Audit should be as concurrent as possible. Scandals and scams are known even while they are being planned and executed. If audit draws attention to them forthwith in a well-publicised manner, such scandals can be halted in mid-stride. Post-mortems are useful but can only be conducted while the patient is dead. It is better to cure the patient and try to keep him alive (Pay Commission 1997).

The Fifth Pay Commission was right. In recent years, there is not a single instance of a major scandal that has been brought to the fore by the audit process. Observations of audit in the Bofors case, Securities Scam, and Disinvestment Scam came long after they had been debated in the media and even in Parliament (Iyer 1997).

There are huge delays at every stage. The CAG sends the Audit Reports to the government, and it is the government which lays the reports before the legislature, and only then, the reports become public. The CAG takes his own time in auditing things, and by the time the reports are finally released, the transactions to which they relate are already several years old. Delays take place during consideration of the reports by the PAC and COPU. There are further delays in the finalization of the reports of the committees, the response of the departments, their consideration by the committees, and the recommendations of the committees to Parliament.

What has been the impact of audit? It is only marginal (Das 2001). And this, despite the constitutional mandate of the institution, its statutory independence from the executive, its high quality of personnel, knowledge resources, the enviable organizational culture, and its diligence—the large number of audit reports that it has generated over the years. The lack of effectiveness of the institution has largely stemmed from how other institutions in the state structure have responded to it: the financial committees of Parliament have been negligent in assisting it while the departments of the government have done their best to thwart it.

CENTRAL VIGILANCE COMMISSION

The Central Vigilance Commission is a five-member body headed by the Central Vigilance Commissioner (CVC). The Commission has a secretary, two additional secretaries, ten directors and four under secretaries. There are thirteen commissioners of departmental Inquiries (CDIs) to conduct enquiries. There is also a technical wing with two chief technical examiners (CTEs) assisted by eight technical examiners and six assistant technical examiners. The total staff strength of the Commission is 279.

The Commission receives corruption complaints against government officials, and gets them investigated either through the Central Bureau of Investigation (CBI) or the vigilance organization in the departments. After an investigation is completed, the Commission is consulted about further course of action—departmental action or prosecution in a court of law or dropping of the case; this is called first-stage advice. In cases in which action for major penalty is instituted after the first-stage advice, the Commission is consulted for second-stage advice on the quantum of punishment. The Commission is also consulted for second-stage advice in cases in which action for minor penalty had been instituted and it is proposed to close the case.

The Commission was established on the recommendation of the Committee on Prevention of Corruption (Santhanam Committee). The Santhanam Committee recommended that anti-corruption work was better done in the department itself and an outside agency such as a vigilance institution could function only in an advisory capacity. So, when the Commission was founded in 1964, the institutional design provided for an advisory role and it is the advisory function that the Commission has continued to discharge. There have been efforts, however, to enhance the power and status of the Commission, particularly in recent years. The Independent Review Committee (IRC) set up by the Government of India in September 1997 with the CVC as its member-secretary, recommended:

- The Commission should be given statutory status.

- Selection for the post of CVC should be made by a committee consisting of the prime minister, home minister, and leader of the Opposition.

- The CBI should report to the CVC about corruption cases. (CVC Annual Report 1997)

The Supreme Court, on the basis of the recommendations of the IRC, passed an order in the Jain Hawala case in December 1997, decreeing statutory status for the Commission. Curiously, it was the judiciary which mandated such a status, although only a statute enacted by the legislature could do that. A Bill—the CVC Bill—has been introduced in Parliament to give effect to the judgement of the Supreme Court and is now referred to the Parliamentary Joint Committee for its comments.

The Parliament will, no doubt, deliberate on the subject and take an appropriate decision, but the question is: will the effectiveness of the Commission improve if it is given statutory status and made independent of the executive? There seems to be no reason for such an inference, because, at no point of time, the functioning of the Commission has been hampered by interference from the government. This is evident from the annual reports of the Commission: the reports have to be laid before each house of Parliament, drawing attention to any recommendation made by the Commission which had not been accepted by the government, and there has not been a single occasion when the Commission has, in its annual report, complained about its recommendations not being accepted by the government. More generally, the Commission's reports have not invited any attention from members of Parliament; clearly, the Commission has not made an impression on the representatives of the people as an anti-corruption institution (Narsimhan 1997).

The Commission does not rank high in public esteem, either. In popular perception, the Commission is seen as a 'somewhat obscure body' (Swami 1998), a 'peripheral body' (Mahalingam and Swami 1998); on the whole, as an institution that is inconsequential.

This is perhaps why the Commission does not receive too many corruption complaints, as the following table shows.

TABLE 4.3
Number of cases received by the Commission

Year	Cases received
1989	3643
1990	3953
1991	3915
1992	3900
1993	4166
1994	4378
1995	3929
1996	4263
1997	4304
1998	5076

Source: Annual Reports, Central Vigilance Commission.

How does the number compare with receipts in other anti-corruption institutions? A comparison with Independent Commission Against Corruption (ICAC), the comparable anti-corruption body in Hong Kong, gives us an idea.

TABLE 4.4
Corruption complaints received by the ICAC

Year	Cases received
1989	2388
1990	2390
1991	2186
1992	2257
1993	3276
1994	3312
1995	2987
1996	3086
1997	3057
1998	3555

Source: Das (2001).

The number of cases received by the Commission has been marginally higher; but the fact remains that in the Corruption Perceptions Index (The Transparency International 1998), Hong Kong is ranked 16th in the list of non-corrupt countries while India is ranked 68th, and India, in any case, has a much larger civil servant population.

The Commission, as we noted, depends on two agencies—the vigilance organization in the departments and the CBI. The vigilance organization in the department is headed by a Chief Vigilance Officer (CVO) who handles complaints of corruption and conducts enquiries. An officer of the department is appointed as the CVO after obtaining the prior approval of the Commission. The CVO looks after other items of work in the department in addition to vigilance work and reports to the head of the department. It so happens that the Commission has very little control over the CVO; for that matter, it does not wield enough clout to get even the post of CVO filled up. In 1992, for example, there were eight departments—including the President's Secretariat and the Prime Minister's Office—where the post of CVO was vacant. There were 71 public sector undertakings, nine banks, and 11 other organizations including Delhi Administration and the Election Commission where the post of the CVO was lying vacant. There were 36 organizations where the post of the CVO had been vacant for three years, and in some of them, for more than 13 years. For the public sector undertakings, at least 25 per cent of the sanctioned posts in the vigilance set-up remain vacant at any given point of time (CVC Annual Report 1997).

The CVC has been given the power to assess the work of the CVO, but the power is only nominal. The CVC records his assessment on a separate sheet of paper which is later appended to the main assessment report. Since the main assessment is done by the official superiors of the CVO in the department, the assessment by the CVC is only of marginal importance. A review of the practice by the CVC himself says that it has not enabled the Commission to assess the work of the CVO in its total perspective (CVC Annual Report 1996). A change in the practice is being contemplated.

The Commission has no control over the CBI, either. The Supreme Court had ordered in the Jain Hawala case that the CBI should report to the CVC. The Court had decreed:

The CVC shall be entrusted with the responsibility of superintendence over the CBI's functioning. The CBI shall report to the CVC about cases taken up by it for investigation, progress of investigations, cases in which chargesheets are filed, and their progress. The CVC shall review the progress of all cases moved by the CBI for sanction of prosecution of public servants which are pending with the competent authorities, specially those in which the sanction has been delayed or refused.

The mandate of the Supreme Court is unequivocal, but since the CBI is a creation of the Delhi Special Police Establishment Act, it is for the Parliament to legislate on the subject. The Parliamentary Joint Committee, consisting of 30 members of Parliament drawn from various political parties, has given its comments on the CVC Bill in November 2000. According to the Committee, the CVC's superintendence of the CBI should be construed in a manner which does 'not amount to undue interference in the agency's functioning'; in fact, the Committee has explicitly prohibited the Commission from directing the CBI to 'investigate or dispose of a case in a particular manner'.

The Parliamentary Joint Committee is obviously reluctant to hand over the superintendence of the CBI to the CVC. Why should that be? Two reasons can be cited. First, the Committee seems to have concluded that the present CVC has exceeded the bounds of his advisory role by issuing instructions to the departments on policy matters, and this, perhaps, explains why the Committee would like the CVC's superintendence of the CBI to be consistent with overall government policy. Second, the Committee would, perhaps, prefer the CBI to be under the central government as is the dispensation now. Such a dispensation gives the government the requisite control over the CBI, if only to ensure that the high functionaries of the government are not exposed to potentially embarrassing investigations.

The question still remains: if the CBI reports to the CVC as mandated by the Supreme Court, would it function more independently? There is no cause for such an inference, because the CBI will continue to take instructions from the government. As Praveen Swami says, 'Even if the CVC is made a statutory body and truly independent Central Vigilance Commissioner appointed, the CBI will continue to retain an uncomfortably close linkage with the Government' (Swami 1998).

There is, very clearly, an agency problem, but what about the rules and the procedures of the institution? In the working of the Commission, the Conduct Rules provide the authority for instituting enquiries, while the Classification, Control and Appeal Rules prescribe the procedure. In addition, there are the Vigilance Manuals—compilations of decisions of the Commission in earlier cases—which provide the precedents.

The Classification, Control and Appeal Rules prescribe elaborate procedures: there are 12 stages in an enquiry. These stages start with the preparation of a charge-sheet and end with imposition of a penalty. As a result, the proceedings tend to be protracted and remain inconclusive for years; the Rules are so demanding by way of procedural correctness and conclusiveness of evidence that it is difficult to punish even the most glaring lapses (Das 2001). The proceedings are also subject to Article 311 of the Constitution which provides that no government servant can be punished 'except after an enquiry in which he has been informed of the charges against him and given a reasonable opportunity of being heard in respect of those charges'. Because of the safeguards in Article 311, most corruption cases go in favour of the delinquent. Article 311 was amended in 1976, permitting a penalty to be imposed on the basis of evidence, but, even in its amended form, the safeguards are so exacting that they tend to protract the proceedings indefinitely.

Both the Conduct Rules and the Classification, Control and Appeal Rules are full of loopholes, and as a result, they provide ample opportunities for exercise of discretion. The Report of the Administrative Reforms Commission had this to say: 'The Conduct Rules and the Classification, Control and Appeal Rules are too brief and perfunctory to be really useful.' The Report pointed out that there were too many loopholes in the procedure (ARC 1967). Considerable discretion is exercised by the functionaries of the Commission—generally by using the loopholes, and also, the safeguards in Article 311—to hand out soft penalties or exonerate the delinquent. The Vigilance Manuals create cushions of safety which are routinely exploited by the delinquent to escape punishment or get away with nominal penalties. Table 4.5 below gives an analysis of the action recommended by the Commission by way of first-stage advice.

TABLE 4.5
Combined CBI/CVO investigation reports

Year	Advice tendered	Action recommended with percentage			
		Prosecution	Major penalty	Minor penalty	Others
1989	1949	39 (2.00%)	522 (26.78%)	182 (9.34%)	1,206 (61.88%)
1990	1998	35 (1.75%)	594 (29.73%)	227 (11.36%)	1,142 (57.16%)
1991	2027	43 (2.12%)	645 (31.82%)	292 (14.41%)	1,047 (51.65%)
1992	2093	48 (2.29%)	845 (40.37%)	277 (13.24%)	923 (44.10%)
1993	2172	46 (2.10%)	797 (36.70%)	291 (13.40%)	1,038 (47.80%)
1994	2234	49 (2.20%)	853 (38.20%)	283 (12.60%)	1,049 (47.00)
1995	1084	15 (1.40%)	349 (32.20%)	138 (12.70%)	582 (53.70%)
1996	2482	84 (3.40%)	955 (38.50%)	247 (9.90%)	1,196 (48.20%)
1997	2817	94 (3.30%)	1,207 (42.90%)	318 (11.30%)	1,198 (42.50%)
1998	2308	64 (2.80%)	936 (40.50%)	194 (8.40%)	1,114 (48.30%)
Total	21,164	517 (2.44%)	7,703 (36.39%)	2,449 (11.57%)	10,495 (49.58%)

Source: Annual Reports, Central Vigilance Commission.

Almost 50 per cent of the cases have ended in exoneration, although these are cases in which the Commission had satisfied itself earlier that there was a prima facie case. In 12 per cent of the cases, the delinquent officials have got away with minor penalties. Prosecution was recommended in only two per cent of the cases. Table 4.6 indicates the recommendations of the Commission by way of second-stage advice.

TABLE 4.6
Recommendations of the Commission as second-stage advice

Year	Imposition of major penalty	Imposition of minor penalty	Others	Total
1989	287 (38.37%)	148 (19.79%)	313 (41.84%)	748
1990	384 (47.12%)	150 (18.40%)	281 (34.48%)	815
1991	426 (42.18%)	162 (16.04%)	422 (41.78%)	1010
1992	384 (41.07%)	171 (18.29%)	380 (40.64%)	935
1993	429 (48.70%)	205 (23.30%)	247 (28.00%)	881
1994	615 (57.00%)	203 (18.80%)	262 (24.20%)	1080
1995	513 (56.60%)	137 (15.10%)	257 (28.30%)	907
1996	659 (57.80%)	158 (13.80%)	324 (28.40%)	1141
1997	1121 (59.60%)	301 (16.00%)	459 (24.40%)	1881
1998	1014 (56.60%)	240 (13.40%)	536 (30.00%)	1790
Total	5832 (52.12%)	1875 (16.75%)	3481 (31.11%)	11,188

Source: *Annual Reports*, Central Vigilance Commission.

Thirty-one per cent of the cases ended in exoneration although these were cases in which the Commission itself had recommended imposition of penalty in its first-stage advice. In 17 per cent of the cases, the Commission has recommended minor penalties. Clearly, the performance of the Commission in its second-stage advice has been as soft in recommending punishment as in its first-stage advice. On the whole, the Commission has not recommended sufficiently deterrent punitive action; it comes across more forcefully when one looks at the penalties recommended by the Commission.

TABLE 4.7
Imposition of penalties

Year	Dismissal	Removal	Compulsory retirement	Total
1989	20	17	12	49
1990	19	22	19	60
1991	20	15	26	61
1992	13	19	17	49
1993	22	17	14	53
1994	30	21	26	77
1995	28	15	4	47
1996	19	10	8	37
1997	25	17	15	57
1998	73	23	20	116
Total	269	176	161	606

Source: Annual Reports, Central Vigilance Commission.

Only 606 government servants have lost their jobs over the ten-year period. Clearly, the punishment awarded in most cases is not exemplary, with the result that necessary deterrence is not established and the stakes for corruption are not raised.

If the rules and procedures are so inhibitive, why hasn't the Commission considered adopting more accessible administrative options? After all, the Commission is also responsible for initiating 'review of procedures and practices of administration in so far as they relate to maintenance of integrity in administration'. A simple administrative option could be that the reporting officers are permitted to record their views on the integrity of the official, and adverse reports received from three separate reporting officers could be used to retire the corrupt official from government employment under FR 56(J). If Article 311 is such an impediment, why has it not been amended? For example, the safeguards in Article 311 could have been diluted for officials who are caught red-handed while taking bribes or who possess disproportionate assets. While the Commission is not enthusiastic about diluting the safeguards in Article 311, the legislature has not been forthcoming either. Interestingly, the only time Article 311 was amended was during the Emergency when the working of the legislature was suspended by the executive.

The CVC Bill suggests a number of measures to make the Commission independent. First, it is proposed that the CVC should be given a tenure and the age of his superannuation fixed at 65. Second, the selection for the post of CVC is proposed to be made by a committee consisting of the prime minister, the home minister and the leader of the opposition. Third, eligibility requirements by way of qualification and experience have been proposed for appointment of the CVC.

A tenure is, of course, a safeguard, but by fixing the age of superannuation at 65, retired judges of the Supreme Court are kept out. The qualification and experience for eligibility are designed in a manner to fit only senior IAS officers. What it means, in effect, is that the position of the CVC is overwhelmingly earmarked for IAS officers. Should one be surprised? Appointing IAS officers as the CVC has been the age-old practice; except for the first CVC who was a former chief justice of a high court, all other CVCs have been IAS officers who were retiring or had retired. What implication does it have for the autonomy of the institution? By appointing superannuating IAS officers, the government would have destroyed the statutory autonomy of the Commission if and when it is given. In other words, through appointments which are by way of placements for IAS officers, and therefore, essentially in the nature of inter-temporal incentives, the government would have been in a position to ensure that the Commission falls in line with its wishes.

The practice also has implications for an institution of restraint such as the Commission; an institution which should, by definition, adhere to norms of self-restraint. The Commission, particularly in the last few years, has not exactly been the epitome of self-restraint: it has relentlessly striven to expand its control over other institutions in the state structure, and has issued instructions to departments on what verges on policy, although, the Commission, in its institutional design, was never intended to be a policy-making body. As we mentioned earlier, the Parliamentary Joint Committee seems to have concluded that the present CVC has overstepped his brief by issuing instructions to the departments on policy matters. It so happens that the Commission is not alone in pursuing an expansionist agenda. T. N. Seshan, an IAS officer, who headed the Election Commission—another institution of restraint—pursued an expansionist agenda rather aggressively in the full glare of media publicity. Could it be that IAS officers, long used to encroaching on others only to give themselves greater prominence and visibility, find it too constricting to pass an opportunity for self-aggrandizement, even when they happen to head institutions of restraint?

Does the Commission have the necessary capabilities for its functions? In the matter of conducting enquiries, the Commission has the required knowledge resources: the commissioners of departmental inquiries have the necessary expertise for conducting enquiries. On the technical side, the Commission has built up expertise which is commensurate with its tasks—the chief technical examiner and technical examiners are drawn from various technical departments of the government such as the Departments of Power, Public Works, Telecommunications, and the Border Road Organisation. On the administrative side, the secretary, additional secretaries, and directors who handle matters relating to first-stage and second-stage advice, are experienced administrators, being on deputation from the Government of India.

The fact that most of the functionaries in the Commission are drawn from such diverse sources, has implications for the organizational culture of the institution. Since an overwhelming part of the senior personnel are on deputation from a variety of departments with radically different backgrounds, educational attainments and experience, an organizational culture internal to the institution has not crystallized.

Since the procedures within the institution verge almost on the judicial, principles of natural justice demand that enquiries be finalized in a time-bound manner. Time limits are prescribed in the Commission for completion of different stages of enquiry. For example, the CVOs are required to complete their investigation within three months; in case of the CBI, the period is six months. But the actual experience has been different. At the end of 1997, investigation reports were awaited in as many as 1355 complaints which had been sent to the CVOs. Of these, 844 complaints were pending for more than three years, and 248 complaints, for periods ranging between one and three years. For the CBI, out of 9 complaints, 4 complaints were pending for more than three y ears (CVC Annual Report 1997).

Delay takes place at every stage of the enquiry, including the implementation of the advice tendered by the Commission. For example, at the end of 1997, there were 1975 cases pending for over six months for implementation of the first-stage advice and 1202 cases for over six months, for implementation of the Commission's second-stage advice (CVC Annual Report 1997). There is delay in the Commission itself. At the end of 1977, there were 2052 cases pending with the Commission, which were brought forward from the previous year. Of these, 156 were complaints, 1214 were investigation reports, and 591 related to enquiry reports and minor penalty cases (CVC Annual Report 1997). No enquiry is completed within the time limit prescribed. The Parliamentary Joint Committee on the CVC Bill was so exercised about the delay in completion of enquiries that it called for a time limit to be prescribed in the law itself within which an enquiry must be completed and decision taken.

Is the Commission effective as an anti-corruption institution? The answer is in the negative. The rules and procedures have not been compatible with the goals of the institution, and the personnel of the Commission have manipulated rules and procedures to make the institution ineffective. But, above all else, the effectiveness of the Commission has been hampered by agency problem: institutions such as the CVOs and the CBI which are designed to assist the Commission, have worked only to subvert its goals.

CENTRAL BUREAU OF INVESTIGATION (CBI)

The CBI is the premier investigating agency of the Government of India in anti-corruption cases. The CBI is headed by a director who is supported by three additional/special directors and fifteen joint directors besides a legal advisor and supporting staff. It has its offices all over the country. It has three main divisions:

- Anti-Corruption Division
- Special Crime Division
- Economic Offences Division

The CBI has a hoary past. During the years of the Second World War, the government set up an investigating unit in the War Department to handle cases of corruption in large contracts; the unit was called Delhi Special Police Establishment. In 1942, its jurisdiction was extended to the Railways, and in 1946, it was made a part of the Ministry of Home and given a statutory basis by the enactment of the Delhi Special Police Establishment Act. After Independence, it developed as a specialized investigating agency and was named the Central Bureau of Investigation in 1963. The CBI derives its investigative powers from the Delhi Special Police Establishment Act, 1946, but such powers are limited to specific offences that are notified by the central government under Section 3 of the Act. The CBI deals with various types of offences: corruption, murder, kidnapping, abduction, and economic offences. Its services are also available for assisting state governments in investigating crimes which have inter-state ramifications. More recently, it has even been given the task of examining documents relating to the date of birth of the chief justice of the Supreme Court. But one feature of the initial design that has endured in the evolution of the institution, is anti-corruption work as its core function.

In the 1960s and early 1970s, there was a change in the nature of politics and administration; they became the source of enormous power, pelf, and patronage. This was so, because, the regulatory regime called for a variety of permits and licenses, and it meant that the ministers and top bureaucrats could collect hefty bribes in the process of granting licenses and permits. This was also the time when politics became an expensive proposition as the electoral process lent itself to manipulation by money power. All this meant that the public offices were used for extracting rent.

Since cases of corruption in high places are investigated by the CBI, the government decided to take charge of the CBI. So, over a period of time, the CBI became an instrument of control; an instrument to protect public functionaries from embarrassing investigations. In other words, the CBI ended up by protecting corruption rather than exposing and punishing it as it was designed to do; in some cases, the CBI was even used to settle political scores.

This is evident from the accusations of bias that are levelled against the CBI. For example, during the CBI's handling of the Jain Hawala case, such allegations were made by politicians and government officials; ironically, the allegations came both from Bharatiya Janata Party and the Congress I, placed at opposite ends of the political spectrum. In the Bihar Fodder Scam, the former Chief Minister Laloo Prasad Yadav alleged that the CBI was used by the ruling Bharatiya Janata Party to settle political scores with him (Swami 1998).

Manipulation of the CBI as an instrument of control is made possible by the provisions of the Delhi Special Police Establishment Act, the CBI's parent Act. Section 4 of the Act vests the power of superintendence of the CBI in the central government. In all cases investigated by the CBI, the government is empowered, even at the stage of investigation, to acquaint itself with details of evidence, which, in essence, means that the government can interfere at the stage of investigation itself and thwart the case (Narsimhan 1997). The Bofors investigation is a case in point. The Delhi Special Police Establishment Act, in vesting the superintendence of the CBI in the government, is not an exception. Legislations such as the Criminal Procedure Code and the Police Acts place all investigation under the control of the government; they are, in fact, a replication of the investigation model of the British state in India. Such a model has also stood the scrutiny of the judiciary: that the government's supervision of investigation also permits operational interference, has been upheld by Justice Desai in the Tata case and by Justice Mukharji in the West Bengal Boys case (Das 2001).

The Supreme Court, however, gave a ruling in the Jain Hawala case in December 1997 that, 'While the Government shall remain answerable for the CBI's functioning, to introduce visible objectivity in the mechanism for overviewing the CBI's functioning, the CVC shall be entrusted with the responsibility of superintendence over the CBI's functioning.' In effect, the Court was handing over the superintendence of the CBI to the CVC, whose independence from the government it had ensured in the same judgement by decreeing a statutory status for the Commission. What did the Supreme Court intend to achieve? Was it to ensure the independence of the investigators in the CBI so as to keep them beyond the pale of government interference? In that case, what does not make sense is the Court's mandate that 'the Government shall remain answerable for CBI's functioning'; such an answerability would logically call for considerable supervision of the CBI by the government. In terms of the Court's order, the government was also empowered to 'take all measures necessary to ensure that the CBI functions effectively and efficiently and is viewed as a non-partisan agency'. The language of the Court's order clearly indicates that the government is given a considerable role in the functioning of the CBI (Mahalingam and Swami 1998).

It makes more sense to see the Court's judgement as one more step in the process of consolidation of its control over institutions in the state structure; it is also in line with the Court's practice in asking the CBI to take up specific cases and report the progress in investigation. In such cases, the judges of the Supreme Court have gone to the extent of personally supervising the process of investigation; in fact, they have been doing the kind of supervisory work which, in terms of the CBI's institutional design, the director of the CBI should be doing. What are the implications of such supervision by the Supreme Court? Ordinarily, investigation is on the basis of information as well as evidence. Courts deal with evidence, not information. It does not make sense, under the circumstances, for regular courts of trial and appeal to associate themselves with stages of investigation which involve assessment of information and its follow-up (Narsimhan 1997).

In defence of the Supreme Court, however, one has to say that the Court has good reasons to be apprehensive about the quality of investigation by the CBI. Such an apprehension has a foundation of facts, because, the CBI has a long tradition of wilfully sabotaging investigation, presumably at the behest of persons being investigated. More often than not, the process is taken to its logical conclusion: a case which is made weak by wilful sabotage, is made weaker in its presentation to the courts, thanks to the quality and malleability of the CBI's prosecutors.

This explains why the CBI's record in detecting and punishing corruption has been so unsatisfactory.

TABLE 4.8

CBI's case records

Items	1972	1992	1997	1999
1. Number of cases investigated and finalized during the year	1790	1412	2820	2763
2. Number of cases prosecuted in the courts	384	505	605	627
3. Number of cases disposed of by the courts during the year	352	237	376	498
4. Number that ended in conviction	300	164	216	249
5. Number that ended in acquittal	52	73	160	249
6. Number of conviction in courts as a percentage of cases investigated and finalized (% of item 1)	16.75	11.61	7.65	9.01

Source: Annual Reports, Ministry of Personnel, Public Grievances and Pensions.

The percentage of conviction in courts is decreasing over the years: from 16.75 per cent in 1972 to 7.65 per cent in 1997 and 9.01

per cent in 1999. What could possibly be a safeguard against such wilfully incompetent investigation and prosecution by the CBI? The Supreme Court, in its judgement in the Jain Hawala case, sought to provide such a safeguard: it decreed that the government should put in place a panel of lawyers to review CBI's work and fix responsibility for unsuccessful investigation and prosecution in each case. How will the Court's mandate impact on the internal incentive structure in the institution? The incentive structure in the CBI is linked to getting a conviction in the courts, and therefore, the CBI filters out a high percentage of cases so as to yield a high conviction rate. The CBI's chosen tactic, as is evident from the history of Bofors or St Kitts investigation, has been to stonewall investigations relentlessly rather than bring prosecution. A panel of lawyers to review the CBI's investigation and prosecution can only be a disincentive against pursuing difficult cases with a low chance of conviction (Mahalingam and Swami 1998).

Now that there is a change of client in the sense that the courts have taken control of the CBI, has the picture changed? Not very much. The judgement of the Supreme Court in the Mukta-Panna Oil Fields case in October 2000 is an example. The case was about the award of an oil-field contract to Reliance-Enron Consortium, and it had been alleged that the CBI's investigation into the bribery and malpractice in the award of the contract was shoddy (*Times of India* 2000). The Court said,

> We note with concern that courts, including this court, have very often relied on this organization (the CBI) for assistance by conducting special investigations. This reliance of the courts on the CBI is based on the confidence that courts have reposed in it and the instances like the one which we are now confronted with are likely to shake our confidence in this organization.

The Court has good reasons to be peeved, because it had earlier mandated a substantial degree of autonomy for the CBI in the Jain Hawala case. In terms of that judgement, the tenure of the director of the CBI was to be for a period of two years and his selection made by an independent committee consisting of the CVC, secretary of the Home Ministry, and secretary, Department of Personnel, Government of India. The Cabinet Committee on Appointments, consisting of the prime minister, the home minister, and the minister for personnel, was to approve the recommendations of the Committee. Will these measures make the CBI independent of the government? The two-year term for the director of the CBI provides some guarantee against political pressure, but it is no fire wall. The procedure for selecting the CBI director, as mandated by the Court, is no guarantee of autonomy, either; this is so, because, the deliberations of the Cabinet Committee on Appointments are, by the very nature of their essential linkages to the senior bureaucrats who service it, a hostage to the interests of bureaucrats who are, more often than not, the subject of the CBI's investigations (Swami 1998).

So the bureaucrats are the key; they are the ones who decide how the CBI as an institution is to be manipulated and thwarted so that it serves their interests. For example, in 1969, the government had issued what is euphemistically known as the Single Directive. The Directive, framed by bureaucrats for bureaucrats, mandates that the CBI obtain government's permission before investigating officers of the rank of joint secretary and above. The Supreme Court struck down the Single Directive in the Jain Hawala case in 1997 on two grounds. First, 'the Single Directive cannot be upheld as valid on the ground of it being permissible in the exercise of the power of superintendence of the Central Government'. Second, 'it cannot be made a condition precedent for initiating investigation'.

Even without the Supreme Court's intervention, the Directive did not make much sense, because the protection it provided to senior bureaucrats also covered cases of disproportionate assets; it taxes one's imagination how acquiring huge assets could ever be construed to be a legitimate part of performance of public duty. In all other cases, the bureaucrats, in any case, cannot be prosecuted without sanction from the government; statutorily, they are protected from vexatious litigation even without the protection of the Single Directive.

The Parliamentary Joint Committee has now recommended that the Single Directive should be put back in its original form despite the Supreme Court's order, because, it is necessary 'to protect bona fide actions at the decision-making level'. According to the Committee, the 'protection' should be restored in the same format which was there earlier and the power of giving approval for taking action against officers of the rank of joint secretary and above should be vested in the central government. The debate over the Single Directive—the Supreme Court striking it down and the Parliamentary Joint Committee restoring it—seems pointless, because, the CBI has, at no stage, been denied permission to investigate top bureaucrats (Mahalingam and Swami 1998). But the sparring yields an interesting insight. It shows how keen are the other institutions in the state structure on controlling the process of CBI's investigation; the fight, essentially, is over who gets the control—the judiciary, the Central Vigilance Commission, or the government?

For an institution which has sparked off such an intense turf war, the CBI has been remarkably exhibitionist. For example, shortly before the CBI Director's controversial removal in 1997, Prime Minister I. K. Gujral cited the government's responsibility to ensure impartial and efficient investigation as a reason for his removal. 'Selective leaks' and 'media-oriented investigations', Gujral told the Chief Minister's Conference, suggested that the CBI had been hijacked by an 'exhibitionist tendency' (Swami 1998).

Does the institution have the necessary capabilities as the premier investigating arm of the Government of India? The CBI has 800 investigating officers and 200 prosecutors. About 75 per cent of the staff of the CBI are drawn on deputation from the police departments, and after they prove their mettle in CBI work, they are permanently absorbed and get normal career benefits within the CBI. Those who do not make the grade, are sent back. Since a large percentage of the staff are from the police department who are inducted into the institution after a very careful and rigorous scrutiny, their investigative capabilities have never been in doubt. In fact, in the late 1950s and early 1960s, the CBI had successfully investigated a number of cases involving high functionaries (Narsimhan 1997). Even now, there is always a demand for the CBI to investigate sensitive cases.

There is a distinct organizational culture in the CBI. This is evident from the fact that when a police officer from the Indian Police Service who has never worked in the CBI is posted to the institution in a senior capacity, the news is greeted with general consternation because he does not partake of the CBI culture. But, since a large part of the staff in the CBI are drawn from the police department of different states, the CBI's culture is substantially diluted; in fact, the kind of organizational culture that should be conducive to doing things in the premier investigative agency of the country, has not evolved. It has not helped that the heads of the institution have not been insiders; their abbreviated tenures have only detracted from the organizational culture of the institution.

Tardy investigation has been the institution's central flaw; a flaw that has often led to disappearance of vital strands of evidence. The delay in the Bofors and St Kitts investigations by the CBI has been so well chronicled in the media that it is now a part of the nation's folklore. Delay in investigation almost derailed the JMM case in which a former prime minister of the country now stands convicted. Although credible information existed that money had been paid in return for votes cast by some MPs in the no-confidence vote in Parliament in July 1993 and the money had been deposited in the banks, the CBI did precious little for years. The CBI started investigating the case seriously only when it was upbraided by the Supreme Court; a conviction was obtained only in 2000.

The well-publicized Jain Hawala case is another example. Diaries indicating massive pay-offs to politicians were seized in the course of a raid, but the CBI paid no particular attention. Action started only when the Supreme Court was moved. Under prodding from the Court that almost bordered on nagging, the CBI investigated the case and filed prosecution. The prosecution eventually collapsed when the Delhi High Court held that the diaries were inadmissible as evidence. But lack of evidence was the real reason why the Jain Hawala case collapsed—the entries in the diaries required some corroboration, and the CBI failed to provide one. The Supreme Court, in fact, took the CBI to task for not having moved against the beneficiaries of the pay-offs on the basis of disproportionate assets if other evidence was not forthcoming (Nayar 1998). In any case, bulk of the key evidence had vanished because of delay in investigation.

Is the CBI effective as an anti-corruption institution? The answer is no. Its record in punishing corruption has been miserable. This is primarily because the CBI has been used to protect corruption rather than expose and punish it. True, the government of the day, by manipulating and thwarting the CBI, has succeeded in protecting its top functionaries from potentially embarrassing investigations, but the CBI's failure has had far-reaching consequences. For one, it has made corruption a no-risk, high-profit activity in the country, and this has determined, to a very large extent, how the incentives for government functionaries—bureaucrats and ruling politicians— are structured. But, more fundamentally, the failure of the principal investigative arm of the government has undermined the legitimacy of the Indian state itself.

On the whole, three clear conclusions emerge from our study of the institutions of internal accountability. First, the statutory/ non-statutory distinction does not appear to have played any meaningful role in the effectiveness of the institution; the CAG with a statutory status has not been any more effective than the Central Vigilance Commission or the CBI. Second, institutional effectiveness is hampered by demand factors which are endogenous to the institutional design—the CAG reporting to the Parliament and the CBI reporting to the government. Third and the most important, the effectiveness of an institution is essentially determined by its interaction with other institutions in the state structure—the manner in which other institutions assist, supplement, thwart, or subvert it.

References

Administrative Reforms Commission (1967), *Report of the Study Team on Promotion Policies, Conduct Rules, Discipline and Morale, vols. I and II*: New Delhi: Government of India.
Appleby, Paul H. (1953), *Public Administration in India: Report of a Survey*, New Delhi: President Press.
Arora, Ramesh. K. and Rajni Goyal (1995), *Indian Public Administration: Institution and Issues*, New Delhi: Wiswa Prakashan.
Central Vigilance Commission (1992), *Annual Report.*
————— (1994), *Annual Report.*
————— (1995), *Annual Report.*
————— (1996), *Annual Report.*
————— (1997), *Annual Report.*
————— (1998), *Annual Report.*
Comptroller and Auditor General of India (1997–8), *Activity Report.*
————— (1998–9), *Activity Report.*
————— (1999–2000), *Activity Report.*
————— (2000–1), *Activity Report.*
Comptroller and Auditor General's (Duties, Powers and Conditions of Service) Act, 1971.
Das, S. K. (2001), *Public Office, Private Interest: Bureaucracy and Corruption in India*, Delhi: Oxford University Press.
Deccan Herald (2000), 'Parliamentary Panel for Clipping CVC's Wings', 23 November.
Hindu (2000), 'Fodder Scam: Probe Urged into CAG Role', 9 November.

Iyer, Ramaswamy R. (1997), 'The Role of Audit in Tackling Corruption', in S. Guhan and Samuel Paul (eds), *Corruption in India: Agenda for Action*, New Delhi: Vision Books.

Joseph, K. P. (1994), 'Decline and Fall of Government Audit', *Economic and Political Weekly*, 5 March.

Kumar, Jeevan D. (1998), 'Audit and Accountability in Administration', Paper presented at the *National Seminar on Administrative Reforms for Good Governance*, 2 November.

Mahalingam, Sudha (1998), 'One More Ordinance', *Frontline*, 20 November.

Mahalingam, Sudha and Praveen Swami (1998), 'Empowering Investigative Agencies', *Frontline*, 9 January.

Ministry of Personnel, Public Grievances & Pensions (1996–7), *Annual Report*.

———— (1998–9), *Annual Report*.

———— (1999–2000), *Annual Report*.

Narsimhan, C. V. (1997), 'Prevention of Corruption: Towards Effective Enforcement', in S. Guhan and Samuel Paul (eds), *Corruption in India: Agenda for Action*, New Delhi: Vision Books.

Nayar, Kuldip (1998), 'Corruption and Complacency', *Indian Express*, 13 October.

Report of the Committee on Prevention of Corruption (Santhanam Committee) (1964), Ministry of Home Affairs, New Delhi.

Report of the Fifth Central Pay Commission, Government of India (1997).

Sathyamoorthy, S. (1990), 'Science Audit—Need, Scope and Challenges', in *Auditing Science and Technology*, New Delhi: Ashish Publishing House.

Swami, Praveen (1998), 'A Step towards Autonomy', *Frontline*, 9 January.

The Corruption Perceptions Index (1998), Berlin: Transparency International.

Times of India (2000), 'SC Bench Spanks CBI for its Little Lie', 24 October.

5

India's Judiciary
The Promise of Uncertainty

Pratap Bhanu Mehta

> You may ask what then will become of the fundamental principles of
> equity and fair play which our Constitutions enshrine; and whether I
> seriously believe that unsupported they will serve merely as counsels of
> moderation. I do not think that anyone can say what will be left of those
> principles; I do not know whether they will serve only as counsels; but
> this much I think I do know—that a society so riven that the spirit of
> moderation is gone, no Court can save; that a society where that spirit
> flourishes no Court need save; that a society which evades its respon-
> sibility by thrusting upon the Courts the nurture of that spirit, that spirit
> will in the end perish.
>
> —Learned Hand

INTRODUCTION

The judiciary in India is a deeply paradoxical institution.[1]
On the one hand the courts have become extraordinarily

[1] India's judiciary is, with some exceptions, a single three tiered system, with
the Supreme Court at the apex. Each state has a high court and district level
courts. The Supreme Court, established in 1950, as a successor to the Federal
Court has broad powers. Under Article 131 it exercises original jurisdiction
in cases involving the government and appellate jurisdiction in a variety of
cases. Under Article 132 it rules on cases involving constitutional interpretation; under Article 133 it exercises jurisdiction over civil cases that involve a
substantial question of a law of general importance. In addition it is an appellate

powerful.[2] Through a creative interpretation of the Constitution, the courts have not only exercised their power of judicial review but have also managed to place limits on the power of Parliament to amend the Constitution.[3] The judiciary has also become an institution of governance. In recent times it has, in the absence of parliamentary legislation, routinely made law; it has made public policy pronouncements; held executive bodies accountable, and has directly taken over the supervision of executive agencies.[4]

---

court for some criminal cases, it has the power to grant special leave to appeal, has writ jurisdictions over questions of fundamental rights, and has the authority to issue advisory opinions.

The high courts act as courts of first and second appeals in civil matters; in addition they have extensive writ jurisdiction and act as superintendents for subordinate courts.

[2] One scholar describes the Indian Supreme Court as 'the most powerful court in the world.' See Dhavan, *The Supreme Court Today*. An American scholar of comparative law, Charles Epps writes, 'the supposed activism of the American Supreme Court seems almost conservative by comparison to the Indian Courts leading decisions.' See his *A Rights Revolution*.

[3] The evolution of constitutional law on this matter has been complex. In *Sankari Prasad* v. *Union of India* (1952) SCR 89, the First Amendment Act, Art. 31A and 31B were challenged on the grounds that no amendments could take away or abridge fundamental rights. The courts ruled that amendments made in exercise of the constituent power of Parliament were not subject to Art. 13 or the fundamental rights they sought to amend. Also see *Sajjan Singh* v. *State of Rajasthan* (1965) 1 SCR 933. Both these judgements were overruled in *I. C. Golak Nath* v. *State of Punjab* (1967) 2 SCR 762 which invalidated any parliamentary amendments that had the effect of eroding fundamental rights. But this judgement had the curious anomaly that it would only have prospective operation. This allowed the First, Fourth, and Seventeenth Amendment, which would otherwise have been invalidated, to stand. In *Kesavananda Bharati* v. *State of Kerala* AIR 1973 SC 1461, a landmark judgement, *Golak Nath* was overruled. This judgement held that fundamental rights were subject to amending power but that Parliament did not have the power to alter the 'basic structure' of the Constitution. This was done largely to prevent a strict interpretation of property rights in Part II to stand in the way of the *Directive Principles of State Policy*. But the judgement, nevertheless abridged Parliament's power to amend the Constitution and was used, in *Indira Gandhi* v. *Raj Narain* to strike down the 39th Amendment.

[4] See in particular, *Vineet Narain* v. *Union of India* (1988), 1 SCC 226. In this case the Supreme Court claimed the power to 'fill the void in the absence

It has cast itself as the ultimate custodian of constitutional values and the highest institution of accountability. On the other hand, with the partial exception of the Supreme Court, most of the institutions of the judiciary remain in a permanent state of crisis. The complaints usually levelled against other institutions of the state—inefficiency, poor enforcement, corruption—are increasingly applied to the judiciary as well. There are twenty million cases pending in Indian courts, of which 3.2 million are pending in high courts.

It appears that this paradox of growing judicial power on the one hand, and the simultaneous corrosion of the operational institutions of justice on the other is a world wide phenomenon. During the 1990s, while most observers were arguing that there had been a global expansion of judicial power, many were also arguing that the civil justice system of most societies, measured on fairly minimal criteria of procedural fairness, delays, and cost, were in a 'state of crisis'.[5] As the editor of what is perhaps the only systematic large scale comparative study of the 'crisis of civil justice' acknowledged: 'A sense of crisis in the administration of civil justice is by no means universal, but it is widespread' (Zuckerman 1999: 12).

Any assessment of the judiciary as an institution would have to therefore explore at least two aspects of judicial power. On the one hand it would attempt to understand the ways in which the judiciary consolidates its independence vis-à-vis the executive/legislature and comes to be seen as a crucial component of the democratic process itself. On the other hand such an assessment would also have to examine the reasons why the administrative functioning of the judiciary itself is relatively poor.

This chapter proceeds in the following steps: In the first section I offer some general reflections on the evolution of judicial review, judicial independence, and judicial activism in India. I argue that India is a case where judicial power more or less creates (and therefore destroys) itself. But even when the judiciary has managed to establish its powers of reviewing legislation and even scrutinizing

---

of suitable legislation' and to provide 'a solution till such time as the legislature acts to perform its role by enacting proper legislation to cover the field.'

[5] The titles of the following books are indicative. See Tate and Vallinder *The Global Expansion of Judicial Power*, and Zuckerman (ed.) *Civil Justice in Crisis*.

constitutional amendments, this fact alone does not mean that a robust constitutional politics is likely to emerge in India any time soon. I suggest that the episodic, uneven, and unpredictable asser-tion of judicial power and the structure of the Supreme Court militate against the emergence of constitutional politics.

In the second part, I argue that the recent court decisions con-cerning how judges to the high courts are to be appointed, are an instance of the judiciary creating its own power. Through these decisions the judiciary has managed to secure its independence from the executive/legislature, but at the cost of shielding itself from public scrutiny. In part three, I suggest that much of the crisis of the Indian civil justice system can be traced to an accumulation of procedural anomalies that create huge perverse incentives for judges and lawyers. Deficiencies in case management are a major factor in causing chaos in Indian courts. The Supreme Court's extraordinary recent experiment with better case management holds considerable promise that these deficiencies can be tackled. But I caution that it may not be easy to enact the success of the Supreme Court at the lower levels. Finally in the fourth part I offer some brief remarks about the ways in which the Indian legal profession can pose both an obstacle to procedural reform and the ways in which its under-institutionalization hampers the system of civil justice.

Before I proceed however, an important *caveat* is in order. This chapter has been written in something of an empirical vacuum. Most Indian legal scholarship tends to be very descriptive and concentrates largely on what is termed as 'black letter law'; there has been almost no serious social science investigation into the Indian judiciary. It is symptomatic of this neglect that Rajni Kothari's classic book *Politics in India* does not even bother to mention the judiciary. The collection of statistics and relevant information is extremely poor. Most courts are in arrears in collecting their statistics, as is the Law Commission. Professional associations like the Bar councils do not have adequate data on their own member-ship, strikes, and so forth. The last good studies of the courts as institutions date from the early to mid-eighties.[6] Such good schol-arship as exists since then has focused largely on constitutional

---

[6] See Baxi, *The Supreme Court in Indian Politics*; particularly impressive is Dhavan, *Justice on Trial: The Supreme Court Today*; Galanter, *Law and Society in Modern India*. A volume, *Fifty Years of the Supreme Court*, Verma and Kusum

interpretation and even in this domain almost exclusively on religion, women's rights, and affirmative action. The Supreme Court's own plea in *P. N. Eswara Iyer* v. *Registrar of the Supreme Court* has gone unheeded:

> Counsel at one stage asked whether there was back up empirical research to warrant the assumptions in the amendment (of certain procedural rules), whether facts and figures about the number and nature of wasted review time of the courts and a host of other related aspects were available. No such material is before us now. It is fair to confess that the scientific method of undertaking research and study into public problems as preclude to legislation is lamentably lacking; and court...management is currently beyond the ken of scientific research. Where awareness is absent, ad-hocism is inevitable.... Here experiential evidence makes do for empirical research.

This more or less sums up the state of research into Indian courts and this chapter, rather than presenting a settled argument, is merely a plea for more research.

I. Independent Judicial Review

It is very difficult to formulate the necessary and sufficient conditions under which independent judicial review takes hold. It used to be a common argument that successful constitutional judicial review is caused and required by strong federalism. The logic for this argument was this: federalism requires an institution to protect complex boundary arrangements; each unit of a federation will, despite incentives to deviate, support the creation and maintenance of some central institution designed to identify non-compliance by others. The logic of this argument was never very persuasive. Why would it necessarily be the case that a state involved in a dispute with a central government would support the creation of another arm of the central government to resolve the dispute? As it turns out in many cases, the nature of the federal arrangement has depended on how judicial power is exercised; and judicial review has often eroded rather than strengthened federalism. In the

---

has just been released. This deals primarily with developments in constitutional law.

case of India, which is, in any event, a more strongly centralized state, one could argue that the nature of judicial scrutiny of the Centre's intervention in the states has influenced the character of federalism itself.

The legislatures and executives have pretty much followed the judicial lead in defining the federal character of the Indian Constitution. It has often been argued that the weakening of Indian federalism during the seventies and eighties was a result of one party dominance of the Centre and that coalition governments increase the prospects of federalism. But a simpler explanation implicating the courts can be offered. Arguably, the advisory opinion of the Supreme Court in 1977, which permitted the dissolution of nine state governments before their term had expired, led to the weakening of Indian federalism, where succession after succession of state legislative assemblies were dissolved. Whatever the other controversies surrounding the Supreme Court's decision in *Bommai*, there has been following that decision, greater reluctance on part of the Centre to impose presidential rule on the flimsiest of reasons. Arguably, the Court has made it clearer than before that there have to be 'substantial constitutional' reasons for dismissing a state government.[7] Even Laloo Prasad Yadav's misrule in Bihar could not quite pass that test. It seems that the character of judicial review could determine the nature and scope of federalism rather than being determined by it.

An analogous argument can also be made about the 'separation of powers hypothesis'. This argument suggested that constitutions which enshrined a strong separation of powers amongst the various branches of government would also in all likelihood have strong traditions of judicial independence and power.[8] The general

---

[7] *S. R. Bommai* v. *Union of India* (1994) 3 SCC 1.

[8] For instance John Ferejohn in his 'Law, Legislation and Positive Political Theory', in Banks and Hanushek (eds) *Modern Political Economy: Old Topics, New Directions*, p. 208 argues that:

Nations with traditions and practices of unrestricted parliamentary sovereignty would tend to have judges that are more or less neutral appliers of law to cases. Conversely, those nations that restrict parliamentary sovereignty, might be expected to develop traditions of judicial independence and power. Judges in parliamentary systems would not emphasize or notice the discretionary or interpretative elements of

presumption has been that judicial review in parliamentary systems should be very weak. But this thesis has never been quite able to explain why strong traditions of judicial review and the exercise of judicial power are appearing in parliamentary systems which have not traditionally had a strong separation of powers even when there has been no change in the formal distribution of powers. Second, these arguments do not quite explain the variance over time in the exercise of judicial power. This variance can often be best explained by the actions of the judiciary itself. The mechanisms by which judicial review comes to be instituted as a regular practice are often judicial decisions themselves. In India, as elsewhere, it is not simply the formal allocation of powers but an evolving constitutional jurisprudence that has enhanced the powers of judicial review.[9] I am not sure we have or can have a general theory of the conditions under which constitutional law will evolve in the direction of asserting greater powers of judicial review. It seems that the degree of independence, especially in democratic societies, that a judiciary has, is itself a creation of judicial power. The thought that 'judicial review causes itself' is probably as good as any answer to the puzzle of judicial power.

The questions to ask would therefore not be: under what conditions do courts exercise extensive judicial review? The answer to that is more or less when they want to. The questions are rather these. First, is there any discernible pattern to the exercise of either constitutional review or judicial activism? What are the kinds of issues which occasion the exercise of the courts' power? Second, what enables the exercise of judicial power to legitimize itself vis-à-vis the executive/legislature. The answer to the first question, in the Indian case, as elsewhere, is that emerging traditions of rights discourse in the court itself,[10] generate strong reasons for judicial review. The emergence of a rights base jurisprudence is a worldwide

---

their decisions. They would see themselves as parliamentary heads....
One would expect this to be true regardless of the history of the legal system.

It is not clear that this hypothesis is empirically sustainable.

[9] See supra. Note 2.

[10] This can also be an artifact of the institutional anomalies of Indian law in some instances. For example, most of the environmental litigation is carried out in terms of 'rights' because the system of tort law is relatively weak.

phenomenon and can take on strong roots even in the absence of a Bill of Rights. But the exact content of this rights jurisprudence has varied considerably. In the Indian case the courts—and society at large—have been less devoted to a civil liberties rights based discourse. Rather, the courts have legitimized such interventions as they have made, based largely on the idea that government ought to be forced to intervene in certain areas to achieve 'substantial goals', whose content is largely defined through the framework set out in the Directive Principles of State Policy. In doing so the courts have had to strike a balance amongst the competing rights at stake. It is far from clear that the courts have evolved any clear criteria or tests to guide competing interests (say between 'environment' and 'development') but the goals of equality have given the courts occasion to flex their judicial might.[11]

Court interventions have been widely seen as legitimate, or at least tolerated, because the representative institutions are widely seen as being immobilized, self-serving, corrupt, and incapable of exercising either their basic policy prerogatives or their powers of enforcement. Even in comparative terms, the exercise of judicial power is increasingly being seen not as a threat to effective majoritarian rule, but as a response to its ineffectiveness. A serious disaffection with majoritarian institutions of accountability make the exercise of judicial power almost necessary. We are resorting to judiciaries basically because we cannot help it.

In India the relationship between the judiciary on the one hand and the executive/legislature on the other has often been contentious. The character of judicial activism has varied considerably over time. In the early years after Independence the courts, much against the wishes of the executive, was seen as wedded to a very traditional and literal interpretation of property rights, aligning itself with the propertied classes and standing in the way of

[11] Even the *Kesavananda* decision, while designed to protect the right of the courts to nullify constitutional amendments, was intended to provide greater justiciability to the Directive Principles of State Policy than to protect Fundamental Rights as was the intent in *Golaknath*. Almost all of the Supreme Court's celebrated 'activist' decisions—a constitutional right to a minimum wage, a right to counsel, a right to livelihood, broad remedies against environmental destruction stemmed from a concern for equality rather than civil liberties. Indeed civil liberties concerns have been palpably weak in Indian courts.

government's land reform legislation.[12] During the same period, the courts took contradictory positions on the protection of Fundamental Rights. Swearing fidelity to 'black letter law' it virtually denied that the Indian Constitution had substantive due process requirements and upheld the state's powers on preventive detention.[13] Yet it also gave serious scrutiny to government regulation of publications. The judiciary was tartly attacked by Nehru for having 'purloined the Constitution'. The executive's behaviour was much as one would predict in a parliamentary system. Armed with its substantial majority in Parliament, and self-confidence in its agenda, the executive under Nehru resorted to constitutional amendments as a means of circumventing the judicial interpretation of the Constitution. Formally a happy resolution was maintained: the judiciary was not denied its power to review legislation for its constitutionality; but faced with a recalcitrant judiciary the government could simply seek to amend the Constitution. During the late sixties and early seventies the judiciary again was seen as standing in the way of Indira Gandhi's development agenda. It struck down the government's scheme for the nationalization of banks, the abolition of privy purses, and made the first strong statement to the effect that Parliament could not, even through constitutional amendment, override the Fundamental Rights elaborated in Part II of the Constitution. This claim was later modified to the effect that Parliament could not, through constitutional amendment, override the 'basic structure' of the Constitution and ever since then the judiciary has insinuated itself as the custodian of the basic structure. The high courts displayed their independence, first by invalidating Indira Gandhi's election on grounds of corrupt electoral practices. Following the State of Emergency proclaimed on 25 June 1975, hundreds of people were detained under an executive order passed under Article 359 according to which Article 21 of the Indian Constitution was suspended. Article 21 provides that no person shall be deprived of their personal liberty except according to the procedure established by law. Judges in nine high courts rejected the constitutionality of this order. But in what is now

[12] On property rights, this period also saw contradictory trends. The Supreme Court, for the most part, seems to have sided with the government on issues relating to property rights, except in a few high profile cases.

[13] In *Maneka Gandhi* v. *Union of India AIR* 1978 SC 597 the court asserted substantial due process rights.

unanimously regarded as one of the darkest decisions in Indian judicial history, the Supreme Court overruled these nine high courts and put the seal of its approval on the state of Emergency.[14] Indira Gandhi's strategy, when faced with recalcitrant courts, was two-fold. On the one hand she resorted to amending the Constitution; on the other she, attempted to 'pack' the judiciary through supersession and transfers. It is one of the ironies of judiciary-executive relationships during her tenure that while arbitrary executive influence in appointments increased, the courts were also formulating far reaching interpretations of the Indian Constitution that would lay the *constitutional* basis for limiting the powers of the executive and Parliament in the future. Ironically, the judiciary emerges out of the Emergency as an even more powerful institution. It managed to legitimize itself, once again, not only as an institution of accountability of last resort but also as an institution of governance. The judiciary seems to have taken cues from Indira Gandhi's populism and made attempts to recast itself in a more populist mode. The Public Interest Litigation (PIL) initiatives, which dispensed with many of the cumbersome formalities of court procedure, attempted to give citizens direct access to the Supreme Court. In these cases judges gave even detailed policy prescriptions that it required the government to fulfil. For instance the courts have required the closing down of business because of environmental concern, building new housing for slum dwellers, even maintaining particular college courses, etc. Some of the zeal that lay behind public interest litigation has abated somewhat; but judges still intermittently use the law created during its heyday to pass policy prescriptions. So much of judicial activism in Indian courts is, as will be explained below, tied to the enthusiasm of particular judges that it is difficult to determine whether this abatement in the zeal over PIL is simply a temporary reprieve or a large trend.[15] But faced with an immobile and corrupt executive, the judiciary again found itself performing such tasks as supervising the role of executive agencies, especially in matters of criminal investigation.

[14] *ADM Jabalpur* v. *Shivakant Shukla AIR* 1976 SC 1207. The four majority judges of a five judge bench were Chief Justice Ray, and Justices Bhagawati, Chandrachud, and Beg. Justice Khanna wrote a famously strong dissent.

[15] For instance Justice Kuldip Singh alone was associated with more environmental activism than the entire judiciary put together. See for instance 1996 *Shiv Sagar Tewari* v. *Union of India* SCC 558.

It should be apparent that the Supreme Court of India is a *politically* significant institution. There is not a single important issue of political life in India that has not been, by accident or design, profoundly shaped by its interventions. The Court itself can be regarded as a powerful actor in Indian politics. Far from being a neutral and distant participant, the courts participate and collaborate in governing India.

The political significance of the courts is not difficult to demonstrate.[16] Most studies of Indian politics pay almost no attention to the courts, but disagreement between the courts on the one hand, and the executive and legislature on the other have been as important a fact about Indian political life as any. The courts have struck down hundreds of central and state laws; during the first seventeen years of its existence, when the Supreme Court was supposedly in its restrained period, it struck down 128 laws. The legislature and the executive have certainly felt its power and acknowledged it. Out of the first forty-five amendments to the Constitution, approximately half were explicitly aimed at reducing judicial power. It is true that the frequent resort to constitutional amendments is an attempt to circumvent the courts' power. On the other hand, the fact that legislatures have never thought it proper to simply ignore court decisions is also extremely significant. Even during the Emergency the government took care to curtail the authority of the courts by legal means rather than by breaching the fabric of the courts' formal authority. This deference has ensured that even constitutional amendments have not been able to alter the basic structure of the Constitution and the formal allocation of powers

---

[16] One of the crucial areas in executive-legislative relations is the power the courts have over stigmatizing or delegitimizing the behaviour of particular politicians. The fact that Indira Gandhi, was accused of corrupt electoral practices meant very little until she was pronounced guilty by the Allahabad High Court five years after the complaint was first filed. Recently the Supreme Court has passed strictures against individual politicians for abusing their discretionary powers when in office and has even gone to the extent of supervising investigations into their doing. But while such judicial intervention in discretionary power and oversight of politicians have elicited groaning they have not yet elicited fear. In part because judicial application of these norms has been intermittent and episodic; it provides a possible opportunity for politicians to get rid of their rivals than an assault on the powers of the political class as a whole.

within it. Even with an executive as ill disposed to the judiciary as Indira Gandhi's government and even with a court as supposedly compliant as the Emergency court, the 'basic structure' doctrine articulated in *Kesavanada* has served the cause of preventing the distribution of powers within the Constitution.

A couple of large conclusions can be drawn from a brief survey of Indian constitutional law. First, the question, 'who is the final arbiter of the Constitution?' cannot be easily answered. The Court has declared itself to be such, but for a variety of contingent reasons its authority to override amendments to the Constitution has not been fully challenged since that decision. In parliamentary systems, there is no theoretical reason to suppose that simply because the courts decide on the constitutionality of a particular matter, that matter ought to be considered settled or removed from the political agenda. The reality of constitutionalism has been that the legislature and the judiciary are likely to remain *competitors* when it comes to interpreting the Constitution. It is by no means settled who has the final word. The decisions of each are more like one link in a long chain of events that can be played out any number of times. Parliament can pass legislation, the courts can determine its constitutionality, Parliament can try to circumvent the courts by amending the Constitution, the courts can pronounce that Parliament has limited powers of amendment, Parliament can...and so on and on.[17] We have not seen a full scale assault on judicial interpretation of what the 'basic structure' doctrine requires during the nineties because of the fragmented political system where no party is in a position to dictate terms to Parliament. In the event of any political party gaining enough power to command the power to amend the Constitution, it is not clear what the outcome of a judicial-legislative tussle is going to be. If indeed, at some point, any recommendations that, the newly constituted Constitutional Review Commission might come up with for changes in the Constitution, are brought before Parliament, the ability of the courts to enforce the 'basic structure' doctrine will be seriously tested. But it bears repeating that judicial supremacy in India is not simply a

---

[17] Perhaps something like this is now underway, though not with respect to constitutional amendments. Parliament passed the Muslim Women's Bill to override the Supreme Court's interpretation of the CPC in the *Shah Bano* case. In a spate of recent judgements the courts seem to be restoring the situation that existed prior to the Muslim Women's Bill.

result of a one time act of constitutional design but is secured through an ongoing struggle.

Second, the courts face a dilemma: The institutional interest of the court is to resolve conflicts over constitutionality while maintaining the legitimacy of constitutional review in the future. Indian judges have, for the most part, been extremely aware of this dilemma. Judges seem to routinely try to anticipate the effects of particular decisions on the popular authority of the court. This makes the major decisions of the court, notwithstanding their own self-presentation, less straightforwardly an application of some high constitutional principle or value. Rather most judgements are a delicate and *political* balancing of competing values and political aspirations; they seek to provide a workable modus vivendi rather than articulate high values. This is not the place to argue this point at any length, but I would submit the hypothesis that most court decisions can be read as modus vivendis of this sort. Even in the *Golak Nath* case, arguably the strongest judgement in favour of the sanctity of Fundamental Rights handed down by an Indian court, made a retrospective exception for three constitutional amendments relating to property rights that it might otherwise have invalidated. Similarly *Kesavananda* case, while making a strong statement to the effect that the 'basic structure' of the Constitution cannot be amended by Parliament, left the door open by being deliberately vague on the content of the 'basic structure'. The *Mandal* decisions simultaneously enlarged the scope of affirmative action, but also put limits on it. Arguably the *Hindutva* decisions, which have been justly criticized for their odd ideological interpretation of Hinduism, can be seen in this light. At one level these judgements reassert the importance of the Representation of People's Act; at another the courts are reluctant to dismiss a popularly elected government simply because of its ideological views.

If one looks upon the courts, despite their assertions of formal powers, as facilitating a kind of modus vivendi, then one can more easily explain why the courts get involved in some matters and not others. For instance, as far as civil liberties are concerned, the courts have been on the whole extremely reluctant to question the presumptive powers of the state in issues like preventive detention and human rights violations. This is because of a perceived sense that Indian public opinion at large shares some of the same security syndromes that drive the state to exercise these powers too frequently in the first place. The courts have, with a couple of exceptions, trod very gingerly on certain classes of religious disputes. First, Indian courts go to unusual lengths to demonstrate that despite calling for reforms in religious practices they are not *anti-religious*. They have interpreted Indian secularism as itself a kind of modus vivendi rather than as a set of clear principles. Second, the courts have on many occasions shied away from taking a clear stand on religious disputes which they see as very clearly controversial. Arguably the fate of the *Babri Masjid* case is a good example. The case itself has languished in Indian courts for fifty years. When the executive sought an advisory opinion from the Supreme Court, it took two years to deliver one to the effect that it was up to the high courts to decide. The courts have been much keener to supervise executive agencies in corruption investigations than they have been to call executive agencies to account in cases of 'communal' violence.

In the Indian case, the court's concern for its own authority has meant a reading of the political tea leaves as it were; the judicialization of politics and the politicization of the judiciary have turned out to be two sides of the same coin. It is not an accident that Indian constitutional law has been relatively unstable, or that the same courts can appear strong and assertive in some areas and not in others. It may be the case that Indian courts have acquired much legitimacy and power not because of the clarity and consistency of an underlying constitutional vision but because of the opposite. One could interpret all of the courts' decisions as a modus vivendi, between competing group values and aspirations which is sufficiently indeterminate and open ended to keep the players motivated enough to play it. In a way the court's legitimacy rests precisely on the fact that in its attempt at providing a modus vivendi, it has given a sufficient number of parties enough partial victories to give them an incentive to keep on playing the game.

If this analysis has any plausibility, one should not too readily assume that there is a simple association between the rise of judicial constitutional review and the emergence of constitutionalism. Constitutionalism is a commitment that the interactions of actors be governed by an authoritative set of rules. But there is no reason for supposing that the authority of any set of rules—whether they delineate formal structures of authority or articulate substantive values—can be fixed and insulated from politics simply as a matter of constitutional design. When we claim that some rules carry such authority we are making a statement less about constitutional design than the fact that there is a consensus in society around those rules. I take it to be the case that for strong constitutionalism to emerge there has to be a prior overlapping consensus on the values such constitutionalism would embody. Constitutionalism is the result of social consensus, not institutional design and is only as robust as the former.

In the Indian case the emergence of constitutionalism is impeded by structural reasons as well. First, enforcement is the Achilles' heel of all Indian institutions, the judiciary included. The judiciary has justified its own power by claiming that the government does not enforce its own laws. Yet, there is little evidence that the judicial intervention leads to better enforcement.[18] Even in cases where the courts were proactive in trying to invite litigation, they were ineffective. As Charles Epps puts it, 'The Indian Supreme Court clearly *tried* to spark a right revolution—*but nothing happened* (Epps 1998: 71).' One of the ways in which the courts institutionalize constitutionalism is through a feedback mechanism that affects the legislature and influences public opinion. The legislature uses guesses about the constitutionality of a particular legislation before enacting it. I take it to be the case that for a constitutional politics to emerge there has to be some relationship, as mediated by the rule making of constitutional judges, between the constitutional rules and the decision-making of public officials. Claims about the judicialization of politics would suggest that under certain conditions judges will construct a set of dialogues and collective conversations about the capacities and limits of state power, which the legislature and civil society will help perpetuate. It is very difficult to make the case that the judiciary has successfully accomplished that goal. It is not clear that the legislature or the executive has, in any sense, internalized judicial law making. Evidence for this is scarce.

There is often a tendency to see the judgements of the court as an artifact of the predilection of particular judges rather than the court as an institution. This is because of a variety of institutional features of the Supreme Court. The average tenure of a Supreme Court justice is relatively short, those of chief justices even shorter;

---

[18] As far as I know there is no study of enforcement of judicial decisions.

the predilection of judges towards writing individual opinions ad nauseam, arguably muddies the law more than it clarifies it. Even in the celebrated *Kesavanada* decision, the judgement runs to over a thousand pages, with eleven opinions 'and as one scholar has rightly written, 'the achievements (of *Kesavananda*) could not obscure the confusion generated by eleven opinions.... A more dangerous example of the dangers of multiple opinions to law and democracy in India would be difficult to find' (Austin 1999: 276).

A further feature, *institutional* feature of the Indian Supreme Court, prevents the emergence of enduring constitutionalism. There is a widespread consensus that jurisdiction exercised by the highest court should always be exercised by the full court (Rao 1966: 219). In India, under Art. 145(3), a 'substantial question of law', arising out of either a reference made by the president or involving an interpretation of the Constitution should be decided by a bench consisting of a minimum number of five judges. While the Court adhered to this mandate during the fifties and sixties, more and more cases involving constitutional interpretation are being decided by smaller benches. There have been many instances where small benches of three judges have declined to refer matters to larger constitutional benches,[19] yet their judgements have had the effect of becoming significant interpretations of the Constitution. The Court's own directive has been that precedents set by larger benches are more binding than those set by smaller benches. Yet it seems that it has become frequent practice for smaller benches to override precedents set by larger benches even when the precedent involves as substantial a case as *Kesavananda*.[20] This feature of the Court's practice has the result of leaving lower courts in a bind about which Supreme Court directive to follow: the most recent or the one articulated by larger benches. A firmer adherence to the principle that constitutional matters should be decided by larger benches would help the clarity of the Court's own constitutional interpretation.

---

[19] *Gujarat Steel Tubes* v. *Gujarat Steel Tubes Mazdoor Sabha* (1979) SC 1914.

[20] Counsel Ashok Desai had argued in the *Hindutva* cases that the courts were unfairly disregarding their own reasoning in *Bommai*. For a more solid instance of the court disregarding judgements made by previous larger benches see *P. A. Shah* v. *State of Gujarat* 1986 SC 486.

It is partly with this problem in mind that proposals have been formulated to either have two courts—one appellate and one constitutional—or to at least have two jurisdictions. The last time this proposal was canvassed in 1979 it was rejected by the Bar, largely because they thought it was a ploy by the government to pack the courts. But there is certainly enough evidence to suggest that the practice of hearing cases in benches has considerably affected the clarity of constitutional principles.[21]

II. Judicial Independence and Appointments

If there ever was an instance of the judiciary creating its own powers out of itself, the recent evolution in the method of appointing justices to the high courts is surely it. The Constitution determines the power and the composition of the judicial branch. The independence of the judiciary is made possible, though by no means guaranteed, by its constitutional position. During the Constituent Assembly debates the idea of an independent judiciary had widespread support. As Ambedkar put it, 'there can be no difference of opinion in the House that our judiciary must both be independent of the executive and must also be competent in itself. And the question is how these two objects could be secured.' One of the key elements in guaranteeing the independence of the judiciary is the tenure, appointment, and transfer of judges. The debate over which method of appointment would best secure the independence of the judiciary was long and protracted with a variety of proposals taken up for consideration. The debate has not abated since.

After due consideration of a range of alternatives the assembly agreed upon Articles 124(2) and 217(1). Judges would be appointed by the president of India in consultation with such judges of the Supreme Court and of the high courts in the states as the president may deem necessary. For an appointment of a judge other than the chief justice, the chief justice of India must always be consulted. Judges of the high court and the Supreme Court can be removed only by an order of the president that is approved by a majority of the total membership and a majority of not less than two-thirds of members present and voting in each house of Parliament. The

[21] Such an argument has also been made by F. S. Nariman in his 'The Growing Uncertainty in the Law: How Consistent are the Decisions of the Supreme Court'.

primary aim of this procedure seems to have been this. On the one hand it avoids a cumbersome appointments process by effectively shutting out the legislature or any other large body. On the other these procedures were aimed at making judicial appointments on the basis of a consensus between the executive and the judiciary. It is very clear from the debates that the founders were suspicious of the idea that appointments to the judiciary be made solely by the executive; nor were they sanguine about legislative involvement. What is even clearer however is their suspicion that they be made solely by the judiciary. The uneasy compromise that Articles 124(2) and 217(1) reflected would be sustained largely by convention than by the clarity of the injunction. The formula still nominally survives though much confusion surrounds the little word 'consult'. In the now notorious *First Judges* case, this was taken to mean that the chief justice had no veto power over the appointments; the *Second Judges* case and the *Third Judges* case reversed this ruling to effectively give the judiciary almost complete control over judicial appointments. The *Second Judges* case reinstated the chief justice's veto power over appointments; the *Third* clarified that the chief justice should act as part of a collegium that consists of the four seniormost judges of the Supreme Court. Under this ruling the executive can ask the collegium consisting of the chief justice and four other justices, to reconsider any of their recommendations. But if the collegium unanimously reiterates its recommendation the appointment must be made. Arguably the *Second* and *Third Judges* cases preserved the spirit of the Constitution in that the Court did not introduce any method of selection that had been considered and rejected by the Constituent Assembly. Nevertheless it could be argued that it has given the judiciary more power than was contemplated by the Assembly.

Even half a century after the promulgation of the Constitution the basic matter of judicial appointments is far from settled. Even in the matter of appointments and tenure, the question of judicial power and independence is open to negotiation and renegotiation between the executive and the judiciary. The basic thrust of the recent *Judges* decisions has been to secure greater judicial power and autonomy over the executive. On the other hand it can be argued with some justice that the net effect of such judicial independence has been to shield judicial decision-making with respect to appointments from any serious and systematic scrutiny.

It is very difficult to get a handle on the question of what difference executive interference makes to the quality of judicial appointments. Each law commission has, from as early as 1954, alleged that there has often been undue executive interference in the appointment of judges. This is widely believed to be the case. Of course at one level it is difficult to *prove* executive influence in any strong sense of the term. But the unspecified nature of many charges makes one suspect that the picture of executive misdemeanour may have been overdrawn, or is largely driven by the power of a few examples and sustained as much as by the public presumption against the executive, and the judiciary's desire to legitimize itself, as by the substance of the charges. One study into the appointment of judges to the Supreme Court found that by and large routine criteria of seniority were applied for elevation of judges from the high courts to the Supreme Court.[22] In an affidavit filed in the *Second Judges* case which practically reinstated the chief justice's veto power on judicial appointments, the government submitted that out of 575 appointments made since the *First Judges* case which allowed the executive more leeway, the government had rejected the opinion of the chief justice of India in only a handful of instances. The public and the Bar alike repeatedly laments the decline in the quality of judicial appointments and certainly there is anecdotal evidence galore for the 'declining quality' of judges. But a couple of points are worth making. These perceptions are also accompanied by a general perception that the quality of the various Bar associations—measured by legal ethics, professionalism, legal skills, educational attainments—has also generally declined. In this sense the claim of 'decline' whatever it means is a claim about the legal profession as a whole and not just judges. Second, it is not clear that this decline is a result of executive influence rather than the judiciary's own internal corrosion. After all even during the heyday of the Emergency when executive interference was supposedly at

[22] Gupta, *Decision Making in the Supreme Court of India*, ch. 3. This study is the only statistical study available of the backgrounds of judges elevated to the Supreme Court. Of the sixty-nine appointments studied more than half of those elevated were chief justices; even in cases were judges were superseded, the supersession never went beyond the fifth seniormost judge of a particular high court except in two cases. One of the juniormost judges to have been elevated was Krishna Iyer.

its highest and good senior judges were routinely superseded in favour of judges whose philosophies and personal inclinations ostensibly comported more with the government's own, it is less than clear that the executive produced 'bad appointments'. To take just one example, Justice Iyer and Justice Bhagwati were elevated to the Supreme Court during Indira Gandhi's tenure. Nobody has ever accused Justice Iyer of being a lackey of the government; and although Justice Bhagwati did abase the judiciary by penning a flattering public letter to Indira Gandhi on her return to power in 1980, his contributions to giving Public Interest Litigation a good deal of momentum were widely lauded at the time. To raise this example is not to deny the fact that many executive initiated appointments have been extremely controversial. It is only to suggest that simply giving occasional examples of the executive's indefensible behaviour is not enough to sustain the claim that the executive role in judicial appointments be diminished.

India has only 2.7 judges per 100 thousand of population compared to a worldwide norm of 6.8 judges. In such circumstances it is astonishing that vacancies to high courts remain routinely unfilled. This fact alone calls for reconsideration of the present mode of appointment of judges. Supply side solutions are not going to be a panacea for the judiciary's inadequacies. But the fact that the judiciary, powerful as it is, has not put enough pressure on the executive to remedy the supply side of the problem, suggests that it has often been concerned with its formal powers more than its effectiveness.

Of course one ought not to conclude that the executive is to be more trusted than the judiciary. My point is rather that judicial preferences in appointments has escaped systematic scrutiny. If the executive does not deserve glory for its appointments, neither is it clear that the judiciary's treatment of itself is much cause for self-congratulation.[23]

But there is a deeper point underlying the continuing controversy over judicial appointments, which applies to a wide range of government institutions. Both executive and judicial appointments will remain objects of controversy for the simple reason that there are no settled criteria for what counts as good judges; or at any rate

[23] Austin, *Working a Democratic Constitution*. Chapter 25 gives all the sorry details of intra-judicial manoeuvring.

there are no criteria that the judiciary itself publicly defends or articulates, beyond the level of platitudes. Nor are there any public forums or bodies in which this debate can be conducted. There are no public reasons given for or against judicial appointments. Take the matter of transfers for instance. Under the current dispensation, judges can be transferred from one state high court to another. The Venkatchaliah Committee that oversaw the largest transfer of judges had insisted that the transfers be in the 'public interest'. But there is seldom any way of determining whether transfers of any particular judges, even when undertaken by the judiciary, are punitive or in the public interest. It is a measure of the Court's own confusion and hesitation on this issue that almost five decades after the Constitution was promulgated, the question of the transfer of judges remains murky. While tansfers began under Indira Gandhi as a mechanism for punishing judges who did not follow the government's agenda, it was soon recommended as a desirable policy goal. Even the Janata government that followed the Emergency, much to the regret of eminent judicial authorities, sought to continue with this policy. There were two primary rationales given for the policy. The first was that many high court judges, had developed close connections during their years of practice with members of the Bar; often their own families continued to practice in the same jurisdictions. These connections, it was argued, were impeding the judges' ability to adjudicate impartially. Members of the Bar were exploiting their connection to seek favours from the courts on every issue from interim orders to final judgements. The transfer policy was, in part, a sort of anticorruption measure. Second, it had long been suggested that it would greatly benefit the judicial process if at least a significant percentage of judges in any given high court, came from outside the state. This would help create uniform judicial standards across the country by providing a mechanism for the transmission of judicial practices and ideas from one state to the other. The Law Commission had recommended that this goal of having out state judges be accomplished largely by new appointments than through transfers. The simple point is that there is very little empirical information on whether these goals were in any way advanced by the policy of transfers. The Court itself seems to have believed this only intermittently and transfers have come in fits and starts rather than through any regularized process. At the moment there is a virtual moratorium on transfers of judges except if they are being elevated to chief justice. The Court still holds the view that the chief justice in any state should be from out of state. But this moratorium on transfers is voluntary rather than binding. It has apparently come about as a conjunction of two desires. Chief justices are reluctant to avoid unnecessary controversy by opening the transfer can of worms. There are also significant sections of the judiciary that feel that a policy of transfers has had an adverse impact on recruitment of judges. It has reduced even further any incentive that top members of the Bar might have for becoming judges, and this fact alone outweighs any possible gains through transfers. But the whole controversy over transfers has operated in an empirical vacuum. The arguments for and against it were entirely a priori. The crucial point is that it is not clear how one even begins to debate this question.

In the absence of any clear criteria, judges have usually, though not always, resorted to the criteria of seniority. The lack of public reason is exemplified by the fact that, like in most state institutions, seniority is a decisive criteria in making appointments. In some ways seniority has considerable advantages as a criteria. It is neutral in the strictest sense, not open to any ambiguity. It gives the rules of selection a certain formal fixity that endures over and above the changes in executive or judicial preference. In deeply divided societies where it might be thought impossible to evolve criteria through public discussion and deliberation, seniority rules are a safe and neutral choice. Indeed in India it has become the norm that departures from seniority in promotion, etc., are *presumptive* grounds for supposing that the norms of fairness have been violated. And the evidence most brought forward to allege violations of fairness involve the claim that seniority has been violated. Norms of seniority, especially in the appointment of chief justices, were established very early on, apparently to the consternation of the executive. But the widespread use of seniority also implies that most other criteria for judicial incompetence, unless displayed in extreme forms, become irrelevant. The resort to seniority rules may in the end reveal the extraordinary lack of self-trust that institutions have in themselves.

The current situation on the appointment of judges seems to me to be unsatisfactory. It secures the independence of the judiciary only by shielding it from any accountability for the appointments it makes. It is clear from the Constituent Assembly debates that the founders did not want to leave the appointment of judges exclusively to one branch. Through the *Second Judges* and the *Third Judges* cases, the courts have, capitalizing on a general suspicion of executive power, virtually shut it out. This outcome seems to me to be unwarranted both constitutionally and empirically.

The simple question is: who shall hold the judiciary accountable for the nature and quality of appointments? This question was insistently raised after the president of India was reported as having suggested to the chief justice that 'due consideration' be given to persons belonging to weaker sections of society like Scheduled Castes and Scheduled Tribes, (and women) who are the beneficiaries of compensatory discrimination in other areas. It seems to me that the president was firmly within his rights to make such a request; the courts have on occasion 'consistent with the requirement of merit' sought to provide for an equitable regional or religious representation in the courts. The judiciary's appropriation of the right to appoint judges does not in the least bit abate questions about the legitimacy of its choices, and the judiciary seems to have avoided rather than confronted the question.

The idea of a national judicial commission for appointments to the higher judiciary has been put forward from time to time. During the Constituent Assembly debates, all such proposals for an independent commission, either to nominate or supervise judicial appointments were explicitly rejected. Such a commission would clearly have the advantage of providing a mechanism for the supervision of the judicial appointments by a body that is wider than the judiciary itself. On the other hand, under current political conditions, the larger the nominating or approving body, the more likelihood there is of deep divisions. It does not seem that the controversies over the legitimacy of judicial appointments is likely to abate any sooner than the deep divisions in Indian society that fuel these controversies in the first place.

III. The Civil Justice System in Crisis

Assessing any civil justice system is an extremely complex matter. A proper assessment of its functioning ought to involve at least three dimensions: the rectitude of the decisions it regularly produces, the time it takes to do so, and the cost involved. It is a perfectly simple requirement of any system of justice that its procedures produce correct results. In the Indian case, as in many others, the degree to which the procedures of the justice system fulfils the requirement of rectitude is almost impossible to determine. In the absence of any hard data, this much can be said: the higher branches of the judiciary are *extremely reluctant* to deny admission of appeals; depending on the jurisdiction as many as seventy per cent of all appeals filed will be admitted. This must be considered a tacit acknowledgement of the courts' recognition that on average there are prima facie grounds for supposing that the procedures of the lower courts are faulty. In one important sense the passage of time is simply part of our assessment of the rectitude of the decision. Again we have no systematic break down of delays by the *type* of cases, but the composition of the dockets is telling in this respect. It appears that more than half of the courts' work is consumed by passing and assessing interim orders. Courts, lawyers, and litigants expect interim orders to be the norm rather than the exception; indeed one case study of the Allahabad High Court found that *seeking interim orders was the point of the litigation.* The fact that interim orders is a proportionately higher percentage of the courts work is also a tacit acknowledgment that delays are the norm rather than the exception.[24] Finally, in terms of cost there are at least two considerations. First, should the justice system be financed by its users, or should the obligation be borne by the taxpayer? Second, what is the relationship between cost and access in any particular justice system? In the Indian case, the court fees etc., are extremely low to ensure access (in the case of some public interest litigation, these were waived entirely).[25]

Most observers agree that the judiciary is considerably under financed. The Indian government has taken Hamilton's description of the judiciary as 'the least expensive branch' as an injunction to be rigorously followed. India has only about ten-and-a-half judges per million population, amongst the lowest rates in the world. The entire expenditure on the judiciary is less than 0.3 per cent of GDP

---

[24] It is estimated by legal experts that, putting aside the frequency of interim orders and appeals, the taking of evidence in Bombay High Court takes an average of five years; the current backlog in Bombay High Court is twelve years for interim orders and even longer for final dispositions.

[25] The Law Commission Report is a sober analysis of this issue.

of which more than half comes from court fees itself. The judiciary has always been in a weak financial bargaining position vis-á-vis the executive; and such increases in spending as it has managed to elicit go largely to increases in salaries. One of the institutional weaknesses of the judiciary is that they do not have a natural political constituency or source of power that can be used to put pressure on the government for more funds. There are still no formal mechanisms by which the financial relationship between the judiciary and the government can be institutionalized in ways that are fair to the judiciary. But even given this constraint there are two striking facts internal to the financial administration of the judiciary. First, it turns out that most high courts are extremely slow at spending even the money they have. Funds sanctioned for infrastrucutral investments like information technology more often than not lapse. A substantial number of courts spend less than their allotted budgets on these items each year. Most of the delays in spending are attributed to the arcane procurement rules of the Government of India. Second, individual judges have almost no control over their own budgets and find it almost impossible to allocate finances efficiently for their own needs. The judiciary has almost no support staff—the idea of law clerks has been proposed for years now but is still pending approval.

To describe the Indian civil justice system, especially at the level below the Supreme Court, as being in a perpetual state of crisis would be an understatement. As an institution, almost all levels of the judiciary exhibit what can only be described as administered chaos. There is unanimity in the view that the court system is administratively inefficient. Judges are excessively passive in an adversarial legal system; excessive party control allows respondents to delay cases with impunity and there are few alternatives for dispute resolution other than an ill-managed trial.

The administrative infrastructure of most courts is woefully inadequate. Records of filings are mostly kept by hand, documents are difficult to trace, judges orally summarize testimony for court recorders, judges are moved around from bench to bench faster than depositions are filed. Judges seem to seldom exercise the power to impose costs for frivolous litigation; interim injunctive relief and adjournments are routinely granted; and the number of possible appeals while a case is still on is large enough to effectively fracture the trial or stay it.

Under the rules that govern the filing of cases, *there are too many points at which the process of civil justice is unnecessarily delayed.* These delays happen despite the rules explicitly designed to overcome them. Probably the single biggest cause of delay that has effects that reverberate down the litigation process is at the very first step. When a complaint is filed in court, the court registrars, usually civil servants, are responsible for determining whether all the procedural requirements have been satisfied. They usually classify the case, are responsible for tracking its progress, and for serving all the relevant notices. There is almost unanimous consensus that the infrastrucutral facilities of the Registrar's office are woefully inadequate. Submissions are still manually filed and tracked and in most courts there seem to be no uniform procedures by which these are handled. Only the Supreme Court has a consistent tracking system facilitated largely by the use of computers.

The Registrar's main job is to screen filing complaints for procedural deficiencies. Again, while systematic statistics are not available a large number of registrars report that somewhere between half and two-thirds of all filings are deficient. Although in principle the lawyers are responsible for deficient filings, it appears that courts seldom dismiss filings on grounds of procedural inadequacies. And even filings rejected on ground of procedural inadequacies can be appealed. Thus it is clear that even simple matters of conforming to court procedures that could be handled by an efficient court bureaucracy end up in court. There are in principle no reasons why the courts should accept inadequate filings that take longer to sort out in court. But the courts mostly take the view—and given Indian conditions rightly so—that plaintiffs should not be penalized because of the incompetence of their lawyers. Since there are no serious mechanisms for controlling incompetent lawyers, deficient filings continue. In some ways, the courts are caught between a rock and a hard place. If complaints are dismissed or not allowed to be heard because of filing deficiencies, a large number of genuine complaints may not make it to court at all.

The organization of information in Indian courts is extremely tenuous. There is very little uniformity in the recording of information, very few standardized forms, and in some cases an inconsistent and non-existent system of classification that makes it very difficult to consolidate cases that involve common issues or common facts. One class of litigation, involving land acquisition disputes, for example, will have as many cases as they are claimants, each with their own lawyers, strategies, etc. Without a proper classification system it will be almost impossible to consolidate similar cases and ensure their speedy disposal. One particularly glaring consequence is that cases remain on the courts' dockets many years after the case has been made redundant. One registrar interviewed estimated that due to delays as many as ten per cent of the cases had become 'non contentious', which means that the litigants were no longer interested but the case remained on the court's docket.

Another consequence of disorganized informational structure is that scheduling of cases in courts and notification of appearance is extremely chaotic. In almost all courts the schedule for appearance is not available until the day or even evening before. In Calcutta High Court, for instance, the schedule of a day's case may be available only at 4 a.m. on the day of the appearance. Cases are usually not rolled over into the next day's calendar. This invariably increases the instances of non-appearance and much of the court's time is wasted simply calling for appearances. The unpredictability of the courts' dockets causes a colossal waste of time all around.

Most Indian courts have very inadequate procedures for taking evidence. The discovery process and the filing of documents all happens physically, in court. The Indian civil justice system has by and large very few out of court discovery processes. This again, takes up more court time than is necessary and makes scheduling enormously complicated. Courts have to coordinate their schedules with the availability of witnesses, and given their own unpredictability have very little legitimacy when they compel witnesses to appear. Again, part of the problem here seems to stem from a lack of trust. The court does not trust the lawyers to effectively monitor each other in out of court discovery processes. The lawyers, in the absence of a professionalized and institutionalized code, have very little trust in each other.

It is not clear what the origins of the practice of the obsession with in-court practices is. In common law systems apparently the judges thought it was important to judge the witnesses' demeanour. But currently this rationale seems bogus. Given the rotation system the probability that the judges who heard the evidence will also render the final judgement is low. Even if it is the same judge, the judgement will be rendered years after the memory of the demeanour is retained in the judge's memory.

One of the peculiar features of the Indian civil justice system at all levels is judicial rotation. Judges are rotated from one panel to another, typically within a period of a couple of months and from one court to another every few years and there is little predictability in their case assignments. One of the more furious debates in legal reform is over non-rotating benches and a fixed calendering system. Under this system a case would be assigned to a judge who will be, barring retirement or departure from his position, responsible for the disposition of the case. The current system has many disadvantages. First, there is considerable reduplication of a judge's time. Judges who have invested in learning about a case will find themselves taken off the case, new judges will have to invest time learning it—and there are no standard procedures by which all this information can be passed along. The possibility that judges can be taken off cases has set up perverse incentives. Many judges feel that the knowledge that a case may be transferred acts as a disincentive to dispose off a matter promptly. Some courts set statistical targets for the disposal of cases. Under such regimes any case which smacks of complexity of any kind will invariably be postponed. Secondly, it seems to be the case that the rotation of judges prevents them from exercising either administrative discipline over their dockets, or exercise authority over the lawyers. It is very difficult to find and collect systematic data on the effects that non-rotating benches would have on disposal rates. But every single case study done of instances where, even for a short period of time, non-rotating benches are introduced, shows a considerable improvement in disposal rates.[26] The matter of non-rotating benches has been mooted many times and each time has encountered stiff opposition from lawyers and Bar associations.

For me one of the big puzzles is how passive judges generally are during the trial process. The judges have within their discretion many powers that if exercised could considerably speed up the process. Extensions, adjournments, and delays are routinely granted

---

[26] The most famous of these instances is the reforms introduced, despite stiff resistance from the Bar, by Chief Justice Satish Chandra at Allahabad High Court in 1980. See Mahajan, 'Allahabad Advocates Facing Dilemma'.

almost as if they are a matter of right. Judges have the authority to frame rules that would govern the conduct of litigation, but most courts seem reluctant to do so. Judges can, under Indian law, make suggestions for settlement, impose costs on non-appearing parties and for frivolous motions, and be more assertive in summoning witnesses and documents. There seem to be three explanations for the judges' reluctance to impose court discipline. One is simply corruption, but it is almost impossible to determine its extent. Even if this were the case (and my own sense is that the incidence of corruption is often exaggerated) it would not explain the general ease by which adjournments are secured. The second is that most judges seek to avoid controversy. They do not want constant appeals against them filed, they do want to acquire a reputation in the Bar for being difficult, just in case it is held against them in promotions. Since adjournments have become the norm, granting them seems the easiest way of avoiding controversy. And finally, the difficulties in the court's own administration make it difficult to take action against lawyers for the non-production of witnesses, etc.

India is also particularly weak in institutionalizing out-of-court dispute settlements. Although conciliation services are available through the Lok Adalats, these are limited to a few jurisdictions like family and accident matters. Indian courts have no obligatory mediation such as compulsory neutral evaluation commonly used in American courts. The conciliation process is hampered by the fact that it involves lawyers rather than the parties themselves. This is a considerable problem in the case of litigation involving government, since lawyers seldom have the authority to settle. But settlement of disputes is rare for a variety of reasons. *Oddly enough, delays in the judicial system, rather than acting as an incentive for settlement, do the opposite.* Any defendant who has received interim relief has very little incentive to settle, if it is unlikely that the ruling will be overturned for some time. The easy availability of lawyers, the low cost of legal services, the absence of cost shifting mechanisms are in principle all designed to facilitate greater access to courts; but they have the consequence of not only increasing litigation but also reducing the incentives for settlement.

Debates over reform of the Indian legal system suffer from three presumptions. One is that since there is too much to be done nothing can be done. The problems with the system appear multitudinous enough to induce a kind of paralysis. This is particularly so because many aspects of these problems interlock with each other to produce a vicious cycle. Lawyers and clients will not accept a fee structure other than one based on court appearance, because that is just about the only thing the Indian civil justice system guarantees. Moves towards contingency fees are unlikely until India develops a more robust system of tort law with some likelihood that judgements will actually be delivered. But until lawyers move to a different fee structure, or the lawyers associations are controlled by better lawyers, they will, at the level of the lower courts, remain substantive obstacles to reform. The second presumption is that the most significant issue in the reform process are mechanisms of enforcement rather than changes in institutional rules themselves. In some cases, this presumption is well-founded: there are a large number of provisions that would enable judges to be more effective if they desired. But from the very first Law Commission, headed by Attorney General Setelvad, to the seventy-ninth, the general presumption has been that a simple investment of resources would be both necessary and sufficient to make a significant impact.[27] The third presumption is that a greater investment of resources, rather than a reform of court management would be required to make a significant impact on the justice system.

Greater investment and better enforcement of internal procedures are by themselves not sufficient. It may turn out that they are not necessary either. The Supreme Court provides a particularly dramatic illustration of this possibility. In October 1994, Chief Justice A. H. Ahmadi introduced a series of reforms to handle matters in the Supreme Court. Most of these reforms had to do with investment in information technology and better classification. The Supreme Court was computerized, a uniform system for the classification of cases was introduced, and the distribution of tasks in the Supreme Court's registry was computerized. These reforms alone, which enabled better case management, reduced the

---

[27] The first Commission explicitly states that the procedures of the court are not a substantial cause of delay. 'The delay results not from the procedure laid down in the CPC but by reason of non-observance of its important provisions, particularly those intended to expedite the disposal of proceedings.' It is only in the One Hundred and Twenty-Fourth Report that problems of court management were given due attention.

backlog of cases in the Supreme Court from 120,000 to approximately 20,000. At the moment the Supreme Court is disposing off cases faster than they are being instituted. At least one weakness of the civil justice system, delay, has been successfully managed at the highest level.

What conclusions can be drawn from this instance of successful reforms? *The most obvious one is what one might call nuts and bolts matter.* In many Indian institutions, a cumulative set of small procedural anomalies can have far reaching impact on the performance of institutions. But there is often little incentive to attend to small but consequential procedural matters.

The place of the recent Supreme Court reforms in the public perception suggests one reason why. These reforms, except amongst the legal community, went virtually unnoticed. Most of the justices heralded as 'saviours of the judiciary' have been lauded for their very public, populist, but largely symbolic, gestures: accepting postcards as writ petitions, calling politicians to account. It seems a pervasive feature of Indian institutional life that such reforming energies as exist within the system either don't attend to, or despair of small reforms that might have a significant impact.

IV. The Legal Profession and the Political Economy of Reform

The single biggest weakness of the Indian justice system is its legal profession. Here again as elsewhere in India, the top of the profession is extraordinary both in legal skill and professionalism. In terms of numbers, India, on last count had 336 lawyers per million of population, apparently a high number by developing country standards. But the quality of the legal profession drops precipitously after the small cream of top professionals and it is the low median that has the most influence on the conduct of law. Marc Galanter's description of the Indian legal profession is as apt today as it was two decades ago:

Among the prominent features of Indian lawyers are their orientations to the courts to the exclusion of other legal settings; litigating rather than advising, negotiating or planning; their conceptualism and orientation to rules; their individualism and lack of specialization. Thus we get a picture of legal services supplied by relatively unspecialized lawyers, involved in little coordination effort, offering a narrow range of services. Relations with clients are episodic and intermittent. The lawyer addresses discrete problems in isolation from the whole situation of the client and uninformed by considerations of long term strategy (Galanter 1989: 283).

While the judiciary is an institution of the state, much of the work it does is determined by the private economy. The judiciary is uniquely at the interface of state and society in many ways. While the state provides with its resources, lawyers and litigants determine how the judiciary is going to be used. The use or non-use of various jurisdictions, the purposes of litigation, the areas of dispute brought to the courts are determined by lawyers and litigants. Of course, as I have suggested many of the incentives for lawyers and litigants are set by the internal rules of the judiciary itself. Nevertheless, it remains the case that the political economy of the legal profession has an extraordinary impact on the ways in which courts are used and over which the courts seem to have very little control. It is thus difficult to disentangle the weakness of courts as institutions from the pathologies of the larger society they find themselves under. One of the striking things that emerged during this research is that almost every single attempt by the courts to reform their procedures in any way that would expedite matters has met stiff resistance from the respective Bar associations concerned. It has proved almost impossible to get systematic data on strikes by lawyers, but it appears that every reform proposal is met with one. Although there is no systematic data, there seems to be a typical response from the Bar whenever reforms are proposed. For instance, Justice Iyer's remark in a famous 1980 case[28] that many oral arguments which take a disproportionate amount of court time could be replaced with written submissions immediately provoked a strike and an extraordinarily high minded defence by the lawyers of their prerogatives. Despite being warned by the chief justice and almost uniformly castigated by the Press, the strike continued till the government, in breach of etiquette that forbids it from commenting on internal court procedures, declared that no such changes would be in the offing. Similar actions have been undertaken when non-rotating benches have been introduced. The issue in all these strikes and boycotts is simple: Lawyers get paid for appearances in court; there is no rationalized system of charging for actual amount of work done. Despite numerous court

---

[28] *P. N. Easwara Iyer* v. *Registrar, Supreme Court*, AIR, 1980 SC 808.

judgements holding members of the Bar in contempt, lawyers' strikes have not diminished. The most recent instance was a strike against the government's far reaching proposal to introduce changes in the CPC. Ostensibly, the lawyers were aggrieved at not having been adequately consulted in the formulation of these reforms, but they were a dramatic illustration of the hostility of the organized Bar to the reform process.

The lawyers objected to many provisions of the new legislation. There is an extraordinary fear of competition from abroad. Most Indian professional associations are hostile to liberalizing the services market, but competition may turn out to be the only mechanism to induce professionalization. Another proposal, to let foreign advocates and law firms practice in India, has proved controversial. This follows from India's agreeing on 1 January 1995 to abide by the General Agreement on Tariffs and Trade; even so, there is as yet no legal obligation to allow foreign firms to practice in India, since renegotiations are on. The principle of reciprocity, which guides the proposal, may exist only on paper, Indian advocates fear. As one lawyer suggested 'Our visa system is liberal, whereas Indian advocates may find it difficult to go abroad and practice in foreign courts. Developed countries have very strict immigration laws. Indian lawyers, for instance, will find it difficult to enter the United States. There will be no reciprocity.' These fears are considerably overdrawn; most foreign firms will have to rely substantially on Indian talent to do their bidding. But it is a measure of the depth of insecurity of the Indian legal profession that it is unwilling to contemplate competition from organized law firms.

Many of the other proposed reforms were largely in the right direction. For instance, this legislation provides for examination of witnesses by commissioners appointed by the courts in order to save the trial judges' time. Although this provision might address the problem of judicial delays, some lawyers fear that it presupposes the commissioners' neutrality. The Bar seems to have hung on to the antiquated notion that Galanter describes above, that only public trials are worth legal work. This lead the lawyers to also oppose provisions for out-of-court settlement. The proposed Act restores Section 89 of the CPC, which was repealed in 1940 and which enables out-of-court settlement of disputes through arbitration, conciliation, mediation, or through the Lok Adalat. This provision too is aimed at helping the courts clear their backlog of cases. Other procedures designed to bind the parties to respond in time included, requiring a defendant in a suit to file a statement within 30 days of summons being served on him or her. Lawyers argue that in many cases, particularly where the government is a litigant, it may not be possible to file a reply within the stipulated period. Tamil Nadu government officials, for instance, have expressed the opinion that where the government is the defendant, it should be given 60 days to file a reply. The Act also sought to restrict second appeals to decrees in respect of amounts exceeding Rs 25,000. (The earlier provision had a threshold of Rs 3000.) As a result, in cases where the decree amount is less than Rs 25,000, the litigant has to go directly to the Supreme Court for appellate remedy; decrees of amounts exceeding Rs 25,000 would have the benefit of an appeal before the high court, subject to there being a substantial question of law involved. Some lawyers claim that the majority of cases under litigation relate to transactions that involve less than Rs 25,000; in such a situation, restricting second appeals to decrees above Rs 25,000 would have the effect of affirming an appellate remedy only for those who have the resources. Even those who argue in defence of the Amendment Act concede this point but claim that this could be corrected through a minor amendment of the Act. The proposed legislation also amends Section 100 A of the CPC in such a manner that appellate remedy against any writ, direction, or order issued under Article 226 or Article 227 of the Constitution will be curtailed. Now writ petitions could be heard by single judges and an appeal against the judge's verdict may be preferred under Clause 15 of the Letters Patent before a Division Bench.

The details of the proposed CPC reform legislation are in some ways fairly humdrum, but they signify a general weakness of the Indian state. There is immense resistance to minor changes that could have far reaching effects; the resistance is largely a consequence of the most insecure sections of the profession having control over organized collective power. Legal reform will be difficult to undertake unless the legal profession becomes more professionalized. Second, it seems that at the moment in most Bar associations effective power is not with the best and most professionalized lawyers but with the worst and least successful. This seems to be part of a general trend in Indian professional associations (including incidentally, the Indian Political Science

Association). The successful ones in the Indian system have very little incentive to be more than nominally active in such associations, while the least successful see these associations as a conduit through which power can be channelled. They have both the capacity, the incentives, and the numbers with them to capitalize on their nuisance value. This is one of the externalities associated with a rapid increase in the educational system with little quality control. The qualifications for being admitted to the Bar are fairly minimal. The result has by and large been an almost complete breakdown of professional self-surveillance. Rectifying this side of the legal profession will be easier said than done. In part the response of the Supreme Court and the Bar Council of India to the problem of deteriorating standards in existing law schools has been to create a handful of new ones without derecognizing the old.[29] This created another privileged layer at the top without addressing the qualities and professionalism of the median on which the health of the system of civil justice ultimately depends.

CONCLUSION

This chapter has argued that the Supreme Court has been extraordinarily creative in its interpretation of the Indian Constitution. It has secured its independence from the executive and has exercised its powers of constitutional review. The Supreme Court in particular carries enormous authority. But despite this, constitutionalism remains a fragile aspiration. For one thing the courts have used their powers to facilitate a modus vivendi rather than articulate clear constitutional principles. The terms of this modus vivendi is greatly determined by the courts' estimate of prevailing political fissures and is likely to shift as the judges' interpretation of Indian public

[29] In fact the Bar Council seems also to be operating under its own archaisms that have no empirical bases. For instance, Bar Council rules explicitly prohibit any full time professor at a law school from engaging in trial practice. Originally this rule was devised for the protection of universities. With low salaries in the university, the argument was that professors would spend all their time with their clients and less with their students. The oppposite possibility was not even considered. This rule would prevent the best legal minds from teaching; those who would be left in teaching would have little or no actual legal experieence and hence would be incapable of giving relevant professional training. This turned out to be the actual consequence of the rule; yet there is stiff resistance to even consider changing it.

opinion shifts. The institutional weakness of the Indian judiciary make it unlikely that judicial principles will carry the due weight of authority in society at large any time soon. The 'constitutional rules' will endure less not only because they are internalized as values that determine behaviour, but also because they provide enough occasions for discretionary manipulation to allow the show to go on. The appalling weaknesses of the Indian civil justice system, below the level of the Supreme Court, and the difficulties of reforming them will only exacerbate this predicament, not resolve it.

References

Austin, Granville (1999), *Working a Democratic Constitution*, Delhi: Oxford University Press, ch. 25, p. 276.

Baxi Upendra (1983), *The Supreme Court in Indian Politics*, Delhi: Eastern Book Company.

Dhavan, Rajeev. *The Supreme Court Today*, Allahabad: Eastern Book Company.

————— (1980), *Justice on Trial: The Supreme Court Today*, Allahabad: A. H. Wheeler.

Epps, Charles (1998), *A Rights Revolution*, Chicago: Chicago University Press.

Ferejohn, John (1995), 'Law, Legislation and Positive Political Theory', in J. S. Banks and Eric Hanushek (eds), *Modern Political Economy: Old Topics, New Directions*, Cambridge: Cambridge University Press.

Galanter, Marc (1989), *Law and Society in Modern India*, Delhi: Oxford University Press.

Gupta, Vijay (1997), *Decision Making in the Supreme Court of India*, Delhi: Kaveri Books.

Kothari, Rajni (1970), *Politics in India*, New Delhi: Manohar.

Mahajan, K. (1980), 'Allahabad Advocates Facing Dilemma', *Hindustan Times*, 21 and 22 May.

Nariman, Fali S. (1998), 'The Growing Uncertainty in the Law: How Consistent are the Decisions of the Supreme Court', *Indian Journal of Law*.

Rao, B. Shiva (1966), *The Framing of India's Constitution*, Select Documents, vol. III, p. 219.

Tate, C. Neal and Torbjorn Vallinder (eds) (1995), *The Global Expansion of Judicial Power*, New York: NYU Press.

Verma, S. K. and Kusum (eds) (2000), *Fifty Years of the Supreme Court of India: Its Grasp and Reach*, New Delhi: Oxford University Press.

Zuckerman, Adrian (ed.) (1999), *Civil Justice in Crisis*, Oxford: Oxford University Press.

6

The Police in India
Design, Performance, and Adaptability

ARVIND VERMA

INTRODUCTION

The police touch the very life of the people. As the coercive arm of the state they are called upon to maintain order and play a role in ensuring rule of the law. By preventing criminal activity and apprehending offenders, the police play a significant role in providing security and dignity to the citizens. The police also impact upon the social, economic, and political situations and thereby contribute to the development and integrity of the nation. Indeed, as Bayley (1969: 11) remarks,

...the nature of police activities provides an important clue to the character of a political regime. A government's evaluation of itself as democratic would hardly be allowed to go unchallenged if the police severely restricted public meetings and political demonstrations or resorted readily to physical force and intimidation in order to prevent crime.

Undoubtedly, the role of the police in India is extremely significant in view of the democratic polity and multi-cultural, multi-ethnic, and large-size diverse population of the country. Through their ubiquitous visible presence and actions, police personnel affect everyone and everything in the society. By a near monopoly of legal force they alone provide for the security of people and enforcement of laws of the country. The officers also determine the manner in which democratic decisions are implemented in the country. In view of the growing violence, extensive social conflicts, and serious threats of terrorist activities, the role of the police is an important factor in the stability of the country. The assurances of equality and dignity to the numerable minorities and weaker sections of the society are also dependent upon the performance of the police. Clearly, the police are a crucial factor in the existence and development of India.

Unfortunately, despite its importance, there have been few empirical studies of the Indian police. In contrast to the voluminous literature on policing that is found in the US and other developed countries, the body of police research in India is meagre. Except for the reports of the National Police commissions of 1904 and 1978 (GOI 1979–83), some reports by state police commissions, symposium proceedings (*Seminar* 1977) and a few books, largely by serving or retired police officers (Lobo 1992; Shah 1992; Singh 1996), the literature on Indian police, especially critical evaluation, is virtually non-existent. The government publishes an annual *Crime in India* that provides official data on the regional distribution of crime and police resources while the media, especially newspapers and magazines, provide journalist accounts of police related subjects. This forms the body of knowledge for the police in India, which obviously is very limited. In view of a shortage of authoritative textual material, I will utilize my experiences in the Indian police where I have served in a senior supervisory rank for almost 17 years. This may induce an element of personal and ideological bias but my attempt will be to remain objective as far as possible.

The aim of this chapter is to describe the design of police institution in India, assess its performance and adaptability in meeting the demands made by a developing society. My study is based upon a historically rooted comparative organizational analysis that draws upon the work of police scholars, analysis of official data, and from my observations. My attempt is to explain some of the structural problems such as corruption and misuse of force in terms of the design features and prevalent organizational practices. The adaptability of the institution is assessed in terms of the police ability to deal with social and political problems confronting the country. The performance is assessed not only by the outcome but also the process and mechanism of implementation. Finally, an attempt is also made to suggest possible avenues of reform for the police institution.

DESIGN: THE HISTORICAL CONTEXT

The Police Act V of 1861 governs the Indian police of the twenty-first century. This itself suggests that the design is outdated and will not match the performance desired in a new millennium. In order to understand the features of initial design and founding conditions that have had an enduring influence, an examination of the historical context in which this instrument was created is essential. The design of police in India 'in the mid-nineteenth century was not independent of the economic, political and administrative realities that existed' (Arnold 1986: 7). Moreover, the police were set up as a colonial force to hold India as 'the brightest jewel in the British crown' and to be 'ruled with a firm hand and ruthlessly, if necessary' (Gupta 1979: 3). The design was tailored to suit the British imperial interests after the First War of Independence in 1857. Even then the organizational set up was not conceived to last more than a short period of time. It is therefore a tragedy that modern India continues to police the country through a mechanism that is not appropriate for an independent, democratic nation.

The design of Indian police was to subjugate the people and it was the war of 1857 that necessitated the urgent need of an instrument to control the vast lands and the diverse people at an economical cost. The need to remould and strengthen the administrative and legal systems developed by the East India Company had become imperative. After facing a real threat of losing power in 1857, the British rulers were determined to ensure complete suzerainty and suppression of all challenges to their power. Although European membership was increased in the army, yet it was clear that the army could be used only for putting down rebellions and for defence of the border. 'The formation of the "civil" police forces was intended to lessen what by the 1850s had come to be seen as a dangerous reliance on the army for internal policing' (Arnold 1986: 13). Accordingly, a police force was needed that could 'develop a sense of fear of authority in the entire population' and 'could serve as the first line of defence' (Gupta 1979: 7). The design could not be expressed in any other terms for the mission of the new police was to ensure that this objective be achieved in a brief period of time.

The reorganization was entrusted to a Police Commission appointed in August 1860 with the avowed aim of making police an efficient instrument for the prevention and detection of crime. Nevertheless, an internal government memo to the Police Commission did not mask the real objectives for the new police force. The Commission was told to bear in mind that 'functions of a police are either protective and repressive or detective' and that 'the line which separates the protective and repressive functions of a civil force from functions purely military, may not always, in India be very clear' (Imperial Gazetteer of India 1909: 380).

People's Police versus Colonial Police

The Indian police system, designed in 1860 was in sharp contrast to the British Bobby who is a celebrated symbol of democratic policing throughout the world. The Metropolitan London police was of course created in 1829 with very different objectives. The main principles behind the reforms by Sir Robert Peel were:

• The police would be a uniformed force but drawn from the local people;

• The force will be totally unarmed;

• It will be accountable to citizens through the office of the home secretary;

• It will be beholden to judicial control; and

• It will work for the prevention of crime by winning the trust and cooperation of the people (Gaines et al. 1996).

This metropolitan system had achieved remarkable success within a short period in controlling crime and winning the trust of the people. The Americans had begun to emulate this system in their own cities—Philadelphia in 1838, New York in 1845, and Chicago in 1854. Yet, the British were not willing to extend this system to their colonies, especially where the Britons were in a minority. Instead, for these regions they created another model, the so-called colonial policing system that was developed in Ireland. The model was guided by the exigencies of trade and profit, considerations other than the interests of the governed people. Brogden (1987) states that such

policing was directly linked to the commercial interests of an expanding capitalism in search of new markets and resources. Colonial police history is essentially the history of that socialization of police work. The British South African Company, the Royal Nigeria Company, and the Imperial British East Africa Company, amongst others, established policing systems. The East India Company spread its police tentacles as far as Singapore (Brogden 1987: 1).

In addition, there were imperialistic and racist considerations too, like the 'glamour and snobbery' (Chakravarty 1989: 231) or the 'cold, bureaucratic, optimistic and racially arrogant' (Edwardes 1967: 176) spirit of the rulers towards the subjugated people. The slightest challenge to any official decree, like singing patriotic songs or displaying native flags was taken seriously. The British Raj in India, though backed by a powerful force was still symbolic, based upon an implied authority and total submission of the people. The Raj was established upon the strength and terror of the police administration in which it was natural that the British would keep direct control and not make officers accountable to the people as done in London. A people's police in India would have made the British Raj redundant.

The colonial model adopted in India is credited to Sir Charles Napier who created a separate police organization in Sindh province after its annexation. This model was based upon the Royal Irish Constabulary that was 'altogether more centralized and coercive than the subsequent British system' (Jefferson 1990). It was a kind of policing that was 'modest' when the 'legitimacy' of the colonial forces was not questioned. But, 'the operational role and intensity of policing was extended' when 'legitimacy was challenged and political instability grew' (Anderson and Killingray 1992). Sir Charles Jeffries sums up the impact of the Irish model on the colonies as follows:

It is clear enough that from the point of view of the colonies there was much attraction in an arrangement which provided what we should now call a 'paramilitary' organization or gendarmerie, armed, and trained to operate as an agent of the central government in a country where the population was predominantly rural, communications were very poor, social conditions were largely primitive, and, the recourse to violence by members of the public who were 'against the government' was not infrequent (Jeffries 1952: 7).

The design of the British police system in India also had roots in the structure developed by the Mughals in the seventeenth century. The colonial model incorporated many features of the Mughal system and officials such as the Daroga, Kotwal, and Faujdar found place in the reorganized British system. 'The British not only borrowed this structure but also took over the feeling tone of the Mughal administration—a mixture of great pomp and show combined with benevolent and despotic intervention' (Cohn 1961: 8). The Police Act clearly intended a repressive police system for the Indian people. Gupta suggests (1979: 7) 'the Act made provision in detail only for two purposes, the establishment and administration, under strict magisterial control, of a single unified force in every province and measures for using it to keep the people of the country effectively repressed.'

Bayley (1969) takes a more pragmatic view and argues that the principles behind the police reorganization were to replace military police with a civilian constabulary that was to be administered by a separate establishment. The chief of police (called inspector-general) was made responsible to the provincial government while the district police chief (superintendent—SP) was placed under the dual control of inspector-general and district magistrate (DM), the civilian bureaucrat. He suggests that the new Police Act (V of 1861), enacted on 22nd March was an attempt to coordinate the imperial police administration with the existing rural policing system. But Bayley (1969) notes that no further structural reforms in police administration in India have been made except for some 'tidying up, tinkering with, and elaborating upon the existing arrangements' (Ibid.: 45).

The Police Act of 1861

The duties of the police officers were incorporated in Section 23 of the Act that stated, 'it shall be the duty of every police officer promptly to obey and execute all orders and warrants lawfully issued to him by any competent authority; to collect and communicate intelligence affecting the public peace; to prevent the commissioning of offences and public nuances; to detect and bring offenders to justice; and to apprehend all persons whom he is legally authorized to apprehend and for whose apprehension sufficient grounds exist.' The order of importance of these duties is significant—to obey orders of superiors and collect intelligence and then followed by prevention and detection of offences. Nowhere does the Act suggest giving service to the people and working closely to gain their trust. This stands in sharp contrast to the duties enshrined in the reorganized Metropolitan Police in England.

There are other sections in the Act too that suggest a repressive nature of the police system. Section 15 provides for the stationing of additional punitive police in any part of the province found to be disturbed from the conduct of the inhabitants. More significantly, the Act provided that the costs of such additional police were to be levied from the inhabitants on the basis of an assessment by the DM. This money was to be realized by distress warrants and sale of confiscated property of the fugitives. Section 17 provided for the appointment of the residents as special police officers to assist the regular police and Section 19 provided powers to punish people refusing to serve as such. Section 30 empowered the police to license the assemblies and processions of people that could be refused on grounds of threat to law and order. Furthermore, since Indians filled majority of subordinate ranks, provisions were made to keep their loyalty under constant supervision. Section 44 required the maintenance of a general diary by the station house officer (SHO) that included details of movements of all police officers posted to the station. 'A close watch was thus ensured on the actions and movements of native police officers from hour to hour and day to day' (Gupta 1979: 9). The senior police officers, who exercised most of these powers thus not only could check the loyalty of their subordinates but also were in a position to wield considerable authority over the general people. Interestingly, Act XLVIII of 1860 amended the policing provisions in the presidency towns of Calcutta, Madras, and Bombay where a large European population was residing. Subsequently, special police acts were passed for each city—Calcutta Police Act of 1866, Madras City Police Act of 1888, and Bombay Police Act of 1902.

The Police Act was accompanied by the introduction of new criminal laws. The Indian Penal Code was enacted in 1860 while the Criminal Procedure Code followed in 1862, the Evidence Act in 1872, and the Criminal Tribes Act in 1868. The Arms Act of 1857 (modified in 1860) was also introduced to disarm the people and prohibit possession of arms without a license. Since criminal elements have always possessed illegal arms, this move was not to curb criminal activities but the ability to pose any challenge to the state. There are some notable features in these laws that suggest a design meant to suppress the people rather than act in accordance with their desires.

The Indian Penal Code of 1860 introduces sections on offences against the state, the army and navy, against public tranquillity, relating to public servants, and contempt of lawful authority, false evidence, and offences against public justice right from the beginning. Offences that affect the lives and property of the people and which are 'the commonest preoccupation of the police and the courts everywhere, were defined only from chapters XVI (Section 299) onwards' (Ibid.: 12). The punishments provided for various offences include death, transportation, solitary confinement, and even whipping, all being 'utterly arbitrary and without any rational, jurisprudential or penological basis' (Ibid.: 13). Similarly, the Code of Criminal Procedures empowered police officers to arrest practically any person and keep him/her in confinement for at least 24 hours. Furthermore, the police can also, on some pretext search any house and summon anyone to the police station. The discretionary powers given to the police were extraordinary and beyond the status afforded by their pay and organizational responsibilities. 'The new police was so shaped in personnel, powers and procedures as to be ever more a terror to the law abiding citizen, but ineffective against the criminal, except by torture and malpractices' (Ibid.: 74).

The new police system was still found to be unsatisfactory even by the British rulers themselves. A Police Commission appointed by Lord Curzon in 1902–3 found that 'the police force is far from efficient; it is defective in training and organization; it is inadequately supervised; [and] it is generally regarded as corrupt and oppressive' (Ibid.: 201). Yet, the British made no substantial changes in the police system and in 1947, independent India inherited a police organization that was shaped by the exigencies of 1857 and governed by the Act of 1861.

Unfortunately, despite Independence and establishment of democracy in the country, this police system has continued unchanged. Indeed, there has hardly occurred 'any significant change in police methods and attitudes' (Arnold 1992) in the organization inherited from the British. The only political initiative to reform occurred with the appointment of the National Police Commission (NPC) in 1978 whose major recommendations have not been accepted by the government. This Commission has also pointed out that the police performance has fallen much short of the expectations of the public because of being constrained to function under an outmoded and 'politically more useful' system (Government of India Report I 1979: 7). It identified politically partisan performance, brutality, corruption, and inefficiency as the clear perceptions of the police institution in the country.

In view of the close collaboration of the administrative organizations and governmental machinery with the British, and the obvious repressive character of the police department in particular, the decision of the new political order to continue with the services of the old structure was perhaps surprising. Considering the bitter and protracted struggle against the British rule in which the police system was used ruthlessly, it seems naturally disturbing to see free India still choosing to continue this British made machinery without fundamental changes (Verma 1998: 227).

DESIGN: INSTITUTIONAL FEATURES

The organizational structure of the Indian police has remained virtually unchanged from 1861. Although, new ranks have been created [deputy superintendent (DySP) in 1905 and director-general (DGP) in 1980s], some financial powers have been enhanced, and training curriculum has been modified to incorporate the constitution and management theories, the institutional features are the same. The police are organized provincially, made accountable indirectly through the home minister and continue to symbolize an oppressive and indifferent state power. Furthermore, 'the proliferation of centrally controlled armed police corps and intelligence agencies' suggests 'the rulers of India since independence have been no more than faithful to their colonial inheritance' (Arnold 1986: 4–5).

Apart from these historical antecedents there are three additional design features that have been instrumental in affecting the police performance. The first is the tradition and growing emphasis on *armed* policing within the system. The second feature is the system of dual control—one exercised by an officer's corps, the so called members of the Indian Police Service (IPS) and the other asserted through the office of district magistrate and the home ministry staffed by officers of the Indian Administrative Service (IAS). The third is the colonial cultural heritage that has not only alienated the police from the citizens but also promoted corruption and unaccountability. These will be described briefly here.

The Tradition of Armed Police

The armed reserve in the police organization was retained even when the recommendation was for the separation of the military and the civilian police. Bayley (1969: 46) observes that 'considering that one of the substantial and senior tasks of government was the preservation of law and order and that communal disturbances, village faction fights, and depredation of sizable robber bands were common occurrences, the continued development of armed police is hardly to be wondered at.'

The armed police model has become a dominant feature of present Indian police system to deal with the public disorder problems (Das and Verma 1998). Indeed, the Indian police have always emphasized law and order maintenance rather than crime control in its functions (Baxi 1980). Every successive government has funded the phenomenal growth of armed police and para-military forces in the country on grounds of escalating violent conflicts, terrorism, and threats to stability. Many specialized police units have been created to deal with communal problems (Rapid Action Force), for providing security to important people (National Security Guards and Special Protection Group) and for preventing cross-border smuggling and terrorism (Border Security Force). There are also separate armed police forces to protect railway properties (Railway Protection Force), to police the Himalayan region (Indo-Tibetan Border Police) and to provide security to the public sector industries (Central Industrial Security Force). A women's battalion in the Central Reserve Police Force has also been created to deal with the increasing number of female agitators (Verma 2000b). Furthermore, every state has also created its own armed units that now consists of 281,987 personnel in its ranks (NCRB 1998). Additionally, every district police also maintains a large contingent of armed unit from its own strength. These armed police forces are only meant for 'law and order' duties and their personnel cannot be used for crime investigation or service functions. Thus, both at the central and provincial levels armed police units far outnumber the ones engaged in crime control tasks.

This has created a difficult situation since the strength of detectives has remained almost constant while the armed battalions have been increasing. The short-term objectives of maintaining order rather than looking into the underlying nature of problems i leading to a dangerous situation. Furthermore, the deployment of armed police does not result in a neutral order maintenance role (Verma 1997). Maintaining order, especially in the democratic framework of the country involves discretionary judgements (described below) that have both political and social implications. Armed police, outside the purview of civilian scrutiny, can and does affect sensitive political issues like elections, communal problems, and public dissent. The central government has powers to deploy armed police units in any 'disturbed' part of the country, overriding the objections of the state governments. This provision has further concentrated powers in the hands of central government. Moreover, the objectives that the police must safeguard in an independent India are based on democratic ideals and freedom. Armed police do not subscribe to these ideals and are not meant to do so either.

Tradition of Dual Control

The second problem is the system of dual control over the police institution. Section 4 of the Police Act states that at the district level the police and SP will 'function under the general control and direction' of the DM. The office of the collector cum district magistrate belonging to the famed Indian Civil Service (ICS and now the IAS) is an older institution than the police system and for more than 100 years the DMs were the main regional representatives of the East India Company. The DMs not only collected revenue on behalf of the Company but also executed its administrative-judicial policies. Indeed, at the district level, the DM was the chief representative of British rule in India. Accordingly, the Police Act sought to maintain the hegemony of this office. But this has made the SP subordinate to the DM for law and order functions and also to the DGP for internal management of the district police. The DMs have been given powers to initiate the confidential reports of the SP, inspect police stations, approve postings of the subordinate officers made by the SP, and have the control over sanction of prosecution.

Furthermore, the DGP is under the suzerainty of the Home Ministry whose secretary is also from the IAS. Thus, the police, and the IPS cadre are controlled by the IAS officers whose pay, perks, and powers have been considerably enhanced to reflect their superiority. Considering that these officers are selected from the same examination system administered by the Union Public Service Commission, and difference of few marks determine allotment to these two services, the rivalry between the two is bitter and of long standing. The SP is a 'colleague' and not a 'subordinate', but the DM gets to determine this relationship. The DGP is the seniormost police officer and second only in importance to the chief secretary. Yet, the home secretary (with considerably less years of service), can thwart the policies and recommendations of the police chief. The IAS inherited the mantle of 'steel frame of India' and has become the most powerful 'union' in the country. Accordingly, proposals and attempts to remove this dual control have been strongly opposed by the IAS fraternity. Indeed, it has been suggested that a reason for non-acceptance of the NPC's reports was the recommendation to abolish the control by the civilian bureaucrats and replace it with an independent security commission (Verma 1998). Tensions between the two services go back to the British period when Woodruff (1954: 53) suggested the SP to be 'something of a diplomat to live beside the District Magistrate'. Altogether, 'it is an arrangement peculiarly English that has continued with pettiness and spite on one side and occasional generosity on the other' (Bayley 1969: 360). The bitter rivalry has prevented institutional reforms for any proposals are evaluated in terms of loss and gain for the two services.

Colonial Cultural Traditions

The third design feature is the colonial organizational culture and norms that have encouraged and sustained venal practices in the police system. The antecedents of these cultural practices lie in the attempts to build glory and unquestioned authority of British rule. The Raj created a life style for the rulers in which 'the "sahibs" and "memsahibs" lived in sprawling "bungalows" and had a retinue of servants for every need' (Verma 2000a). There were *khansama*s (chefs) to cook their meals and *aayah*s (maids) to look after their children (Woodruff 1954). Summers were spent at the hill stations to escape the heat and dust of their burden while the winters were meant for tiger hunts, cricket, and entertainment by the exotic Maharajahs. The British built few hospitals and schools but the police stations and buildings were imposing structures in Victorian architecture (Metcalf 1994). 'Most police stations also had a large compound with curving path to the gate manned by an armed sentry, a structure to keep the people in awe and at a distance' (Verma 2000a). Ostentatious pageantry and grandeur of the senior officers was an obvious, visible form of authority. The morning parade and salute to the commanding officer, the armed sentry at the superintendent's gate, and armed escort on their tours were symbols that placed the officers on a high pedestal. A deliberate paternalistic style of governance was created in which a few selected officers took all the decisions for the people (Griffiths 1971). Woodruff (1954) indeed has called them the 'guardians'. This style of governance created a cultural setting in which the administrators were way above those being ruled and this distance was deliberately maintained. There was no way in which any citizen could dare to approach the senior officer thereby leaving no avenue of complaint against the brutalization and corruption of the institution. This organizational ethos, the indifferent styles of administration, and its deliberate alienation from the citizens all contributed greatly towards corrupt practices within the police.

The tiger hunts and lavish entertainment were adjunct to this myth, one that further institutionalized corruption within the ranks. These entertainments were made part of the organizational practices in which the officers on tours would combine business with sports and pleasure. It was usual for the British officers to combine inspection of the police station with a tiger hunt and the subordinate officers not only had to get the records updated for inspection but also arrange food and shelter for the large number of members of the hunting party (Rao 1996). In present day India, tiger hunts have naturally been banned but the Raj lives on. The organizational culture and practices remain the same. The same traditions of grandeur and lavish living style of the senior officers are still quite visible. 'Instead of tiger hunts there are New Year parties, picnics and official "get together" with family and friends, at "Dak Bungalows" (government rest houses). The entertainment of senior officers by the subordinate staff is even now an established practice in the police departments and beyond a token payment all other expenses are passed down to the subordinate officers' (Verma 1999).

The British made traditions continue and the practice of glorifying senior officers still survives. In many provinces like Uttar Pradesh and Bihar, senior police officers are still addressed as 'Huzur Bahadur', the brave gentleman, or 'Kaptan Sahib', the lordly captain, titles used during the British period. Personal drivers, bodyguards, even armed guards for the residence and families are common appendage for senior police officers. Independent India's police (and civil bureaucrats) display with pride their association and continuance of the British legacy. Most police offices maintain a 'succession list' (names and tenure of officers from the past) coming down from the British to the present period.

The police stations and other offices still function from the same bungalow type buildings while the palatial mansions built for British officers now house the present senior officers. Implications of these continuing cultural traits are clear: the police of independent India are no different from the old police system and the IPS is the inheritor of the baton passed down by its British predecessors. The wide gulf between the 'rulers' and the ruled continues and the class hierarchy even within the force is strictly maintained. Constables and even middle level officers do not sit down in front of the SP. IPS officers still use police constables as personal orderlies who serve as their domestic servants. It is not uncommon for police station personnel to take care of the comforts of the senior officers. Thus, official vehicles, telephones, and staff are used for personal purposes, subordinate officers escort the children to school or the spouse for shopping and making social visits. It is a common sight in India to find a police officer's family being accompanied by police personnel or even armed guards and this hardly raises any questions. In several places it is not uncommon to find a large number of police personnel engaged at the farms and personal establishments of the senior officers.

India is unashamedly an elitist society (Sen 1986) but elitism within the superior bureaucratic services is scandalous. Such blatant misuse of official resources and other corrupt practices, in the name of cultural traditions are rarely commented adversely or even considered deviant since these have been going on for a very long time. The final outcome of these practices is a quiet acceptance of corruption and undesirable practices within the institution. Clearly, an instrument designed for colonial rule can hardly give desirable performance in an independent, democratic society.

IMPACT OF SOCIAL AND POLITICAL CHANGES ON THE POLICE

After Independence the functions of the government have increased manifold. Whereas the British rulers were largely concerned with the collection of revenue, maintenance of order, and administration of law, the present day governmental responsibilities include providing food and shelter, education, health and welfare, gainful employment, community development, improving agriculture, developing cooperatives, banking, marketing, communications and public sector undertakings. Almost every aspect of internal social, economic, and political development is the concern of elected governments. Consequently, public dissatisfaction with the quality of life issues whether directed at the failure to provide food at reasonable prices, affordable education, health, infrastructure, or even subsidies to stabilize the market are now directed at the government. Police as the strong arm of the law have to bear the brunt of these expressions that spill out into the streets as demonstrations and agitation against government policies.

Social and Political Conflicts

Akbar (1985) suggests that India is besieged by social strife. The communal division between Hindus and Muslims has continued despite division of the country. The caste conflicts especially in Bihar have led to horrible mass killings since the sixties (Sinha 1991). There have been ethnic and regional conflicts in virtually every part of the country. The nascent democracy has also been rocked by serious political conflicts. Agitations against government policies continue to cause widespread disruptions and violent clashes. Industrial strikes, student problems, and job reservation issues have also created severe law and order problems. India is an open society with a democratic polity where freedom of expression is guaranteed by the Constitution. Agitations to prevent governments from functioning or to demonstrate public support for a cause are common political activities (Verma 2000b). Many of these political actions turn violent and cause destruction of property and loss of life. While manifestly an essential feature of the democratic means of protest, most of these forms in their articulation very often involve a degree of violence, either on the side of protesters or by the police trying to prevent the conflict (Verma 1997). These social and political conflicts are so serious that for Indian police maintenance of order is of paramount importance.

In a democracy, free and fair elections are necessary for the legitimacy of the government. However, the electoral process is increasingly being marred by violence. Booth capturing (forcible casting of vote in favour of a particular candidate) and deliberate prevention of genuine voters from exercising their franchise has become a serious problem in many parts of India (Jha 1997). There are many groups too who oppose elections on ideological grounds and attempt to prevent them from taking place. Even elections to village councils, municipalities, unions, and other smaller public bodies are affected by violence. In the national elections of 1999 an estimated 130 people had been killed in electoral violence (Election Commission of India 1999).

Unstable social, economic, ethnic, religious, and political conditions have forced modern India to lay more stress on order maintenance than due process of law. This is reinforcing the perception that the rule of law is possible only in an orderly state and thus the ideal of a civilian police force has not materialized in practice. Furthermore, even if the existing police institution is not entirely malignant it generally serves the interests of the propertied and ruling class. This blocks the cooperation of the people, which is so essential for democratic policing. The outcome of sociopolitical changes after Independence has been to considerably politicize the police institution.

Politicization of the Police

There is growing politicization of the public institutions in the country. Potter (1986: 198) states that 'political 'pressure' or 'interference' [is] a central preoccupation amongst the administrators. By several accounts (Das 1998; GOI 1979) police leaders enjoyed considerable operational freedom till the mid-sixties. The situation deteriorated rapidly after the elections of 1967 when Congress lost power in many states and coalition governments arrived on the Indian political scene. The political struggle to hold on to power or gain power now overshadows everything else and this has affected the public institutions directly (Mitra 1998). The political interests in the police departments have virtually destroyed the autonomy of the police leadership in administering the department. The NPC commented harshly on this interference in police work and cited several instances of unwarranted and blatant political misuse of the police organization (GOI 1979). At present, when Indian politics itself is functioning with no holds barred, this interference in police functions has of course increased substantially. In an era of ideologically different political parties forming a government, direct diktats to the officers have naturally increased since every small time politician has become important in the coalition.

The day-to-day political interference in the work of police officers is now a regular media story (Aggarwal 2000; *Indian Express* 1998; *Times of India* 1999). A public impression clearly exists that police are unable to discharge their duties properly because politicians do not let them function fairly, impartially, and in the best interests of the people. The courts have passed several adverse comments on the attempts to throttle police investigations into several scandals (Mahalingam and Swami 1998). The large scale transfers and postings of all ranks of officers on grounds that smack of political considerations (*Times of India* 1999), the helplessness of police chiefs as displayed by their frequent humiliations by the chief minister's office (GOI 1981; *India Today* 1979a), and the inability of the police leadership to discipline officers who are politically connected (Raj Kumar 2000), all present evidence of a police department that is ruled by political expediency rather than any established procedures and norms.

Furthermore, police functioning is dictated more by politics than by law or administrative guidelines (*India Today* 1979b). Whether it is taking action against the politicians involved in criminal acts, or making arrests of anti-social elements or controlling order maintenance problems, the supervisory officers have to tread very carefully. Their judgements are contested by politicians who attempt to make political capital out of every incident. For instance, even making an arrest on a warrant issued by the court, precaution has to be observed. An arrest of a backward caste offender by a forward caste officer is potentially explosive and frequently introduces factors unrelated to the criminal behaviour for which the arrest was being made. Similarly, in preventing a demonstration from turning riotous, the lathi charge or other use of force invite criticisms that are dictated more by politics than by legal issues (Verma 1997). All these situations have created an atmosphere where political interference is not only present on a large scale but is also apprehended affecting the normal functioning of the police officers.

The appointment and continuation of the police chief is dependent upon his usefulness to the chief minister (Stracey 1981) and even the posting of the lowest ranking constable is done at the behest of the politicians. These political appointments have aligned personnel with one or other set of politicians. Officers openly declare their loyalty and take pride in this association (GOI 1981; Singh 1996). With every change in the fortunes of the politicians, the rise and fall of 'their' police officers also follow a similar path. Those officers who refuse to tow the line immediately feel the pinch. They are summarily transferred to innocuous posts, shuffled around from one distant corner to another, and overlooked for prestigious jobs, foreign jaunts and from key decision making posts (*Times of India* 1999). Their 'plight' is enough to make most of the others fall in line quickly. The police departments have become totally subservient to the political manipulations of the ruling parties and powerful politicians. Kohli (1990: 217) suggests that such politicization is 'having unanticipated and unfortunate consequences: when leaders (politicians) now need to call on the police arm of the state, that arm is relatively limp.'

THE 'AGENCY' PROBLEM

The Indian police also suffer from numerous 'agency' problems that hamper the proper functioning of the institution. The police are a state subject and are organized provincially. This has created mammoth size departments where internal management is becoming extremely difficult. For instance, the following Table 6.1 illustrates the size of the police departments in some selected provinces and cities of the country:

It is becoming difficult to administer such large departments. Manual record keeping systems, antiquated administrative rules and norms are making the management extremely demanding. Lack of proper procedures and actions taken for political appeasements further open avenues for grievances. It is becoming increasingly common to challenge government decisions for these are not fair or well considered. Personnel management in police (and other

TABLE 6.1
Size of police departments

States	Total strength	% Armed (1997)
Andhra Pradesh	66,650	17.4
Bihar	63,933	30.6
Gujarat	51,807	23.9
Karnataka	51,881	18.3
Madhya Pradesh	64,858	45.1
Maharashtra	128,191	11.7
Rajasthan	58,004	19.6
Tamil Nadu	74,655	15.3
Uttar Pradesh	136,595	25.8
West Bengal	61,814	37.7
Metropolitan cities		
Bangalore	7666	49.9
Bombay	30,482	26.0
Calcutta	16,078	48.7
Delhi	42,251	25.2
Hyderabad	9009	26.3
Madras	8672	42.4
Total (All-India)	1,058,283	29.4

Source: National Crime Records Bureau—*Crime In India* 1998.

departments) is mired in thousands of court cases challenging transfers, postings, appointments, pay scales, and promotion decisions.

Centralization of Powers

Another problem is the concentration of decision-making that is affecting the performance. Although transfer and posting of subordinate officers within the district is done by the SP or the DIG, posting of officers to the district is done from the police headquarters. Funds, resources like vehicles, and communication equipment are also provided from a central pool. Moreover, important investigations, vigilance, intelligence collection, armed battalions, railway police, and even supply of stationery and clothing are centrally controlled. Thus, institutional power is concentrated in the hands of few officers sitting in the headquarters while the field officers are denied funding and independence of action.

There are many ways in which this centralized command structure works against the local or special interests of the districts and sub-divisions. This is seen in the policy of transfer and posting of subordinates that are framed at the headquarters. For instance, after training at the academy, sub-inspectors are posted to a particular district for a period of 6–8 years. Due to an old rule this posting cannot be done at the officer's home-district where it is feared he may be influenced by family association. This rule is relaxed for large cities and metropolitan areas and officers with 'connections' manage to get themselves posted to these and other 'lucrative' areas. Furthermore, regions that require dedicated and good officers, like the tribal districts, generally suffer since nobody wants to go there and if posted find godfathers to get them out quickly. Over a period of time, the situation becomes very aggravated since many districts have excess officers who refuse to move out and many have a shortage. The districts of Palamau, Gopalgunj, and Saharsa in Bihar are examples where only the 'discarded' officers get posted or those who are unable to exert any external influence. It is not surprising that these districts have now been seriously affected by Left-wing extremism with years of neglect and indifference. It is also not surprising that training has been adversely affected since officers are not willing to be posted to police academies.

As described above, a culture of distrust of the subordinate officers has continued from the British period. Accordingly, elaborate rules were made to ensure closer supervision over their actions. Numerous reporting systems have been developed to account for every activity of the investigating officer of the police station. This record keeping system has become so complex that few officers can neither maintain its integrity nor keep it up-to-date. Considering that most of the police records are still being kept manually the result has been a system that does not provide any useful information but has become simply a tool for the senior officers to threaten the subordinates.

At present, in the state of Bihar there are over 250 different documents that have to be maintained at the police station. Each officer is required to maintain a personal diary to record each and every action on a continuing basis. The record system is so designed that every document is inter-connected and has overlapping columns. This is seen as a way to ensure that all transactions are faithfully recorded since inter-connectivity ensures several documents to be tempered simultaneously. Nevertheless, precisely this is happening. Officers become adept in making false or late entries and yet maintaining the inter-connectivity of all the records (Verma 2000). The criminal record system of Indian police is not only an outdated system but also one that serves only the departmental and political objectives and is otherwise worthless.

Official statistics are convenient data sets to project any kind of desired situation. As any police manager knows, the data can be easily used to imply either of the cases: these can be used to suggest that crime has been rising (as done when the need is to demand more funds) and these can also simultaneously be used to say that the crime has been 'under control', when the media and politicians take notice of some sensational cases (Verma 2000).

Class Distinctions Within the Organization

Another agency problem is a three-tier organizational structure that has developed distinct class divisions. There is a wide gulf between the IPS, the middle tier investigating ranks of sub-inspectors and inspectors, and the lowest ranks of constabulary. Constables comprise 80 per cent of the force while the middle ranks constitute around 19 per cent of the personnel. Yet, all the power and privileges are concentrated in the hands of the IPS officers. The constabulary has not been entrusted with any status and responsibility in the organization. Their functions are largely to provide sentry duties, act as guards, provide visible presence of police through patrolling, and do odd jobs for the department. They have a low status, not much of education, and are paid poorly even by Indian standards. The NPC in its Report I described the poor working conditions of the constabulary and pleaded for their amelioration (GOI 1979).

The subordinate officers are more educated; enjoy some power and benefits of office. They undertake all the work related to investigation, inquiry, and collection of intelligence. Despite the fact that the bulk of policing is done by this cadre, their say in the organization is severely restricted. Even in investigations the final decision remains that of the SP who is an IPS officer. The investigating officers have few promotional avenues and negligent financial or administrative powers. Since they are at the cutting edge of policing the majority of complaints and pressures fall upon them. The poor working conditions in the police stations where they operate, the continuous demands of their job, and constant admonitions from their superiors makes their tasks perhaps the most stressful in the organization.

As expected in such a system, the class divisions between the three tiers are unscalable. A constable can rarely hope to reach the middle rank of an investigator while the sub-inspector can at best hope to retire as a DySP. The office of SP or entry into the IPS is impossible to reach for the two lower tiers. Consequently, the status of the IPS is so elevated that a police constable or even a sub-inspector cannot even sit at the same table with them. The military type hierarchical system is as powerful in the police as in the army. The direct consequence of this division is a complete lack of communication between the three tiers. A SP has to develop alternative sources of intelligence since information from below is suspect and many times even tainted. Every case has to be supervised personally before evidence collected by the investigators is accepted. This not only introduces considerable delay in processing of the cases but also forces the investigators to produce evidence 'desirable' and 'acceptable' to their superiors. The investigation is thus dependent upon the whims and desires of the SP and senior officers rather than upon the work done by the field officers.

PERFORMANCE MEASURES

It is important to know about police performance to assess that public money is well spent and to 'hold police managers accountable for improving organizational performance' (Alpert and Moore 1993: 110). Brodeur (1998: ix) suggests that evaluation is also a 'powerful instrument for revealing the assumptions underlying policing programs'. Performance measures further help to verify claims that new initiatives have given results and assess where improvements need to be made. Yet, there are no easy methods to assess police performance. The ways of measuring police accomplishments are hotly debated and there is no consensus amongst the researchers and practitioners.

There are three types of programme evaluation methods prevalent within the police institution. First, day-to-day monitoring by police supervisors is an internal evaluation mechanism and part of routine police work. However, it varies from one department to another and there is no uniform standard across the country. The second is a research evaluation, an external mechanism that may be carried out for specific purposes. Sadly, such a process has not found much support within the police establishment. The Bureau of Police Research and Development (BPRD), a government run organization is meant for such research initiatives but it has not undertaken any major evaluation in the last fifty years. Finally, there is also the mechanism of using market-based forces for evaluation just as done in the private sector. Comparing the police services with that of the private security agencies in the country, or determining the satisfaction of citizens through specially designed surveys are some techniques, which again have not been used in the country.

Process and Impact

However, before evaluating the performance of the Indian police there is a need to understand the distinction between a process and its impact. There are a large number of functions that are carried out by police officers on a routine basis: patrolling, surveillance, investigation, dispute resolution, guard and escort duties, and enforcement of laws and maintenance of order. Rather than assess these in terms of their outcome, such as, if an offender has been apprehended, a criminal incident results in conviction or a dispute settled amicably or even a disorderly situation brought under control, the *manner* of implementation also needs to be considered. Implementation is assessed with the view to see if the design was properly conceived; did police maintain order in accordance with the legal procedures and without laying the seeds of future conflict or simply used excess force to disperse the crowd. This necessarily calls for an examination of the best method to deal with a situation that really cannot be judged after the events. It is difficult to lay down procedures that can deal with any emerging problem. Every situation is unique in itself and needs continuing assessment to determine the best strategy to deal with the problem.

Moreover, in the case of policing the attention is always focused upon the failures and not on the hundreds of incidents that are settled routinely by the police every day. Thus, the attention is always upon the outcome, what is the end result rather than the process and form of implementation used by the police to control the problem. For instance, the impact is measured through aggregated figures—did annual crime go up or down? Nevertheless, focusing only upon the impact diverts attention from many other equally significant issues. The COMSTAT programme launched by the New York police lowered the crime figures but alienated youth and minorities since the focus was upon quickly apprehending the suspects in criminal cases (Brodeur 1998; Pepinsky 2000). In particular, there are four standard evaluation measures commonly used to assess the performance of the police. These are the reported crime rates, the overall arrests figures, the so-called clearance rates (based on cases reported and ending in prosecution), and finally the time taken to respond to a situation. These measures are generally outmoded and unsuitable for measuring police functions. There is now a considerable literature to suggest that these measures reflect a reactionary model of policing and fail to capture some of the significant contributions and failures of police officers (Brodeur 1998; Whitaker 1984). Furthermore, these measures divert attention from the problems of assessing individual performance. These do not help in answering what is good police work and how to recognize it. These also focus on police malpractices—negative performance in terms of complaints and failures rather than the success of dealing with citizen problems in an unobtrusive way. Furthermore, most police work is dispersed and is of low visibility. It creates large areas of discretion about which there is no information except when the discretion turns sour and draws attention in the form of a complaint or failure. Accordingly, these four standard performance measures are inappropriate to determine what was really done by officers responding to the incidents. However, the process of policing is difficult to assess in India since there are no ethnographic observational studies of police in action. The manner in which officers handle crowds, political agitations, citizen complaints, etc., are unknown except when these are mishandled and media highlights the failures.

Performance based on Official Statistics

The statistics compiled from the police sources are not without their limitations. Crime statistics are not a valid measure of police performance. Criminologists have frequently and bitterly debated whether crime figures are valid or reliable measures of the actual amount of crime in the society (Wolfgang 1963; Biderman and

Reiss 1967; Wheeler 1967; Black 1980; Hindelang, Hirschi and Weiss 1979; Bottomley and Pease 1986; Coleman and Moynihan 1996). Citizens fail to report crimes thinking it is too trivial in nature, or that police can do very little about it. Particularly, in India image of the police as being corrupt, incompetent, disinterested precludes many citizens from going to the police station to register a criminal offence. The police themselves discriminate in recording complaints and minimize offences to present a favourable image of controlling crime (Verma 1993). Strict supervisions and strong leadership advocating true registration have invariably shown higher number of crimes in a given period (Saxena 1987). In 1971–3, the police chief of Uttar Pradesh made a determined effort to record public complaints and this saw crime figures shooting up.

There are many problems of internal validity also associated with police statistics (Wolfgang 1963). Their classification system is inherently defective as in designating an act as a serious offence. Typically, physical harm is deemed grievous or non-grievous in police reports strictly in accordance with their legal definitions. Only the former is considered serious even though the latter type of case may be more harmful to the victim due to their psychological effects. Similarly, in considering the seriousness of property stolen, embezzlement has been omitted but pick pocketing is included in the count. Auto thefts are still not separated from the general theft of property, and no distinction is made between different types of properties, for example between cars and two wheelers, which are different on the basis of modus operandi of the act. There is no system of attaching *weights* to the offences and each is counted as a single unit even if one is a theft of Rs 50 and the other a homicide. Due to this practice, property offences are given overwhelming prominence in the total count and an increase or decrease in this type of crime alone, affects the overall trend of criminal statistics.

Perhaps, the most severe problem is one of 'multiple offences' where only the serious violation is counted. Thus, in a robbery case, the damage to property, physical injury, trespassing and other such crimes are not counted as separate crimes. Similarly, an offence involving several victims is also condensed into a single offence. This may explain why Kashmir, where terrorists have frequently killed several people in a single attack still reported lower number of murders (753) than UP (7756), MP (3463), and Bihar (5354) in 1997 (NCRB 1998). The calculation of the *rate* of crime is also approximate since population census counts are done once every ten years and for other years, estimation is made on the basis of population growth rates. Invariably, crime rates in India show a decline for the eleventh years, 1951, 1961, 1971, 1981 and 1991 since the actual, and therefore greater count of population is done at the end of the decades of 1950, 1960, 1970, 1980, and 1990!

This rate represents the risk ratio for a person in the population, but as is well known, a large section of the population has little connection to criminal activities. Small children and old people for example, make no contribution to criminal behaviours and in India, even females should not be counted since their percentage contribution to criminality, despite growth remains about 5.1 per cent (NCRB 1998). Finally, there is no procedure for taking into account the standard errors involved in these statistics. The differences in procedures over large geographical regions and styles of functioning inherent between organizations create widely different variances due to which these numbers are not at all comparable (Wolfgang 1963). Furthermore, NCRB also classifies offences under the Indian Penal Code (IPC) or the Local & Special Laws (L&SL) that leaves an abnormally high percentage under the head 'Others'. The percentage of crimes in this category is 42.2 for IPC cases and astonishingly high, 78.6 for L&SL cases for 1997. Naturally, these large numbers are thus lost for analysis for what can one make out of behaviours described as others!

The analysis of bare statistics, though promising, ultimately has limited utility for evolving policies to control criminal behaviours. The investigators require information about the *characteristics* of the offenders and the *circumstances* of the perpetuation of the act itself. For only this type of data can help in designing strategies to combat crime incidences. The knowledge about the persons arrested for criminal behaviour like their ethnicity, social status, caste, and family background and their treatment in the court of law are crucial for policy planning perspectives. It is necessary for any evaluation and subsequent change in the functioning of the Criminal Justice System in the country. Police effectiveness cannot be diagnosed without taking into consideration, the trial of criminal cases in the courts of law. Also, police preventive measures cannot be formulated without a knowledge of the operation of bail provisions, the incarceration periods, and nature of punishment meted out by the courts. All these and many other types of information are required for the proper evaluation of performance but are simply not available. Police agencies do not maintain records of offenders after their arrest and statistics from the prisons and courts are not published by the government. Victim Surveys and Self-Report data sources are an alternative and perhaps better ways of measuring crime but no large-scale effort has ever been made to obtain figures separately from the police department. For all these reasons official crime figures are inappropriate to measure police performance in terms of criminal incidents.

Crime in India

Nevertheless, how does the Indian police fare in terms of its own data? Unfortunately, in these measures too the Indian police output is extremely poor and even alarming. The following evaluation is based upon the data prepared by the National Crime Records Bureau (NCRB 1998), a government organization that collects figures from each of the states and compiles them into an annual report, called *Crime in India*. According to the report for the year 1997, crime trends in the country are as follows:

The total criminal incidents in the country are increasing steadily. As many as 64,11,259 incidents were reported in 1997 that marks an increase of 28.3 per cent over 1987. The rate of these crimes, taking population as the denominator suggests an increase of 5 per cent over 1987 that is more than the rate of population growth over this period. However, as Table 6.2 informs, the incidents recorded under the IPC have increased by only 22.2 per cent as compared to 30 per cent increase in the incidents recorded under L&SL. Indeed the rate of IPC crimes has come down to the level of 1987. IPC crime heads are heavily influenced by property crimes like burglary and theft and these incidents have been showing a declining trend over the past four decades. From a two-third share of 67.1 per cent in 1953 the proportion of these crimes has come down to 22.7 per cent. There is no explanation for this decline except that it reflects police practices.

This becomes obvious when we learn that violent crimes like murder, rape, kidnapping, and injury, especially against women are all increasing over the years. In 1997, 249,200 violent incidents were recorded. There were 37,543 murders recorded by the police in 1997, which is an increase of 31.7 per cent over the 1987 figures.

TABLE 6.2
Crime rates recorded under IPC and L&SL

Year	Estimated mid-year population* (in lakhs)**	Incidence			Rate			Percentage of IPC crimes to total cognizable crimes
		IPC	L&SL	Total	IPC	L&SL	Total	
1987	7814	1,406,992	3,589,326	4,996,318	180.1	459.3	639.4	28.2
1988	7966	1,440,356	3,765,669	5,206,025	180.8	472.7	653.5	27.7
1989	8118	1,529,844	3,847,665	5,377,509	188.5	474.0	662.4	28.4
1990	8270	1,604,449	3,293,563	4,898,012	194.0	398.3	592.3	32.8
1991	8496	1,678,375	3,370,971	5,049,346	197.5	396.8	594.3	33.2
1992	8677	1,689,341	3,558,448	5,247,789	194.7	410.1	604.8	32.2
1993	8838	1,629,936	3,803,638	5,433,574	184.4	430.4	614.8	30.0
1994	9000	1,635,251	3,876,994	5,512,245	181.7	430.8	612.5	29.7
1995	9160	1,695,696	4,297,476	5,993,172	185.1	469.2	654.3	28.3
1996	9319	1,709,576	4,586,986	6,296,562	183.4	492.2	675.6	27.2
1997	9552	1,719,820	4,691,439	6,411,259	180.0	491.1	671.2	26.8
Percentage change in 1997 over 1987	22.2	22.2	30.7	28.3	0.0	6.9	5.0	-5.0
Compound growth rate per annum	2.0	1.8	2.7	2.4	-0.2	0.6	0.4	-0.6

Source: National Crime Records Bureau—Crime in India 1998.

Uttar Pradesh (7756) and Bihar (5354) reported the two highest proportions in the country. Property disputes, class conflict, and caste conflict were some of the main reasons for murders in Bihar while UP was high for the category of personal vendetta or enmity. The number of cases of rapes have also increased by 79.1 per cent during the decade 1987–97 with Bihar, UP, and MP being the main contributors. Similar is the case of kidnapping where the increase is 43.6 per cent over 1987. Since violent crimes cannot be ignored the officers tend to neglect smaller incidents of theft and burglary. This has the effect of reducing overall crime rates and helps show police in control of the situation.

The inability of the police to control deviant acts may be seen by the increasing trends in crimes against women and children. Even NCRB acknowledges that crimes against women are increasing and adds, 'sizable number of crimes against women go unreported due to the social stigma attached to them' (NCRB 1998: 14). It is educative to learn that police investigations were incomplete in 74.6 per cent of offences registered under Dowry Prohibition Act. Out of four cases for trial under the Sati Prevention Act during 1997, three were compounded and one remained pending. Thus, even when crimes against women were being registered their outcome was not satisfactory. It is also alarming to note that 28.8 per cent of rape victims were children.

Police performance in investigating crimes has been poor by its own records. Over the decade around 20 per cent of the reported cases remain pending for police action. The figure has gone up from 15.8 per cent in 1961 to 23.8 per cent in 1997. Bihar and Maharastra show the largest pendency while Terrorist and Disruptive Activities Act (TADA) cases (where presumably nation's security is involved) continue to show the highest pendency of 70.9 per cent of all the crimes. NCRB reports that almost 93 per cent of the investigated cases result in submission of chargesheet against the accused. It is significant that for the same period almost 80.5 per cent of the cases remained pending for completion of trial in the court. It is also significant to note that the ratio of conviction to total cases tried in the courts in 1997 was 38.2 per cent. This suggests that the courts are not upholding police findings and perhaps most of the chargesheets are either being submitted in haste or with little evidence. Since filing of the chargesheet is the decision by the SP it is clear that this is being done to improve police statistics.

Recovery of stolen property is another way to assess police performance. In 1997, property worth 33,514 lakh was recovered against stolen property of 131,216 lakhs, a proportion of 25 per cent. Interestingly, the highest percentage of recovery was for 'cycles' (52.5 per cent) and low for motorcycles and scooters (34.2 per cent). Since the latter are insured their loss is invariably reported and thus form a more valid measure of police achievement. For Indian police this figure is low. Police statistics begin to crumble when we examine the data for juvenile delinquents. Table 6.3 gives the figures for the states of the country.

It is interesting to note that the largest populated state of UP, which records high figures for violent and property crimes, has

TABLE 6.3
Juvenile delinquency cases

States	No. of cases (1997)
Andhra Pradesh	696
Arunachal Pradesh	24
Assam	172
Bihar	563
Goa	23
Gujarat	278
Haryana	489
Himachal Pradesh	57
Jammu & Kashmir	0
Karnataka	479
Kerala	56
Madhya Pradesh	2572
Maharashtra	2374
Manipur	0
Meghalaya	38
Mizoram	45
Nagaland	5
Orissa	108
Punjab	10
Rajasthan	711
Sikkim	4
Tamil Nadu	3020
Tripura	5
Uttar Pradesh	43
West Bengal	4

Source: National Crime Records Bureau—*Crime in India* 1998.

only 43 cases of juvenile delinquency. Bengal has just four cases, which is less than the numbers for Goa, and sparsely populated Arunanchal Pradesh. Either there are little saints in these two states or else the police figures are totally incorrect. When small cities like Vadodara (99), Pune (104), Jaipur (87) record more juvenile cases than the large metropolis of Calcutta (only two cases) the figures seem grossly incorrect. We begin to understand police practices when we learn that 9,89,292 people were arrested for 'other crimes' under IPC, that highest arrests were for riots followed by injury where police discretion plays an important role. Similarly, 'other' category in L&SL cases account for 75 per cent of the arrests.

Some information about police misbehaviour is also available. There were six cases of rape under police custody in 1997. It is disturbing to note that of the 12 cases pending trial for custodial rape, only one case was heard and it ended in acquittal. In 1997, police resorted to firing on 790 occasions in which 467 civilians were killed. Amongst these were 200 incidents of 'riotous mobs' and 169 were classified under the category 'other' for which no further information is available. Significantly, police firing incidents have increased by 3.3 per cent over the previous year. During 1997 there were also 123,523 citizen complaints filed against police officers in which 35,071 were declared unsubstantiated and 1501 cases were sent up for trial after the inquiry which amounts to 1.21 per cent of the total complaints. This data suggests citizen complaints are not being inquired seriously. Again, no serious attempt appears to be made to deal with delinquent officers.

Despite increase in crimes, police strength has remained constant resulting in increasing workload for the officers. The number of police personnel per unit population of 1000 was 1.3 that has remained static from 1987. During this period crime rate has gone up from 639.4 to 671.2 resulting in higher workloads. The national average workload for an investigator is around 60.7 cases a year. The average expenditure per policeman was Rs 77,401 per year for all category of personnel. Clearly, Indian police officers are over-worked and lowly paid.

RULES VERSUS DISCRETION

Police work involves considerable discretion. The exercise of police discretion has been a subject matter of close scrutiny amongst criminal justice scholars in the US (Bottomley 1973; Davis 1969; Reiss, 1974; Skolnick 1994). Discretion is said to be influenced by policing style (Wilson 1968), the operational environment (Skolnick and Bayley 1986; Mastrofski, Ritti, and Hoffmaster 1987), and is related to a variety of community factors including the political culture (Pepinsky 1984). The nature of criminal law, work environment, police culture, and lack of specific guidelines form some of the underlying sources of discretionary powers of the police officers (Davis 1975; Lipsky 1968). Further, challenge to officer's authority, seriousness of crime, circumstances of the case, the demeanour and personality of the complainant, relationship with the offender and even the race of the suspect influence police discretion (Black 1980; Powell, 1981; Uviller, 1984; Smith, Visher, and Davidson 1984; Bayley, and Garofalo 1989; Kappeler, Sluder, and Alpert 1994; Klinger 1994). These discretionary judgements determine the nature of the complaint, settlement of dispute, when, where and who to arrest and even which laws to enforce. Such decisions effectively make police into policy makers and 'street corner politicians' (Davis 1975) who act as 'gatekeepers' of the criminal justice system (Alpert and Dunham 1992).

Unfortunately, there is not a single study that has examined the nature and exercise of discretion by the Indian police in citizen encounters. An overwhelming number of police actions are directed against the lower classes, the police focus remains on property crimes, and there is widespread use of force against citizens. All these characteristics suggest that US research findings bear similarity to the Indian situation. Apart from the general discretion in law enforcement and criminal investigations, the Indian police also exert considerable 'situational' discretion in handling law and order responsibilities. Use of discretion in controlling an unruly crowd, for example, is guided by variables, 'such as the physical setting, relationship between the police and people, objectives of those leading the crowd, number of participants and media attention to the situation' (Verma 1997: 66).

Discretion in Law

Since 'all legislation leaves room for interpretation' (Bottomley 1973: 38) Indian laws too provide considerable discretionary judgements to the police officers. The Criminal Procedure Code (CrPC) exemplifies such varying interpretations. The CrPC has delegated considerable scope for discretion to the police in matters of arrest, search, seizure, and other functions. Sections 41 to 56 of this code describe the general powers of arrest without seeking warrant from the magistrate (Mitra 1960). Thus, Section 54 CrPC states '...any police officer may arrest... without a warrant... such person who has been concerned in any cognizable (indictable) offence or... against whom... reasonable suspicion exists of his being so concerned... (fourthly)... in whose possession anything is found which may reasonably be suspected to be stolen property.' This affords considerable discretion for what constitutes *reasonable suspicion*, even in subsequent clarifications has not been spelt out and are said '... to depend upon circumstances of the particular case' (AIR 1950 M.B. 83). Furthermore, clause four has extended this discretion and has stipulated that no formal (citizen) complaint is necessary for a police officer to arrest a person under this clause.

Moreover, police have been given authority to arrest even to *prevent* its occurrence. Thus, Section 151 CrPC states that, '...a police officer knowing of a design to commit any cognizable offence may arrest... the person so designing, if it appears to the police officer that the commissioning of the offence cannot be otherwise prevented...' Though, the courts have laid down that, '...where no emergency for arrest which this section contemplates is shown to have existed, the attempt to arrest on part of the police is not only 'not strictly justifiable by law' but is illegal' (*Gaman* v. *Emp.* 1930), police officers have wide optional powers under this section. In a subsequent ruling the judges too have acknowledged that '...It is not open to the Honorable Court exercising jurisdiction... to go into the question whether in fact the police officer was justified in concluding that the necessity contemplated by this section really existed. The discretion is vested solely in the police officer and that discretion cannot be questioned' (Om Prakash 51, CrLJ 143 Madras).

The provisions of search are even more discretionary in their nature. Section 165 CrPC states: '...whenever an investigating officer has *reasonable* grounds for believing that anything... may be found at any place... and that such thing cannot in his *opinion* [both italics added] be obtained without undue delay, ...he may after recording the reasons... cause search to be made... even by a subordinate officer, duly authorized by him'. Again, the Indian law merely uses the terms 'reasonable grounds', for providing authority to the police officer, who moreover, can conduct this search if in his *opinion* there is no time to seek a search warrant. Even in later clarification, the courts have held that once it is found that the evidence of the recovery of articles is reliable, '...the illegality of the search however does not make the evidence of seizure inadmissible...' (AIR 1965 Orissa 136–7). The fact that search was illegal would not vitiate trial and further more '...conviction on basis of discoveries made in such search can be made...' (AIR 1955 NUC M.B. 3862 DB). Thus, in sharp contrast to the American jurisprudence, the *Mapp* v. *Ohio* (1961) exclusionary rule, Indian law makers have permitted police to exercise considerable personal judgement in conducting searches in course of their investigations. In fact, Section 166 CrPC extends the power to have such searches carried outside the jurisdiction also, through another police officer of that area. Consequently, Indian police rarely attempt to obtain search warrants for they can always search a place under any *current* ongoing investigation of a case.

Discretion by Rank

The lowest ranks exercise the largest discretion (Davis 1969). In the Indian police, constables are at the bottom of the hierarchy and form almost 80 per cent of the total strength. They enjoy little legal powers and their role has also been limited to guard and escort duties, running errands, and walking the beat. The qualifications for becoming a constable have also been low, barely literate (grade 4 in Bihar) and their training does not go beyond drill and arms handling. Their working conditions have also been miserable as well as their status in the department and in general society. A police constable is paid the same amount as a fourth grade employee like a peon in a government office. The Indian police constables present a woeful lot: loosely dressed, overworked and uncouth and still able to exercise extraordinary powers.

Constables have considerable discretion since they are the first at the scene of incident and more in contact with the citizens. For instance, they are generally sent to deal with disputes, make local inquiries, and handle the disorder problems in the initial stage. Thus, they get to decide if an incident merits further action by an officer, make an assessment about the nature of the problem and involvement of individuals. In a survey of police personnel of Delhi, to the question 'If offence is not serious it is OK to let go of the offender', 45.9 per cent of the constables agreed whole-heartedly. Almost 71.8 per cent personnel supported the statement 'Dispute is best handled informally by warning.' The survey found that constables were exercising considerable discretionary powers, settling disputes and resolving social conflicts without any recog-nition nor departmental guidelines (Griffith, Murphy, and Verma 2000).

The recording of a crime incident is governed by Section 154 CrPC that authorizes a police officer to register a citizen complaint if it involves a criminal offence. This accords considerable discre-tionary powers to the subordinate officers who decide to register a case or settle the problem otherwise. Furthermore, few citizens understand legal definitions and again officers make the decision about determining the nature of the crime under a specific criminal statute. Thus, whether a case is registered as a theft, burglary, or simple assault depends upon the discretion of the officer. Once an FIR is recorded it can be changed only by a supervisory officer or during the trial stage. The consequence of all these factors is that registration of crimes is largely a function of discretionary judge-ments by the police officers. In view that their performance is evaluated in terms of the rise and fall of crime statistics, it is little wonder that few crimes are recorded and many are minimized in terms of the seriousness of the charge. Since FIRs determine all subsequent police action this discretion has substantial impact upon the police institution.

The situation in the higher echelons is no different. The post of SP has historically been one of the chief executive in the district and one who wields large power in the police organization. The discretionary powers of the SPs are considerable especially in matters of posting of subordinate officers, in distributing scant resources, and in controlling the final outcome of the cases. SPs also play an important role since their decisions affect political developments and increase or decrease law enforcement in an area. Hence the posting of the SP is a political decision generally taken by the chief minister of the state. This also enables the SP rank officers to build relationship with politicians that may cut across the powers of the DGP or any other superior officers. During the election periods it has become common across the nation to transfer and post SPs since they exercise large discretionary powers in the holding of the elections.

In view of the fact that most elections are hotly contested and are marred by violence, the police officers exercise considerable discretion in making security arrangements for the election booths. They determine the 'sensitivity' of the booths according to the likelihood of expected violence in its vicinity. This is calculated on the basis of past violence, current disputes, and also intelligence reports. Depending upon the scale, the SP decides the *nature* and *amount* of force to be deployed at these booths. That is, in what strength the units should be armed, unarmed, auxiliary, or simply 'symbolic' like the village watchman. In addition, patrolling parties and reserve backups are also maintained. In view of the scale of requirements many polling booths are still left unguarded. Since the presence of armed police provides greater security and its absence creates opportunities for booth capturing or preventing others from reaching and casting their votes, force deployment becomes a crucial decision. It determines the *location* and *amount* of violence that can take place considering that the likelihood of violence is practically everywhere. During the election period, police authorities also make large scale preventive arrests to control unruly elements from vitiating the election process. In India today, all the political parties have been criminalized and nominate those who can forcibly win the elections. This situation makes police actions very critical for these determine which party would 'lose' more men in comparison to other parties. These decisions are extremely crucial in influencing the overall outcome of the elections since loss or gain of even 10 per cent of the booths affect the final results (Verma 2000b).

As an illustration of discretion consider the case of national elections of 1999 which involved an estimated 600 million voters and around 15–20 thousand candidates. There were more than three million polling booths and it cost an estimated $(US) 250 million. Furthermore, almost 2 million police and para-military forces were deployed along with almost 1 million civilian personnel for security purposes (Election Commission of India 1999). The elections were spread over a period of 20–30 days in order to facilitate the re-deployment of forces from one area to another. In April 1999, when the national elections became imminent, Bihar and UP governments transferred almost a hundred senior police officers including the chief of police (*Times of India* 1999).

Clearly, the political process is affecting and being affected by the discretionary judgements of the police officers. On the one hand this has given considerable unaccounted powers to the individual officers and on the other, it has politicized the institution. Politicians understand the importance of discretion and use the police to exercise it in their favour. Accordingly, the transfer and posting of police officers have become completely politicized for these determine whose favourite gets into which position. This creates situations in which individuals matter in the organization. An entrenched SHO is able to thwart the efforts of the superintendent by going slow with the investigation. By stopping a specific group of people and checking their baggage, a constable can bring discredit to the efforts of the management to build bridges with this community. By delaying the arrest of an offender an officer can fuel tension between two warring communities. The rules that govern registration of criminal cases and citizen complaints can be used through discretion to build evidence against a particular group thus making the rules work at cross purposes. Since police actions affect social, economic, and political developments the whole organizational dynamics is now affected by the discretion exercised by individual officers.

COMPATIBILITY OF RULES WITH INCENTIVES AND GOALS

A sound policing policy would depend on balancing different ideas and negotiating the competing interests and logic of these different institutions. However, the system of dual control over the police and the old, bitter rivalry between the IAS and the IPS has made many rules and procedures incompatible with objectives of the institution. Both the IAS and IPS officers have their own interests and end up in competition rather than cooperate with one another as intended by the design of the institution.

The IAS and IPS Rivalry

As described above, in the colonial set up of the nineteenth century, the police have been made subservient to the DM. However, the implementation of this provision has gone beyond the original design of the institution. Not only was the SP subordinated to the

DM, (in some states medical bills of police officers have to be countersigned by the DM) but this subordination was followed at all the bureaucratic levels. A Home Ministry was created and its secretary assumed greater powers than the chief of state police. At the regional level the divisional commissioner was elevated over that of the deputy inspector general (DIG) and even at the sub-divisional level the DySP was subordinated to that of sub-divisional magistrate (SDM). What exacerbated the issue was also the fact that all these officers belonged to the Indian Civil (now the Administrative) Service while the police officers were members of the Indian Police (now the IPS). Thus, everywhere in the country, at every level the IAS has assumed superiority over the IPS and all decision-making at the policy level has been usurped by the IAS officers. Consequently, a great rivalry runs between the two services that have hindered the growth of professional policing in the country.

The IAS organization is able to control the entire functioning of the police department without being accountable for its operations. The service rivalry has also resulted in petty bickering and necessary schemes being blocked because these are seen as competitive to the status of the IAS officers. For instance, for a long period of time the SP was provided a jeep instead of a car on grounds that his work involves going to rural areas! The DM, despite being in charge of rural development still had an official car. The metropolitan cities are suited to the police commissioner system where the commissioner has powers of regulation necessary to administer the law and order management in the area (Chaturvedi 1985). However, this reduces the status of the DM as all the focus shifts to the police commissioner. In view of this situation, the IAS lobby has blocked the extension of this commissioner system to many metropolitan cities such as Kanpur, Lucknow, Patna, Jaipur where this system would have been more appropriate. The IAS lobby has also thwarted requests for increasing the financial powers of the police officers for that too is exercised by the home secretary. In reality, this has implied that a police chief does not have the authority to purchase much needed resources for the department. Interestingly, in name of speedier development, extensive financial powers are nonetheless given to lower functionaries as the block development officer and sub-divisional officer, who are much junior even to the SP. The IAS has also concentrated all rule making power in the hands of the Home Ministry and thus away from the IPS. Thus, even proposals like transfer, posting of officers, their promotions or punishments, placement of forces for law and order maintenance are all handled by the IAS officers. This has not only hampered the growth of professional policing in the country but has also weakened the DGP whose orders are circumvented or even overturned by a deputy secretary of the Home Ministry.

Apart from harming the professional growth of the police institution, the system has also diverted the DM from developmental work. Most DMs are engaged in law and order problems getting very little time for other activities. Consequently, land survey, construction of infrastructure and even collection of revenue has suffered since these are exclusive domains of the DM. In Bihar, land settlement has not been done for several decades that has escalated social conflicts and spawned Left-wing extremism. In the ravines of Ganga, land measurement has to be done every year because of shifting course of the river. Non-attention to this work by the DM has left large tracts of land under dispute creating serious law and order problems in the districts of Begusarai, Bhagalpur, and Munger.

A professional police officer generally focuses upon the operational issues of a social problem. For example, the growth of Left-wing extremism in Bihar is largely due to the failure to implement land reforms and development schemes for the weaker sections. These failures have driven the people towards the radical groups who promise instant seizure of land and settlement of the disputes. The police have seen this as a problem of law enforcement and order maintenance. Acceding to police demands governments have created special battalions and strengthened existing units apart from increasing the budgets for intelligence machinery. Such repressive measures have further driven the people towards extremist groups. The IAS and the IPS have not been able to evolve a joint strategy that can assure development along with impartial law enforcement. For instance, police operations have been hampered due to lack of roads and bridges in rural areas. The funds to build infrastructure are given to the DMs who have not worked any common strategy to construct them in accordance with police needs. Consequently, despite huge expenditure police penetration into affected areas has not improved. Kohli (1990: 218) reports that due to the 'underdevelopment of transportation and communication networks, police seldom could reach the scenes of disturbances quickly.'

However, this division has had both benign and malign effects. The involvement of multiple institutions has dispersed power, provided a series of checks and balances, and permitted self-correcting mechanisms to come in play. Despite the severity of terrorism in Punjab, economic activities continued and helped bring the state to normalcy (Joshi 1993). On the other hand this very complexity often thwarted effective implementation, innovation, and change. It took a long time for an effective strategy to emerge in Punjab. In Bihar, Assam, and Andhra Pradesh, the problems of extremism and terrorism are continuing with no coordinated strategy in sight.

AUTONOMY AND ACCOUNTABILITY

Both the IAS and the IPS have traditionally enjoyed high status in the society. At the district level, the DM and SP have been the number one and two state functionaries. They still enjoy preeminence in local functions and in the minds of the people. Both services have garnered many unofficial perks for their offices. For instance, officers enjoy free accommodation, chauffeured cars, body guards, retinue of orderlies, and extensive lands attached to their bungalows. In many districts, the produce from the lands (carried out by official personnel) earns more than the annual salaries. There is also considerable glamour attached to these posts with armed guards and ceremonial functions that maintain their high status in the local community. Accordingly, SP of a district is the most coveted posting in the police department and there is considerable 'competition' to get these posts. Furthermore, officers make all kinds of compromises and build links with the politicians to retain these posts as long as possible.

In the police organization there are other posts that are coveted for their power, perks, or for attracting the public and media attention. Thus, posts such as that of the range DIG, regional IG, head of the CID, Special Branch and the administration of the Headquarters, or those of the armed battalions, Railways and resource allotment are most coveted amongst the officers. It may be noticed that training institutes, auxiliary forces, and many other sections like that of prosecution and inspection are considered 'punishment' postings since these have none of the perks described above. At the central government level, postings in the CBI and the IB are considered attractive in comparison to that of Bureau of Research and Training, Crime Records Bureau, and even the central armed battalions such as the CRPF, BSF, and the ITBP. Furthermore, even within the CBI and the IB, there are only a handful of posts that are desirable since these give access to political circles or provide avenues for foreign travel. A newly created unit, called the National Security Guard has also assumed importance since the NSG is responsible for providing security to the prime minister and other dignitaries. This enables many officers to build rapport with powerful politicians and thereby jump to the 'good' postings or get important assignments. As expected all these culturally created modes of behaviour lead to manouevring and cross-sectional linkages that break the established bureaucratic chain of command. Ever since retired IAS and IPS officers have begun to be posted as governors, ambassadors, and advisers the drive to build politically useful links have taken a big priority amongst the police officers. Right at the beginning of the careers, these manouevrings begin destroying the élan of the officers' code and heavily politicizing the police services.

It has also taken a sinister turn through another means. Since caste affiliations are important in Indian politics, officers build bridges with their caste politicians and essentially allow use of their office to make gains for their political mentors. It is not surprising that till the eighties, when Congress party was ruling the state of Bihar most of the chief ministers were from the so-called 'forward castes'. Thus, all the important posts in the department were occupied by the forward castes like Jhas, Singhs, Sharmas, and Sinhas. However, when the Janata Dal came to power in 1990, officers of the so-called 'backward castes' immediately gained the favour as the new chief minister was a Yadav, a backward caste. This trend is seen in every state of the country. In the state of UP, when a Brahmin chief minister gave way to a Yadav caste chief minister, officers from the Yadav and other backward castes ascended all the important posts, replacing forward caste officers. This was then accompanied by massive changes all over the department in which the officers of these castes were posted as in-charges of police stations, circles, and other important subordinate ranks. When the political scenario changed with the ascension of a 'Harijan' chief minister the shake up in the bureaucracy including the police department was predictable. The Phoolchands and Paswans belonging to the Scheduled Castes now in turn replaced the Yadavs and Kurmis who had replaced the Singhs and Sharmas. When subsequently the Bharatiya Janata Party (BJP) formed the government, Mayawati, former chief minister of UP openly alleged that 'dalit' officers, close to her party had been denied important posts in the government and on that basis broke away from the BJP alliance!

Moreover, young entrants to the IPS (and IAS) are also being showing farsighted visions for their career enhancements. They are not only marrying into rich families but also preferring those that are politically connected. Hence, over the years a powerful net is developing where close links have developed between the politicians, business class, and bureaucrats that have also been cemented through marriage alliances. The case of a senior officer in the former Prime Minister Atal Bihari Vajpayee's office is illustrative in this regard. This person was the secretary of the Prime Minister, his brother-in-law was a police commissioner of Delhi, his father-in-law was the chief minister of Bihar and his family is the largest land owners in Bihar. He also has many other family members who are in the bureaucracy, working for large business houses and in politics. There are many other such families that have used their links in the bureaucracy, politics, and business to promote their members.

The end result of such bureaucratic-political and economic alliances is extremely dangerous. It has destroyed the autonomy of police organization and also made it into a tool of private interests. The 'politicization of the force' as it is euphemistically described, has induced new forms of corrupt practices within the organization. Police power is now openly used to subdue political opponents, to turn a blind eye towards criminals and lumpen elements aligned with the politicians, to ensure deliberate hindrance in the investigation of corruption cases against specific personalities and the misuse of police power to ensure electoral victories. The [mis] use of the police for political purposes has become an accepted part of the administration. The special branch within the police department, responsible for intelligence collection has been virtually converted into the chief minister's watchdog. Intelligence is openly collected against political opponents both outside and within the party. It is also not unusual for this branch of the police to analyse and recommend names of those people who would be loyal to the chief minister and suggest electoral strategies. This branch is also provided with large funds to gather intelligence but it is known that such funds are also used to buy political opponents and for furthering the interests of the chief minister.

The officers are pressured to cover up political shenanigans and corruption. Thus, the selling of public lands and railway stations by the forward caste chief minister Jagannath Misra, despite public outcry, could not be prosecuted and investigators used every trick to stall the proceedings against him (Shourie 1983). At present, the so-called fodder scam, in which the former chief minister Laloo Yadav and his close relatives have been accused of cheating the public treasuries of almost 20 million dollars is similarly stalled (Jha 1997). Corruption in high places is not unknown in India but the nexus between the police and politicians has ensured that proper investigations in such cases are never undertaken. Even at the federal level the situation is not any different. Recently, in the so-called Hawala cases the Supreme Court had to pass strictures against the government and direct the federal investigation agencies not to listen to the ministers to ensure that investigations are carried out fairly (Rao 1996).

Such bureaucratic, business, and political alliances have destroyed the autonomy of the police institution. The police have become a tool for furthering specific objectives. Kohli (1990: 279) suggests that the naxalite 'movement would not have gained strength but for the fact that the UF government, especially the CPM, decided to keep the police out of the conflict.' In 1975–7 brute police power was used for forcible sterilization, clearance of slums, and arrests of political opponents of Indira Gandhi. Police have become a useful instrument in political battles too. Thus, the destruction of mosque at Ayodhya and the killing of Sikhs in Delhi could go cn by shackling and preventing timely police action. In the communal riots at Bhagalpur and Bombay, police openly played a partisan role at the behest of ruling party functionaries. There are many such examples all illustrating the decline in autonomy and politicization of the police institution.

Need for Accountability

An institution that is no longer in control of itself can hardly be accountable to the people. Moreover, as mentioned above in the colonial design there is no provision of local accountability. At present, the only elected official able to assert some degree of control over the police is the home minister who is too remote an authority for effective redressal of citizen grievances. Thus, the problem of accountability of the police institution is a serious one. The NPC pointed out in its First Report (GOI 1979):

One of the fundamental requisites of good government in a democracy is an institutionalized arrangement for effectively guarding against excesses or omissions by the executive in the exercise of their powers or discharge of their mandatory duties which cause injury, harm, annoyance or undue hardship to any individual citizen.

The system of accountability must not only include departmental checks and balances but also an effective inquiry procedure into any specific complaint of an alleged excess or omission, for its individual and organizational lapses, for exposing it promptly to ensure public confidence and for a corrective as well as penal action. The arrangement is especially necessary in case of the police which have vast scope for discretionary powers by a large number of its personnel and which affect the rights and liberties of individual citizens in daily life. Powers of arrest, search, seizure, institution of a criminal case in court, preparation of reports that have long term implications on the alleged anti-social conduct of any citizen, create vast scope for misconduct by police personnel.

Apart from direct acts of misconduct, police officers cause extreme annoyance to public by not performing their mandatory duties too. A large number of persons are affected by the malady of non-registration of complaints when crimes are reported at the police stations. Even when cases are registered, slackness and indifference in follow-up action is another cause for public complaints. Police ineffectiveness in dealing with deviant elements and other persons believed to be responsible for criminal behaviour, is yet another cause for public criticism against police. Unfortunately, a majority of the persons who are aggrieved on account of police inactivity or indifference belong to the weaker sections of society. Their lack of resources make them helpless to pursue their complaints with senior officials or in different places.

The NPC found that in 1977, out of a total of 68,275 complaints inquired by the departmental officers, allegations were substantiated either wholly or partly in 4797 complaints only, which amounts to mere 7 per cent. The complaints against the police have also been extremely serious. Police officers have been charged with deliberately blinding suspects in Bhagalpur and faking encounter killing of 'dacoits' in UP. Rapes and unnatural deaths in police custody are also frequent occurrences. Yet, despite the passage of more than five decades after Independence, few police officers have been convicted for their involvement or omission of duty. Torture, deaths in police custody, and high-handed acts especially against the weaker sections are also frequent complaints. Still no procedures have been formulated within the department, which could check these and other such malpractices. The need for an effective institutional machinery to deal with public complaints against the police is in fact a long standing requirement, which has been expressed by citizen forums, media, and concerned human rights activists.

The System of Accountability

The basic procedure in India for inquiring into citizen complaints against police officers is largely one of departmental inquiry. In the present system a public complaint against an officer is placed before the SP for further action. If the SP is convinced of its genuineness, an explanation is called from the concerned officer. In case this 'preliminary' defence is found unsatisfactory, the SP either inflicts a 'minor' punishment or else if the charge is serious, draws up a departmental proceeding. An officer not below the rank of inspector holds such an internal inquiry and its progress is reviewed periodically. If the charges are substantiated, the SP in most cases is empowered to inflict 'major' punishment but in case of dismissal, the orders have to be confirmed by the next higher ranking officer. The 'guilty' officer has the right to appeal for expunction of the punishment or for its reduction.

This procedure of departmental inquiries has several inherent drawbacks and can be criticized on the following grounds:

(i) The inquiry officer is generally favourably disposed towards his own subordinates and may believe that exposing the misconduct will disgrace his own supervision.

(ii) He also fears unpopularity within the organization and thus prefers to avoid going against his subordinates.

(iii) If the allegations are made against a police officer who has the reputation for getting the work done, the inquiry officer is hesitant to initiate any in-depth investigation.

(iv) In several cases, the inquiry officer is himself corrupt and dishonest.

(v) In most inquiries witnesses are treated casually and indifferently, sometimes even with hostility.

(vi) The propensity to suppress the alleged misconduct increases when it is said to have occurred in the course of duty. Examples are : allegations of torture when the suspect is interrogated during investigations, excessive use of force during arrests or in controlling unruly mobs, etc.

(vi) In some cases there is a straightforward conflict of evidence between the complainant and the subject officer(s). In such cases the inquiry officer commonly tends to believe a fellow officer rather than a stranger victim.

(vii) There is a general feeling amongst the police that only a police officer could fairly assess the stress and provocation of police experiences. The misconduct is then considered as one that may be condemnable by outsiders but is definitely understandable if not completely condonable by the fellow police officers.

In addition, the problem gets compounded by the formality of procedures, delaying tactics employed by offending officers, frequent transfers of conducting or supervising officers, and excessive workloads of normal policing. The result is that departmental inquiries take considerable amount of time and effort to be completed. By then the complainant has been so harassed or intimidated that its efficacy is lost. Even if departmental inquiries are conducted expeditiously and with due precautions by intervention of the SP the aggrieved person remains dissatisfied about its impartiality and objectivity.

Other channels of control have also been built into the police system in order to provide some form of external review. The principle of general control and supervision by the DM was to make police beholden to a 'civilian' authority in order to have an external check on its actions. Police department too has been placed under the civilian bureaucratic control of the Home department in order to introduce alternate avenue of control apart from the police hierarchy under the chief of police. The independent judiciary is of course a separate institution to which police is beholden for all its actions.

In practice, these external controls hardly operate and if at all, very ineffectively. The NPC found that the public trust is placed more in the SP than in the offices of DM or other civilian bureaucrats. In fact, most complaints received by the DM or in the Home Office are routinely passed to the corresponding police officers for inquiry and little effort is ever made for independent inquires. In rare cases when elected representatives make an issue of some citizen's complaint, both the police managers and bureaucrats close rank to safeguard 'executive responsibilities' (Singh and Vajpeyi 1981: 143).

The judiciary is trusted more but the procedures of instituting inquiries by members of the bench are cumbersome, slow, and can only be initiated by government directives. Generally, in serious cases of police misconduct there is always a demand for judicial commission which is looked upon more favourably. In several instances, the very demand for judicial commissions when not conceded by the government have become the main issue around which further tension and pressure build up and escalate the law and order situation regardless of the nature of original incidents. In rare cases where ultimately the government conceded setting up of such commissions, it either weakened them by not providing logistical support or did not accept their findings. The Justice Shah Commission which looked into police excesses during the 'Emergency' period of 1975–7 and the Justice Chawla Commission which inquired into the Delhi riots of 1984 in which Sikhs were killed, both failed to punish guilty policemen for these reasons.

The NPC proposed a major policy framework for police accountability. Among several of its recommendations there was one stipulating that certain serious misconducts of police should mandatorily be inquired by senior judges. It asked for the setting up of a District Inquiry Authority, headed by a senior judge of the district court who would conduct such inquiries upon receiving information from the SP. It also proposed that such inquiry reports including the action taken by the state government or the police department should be made public. The NPC also proposed an autonomous State Security Commission to control and supervise the police department in every province. The objective was to create an organizational structure to prevent direct political interference in the functioning of the police departments. The proposal was to make the home minister as the chairman of this body with some members of the opposition party, eminent jurists, and public figures being the other constituents. This security commission was to function similar to the police boards, with the chief of police enjoying complete responsibility for the operational and disciplinary matters of the force. The role of the Home Ministry run by the IAS was sought to be annulled and the control was to be transferred to an independent board. The National Police Commission argued that by keeping the home minister as the chairperson, the political control by the government (ruling party) will be maintained but this arrangement will shield the police from direct day to day interference that had become common. The police chief, assured of a tenure, would have the freedom to mould the force into a professional body and be held accountable for its performance. The autonomous State Security Commission will ensure accountability of the police. As we know, these recommendations of the NPC are not acceptable to any political party and as yet have not been implemented. Police unaccountability remains a major problem for the people.

Self-Restraint and Exit

The role of the police is not well defined and has generally been expanding. The colonial model was designed for the maintenance of the interests of the ruling class and keeping the sovereignty of the British. Independence brought many new challenges—that of social conflicts, terrorism, communal disturbances, and special needs of the minority and weaker sections. The tendency of the state to control unwanted behaviour by criminalizing it has invariably expanded the areas of police action. Thus, laws abolishing untouchability, dowry, child labour, trafficking in women, and misuse of the internet have expanded police powers. The expansion in armed units has already been described above. New units in the name of 'protection of weaker sections,' 'Harijan', and 'women' police stations and even 'tourist police' have been created within state police organizations. These have been done without taking into account the capabilities and efficiency of the police institution. On the other hand, the police institution has successfully thwarted attempts to scrutinize its operations, hold it accountable, and make it honour the rights of the citizens. The growth in the activities of an emerging democratic state has been paralleled by the expansion of the bureaucratic machine. In particular, the expansion of the IPS has only been second to that of the IAS. They have expanded their rank structure from inspector-general to director-general (a secretary level post); enhanced their promotional avenues, garnered many resources, and enlarged their perks. The IPS has also usurped all the senior command posts related to internal security and enforcement of criminal laws in the country. Not only all the para-military forces like the BSF, CRPF, ITBP, and others, but also the intelligence gathering and investigating agencies like the IB, RAW, and the CBI are commanded by IPS officers on deputation. Furthermore, organizations like the Institute of Forensic Sciences, research establishments like the Bureau of Police Research and Development and large prisons (like Tihar) are also controlled by the IPS. In many states the IPS officers have also prevailed upon the governments to create ex-cadre posts in public relations, publishing, and even public sector industries. The expansion has given the IPS a vast say in the administration of the country that was perhaps not envisaged in the design. Perhaps, this may be the reason that in matters of security a professional, detached viewpoint has not emerged. The IPS (and the IAS) have silenced other voices in the country.

ORGANIZATIONAL CAPABILITIES

The capability of the police institution lies in the quality of its personnel. The administration of justice and security of the people depend upon the professionalism of the police officers. However, recruiting and training matters are sadly neglected within the police institution. It is an obvious fact that despite voices being raised for more than two hundred years, the issue has not received serious consideration from the government. The status of the constable remains low and minimum educational qualifications have been set at barely literate standards. Most training institutes are in dismal shape. Many do not have adequate facilities, there is a dearth of qualified instructors, and training schedules are not followed. Although, on the recommendation of several committees, the training curriculum has been enhanced, in reality there is virtually no training except for physical and arms drill. Every police person is required to learn about the Constitution, human rights issues, get a full year instruction in criminal and procedural law, and learn about basic science, history, and geography of the country. However, most subordinate police officers come out of the academy just as they had gone in. Furthermore, the probationers are frequently sent out on law and order duties disrupting their training. There are few assessments of training procedures and little by way of external evaluation. Most of the training takes place in the field where recruits learn from the older officers and pick up undesirable modes of behaviour.

It may be pointed out that training of IPS officers is on the other hand extremely impressive. The National Police Academy at Hyderabad is comparable to any police academy in the world and provides excellent instruction to the men and women selected for this prestigious service. But this again points towards the elitism prevailing in the bureaucracy and preferential treatment for senior ranks.

The pay for the police officers have not been commensurate with their responsibilities and powers. The working conditions for subordinate ranks have always been dismal. Most of the investigating officers have a low social status and their working time extends beyond 10–12 hours every day. Housing for the police barely reach 2–3 per cent of the personnel and no provisions have been made for over-time work, transport, and promotions. During elections, religious festivities, and agitations, which are common, police station officers work for more than 14–15 hours continuously. Yet, their emolument, perks, and organizational support are negligent. Most stations and other police buildings are in poor shape, generally decrepit and urgently needing repairs. There are few vehicles for the police stations and communication equipments like wireless sets and telephones are in short supply. The poor training and neglect of working conditions have seriously affected the capabilities and professionalism of the police personnel.

Lack of Institutional Memory

While discussing the institutional capabilities two other issues need to be pointed out that have destroyed the competence of the Indian police. As mentioned above, right from the beginning, an elaborate record keeping system was developed to ensure accountability of the subordinate officers and to keep control over the jurisdiction. These records did serve to build institutional memory and became the basis of criminal investigations. For a long period of time the Indian police have been maintaining records of people suspected, arrested, interrogated, prosecuted, and convicted of criminal offences. Since all investigations are based upon the principle of modus operandi, these records served a useful purpose in keeping surveillance over suspects and in apprehending the offenders. However, after Independence when politicization of the police became common everywhere, this practice has slowly declined. There are two reasons for it. First, the police personnel are being shifted and transferred so rapidly that they hardly have time to maintain the records. At the level of senior officers this has become even more problematic since regular inspection and updating of records are not being stressed in the department. Second, the inability of supervisory officers to control their politically connected subordinates have also created an environment where delinquency is not being controlled. Hence, there has been a general neglect in record keeping and building institutional memory.

Furthermore, most of the records are still manually maintained and over the years it has become impossible to obtain any meaningful information from them. The police departments have also not shown any initiative in building institutional memory and devising new ways of collecting, processing, and disseminating information. For instance, despite the fact that Left-wing extremism has been prevalent since the early sixties, no separate records have been evolved to take account of these so called 'naxalite' cases. With the passage of years it is now almost impossible to build a record of all the naxalite cases reported in different parts of Bihar, Orissa, or Andhra Pradesh. Similarly, despite the concern for communal cases, police do not designate such cases as a separate category. Consequently, police records do not provide any useful *operational* information that could help assess a problem and devise effective strategies. The record system has continued unchanged from the British period and little effort has been made to modernize the procedures.

This may also be gleaned from *Crime in India* where one cannot find information about communal cases, terrorist incidents, socioeconomic background of people arrested for criminal charges, or even the temporal distribution of criminal incidents. All these shortcomings reduce the capabilities of the institution in devising effective strategies. The unfortunate result is that officers begin to take short cut methods—kill suspects in encounters since they are unable to build evidence against them; arrest people randomly; and use third degree methods to extort confessions. The incidents of brutality and custodial deaths can be traced in part to the declining capabilities of the police institution.

ORGANIZATIONAL CULTURE

The police have their own subculture: one of secrecy and violence. In a well-known study, Westley (1970) identified a distinct police subculture in which hostility towards the citizens, group solidarity, and secrecy were paramount. According to this study most police officers view the citizens as enemy and they feel justified to protect fellow officers from external criticism. Skolnick (1994) described a distinct working personality characterized by exercise of authority and threat of danger. Research indicates that police officers meet citizens on a selective basis generally encountering only those who have a problem or resent police intrusion. In the face of perceived citizen hostility it becomes natural for the officers to rely upon their colleagues for support and understanding. Officer behaviour is thus affected by their working environment, organizational culture, street experience, and demands of their jobs which affect their behaviour and functions. Furthermore, Westley reported that the feeling of group solidarity also became the basis for justifying violence against the people and a majority of the officers rationalized the illegal use of force.

Sparrow (1988) suggests that peer group sub-culture in the police institution is strong and generally resistant to change. Police corruption and brutality are also linked to the occupational subculture. Group solidarity initiates officers into corrupt activities or in covering the deviance of other officers. Westley (1970) found that officers were willing to lie to cover the illegal acts of their colleagues. In the comparative study of Delhi Police it was found that 71.4 per cent of officers thought they could only trust their fellow officers (Griffith, Murphy, and Verma 2000). The Mollen Commission (1994) reported a 'code of silence' amongst the officers of the New York Police Department. This code of silence sustains misconduct. The Christopher Commission report on Los Angeles riots (1991: 168) found that there was 'an unwritten rule that you do not roll over, tell on your partner, your companion'. Police sub-culture then becomes a serious obstacle to organizational accountability.

Niederhoffer (1967) further reports that police culture is dominated by cynicism and authoritarianism. He argues that police officers are cynical about the external world and their own organization. Cynicism tends to develop 'conventional social values, cynicism, aggression, superstition, and a tendency to stereotype, to project personal values onto other and to define the world in terms of good versus bad people' (Walker 1999: 327). Muir (1977) has also suggested a positive aspect of police personality—one of detachment and impersonal behaviour that shields the officers from unpleasant features of their work.

Most of these characteristics are applicable to the Indian police. Although a formal study of police perceptions has not been done in the Indian context, a large sample of police officers from Delhi (957 personnel chosen randomly from all ranks) appear to suggest the broad findings of the above mentioned traits (Griffith, Murphy, and Verma 2000). To the question 'Police work gives a chance to punish lawbreakers' elicited agreement by almost 87.7 per cent of the respondents. Officers sticking with one another is prevalent in the Indian police also. To the question 'first loyalty must be to fellow officers' 74.7 per cent of the officers agreed while 69.6 per cent believed that 'they can only trust other police officers'. More significantly, 86.4 per cent said that 'it is important to stick together'.

Organizational Deviance

Organizational culture impacts strongly upon the misconduct, brutality, and corruption within the ranks of the police. Pervasive corruption and brutality flourishes because of organizational culture that evolves in the system through several kinds of practices, beliefs, and value systems (Sherman 1978). The British for the purpose of establishing their Raj assiduously built the sub-culture of the Indian police. The police were meant to suppress any dissent against British rule, a situation that gave unlimited power to police officers. Consequently, corruption and brutality became endemic and rampant in the police department (Verma 1999). At present their unsavoury reputation for extortion and corruption is perhaps even more widespread and brazen than ever before. Every rank, from the lowest 'chowkidar', the village watchman, to the highest ranking DGP is known to have tainted hands (*Times of India* 1997a). The investigating officers extort money from complainants, witnesses, and naturally the accused. The constabulary extorts money from hawkers, footpath dwellers, truck and bus drivers (Anandan 1997; *Indian Express* 1997). Regular extortions in every police station (so-called *hafta*) are common public knowledge. Traffic constables collect money from truck drivers in front of everyone (*India Today* 1998). Corruption within the ranks of IPS is also widespread. Senior officers make money from transfer and postings of subordinate officers, take bribes, and give favours (*Times of India* 1996; *Indian Express* 1999). They demand cuts from vendors supplying uniforms, office equipment, and vehicles to the department; even extort from the business houses and subvert investigation of cases on pecuniary or political considerations (Kumar 1996). Corrupt practices are now part of the Indian police system and are found in every department, in every rank, and in every police institution including training colleges. The malaise has spread all over the country and in every aspect of policing.

The IPS officers, who themselves misuse public funds and demand services from the subordinates, are unwilling and unable to provide any control over the mercenary actions of their subordinates. They have little legitimacy and moral strength to take firm action against the extortion indulged by their officers. Most share the booty while a small minority remains at best passive and indifferent towards these corrupt practices. The elitist nature of the police leadership, the unaccountability to the people, and outdated management practices has all combined to make corruption ubiquitous and even acceptable within the organization (Verma 1999).

A strong code of silence prevails within the Indian police institution also. Despite citizen uproar and media publicity against fake encounters, deaths, or rapes in police custody, little action has ever been taken against the guilty officers. All these actions are well within the knowledge of even supervisory ranks and cannot continue unless there is passive acquiescence from the top. The blinding at Bhagalpur, the several cases where people disappeared from police custody, the encounter killings in the name of dacoity operations in

UP, against naxalites in Bengal, Bihar, and Andhra Pradesh, and Sikh terrorists in Punjab, all suggest a culture of brutal and unaccounted force that has sanctions from the highest quarters. The elitist nature of the police leadership, the politicization of the department, the unaccountability to the people, and outdated management practices has all combined to create organizational deviance. Extortions and use of brutal force have gone beyond the stage of a few bad apples. These are practiced openly and without fear of punishment. The organizational culture of the Indian police has spawned a deviant institution.

Organizational Adaptation with Changing Time

The capacity of the Indian police organization to adapt to the changing times is limited. The departmental policies and power struggle within the police organization have severely limited its capacity to deal with emerging challenges. The considerations of caste and political affiliations begin to play a role whenever any attempt is made to change procedures, administrative functions, or change in responsibilities. The allotment of posts within the department is guided by caste equations and political considerations. A certain number of officers belonging to specific castes 'have' to be posted to the high profile offices at all levels in order to placate the caste lobbies. The consequences are that many management problems are created in order to placate the caste and political interests with detrimental effect upon the organization. For instance, in the districts of central Bihar, caste considerations have played havoc with the police administration. Despite the continuing mayhem from Left-wing extremism and caste conflicts for more than two decades, a concerted effort has not been made to post competent and proven officers to combat the problem. Postings are guided by considerations other than the efficiency and needs of the organization. The pressures from caste and political lobbies compromise attempts to send impartial and competent officers. This seriously affects the ability of the department to combat growing violence in a concerted manner.

These problems exist at the national level too where transfers and postings in important units like the BSF, CRPF, ITBP, and NSG are determined by extraneous considerations. Officers resist postings in hot spots like Kashmir and Assam while seeking those at Delhi and large metropolitan centres through political support.

The organizational malaise in these units is also spreading. These also suffer from paucity of resources, lack of training, and failure to induct new technology. Their operation is insulated from external review in the name of security and despite a revolt by the units of CISF very little is known about their internal administration. The CBI has been politicized too and has dragged its feet in investigating prominent politicians or bureaucrats. Almost all police agencies have failed to adopt new ideas or methods and have remained reactive in their orientation. The old practices continue without any examination of their relevance to the present time. For instance, induction of computers, Geographical Information Systems, Offender Profiling and Computer Aided Dispatch system, registration of citizen complaints through an automated systems have still not found a place in police operations despite availability of these technologies in the country. Although new forms of crimes—cyber crimes, computer hacking, child pornography, white collar, and environmental crimes—have begun to threaten the nation, police practices still remain the same. There is little attempt to develop a long term strategy and prepare the police to face the challenges of the new millennium.

CONCLUSION

Institutions are important in the life of a nation. In India, where a nascent democracy is shaping the lives of millions of diverse people, in a land ravaged by centuries of colonialism and exploitation by the ruling classes, the need for a well functioning institution is undisputed. The police institution is obviously one that is important in the democratic system of the country. The security and well being of the citizens is dependent upon the police. Yet, the police institution in India is in a dire state: disorganized, inefficient, corrupt, and partisan in its operations. It is unable to perform in accordance with the expectations of a democratic society. The fault lies in the design and inability to adapt to the changing circumstances that have emerged after Independence. It has failed to deal with social conflicts and prevent growing violence. The force has become heavily politicized and its leadership has been reduced to a rubber stamp.

Ultimately, the reform of the police lies in the hands of the politicians who have not shown any interest in changing the institution. The need to have a malleable police force that can be used for partisan interests overcomes any political will to change the institution. Yet, failure is also that of the police leadership that has not shown any inclination to reform the institution. Despite having the advantage of public acceptance and status, the IPS has failed to provide leadership to the force. The growing corruption and catering to political interests have compromised most of the IPS officers. The officers' corps has lost its élan and the failures of the police institution are as much the result of extraneous influences as those of the officers who do not stand up for their organization. Indeed, no reform seems possible at the present period since the politicians, the IPS, and the IAS officers all have vested interests in maintaining the status quo.

The reform can only come from the pressure exerted by the people and other institutions. The judiciary, National Human Rights Commission, media that now also includes satellite based electronic communication systems—the internet and the cable TV—academic community, and several kinds of citizen groups have an interest in reforming the police. At present, some of these institutions and citizen groups like the People's Union for Democratic Rights, the People's Union for Civil Liberties, the Andhra Pradesh Union of Civil Liberties, Majdoor Kisan Sangharsh Samiti have achieved some success. These have forced the government to be accountable for its policies and actions.

Unfortunately, non-governmental organizations and human rights groups have not been involved in supporting the development of public institutions. Most have suffered at the hands of the police and are naturally antagonistic towards it. This is distressing for these groups—with their grass root contacts and experience of work amongst the downtrodden can provide greater insights and more practical ways for reforming the police. The need to challenge the assumptions behind the police functions and roles is something that can come only with 'public exposure and debate that can force a sharpening of definitions, procedures and conclusions' (Gilsinan 1991: 214). Despite fifty years of democracy, public institutions are still beyond the scrutiny of social scientists and other external reviewers. Despite some research supported by the NPC and BPRD, an environment has not evolved to promote a continuing association between the police and the academic community. Disassociation of the social scientists has prevented the development of an appropriate *research methodology* and *reliable data sources*. There is no tradition for the police and other criminal justice organizations to open their records, activities, and deliberations for public scrutiny. The police agencies still fear 'opening up' and academic research on justice issues remains almost non-existent in the country. This may be contrasted with the research unit of the British Home Office where pioneering work on situational crime prevention techniques has been done (Clarke 1992). Similarly, the work of the 1967 President's Commission in the US 'generated a fresh intellectual discussion of major components of criminal justice' (Conley 1994: xiii). This Commission not only sponsored important field research on police activities, it also initiated an unprecedented contribution of literature on the police. Its impact 'launched the police establishment on a giddy, if brief adventure with forces that blew down the walls insulating the police world' (Bouza 1985: 255).

The impact also led to the realization that instead of designing 'what the police can do about the crime problem, the police need research about the community problems to determine its tasks' (Reiss 1985: 65) and further that 'research should be the core of policing' (Goldstein 1979). Focusing upon quality of life issues also helps combat crime and disorder (Wilson and Kelling 1982). The role and function of not only the police organizations, but all other criminal justice agencies in Britain, US, and most developed countries have been widely studied, examined and probed by scholars, academicians, research institutions, and citizen groups. The consequent public inspection has undoubtedly implied greater accountability, responsibility, and openness on the part of bureaucratic organizations, a situation ensuring the democratic functioning of the governmental bodies.

The association of the universities and autonomous institutions with the criminal justice agencies in India can be similarly conceptualized. This will have the advantage that indirectly through the research agenda a process can be generated that could contribute to public accountability, performance appraisal, and checks on the misuse of power. The failure of the police institution can perhaps be addressed by seeking strategies beyond the bureaucratic, managerial approaches. It is an approach that can come from a broad based research agenda. This appears to be the best hope for reforming the police institution.

References

Aggarwal, Rajendra (2000), 'Araria saw 12 DMs, 10 SPs in 10 years', *Times of India*, 23 June.

Akbar, M. J. (1985), *India: The Seige Within*, Harmondsworth: Penguin Books.

Alpert, G. P. and M. H. Moore (1993), 'Measuring Police Performance in the New Paradigm of Policing', in G. Alpert and A. Piquero (eds) *Community Policing: Contemporary Readings*, Prospect Heights, IL: Waveland Press.

Alpert, G. P. and R. G. Dunham (1992), *Policing Urban America* (2nd edn), Prospect Heights, IL: Waveland Press.

Anandan, Sujata (1997), '"Hawkers" Saviour is Fighting for Life', *Times of India News Service*, 8 January.

Anderson, David M. and David Killingray (eds) (1992), *Policing and Decolonisation: Politics, Nationalism and the Police: 1917–65*, Manchester: Manchester University Press.

Arnold, David (1986), *Police Power and Colonial Rule, Madras 1859–1947*, Delhi: Oxford University Press.

————— (1992), 'The Demise of British Rule in India', in David M. Anderson and David Killingray (eds), *Policing and Decolonisation*, Manchester: Manchester University Press, pp. 42–61.

Baxi, Upendra (1980), *The Crisis of the Indian Legal System*, New Delhi: Vikas.

Bayley, David. H. (1969), *Police and Political Development in India*, Princeton, NJ: Princeton University Press.

————— and James Garofalo (1989), 'The Management of Violence by Police Patrol Officers', *Criminology*, vol. 27, no. 1, pp. 1–25.

Biderman, A. D. and A. J. Reiss (1967), 'On Exploring the "Dark figure" of Crime', *Annals of the American Academy of Political and Social Science*, vol. 374, pp. 1–15.

Black, Donald (1980), *The Manners and Customs of the Police*, New York: Academic Press.

Bottomley, A. K. (1973), *Decision in the Penal Process*, London: Martin Robinson.

Bottomley, A. K. and K. Pease (1986), *Crime and Punishment: Interpreting the Data*, Milton Keynes: Open University Press.

Bouza, Anthony V. (1985), 'Police Unions: Paper Tigers or Roaring Lions?', in William A. Geller (ed.), *Police Leadership in America: Crisis and Opportunity*, Chicago, Illinois: Praeger Publishers.

Brodeur, Jean Paul (ed.) (1998), *How to Recognize Good Policing: Problems and Issues*, Washington, DC: Police Executive Research Forum.

Brogden, Michael E. (1987), 'The Emergence of the Police—The Colonial Dimension', *British Journal of Criminology*, vol. 27, no. 1, pp. 4–14.

Chakravarty, Suhash (1989), *The Raj Syndrome: A Study in Imperial Perceptions*, New Delhi: Penguin Books.

Chaturvedi, S. K. (1985), *Metropolitan Police Administration In India*, Delhi: B. R. Publishing Corporation.

Christopher Commission (1991), *Report of the Independent Commission to Investigate the Los Angeles Police Department*, Los Angeles: City of Los Angeles.

Clarke, Ronald V. (ed.) (1992), *Situational Crime Prevention: Successful Case Studies*, New York: Harrow and Heston.

Cohn, S. Bernard (1961), *The Development and Impact of British Administration in India*, New Delhi: Indian Institute of Public Administration.

Coleman, Clive and Jenny Moynihan (1996), *Understanding Crime Data: Haunted by the Dark Figure*, Buckingham: Open University Press.

Conley, John A. (1994), 'Introduction' in John A. Conley (ed.), *The 1967 President's Crime Commission Report: Its Impact 25 Years Later*, Cincinnati, OH: Anderson Publishing Co.

Das, Dilip K. and Arvind Verma (1998), 'The Armed Police in the British Colonial Tradition: The Indian Perspective', *Police Studies: The International Review of Police Development*, vol. 21. no. 2, pp. 354–67.

Das, S. K. (1998), *Civil Service Reform and Structural Adjustment*, Delhi: Oxford University Press.

Davis, K. C. (1969), *Discretionary Justice—A Preliminary Inquiry*, Baton Rouge: Louisiana State University Press.

————— (1975), *Police Discretion*, St Paul: West Publishing.

Edwardes, Michael (1967), *British India 1772–1947: A Survey of the Nature and Effects of Alien Rule*, London: Sidgwick & Jackson.

Election Commission of India (1999), *Elections 1999: Facts*. www.eci. gov.in.

Gaines, L. K., V. E. Kappeler, and J. B. Vaughn (1996), *Policing in America* (2nd edn), Cincinnati, OH: Anderson Publishing Co.

Gilsinan, James F. (1991), 'Public Policy and Criminology: An Historical and Philosophical Reassessment', *Justice Quarterly*, vol. 8, no. 2, pp. 201–16.

Goldstein, Herman (1979), 'Improving Policing: A Problem-Oriented Approach', in *Crime and Delinquency*, 25 (April), pp. 236–58.

Government of India (1979–83), *Reports 1–8 of the National Police Commission*, Ministry of Home Affairs, Faridabad: Government of India Press.

Griffith, C. T., C. Murphy, and Arvind Verma (2000), ·*Comparative Study of Police Perceptions in Canada, Japan and India*, unpublished report.

Griffiths, Percival Joseph, Sir (1971), *To Guard My People: The History of The Indian Police*, London: Benn.

Gupta, Anandswarup (1979), *The Police in British India: 1861–1947*, New Delhi: Concept Publishing Company.

Hindelang, M., T. Hirschi, and J. G. Weiss (1979), 'Correlates of Delinquency: the Illusion of Discrepancy between Self-Report and Official Measures', *American Sociological Review*, vol. 44, pp. 995–1014.

Imperial Gazetteer of India, Part IV, reprint 1909.

India Today (1979a), 'The Police: Overworked, Underpaid, Demoralized but Militant', New Delhi, 16–30 June, pp. 44–50.

————— (1979b), 'Law and Order: Crime and Politics', New Delhi, 1–15 November, pp. 80–90.

————— (1998), 'The Ugly Indian', vol. 23, no. 34, 18 August, p. 28.

Indian Express (1997), '5 policemen suspended for extortion at airport', Thursday, 25 September.

————— (1998), 'UP-wardly mobile', 2 July.

————— (1999), 'IG Gets One-Year Jail for Corrupt Practices', *Express News Service*, Friday, 15 January.

Jefferson, Tony (1990), *The Case against Paramilitary Policing*, Buckingham, England: Oxford University Press.

Jeffries, Charles, Sir (1952), *The Colonial Police*, London: Max Parrish.

Jha, Sachchidanand (1997), 'Laloo is likely to be Chargesheeted', *Times of India*, 8 January.

Joshi, Manoj (1993), 'Combating Terrorism in Punjab: Indian Democracy in Crisis', *Conflict Studies*, vol. 261, May.

Kappeler, V. E., R. Sluder, and G. P. Alpert (1994), *Forces of Deviance: Understanding the Dark Side of Policing*, Prospect Heights, IL: Waveland Press.

Klinger, D. A. (1994), 'Demeanor or Crime? An Inquiry into Why "Hostile" Citizens are More Likely to be Arrested', *Criminology*, 32, pp. 475–93.

Kohli, Atul (1990), *Democracy and Discontent: India's Growing Crisis of Governability*, New York: Cambridge University Press.

Kumar, Ajay (1996), 'Bihar Govt Rules out Quick Action against IPS Officials', *Indian Express*, Patna, 1 September.

Kumar, Raj (2000), 'Laloo keeps "uniformed friend" happy', *Times of India*, 22 June.

Lipsky, Michael (1968), *Street Level Bureaucracy: Dilemmas of the Individual in Public Services*, New York: Russell Sage Foundation.

Lobo, John (1992), *Leaves From A Policeman's Diary*, New Delhi: Allied Publishers.

Mahalingam, Sudha and Praveen Swami (1998), 'Law Enforcement: Empowering Investigative Agencies', *Frontline*, vol. 14, no. 26.

Mastrofski, S., R. Ritti, and D. Hoffmaster (1987), 'Organizational Determinants of Police Discretion: The Case of Drinking and Driving', *Journal of Criminal Justice*, vol. 15, pp. 387–401.

Metcalf, Thomas R. (1994), *The New Cambridge History of India: Ideologies of the Raj*, Berkeley: California University Press.

Mitra, B. B. (1960), *The Code of Criminal Procedure* (13th edn), vols 1 & 2, Calcutta: Eastern Law House.

Mitra, Chandan (1998), *The Corrupt Society: The Criminalization of India from Independence to the 1990s*, New Delhi: Penguin India.

Mollen Commission to Investigate Allegations of Police Corruption (1994), *Commission Report*, p. 47.

Muir, W. (1977), *Police: Streetcorner Politicians*, Chicago, IL: University of Chicago Press.

National Crime Records Bureau (1998), *Crime in India—1997*, Faridabad: Government of India Press.

Niederhoffer, Arthur (1967), *Behind the Shield*, Garden City, NY: Anchor Books.

Pepinsky, Harold E. (1984), 'Better Living Through Police Discretion', *Law and Contemporary Poblems*, vol. 47, no. 4, pp. 249–67.

———— (2000), 'Living Criminologically with Naked Emperors', *Criminal Justice and Policy Review*, vol. 11, no. 1, pp. 6–14.

Potter, David C. (1986), *India's Political Administrators: 1919–1983*, Oxford: Clarendon Press.

Powell, Dennis D. (1981), 'Race, Rank and Police Discretion', *Journal of Police Science and Administration*, vol. 9. no. 4, pp. 383–94.

Rao, T. Padmanabha (1996), 'SC Upholds CBI probe into Fodder Scam', *Hindu*, 20 March.

Reiss, Albert J. Jr (1974), 'Discretionary Justice in the US', *International Journal of Criminology and Penology*, vol. 2, pp. 181–205.

———— (1985), 'Shaping and Serving the Community: The Role of the Police Chief Executive', in William A. Geller (ed.), *Police Leadership in America: Crisis and Opportunity*, Chicago, Illinois: Praeger Publishers.

Saxena, N. S. (1987), *Law and Order in India*, New Delhi: Abhinav Publications.

Seminar (1977), 'The Police: A Symposium on the Problems of Law and Order in a Democracy', #218, October, Bombay: R. Thapar.

Sen, Amartya (1986), 'How Well are India and China Doing?', in Iqbal Khan (ed.), *Fresh Perspectives on India and Pakistan*, Oxford: Bougainvillea Books, pp. 85–97.

Shah, Giriraj (1992), *The Indian Police : A Retrospect*, Bombay: Himalayan Publishing House.

Sherman, Lawrence W. (1978), *Scandal and Reform: Controlling Police Corruption*, Berkeley: University of California Press.

Shourie, Arun (1983), 'Justice in Bihar', *Indian Express*, 18 April.

Singh, Baljit and Dhirendra K. Vajpeyi (1981), *Government and Politics in India*, New York: Apt Books Inc.

Singh, N. K. (1996), *The Plain Truth: Memoirs of a CBI Officer*, New Delhi: Konark Publishers.

Sinha, Arun (1991), *The Struggles of the Poor*, London: Oxford University Press.

Skolnick, J. H. (1994), *Justice Without Trial: Law Enforcement in a Democratic Society* (3rd edn), New York: Macmillan.

————— and D. H. Bayley (1986), *The New Blue Line: Police Innovations in Six American Cities*, New York, NY: The Free Press.

Smith, Douglas A., Christy A. Visher, and Laura A. Davidson (1984), 'Equity and Discretionary Justice: The Influence of Race on Police Arrest Decisions', *Journal of Criminal Law and Criminology*, vol. 75, pp. 234–49.

Sparrow, Malcom K. (1988), 'Implementing Community Policing', *Perspectives on Policing*, No. 9. Washington, DC: Government Printing Press.

Stracey, Eric (1981), *Odd Man In: My Years in The Indian Police*, New Delhi: Vikas.

Times of India (1996), 'D-G Prisons of Haryana Held For Bribery', 12 December.

————— (1997a), 'Senior TN Police Officer Arrested on Corruption Charges', 5 January.

————— (1999), 'IPS Officers being Shifted on 'Partisan' Considerations: Trusted Officials Given Important Districts', 30 April.

Uviller, Richard H. (1984), 'The Unworthy Victim: Police Discretion in the Credibility Call', *Law and Contemporary Problems*, vol. 47, no. 4, pp. 15–33.

Verma, Arvind (1993), 'The Problem of Measurement of Crime', *Indian Journal of Criminology*, vol. 21, no. 2, pp. 51–8.

————— (1997), 'Maintaining Law and Order in India: An Exercise in Discretion', *International Criminal Justice Review*, vol. 7, pp. 65–80.

————— (1998), 'National Police Commission in India: Analysis of the Policy Failures', *The Police Journal*, vol. LXXI, no. 3, pp. 226–44.

————— (1999), 'Police Corruption in India: Roots in Organizational Culture', *Police Studies: The International Review of Police Development and Management*, vol. 22, pp. 264–78.

————— (2000), 'Lies, Damn Lies and Police Statistics', *Indian Police Journal*, vol. XLVI. nos 2–3, pp. 29–36.

————— (2000a), 'Consolidation of the Raj: Notes from a Police Station in British India: 1865–1928', *Criminal Justice History*.

————— (2000b), 'Policing of Public Order In India', *International Journal of Police Management and Science*.

Walker, Samuel (1999), *The Police in America: An Introduction* (4th edn), New York: McGraw-Hill.

Westley, W. (1970), *Violence and the Police: A Sociological Study of Law, Custom and Morality*, Cambridge, MA: MIT Press.

Wheeler, S. (1967), 'Criminal Statistics: A Reformulation of the Problem', *Journal of Criminal Law, Criminology and Police Science*, vol. 58(3), pp. 317–24.

Wilson, James Q. and G. Kelling (1982), 'Broken Windows: Police and Neighborhood Safety', *Atlantic Monthly*, vol. 249, pp. 29–38.

Wilson, James Q. (1968), *Varieties of Police Behaviour: The Management of Law and Order in Eight Communities*, Cambridge Mass.: Harvard University Press.

Whitaker, Gordon P. (ed.) (1984), *Understanding Police Agency Performance*, Washington, DC: US Dept. of Justice, National Institute of Justice.

Wolfgang, M. E. (1963), 'Uniform Crime Reports: A Critical Appraisal', *University of Pennsylvania Law Review*, vol. 111, pp. 708–38.

Woodruff, Philip (1954), *The Men Who Ruled India: The Guardians*, New York: Schocken Books.

7

Civil Service

An Institutional Perspective*

K. P. Krishnan and T. V. Somanathan

The higher civil services in India—A primer

The 'higher' civil services in India, also known as the Class I or Group A services, are of three main types. *All India Services* are those whose members serve both *Union* and *State Governments*. *Central Services* are those whose members work under the *Union Government* only. *State Civil Services* are the higher services of *state governments*.

There are three All India Services—the Indian Administrative Service (IAS), the Indian Police Service (IPS), and the Indian Forest Service. The IAS and the Indian Foreign Service (IFS), a Central Service, are considered the most prestigious as judged by preferences of examination candidates and general public perceptions. Their pre-eminence is derived partly from a very slight edge in pay scales and slightly faster promotions, but more from their job content—the glamour and travel opportunities of the foreign service and the breathtaking variety of job content of the administrative service.

The IAS is a 'mandarin'-type civil service, comparable very broadly to the examination-recruited higher services in Britain, France, or Japan. Where it differs from many other 'mandarin' services is in the lateral mobility of IAS officers. Not only do they work at several different levels of government—Union, State, Local and Public Sector Corporations—but they also move across ministries and functions to a much larger extent than in most other mandarin civil service systems. In this latter respect the IAS is closer to the

---

* The views expressed in this chapter are purely the personal views of the authors and should in no way be construed as representing the views of the concerned government(s)/organization(s).

career component of the US Senior Executive Service (SES).[1] IAS officers do, however, specialize by geographical area—a necessity in a country with such diversity of language, culture, religion, and custom.

Recruitment is primarily through a very stiff competitive examination at a young age, typical of mandarin-style services. Candidates coming through the competitive examination are referred to as 'regular recruits' or 'direct recruits'. Two other streams of entry exist (known as 'promotion' and 'selection') which follow less rigorous procedures—these allow state civil servants to be promoted into the IAS. This is another feature of the IAS which resembles the American SES (though the IAS pre-dates the SES by 30 years). The recruitment examination is conducted by the Union Public Service Commission, an apolitical body, and is a common examination covering the IAS, IPS (but not Forest Service) and most non-technical Central Services. Successful candidates are allotted to services on the basis of their preferences and examination ranks. Most candidates choose the IAS/IFS as their first two preferences (not necessarily in that order) and thus those selected for these services are usually the highest ranked.

IAS officers are allotted to state cadres in which they specialize, learning the state language, customs, laws, etc., and clearing examinations in these subjects. They undergo a two-year training, about half of which is spent in the National Academy of Administration, Mussoorie, undergoing a rigorous multi-disciplinary course of examinations and assignments. One year is spent in on-the-job training in the state of allotment, including long stints in rural areas. Part of their career is usually spent in the union government.

Though the IAS came into existence in 1948, it inherited the mantle of the colonial Indian Civil Service and members, especially in the early years, saw themselves as successors of the ICS and its traditions.

Key administrative and police positions in state governments are designated as 'cadre posts' signifying that they may only be held by officers of the IAS/IPS. This is a deliberate feature of the All India Service system intended to promote quality, impartiality, integrity, and an all-India outlook. Thus the Secretaries (equivalent to 'permanent secretaries' in most Commonwealth countries) of most state ministries and the head of the civil service (the Chief Secretary) are always IAS officers, and the senior-most police officers (Inspectors-General) and the head of the state police (Director-General of Police) are always IPS officers.

I. INTRODUCTION

Is the limited effectiveness of the civil service, one of the principal institutions of governance, a critical factor that explains independent India's modest record in governance and development? This chapter is an attempt at answering this question by examining the

[1] Barbara Nunberg, 'Managing the Civil Service: Reform lessons from advanced industrialized countries'.

initial design of the institution, the changes in it over time, its performance in terms of contribution to governance and development, and adaptability.

This chapter is organized as follows:

This introductory section examines definitional issues and sets out the scope of the study. Section II looks at the formal design of the institution, concentrating mainly on the initial design after Independence, but also touching upon on some changes to the formal design which have occurred since. Section III attempts an assessment of the current state of effectiveness of the civil service against criteria laid out in Section I. Section IV examines the differences between the initial and formal design and the changes made during the actual implementation of the design, and the effects of those changes on institutional performance. Section V is an analysis of the actual incentive structure facing members of the civil service, as a result of the current combination of elements of the formal design and the informal realities of implementation. Section VI (the concluding section) starts with a very brief summing up of the consequences of both the design and its actual implementation on institutional performance. It then sets out some ideas and recommendations for improvement.

A few prefatory remarks on methodology are necessary. The study uses and quotes published data and data available in the public realm wherever possible. In reaching some of its key insights, it relies also on the authors' own knowledge of the institution, and responses to structured interviews. However, as loyal civil servants and faithful adherents to the Conduct Rules, the authors have limitations in the degree to which they can use such information. A few 'case studies' are cited; *all the case studies are real and factual*, not hypothetical. In those cases where the facts are public knowledge, names have been given. In those cases where the facts are not publicly known and where release would not be proper, they are withheld. The study thus has the advantage of access to insights not available to an outside researcher, but the corresponding limitation that full 'citation' of information sources is not possible.

Definitions and Scope

'Civil service' in India is a much researched and written upon topic. The subject has been examined from a variety of points of view.

This chapter will look at this institution mainly, though not exclusively, from the perspective of 'new institutional economics'.

New Institutional Economics

In the tradition of Douglass North[2] and others of the same school 'institutions' is defined to include all 'humanly devised actions that determine the structure of incentives'.[3] The importance of institutions in determining the performance of the economy derives from the fact that they collectively shape the motivations of individuals, groups to save, innovate, take risks, and cooperate. Based on this definition, the broad approach of the analysis of how 'institutions' impact governance and development is as follows:

- Information is not costless. Transaction costs are a major determinant of economic activity, competitiveness, and growth.

- Transaction costs are affected by the 'effectiveness' of the prevailing institutions.

- In accordance with the definition above, institutions (as distinct from organizations) are the laws, policies, procedures, rules, and customs (both formal and informal) within which organizations must operate.

- The interaction between institutions and organizations is the key to 'institutional effectiveness'. A move to a more effective set of rules etc., implies lower transaction costs and hence higher levels of economic activity.

- The effectiveness of organizations and their interaction with the regulatory framework depends primarily on the people of the organization (the civil service in our case).

- The civil service should therefore be looked at, analysed, and evaluated in terms of its contribution to more effective institutions and reduction in transaction costs.

Such an approach (a neo-institutionalist perspective as the author calls it) leads Kozo Yamamura to conclude that the government especially its central bureaucracy can play an important role in

---

[2] North, Douglass 1990, *Institutions, Institutional Change and Economic Performance.*

[3] Ibid., p. 3.

determining the performance of an economy.[4] This is so because the government can be the most effective definer of institutions and enforcer of property rights, and thus can determine how efficiently resources in the society are used. It can also play active roles in shaping and inculcating ideology, values, and social norms to reduce the costs of cooperation.

Effectiveness of Civil Service

In this sense therefore 'effectiveness' of the 'civil service' should be defined as the contribution of the civil service to the reduction of transaction costs for economic entities. This could happen through the role of the civil service in:

• the maintenance of democracy to the extent that democracy is considered as necessary[5] or desirable for economic development;[6]

• the maintenance of order so that economic activity goes on unimpeded, as disturbances to public order lead to delays and uncertainty and an increase in costs;

• creation and maintenance of a system of property rights so that the cost of contract enforcement is reduced;

• the regulation of markets (to the extent regulation is needed for a well-functioning market economy).

These are what may be called 'passive' or background roles of the 'civil service' in creating/supporting effective institutions. In addition to this in the Indian context, there is also a more 'activist' role that was assigned to the civil service in directly participating in and catalysing economic development.[7] Prominent here would be the role of the civil service in

• poverty alleviation;

• social empowerment; and

[4] 'The Role of Government in Japan's "Catch-up" Industrialization. A Neoinstitutionalist Perspective', by Kozo Yamamura, pp. 102–6 in *The Japanese Civil Service and Economic Development: Catalysts of Change* by Hyung Ki Kim et al. (ed.).

[5] 'The State in a Changing World' WDR *1997*, WB.

[6] Sridharan R., 'India: Good Governance and Political Culture'.

[7] We will use the term 'economic development' and 'economic growth' synonymously with 'poverty alleviation' etc.

• industrial and trade administration (going beyond the 'market regulation' role).

The difference between the first and second set of roles is broadly in terms of whether it supports and strengthens the functioning of markets or intervenes in the functioning of the market mechanism. The intervention could be on the ground of 'market failure' in the standard economic sense or on the ground that the consequences of the free functioning of the market are not acceptable politically or socially as determined by India's policy makers.

This brings up a larger issue. While the neo-institutionalist definition is a useful one, and provides the main anchor for this chapter, it has its limitations. Firstly, the institutional economics approach has the drawback of being too narrowly rooted in *economics*. For instance, one could argue that democracy or secularism and the freedoms that go with them have *value in themselves*, and not merely because they are necessary for economic development. Indeed there are those who argue—like Lee Kuan Yew, the former Singapore prime minister—that democracy in India reduces economic development. Taking a purely economic approach, one could argue that the role of the civil service in preserving democracy does not add to 'institutional effectiveness'. Likewise, maintenance of public order cannot be viewed purely as a reduction in 'transaction costs' or a means of promoting economic activity—it has social value in itself.

Secondly, the institutional economics approach, with its emphasis on enforcement of contracts and maintenance of property rights, confines itself to one school of economic thought. Land reform (of the coercive variety), for example, destabilizes well-established property rights and yet, can be shown in certain circumstances to make a positive contribution to economic development.

Thirdly, if one accepts that the civil service in a democracy is, and should be, subordinate to the elected political executive, it is difficult to argue that one can measure its 'institutional effectiveness' purely in terms of its role in promoting a particular kind of economic policy. How does one judge a civil service which—with effectiveness—implements policies of a democratically elected government that increase transactions costs (for example, through the creation of a complex licence-permit raj or through policies of, say, a communist government which assign the government a role completely inconsistent with free market economic policy)?

Faithful implementation of the policies of an elected government insofar as they do not contravene the law or the Constitution is surely the mark of an effective, not ineffective civil service. Clearly, an 'institutional economics' approach alone is insufficient. This chapter will therefore adopt a somewhat eclectic approach and look at 'effectiveness' in terms of performance with respect to three parameters:

• promoting economic development under a 'neo-institutionalist' perspective;

• preserving India's constitutional order, including democracy, secularism, and the rule of law (being 'good' in themselves, regardless of their effect on economic development);

• faithfully translating the will of elected governments into policies and then implementing them effectively.

It is almost immediately obvious that 'effectiveness' under one parameter does not always mean 'effectiveness' under another—which is one of the problems this chapter, and indeed, any analysis of civil service effectiveness, will have to grapple with.

II. FORMAL DESIGN

Given the basic constitutional and political features of the Indian governmental system, the civil service was and is a creature of the Constitution and laws flowing out of it. It drew its functions, powers, rights, and duties from these sources. The 'passive' and 'active' roles outlined above, required a civil service system in India (as elsewhere) to possess the following major characteristics:

• impartiality and neutrality[8]
• integrity in terms of being corruption-free
• adequate capacity and knowledge

It can easily be shown that each of these features is necessary not only to reduce transaction costs and thus lead to greater levels of

[8] Hyung-Ki Kim in 'The Civil Service System and Economic Development: The Japanese Experience', refers to the need for the insulation of the civil service and the public services from the political world and from societal interest groups.

economic activity, but also to be effective under the other two parameters identified.[9]

WHAT IS 'CIVIL SERVICE'?

In the context of a general approach to studying civil service reforms, Stevens has suggested that it is best to 'start with a broad canvas and take stock of the public service as a whole, narrowing the focus as appropriate'.[10] The identification or categorization of the 'civil service' could be based on one or more of the following criteria:

• All those who draw their pay and allowances from the Consolidated Fund of India or the Consolidated Fund of the states ('government servants' in the strict sense of the term) or

• In addition to those covered by the above criterion, include those who draw their pay and allowances from organizations that are funded entirely or substantially out of the above Consolidated Funds or

• Those who perform functions of the 'state' independently of the sources of their pay and allowances,

Conceptually the last definition is appealing. Adoption of this definition would mean that besides employees of the central and state governments, employees of local bodies (Urban Local Bodies, Zilla Parishads, etc.) energy and water utilities, most public sector undertakings, statutory bodies like the Employees State Insurance Corporation, etc., would get covered. This is not a perfect definition admittedly and can be criticized on the ground that it includes employees of industrial undertakings, etc. who are not traditionally associated with the term 'civil service' and whose functions are not those which necessarily have to be performed by the state. However, the counter-argument is that one should include all those who are performing functions, which the 'state' has decided it should perform. This accords with the legal concept

---

[9] Chapters 2 and 3 of 'The State in a Changing World', make these points well.

[10] Mike Stevens, 'Preparing for civil service pay and employment reform: A primer' in David Lindauer & Barbara Nunberg (eds), 'Rehabilitating Government'.

of 'state instrumentality' contained in Article 12 of the Constitution of India[11] as interpreted by the judiciary, though traditional political science and public administration literature did not include employees of industrial undertakings, etc. in the definition of 'civil service'. Starting[12] with a judgement, which only included 'authorities' created by a statute for categorization of an organization as 'state', the judiciary moved[13] to a definition, which said that it did not matter whether a body/agency was created by or under a statute or was a company, etc. What mattered in deciding whether a corporation/agency was an instrumentality of the government is to see whether: .

- the entire share capital of the body is held by the government or
- it receives financial assistance from government or
- it enjoys monopoly status conferred or protected by the state or
- there is deep and pervasive state control of the organization or
- the functions of the body are of public importance and clearly related to government functions.

Hence employees of all those agencies of the government against whom fundamental rights can be enforced, excluding the judiciary and members of the armed forces (who though public servants are clearly not 'civil servants') but including the police and members of the paramilitary forces, are covered in this definition of civil service. This is the sense in which we will use the term 'Indian civil service'[14] in this chapter. Such an inclusive definition is also

---

[11] Article 12 of the Constitution of India reads as follows: 'State', unless the context otherwise requires, includes the Government and Parliament of India, and the government and the Legislature of each of the states, and all local or other authorities within the territory of India or under the control of the Government of India.

[12] *Rajasthan State Electricity Board* v. *Mohan Lal* AIR 1967 SC 1857 affirmed in *Sukhdev* v. *Bhagatram* AIR 1975 SC 1333.

[13] The judgement of the Supreme Court reported in *Ajay Hasia* v. *Khalid Mujib* AIR 1981 SC 487.

[14] The distinction between the 'Indian civil service', with a small 'c' and small 's' and the Indian Civil Service (ICS), the predecessor of the IAS is to be noted.

used by many other scholars like Kim (1996). Based on this definition, the position on the strength of the civil service in India is as given in Table 7.1.

TABLE 7.1
Employment in the organized sector in India (in lakhs)

Year	Central govt	State govts	Quasi govt	Total*
1953	1.50	2.20	0.10	4.10
1961	2.09	3.01	0.77	7.05
1971	2.77	4.15	1.93	10.73
1981	3.20	5.68	4.58	15.48
1988	3.38	6.78	5.95	18.32
1989	3.39	6.89	6.00	18.52
1991	–	–	–	18.97

Source: Das, Civil Service Reform and Structural Adjustment.
Note: * Including local bodies.

What stands out in Table 7.1 is the large absolute number of civil servants. Table 7.2 lists the Group A Services of the central government. Though the authors are aware that this list is neither exhaustive nor current, the list has been quoted here to draw attention to the variety in the composition of the organized civil services.

In addition to these services, are the 'All India Services' (AIS) constituted as per Article 312 of the Constitution of India (see beginning of the chapter). Apart from the Central Group A services and the AIS, there are State Group A services. Then there are Central Secretariat Services Groups B to D, and similar services in most States and Union Territories. In addition both the central and state governments recruit teachers, doctors etc., and the entire set of local body (urban and rural) employees too who constitute part of the 'Indian civil service'. Likewise employees of central and state public sector undertakings and staff of nationalized banks, industrial undertakings, etc., fall within the wider definition.

Given the other institutions which are a part of this study and its overall thrust, we propose to restrict our analysis to the AIS and

TABLE 7.2
Central Civil Services—Group 'A'

	Authorized strength (duty posts as on 1.1.1992)
Ministry of Civil Aviation	
Three Group A Services	361
Ministry of Defence	
5. Defence Aeronautical Quality Assurance Service	258
6. Defence Quality Assurance Service	687
7. Indian Naval Armament Service	90
8. Defence Research & Development Service	5405
9. Indian Ordnance Factory Service	1682
10. Indian Ordnance Factory Health Service	214
11. Indian Defence Estate Service	118
12. Indian Defence Accounts Service	329
13. Military Engineer Services (civilian component)	1760
Ministry of Energy	
14. Central Power Engineering Service	581
Ministry of External Affairs	
15. Indian Foreign Service Group 'A'	733
Ministry of Finance	
16. Indian Revenue Service	2144
21. Indian Economic Service	515
22. Indian Civil Accounts Service	149
Ministry of Health and Family Welfare	
23. Central Health Service (General duty cadre)	4921
Ministry of Home Affairs	
24. Border Security Force	2323
25. Medical Officers Cadre of BSF	311
26. Central Reserve Police Force	1886
27. Medical Officers Cadre of CRPF	335
28. Indo-Tibetan Border Police (GD Executive Officers' cadre)	456
29. Medical Officers of ITBP	137
30. Central Industrial Security Force	698
Department of Company Affairs	
31. Central Company Law Service	

TABLE 7.2 *contd*

TABLE 7.2 *contd*

Ministry of Water Resources
35. Central Water Engineering Service   786

Ministry of Labour
36. Central Labour Service   360

Ministry of Law & Justice
37. Indian Legal Service   118

Department of Mines
38. Geological Survey of India   2476

Department of Railways
39. Indian Railway Service of Engineers   2132
40. Indian Railway Service of Mechanical Engineers   1254
41. Indian Railway Service Signal Engineers   872
42. Indian Railway Service of Electrical Engineers   1074
43. Indian Railway Stores Service   515
44. Indian Railway Traffic Service   1079
45. Indian Railway Personnel Service   448
46. Indian Railway Accounts Service   651
47. Indian Railway Medical Service   2292
48. Indian Railway Protection Force   243

Ministry of Science & Technology
49. Indian Meteorological Service   438
50. Group 'A' Service of Survey of India   358

Department of Surface Transport
51. Central Engineering Service (Roads)   214
52. Border Roads Engineering Service   580

Department of Statistics
53. Indian Statistical Service   528

Ministry of Commerce
54. Indian Supply Service   133
55. Indian Inspection Service   114
56. Central Trade Service   213

Ministry of Urban Development
57. Central Engineering Service   680
58. Central Electrical & Mechanical Engineering Service   194
59. Central Architects Service   171

Source: Website of the Department of Personnel & Training GOI (http://persmin.nic.in/2.1.6.html.

within these the Indian Administrative Service (IAS). The reasons for this are as follows:

• Covering all services as defined and described above would render the exercise unmanageable. The variety of functions performed and the countless categories that get included will make the study that much less useful.

• A number of the Central Civil Services (CCS) are part and parcel of technical or functional departments. For instance though recruited by the Union Public Service Commission through the same Civil Service Examination, officers of the Railway services, the P&T services, the Income Tax and Customs Services, the Indian Audit and Accounts Services are all officers of one department/ agency/organization of the GOI for the rest of their lives and a bulk of them would spend their entire careers in the department/agency/ organization.

• The study is separately focusing on many of these departments (namely the CBDT, CBEC, C & AG, etc.) and hence issues relating to the personnel of these departments would get covered there.

• The other Central Civil Service is the army of support staff and a small cadre of Central Secretariat Service officers who man the secretariat at the lower and middle levels.[15] In terms of numbers and their non-occupation of a significant number of control posts, a study of this cadre though useful otherwise, would not serve our purpose.

• On the other hand the AIS is a compact entity. The strength of serving officers belonging to the three All India Services is in the region of a little over 12,000.[16]

• Besides the small numbers, the AIS has major reasons to commend itself to be a surrogate for the civil services. The AIS

[15] For instance as on 1 July 1999, the three Central Secretariat Services consisted of 25,900 persons of which officers of the rank of under secretary and above were less than 800 of whom most were under/deputy secretaries.

[16] As per the Annual Report 1999–2000 of the Ministry of Personnel Public Grievances and Pensions of the GOI, the authorized cadre strength of the IAS was 5334 of which about 4881 were in position in 1999. Likewise as per the Annual Report 1999–2000 of the Ministry of Home Affairs the cadre strength of the Indian Police Service is 3442. The corresponding figure for the Indian Forest Service is approximately 3300.

officers between themselves man almost all of what can be called critical or 'control' posts of the Government of India *as well as* state and local governments. Though they are allotted to state cadres the Union government continues to retain a major say in their service conditions. They handle a wide variety of tasks and cover the entire gamut of functions performed by the 'Indian State'. For example the C & AG who heads the department to which the officers of the IA&AS belong is an officer of the IAS. Though notionally he ceases to be a member of the IAS when he is appointed to this post, he is perceived as an IAS officer by both the department and outsiders. Likewise, the secretary of the Department of Revenue of the Ministry of Finance under which the two tax boards function is an officer of the IAS. The chairmen of the Securities & Exchange Board of India, the Forward Markets Commission and the Board of Industrial and Financial Reconstruction, and numerous other regulatory bodies are drawn from the ranks of the IAS. The heads of the Central Bureau of Investigation, the Central Reserve Police Force, the Border Security Force and the Central Industrial Security Force, etc. are from the IPS. Table 7.3 below brings out the dominance of the AIS and more particularly the IAS in the central government. Given the focus of this study (the central government) we have not shown the numbers for any state government. But the dominance of the AIS generally, and the IAS specifically, in the context of a state government is even greater.

INITIAL DESIGN

The Constitution is a good starting point for an examination of the initial design. Services under the Union and the state are dealt with in part XIV of the Constitution. In this or any other part of the Constitution, we find no explicit reference to the role and functions of the 'civil service'. Good pointers however to what was envisaged are the chapters dealing with 'executive' functions.[17] There are implicit references to the role and functions of the 'civil service' in the Directive Principles of State Policy (part IV of the Constitution, hereinafter referred to as DPSP). Equally instructive are some of the initial Five Year Plan documents which make interesting reading

[17] Chapter 1 of part V of the Constitution deals with the 'Union Executive' and Chapter 2 of part VI deals with the 'State Executive'.

TABLE 7.3
Distribution of officers serving in the central government by service
(as on 1 November 2000)

Sl. no	Service*	Secy level	Addl Secy level	Jt Secy level	Director level	Dy Secy level	U Secy level	Total	% of total
1	IAS	95	73	275	211	122	11	787	33.59
2	IPS	18	9	86	46	39	0	198	8.45
3	IFt.S	1	0	1	22	7	0	31	1.32
4	IA&AS	2	1	14	7	19	0	43	1.84
5	ICAS	0	0	2	2	8	0	12	0.51
6	IDAS	0	2	10	20	7	0	39	1.66
7	IES	0	0	2	34	12	0	48	2.05
8	IStS	0	0	0	13	7	0	20	0.85
9	IFS	6	0	9	6	3	1	25	1.07
10	ICES	2	6	7	13	15	0	43	1.84
11	ITS	1	4	12	31	30	0	78	3.33
12	IPoS	1	0	8	15	11	0	35	1.49
13	IIS	0	0	0	9	10	2	21	0.90
14	Rly. services	10	1	5	22	11	0	49	2.09
15	CPES	0	0	0	0	3	0	3	0.13
16	CWES	1	0	0	0	0	0	1	0.04
17	CES	0	0	1	3	3	0	7	0.30
18	IDEtS	0	0	1	5	2	0	8	0.34
19	ILS	3	2	0	0	0	0	5	0.21
20	CSS	0	4	35	104	112	529	784	33.46
21	ISS	0	0	1	0	3	0	4	0.17
22	CCLS	0	0	0	2	0	0	2	0.09
23	IInS	0	0	0	1	0	0	1	0.04
24	ITeS	3	0	0	1	1	0	5	0.21
25	IOFS	0	0	4	11	6	0	21	0.90
26	ICoAS	0	0	0	3	6	1	10	0.43
27	CTS	0	0	0	0	6	1	7	0.30
28	Others	14	3	1	16	16	6	56	2.39
	Total	157	105	474	597	459	551	2343	
	Percentage of IAS officers to total	60.51	69.52	58.02	35.34	26.58	2.00		33.59
	Percentage of CSS officers to total	0	3.81	7.38	17.42	24.40	96.01		33.46

Source: Department of Personnel & Training, Government of India.
Note: * See Table A7.1 for the full names of the Services listed out in the table.

and are indicative of the thinking of the founding fathers. In the very First Five Year Plan it was said 'a national plan has to be an expression of a basic unity of purpose in the community. It is this unity, which would constitute the ultimate sanction behind the plan, give it force and evoke the necessary sacrifice and effort on the part of the members. Joined to this unity of purpose must be *an effective power in the hands of the state to be exercised with the necessary persistence and determination in order to ensure the further-ance of accepted ends. Constructive use of this power calls for integrity, efficiency, and responsiveness in administration.'* (emphasis supplied.)[18] The same paragraph goes on to talk about the 'changes in admin-istration appropriate in the context of the new role of the state'. For our purposes therefore what becomes relevant are the following features of the initial design:

• a big role for the state and therefore for the 'civil service' in the economy;

• the 'civil service' is now cast in the role of a 'development agent' from being a purely 'regulatory agent' earlier.

On the social development front, the First Five Year Plan said explicitly what the Constitution only referred to implicitly. As pointed out by Professor Tope (1992)[19] the DPSP outline the ideal of the 'welfare state'. They enjoin the 'state' to frame its laws in order to ensure social and economic justice. The DPSP and the Constitution sought to achieve this objective by:

• a vast increase in the range and details of government regulation of privately owned economic enterprise;

• the direct provision of services by government to individual members of the community—unemployment and retirement ben-efits, family allowances, low cost housing, medical care, etc. and;

• increasing government ownership and operation of industries and business.

However the plan document said pointedly that 'one of the impor-tant methods of bringing about progressive social change is social

[18] Planning Commission, 'The First Five Year Plan Document', ch. I, para. 7.
[19] Tope, *Constitutional Law of India*, pp. 357–8.

legislation'.[20] Though the document refers to the importance of public opinion and enlightened understanding, etc. the basic approach is to *bring about* social change that is considered desirable and in the public interest if necessary by the use of state authority and force. Therefore what becomes relevant for our purpose here are the following:

• legislative action as an important instrument for effecting social change;

• and as a consequence the civil service was to take on the role of 'enforcer' of these pieces of legislation and become an agent of 'social change'.

Though the basic civil service function continued to be securing public order and enforcement of laws, the nature of the laws changed drastically after Independence. From a position of minimal interference in the social order, the situation became one of redefining the social order by proactive use of state power. Therefore the neutral enforcement of rules and maintenance of order—the role traditionally associated with the civil service generally and in India till then (the *passive role* in reducing transaction cost as per our terminology) was clearly pushed to the background and the development catalyst and change agent role (the *activist* role in our classification) became more important. This very far-reaching change in the role of the civil service was not accompanied by any fundamental change in the basic civil service system in terms of recruitment, training, etc., except that the service comprised a greater proportion of Indians than before Independence. The plan document clearly recognized this when it said that 'from the maintenance of law and order and the collection of revenue, the major emphasis now shifts to the development of human and material resources, and the elimination of poverty and want'.[21] The review of the achievements during the First Plan period carried out by the Planning Commission confirmed and reiterated this view when it said that 'in the transformation of the economy in the light of the objectives and priorities accepted, the state will have to play the crucial role' and that 'during the plan period there has been

---

[20] Planning Commission, 'The First Five Year Plan Document', ch. XXXVI, para. 26.

[21] Ibid., ch. V, para. 2.

considerable enlargement of the responsibility of the state in the economic field'.[22]

Continuing in the same vein the Second Five Year Plan identified 'the principal administrative tasks during the Second Five Year Plan' as:

• carrying technical/financial/other aid to small producers as in agriculture/national extension/community projects and village and small industries;

• efficient management of public enterprise in industrial and commercial undertakings, transport services, and river valley schemes;

• strengthening the cooperative sector of the economy especially cooperative, financial, marketing, and other institutions.

Features of the Initial Design

In accordance with the initial scheme discussed above, the AIS was to:

• be all India not only in name but in character,
• have dual control by state and central governments,
• be selected purely on the basis of merit,
• be selected by an apolitical authority formally outside the political/administrative hierarchy of the government, and
• be protected from arbitrary punishment.

There are other additional features of this system which reinforce the above features. These will be addressed in the last part of this section. However, to completely understand the initial design it is necessary to dwell a little on each of the above features.

All India Character

Though it is often said that the IAS was essentially continuing the already entrenched ICS tradition, it was not entirely so. As pointed

[22] Planning Commission, 'Review of the First Five Year Plan', ch. 1, para. 21.

out by V. Subramaniam[23] 'it (the creation of the IAS) was also a clear act of deliberate choice and not just continuing the ICS tradition by inertia though Sardar Patel himself used the argument of continuity. The ICS was reduced to less than 300 and the IP was thin on the ground and both could have been wound up with due compensation or absorbed.' Hence as he points out Patel's decision to *recreate* them as IAS and IPS was deliberately taken. Patel's strong advocacy of this at the conference of the Provincial Premiers in October 1946 deserves repetition to fully understand the thinking behind this.

My own view, as I have told you, is that it is not only advisable but essential if you want to have an efficient Service, to have a Central Administrative Service in which we fix the strength as the provinces would require them and we draw a certain number of officers at the Centre, as we are drawing at present. This will give experience to the personnel at the Centre, leading to efficiency in the administration of the district, which will give them an opportunity of contact with the people. They will thus keep themselves in touch with the situation in the country and their practical experience will be most useful to them. Besides, their coming to the Centre will give them a different experience and wider outlook in larger spheres. A combination of these two experiences should make the Service more efficient. They will also serve as a liaison between the provinces and the Government and introduce a certain amount of freshness and vigour in the administration both of the Centre and the Provinces. Therefore my advice is that we should have a Central Service.[24]

Having got the support of the Premiers, Patel ensured that the Constituent Assembly agreed to this and made this a part of the Constitution. In an oft quoted passage from his famous intervention in the Constituent Assembly discussion on this, Patel said 'you will not have a united India if you have not a good All India Service, which has the independence to speak out its mind, which has a sense of security that you will stand by your word... if you do not adopt this course, then do not follow the present Constitution'. In conclusion he said 'there are many impediments to this Constitution.

---

[23] V. Subramaniam, 'Some Administrative Aspects of Federalism in the Third World.'

[24] Report of the Premiers Conference, October 1946. Note that the term 'Central' in this context refers to what are now called All India Services, serving both Union and states.

But, in spite of that, we have in our collective wisdom come to a decision that we shall have this model wherein the ring of Service will be such that will keep the country intact'.[25] Given the partition of the country and the problem of the various Princely States, the 'all India' character of the Service was a matter of passion with Patel. But this was not an isolated view of just one individual but a central theme of the Constitution. In providing for only an Indian citizenship (no separate state citizenship), not giving states a right to secede, including numerous subjects in the Concurrent List to ensure national uniformity, provisions relating to free trade and commerce within India in part XIII of the Constitution, etc., the founding fathers clearly indicated their national view of matters. The creation of All India Services was a logical concomitant of this. The First Five Year Plan also said that 'in particular it is important to ensure both at the Centre and in the States, that individual economic programmes and proposals are carefully related to the requirements of national planning and the *common national interest should always prevail over sectional and local claims*'[26] (emphasis supplied).

As regards civil services, in addition to the preservation of the unity and integrity of the country, underlying the all India character, was the idea of working into the system 'objectivity' and 'neutrality' into the functioning of the state bureaucracies. Regional and casteist forces were already on the rise and given the enormous power that the civil service was proposed to be vested with, it was necessary that 'control posts' were occupied by persons who were less likely to be amenable to local pressures. The combination of the all India character of the service and the allocation as per Rules of a large number of outsiders to a state cadre were 'designed' to ensure a higher level of objectivity and neutrality in a system which was likely to be subject to enormous regional and local pressure. [We will revert to this question of the Rules regarding 'insiders' and 'outsiders' in a state cadre to show how the vision of the founding fathers has been distorted and narrow, partisan, local considerations which were kept out by design have crept into the system in the eighties and nineties.]

[25] Both quotations are from the Constituent Assembly of India Debates, vol. X, no. 3, 10 October 1949.

[26] Planning Commission, 'The First Five Year Plan Document', ch. V, para. 6.

Dual Control

For historical reasons well brought out in various writings, by the time of Independence, the idea of a strong Centre was more or less well accepted within the Congress party as well as the mainstream political opinion in India.[27] As V. Subramaniam points out 'quite apart from this basic predilection for a strong Centre, all the events of 1947 and 1948, such as the flood of refugees, the hostility of Pakistan and the Kashmir problem, generated a climate of opinion favouring a strong Centre. In terms of administration, the Second World War had already released some centralizing tendencies'.[28] It was in this background that Patel pushed the Provincial Premiers and later the Constituent Assembly towards an AIS that will be recruited centrally (selection by the Union Public Service Commission [UPSC] with coordination by the Ministry of Home Affairs [MHA] and later by the Department of Personnel and Training [DOP&T] of the Government of India) with major disciplinary and service control and cadre management powers vested in the Union government but which will principally serve the provinces (state governments). Despite pressure to provincialize the control of the Service, Patel did not yield ground and ensured that 'dual control' was retained.

Given that a large number of rural development and social development related subjects were in the State and Concurrent Lists of the Seventh Schedule of the Constitution, it was the state executive which was likely to be called upon to implement most of these development schemes as well as enforce the social legislation. Hence there was a high likelihood of the civil service arm of the state executive coming in conflict with the dominant political interests in the state. Given that these interests are likely to have good access to the ruling set up in the states, it was necessary to insulate the state executive from arbitrary action by the ruling politicians of the state. Therefore the dual control system put in place in the Constitution was a necessary element of the constitutional scheme of division of powers and the need for a strong and neutral permanent state machinery. (Indeed we would argue that in Westminster-style constitutions without separation of legislature

[27] V. Subramaniam 'Some Administrative Aspects of Federalism in the Third World', pp. 47–59.
[28] Ibid.

and executive, there is an absolute need for a neutral civil service; in presidential systems where the legislature is independent and ratifies executive appointments, a neutral civil service is perhaps less essential. Evidence from other countries seems to support this hypothesis with most parliamentary democracies having independent civil services.) However, given the need to vest administrative control of the AIS with the state governments for operational reasons there were inherent limitations on the extent of this 'insulation'. [As we will see presently, this administrative control has often been used/abused very creatively by the political executive to completely subvert the constitutional design.]

Merit Based Selection

Article 312 of the Constitution of India empowers Parliament to create more All India Services (AIS) on the fulfilment of certain conditions. The existing Indian Administrative and Police Services were deemed to be Services created by Parliament under this Article. Section 3 of the AIS Act passed by Parliament in 1951 and the Rules made by the government namely the IAS (Recruitment by Competitive Examination) Regulation 1955 and the IAS (Appointment by Promotion) Regulations 1955 and the IAS (Appointment by Selection) Regulations 1965 prescribe the selection process for the IAS. Similar provisions exist for the IPS and the IFtS.

By and large even the worst critics of the higher civil services would concede that the competitive examination and interview based selection process for the AIS is fair and merit based. There are bound to be different views on what constitutes 'merit' and whether the present examination system is an appropriate test of the knowledge and skills required for a career in the civil service.[29] For example Raj Singh says (as quoted in S. K. Das 1998) that most good students in India join engineering and medicine after school and hence the overwhelming proportion of liberal arts graduates in the civil service qualifiers list is indicative of inadequate merit. However the following tables and data from annual reports of the Union Public Service Commission (UPSC) go some way in

[29] Singh, 'Indian Bureaucracy and Development', *Indian Journal of Public Administration* XXXIV, 2 for instance says that the examination system is not a good test of academic merit.

establishing the merit argument. Even the argument advanced by Raj Singh does not hold any more. For example, of the 738 candidates recommended for appointment based on the 1996 civil services examination, 189 were engineers and 37 were doctors. Many were from Indian Institutes of Technology and some were from Indian Institutes of Management.

TABLE 7.4
Success rate for the Higher Civil Services in the examination

Year	No. of applicants	No. actually appeared	No. selected	% selected
1950	3647	2797	240	8.58
1960	10,376	5873	333	5.67
1970	11,710	6730	428	6.36
1980	89,277	56,375	747	1.32
1990	309,300	158,074	940	0.59
1993	215,034	114,684	790	0.68
1996	244,472	120,712	738	0.61

Source: p. 154 of Das (1998) and UPSC *Annual Reports.*

The selection has been from a fairly large pool of candidates.[30] Of the selected candidates 37.61 per cent are from five institutions which are among the highest rated in the country namely Delhi University, IIT Delhi, Jawaharlal Nehru University, Rajasthan University, and IIT Kanpur. Of these candidates 62.6 per cent are first divisioners. On the whole, the first division success ratio for both the higher and pass degrees is much higher than the other divisions. The only cause of concern on the examination front has been the rare instances of alleged leakage of question papers at some centres. Overall, the integrity of the selection process has been built up and preserved over time.

Selection Body

As Tope (1992) points out 'recruitment to the public services in a country which enjoys a parliamentary system of government is

---

[30] However, the increased number of attempts which candidates are allowed inflates the apparent size of the pool, as Das (1998) points out.

TABLE 7.5
First divisioners vis-à-vis others in the Civil Services examination 1996

		Candidates appeared		Candidates qualified	
		First divisioners	Others	First divisioners	Others
Higher degrees	Number	2952	1956	361	137
	Percentage	60.15%	39.85%	72.49%	27.5%
Pass degrees	Number	1462	1728	137	104
	Percentage	45.83%	54.17%	56.85%	43.15%

Source: Annual Report of the UPSC 1997–8 (Appendix VIIA pp. 71).

always a matter of vital importance. Such recruitment must not be made from the point of view of party interest, because such a system will affect efficiency and continuity in public services.' Hence it is necessary to have an independent body charged with the task of recruitment. This is done by the creation of Public Service Commissions (PSC).

Article 315 of the Constitution provides for the establishment of a PSC for the Union and for states. The Constitution in Articles 316 and 317 provides for measures to ensure independence of the PSC from the ruling government by:

• requiring the intervention of the Supreme Court for the removal of a PSC member,

• prohibiting the holding of another office of profit in governments by a retired member of the PSC,

• protecting the service conditions of PSC members from adverse changes after appointment.

Article 320 of the Constitution casts a duty on the UPSC to conduct examinations for appointment to the civil services.

Protection against Arbitrary Punishment

The Constitution, in keeping with Sardar Patel's emphasis on a competent civil service which would 'speak its mind freely', had strong legal protection against arbitrary punishment, enshrined in Article 311 of the Constitution. The scheme and its logic were analogous to the objectives of the 'tenure' system in US universities—to allow the free and frank exercise of authority and expression of opinion, without fear of political reprisal.

Article 311 is sometimes viewed as a barrier to discipline and efficiency in the public service. This view is not supported by a reading of the article itself, which merely prescribes *procedural* safeguards. It does not in any way restrict the government from imposing any punishment on any kind of civil servant. It merely requires that the civil servant be informed of the charges against him and be given an opportunity to defend himself. It also provides that no severe punishment (dismissal, removal, demotion) can be imposed by an authority subordinate to the authority which appointed him. These are simple and unobjectionable rules of natural justice. In respect of the All India Services—whose members are appointed by the president of India, it has the practical effect that major punishments can only be imposed by the central government, giving officers a protection against *mala fide* or arbitrary actions by state governments. However, the scope of the protection has been greatly expanded by judicial interpretation, probably going for beyond what the constitution-framers had in mind.

Other Elements

There are other elements like common general training for all the cadres of the IAS in a common training centre, the age of recruitment and number of attempts permitted in the examination, and an attractive pay scale which went into the making of the IAS. As per the original thinking, in line with the euphoric nation-building mood of the founding fathers, and the expectations of the government from civil servants, the upper age limit was kept low so that young people infused with a sense of idealism and public service would constitute the bulk of the service. [This requirement has since been modified considerably, as described later in this chapter.]

Special Considerations

Two other features of the initial design deserve mention here.

Promotion from State Cadres

The initial design envisaged promotion of officers from the 'State Civil Service' (the rough generalist equivalent of the IAS at the state level) and officers of other state services into the IAS (and likewise of state police officers into the IPS). While intended to give states a means of 'representation' in the service, it implicitly also recognized the value of practical experience and the fact that 'merit' can be found from more than one source. This was intended for the best among the state civil servants.

Reservations

One exception was made to the general rule of meritocracy and uncompromising entry standards. This was to provide for reservation of seats in the IAS for candidates belonging to the Scheduled Castes and Scheduled Tribes on affirmative action grounds.

The Initial Design—An Assessment

Figure 7.1 is a pictogram depicting the key features of the initial design of the IAS.

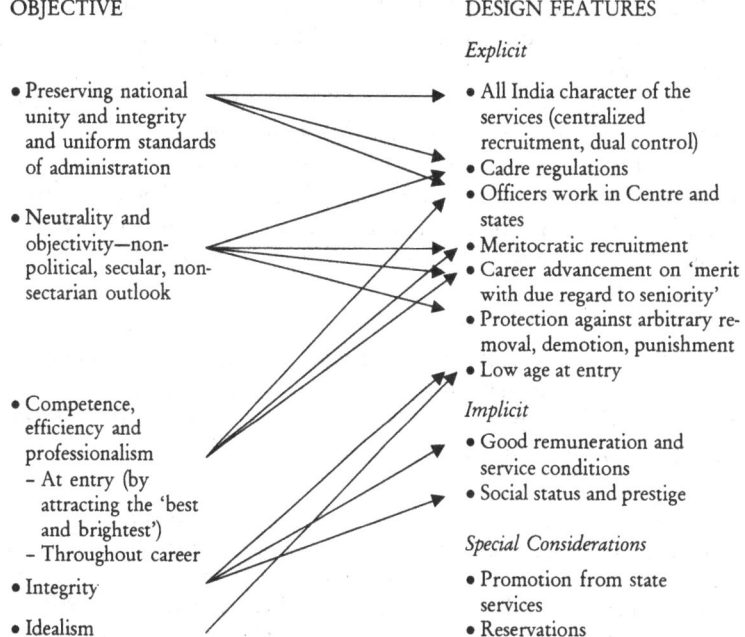

OBJECTIVE

- Preserving national unity and integrity and uniform standards of administration

- Neutrality and objectivity—non-political, secular, non-sectarian outlook

- Competence, efficiency and professionalism
  - At entry (by attracting the 'best and brightest')
  - Throughout career
- Integrity
- Idealism

DESIGN FEATURES

Explicit

- All India character of the services (centralized recruitment, dual control)
- Cadre regulations
- Officers work in Centre and states
- Meritocratic recruitment
- Career advancement on 'merit with due regard to seniority'
- Protection against arbitrary removal, demotion, punishment
- Low age at entry

Implicit

- Good remuneration and service conditions
- Social status and prestige

Special Considerations

- Promotion from state services
- Reservations

FIGURE 7.1: The Initial design of the All India Services in the Indian Constitution

Most of the features of the design clearly tend to support a civil service that is effective in the neutral, honest, uniform, and predictable enforcement of the law (our first and foremost criterion), and in the preservation of a democratic polity. The third criterion of effectiveness—faithful implementation of the legitimate political will of the elected executive—is not explicitly addressed; indeed it appears this was not seen by the founding fathers to be a problem given the clear and unequivocal primacy of the political executive over the civil service. The provisions on induction of state civil servants and reservation had different design objectives, namely giving states and the weaker sections respectively a sense of 'representation' in the nation's premier service.

Explicit Changes to the Design

Increased Promotion from State Services

The proportion of state service officers promoted to the AIS used to be 25 per cent of the cadre strength for each state.[31] This was increased to 33.33 per cent (with a consequential decrease in the direct recruitment quota) in 1977. Following representations by the state service officers, in January 1998, amendments were issued to the IAS (Cadre Rules) 1954 and IAS (Fixation of Cadre Strength Regulations) 1955 to include 'state deputation reserve' and 'training reserve' towards the computation of the promotion quota. The result of the amendment was transfer of a little over 250 posts from the direct recruitment quota to promotion quota in the IAS and similar results for the other two All India services.

Increase in Reservations

Since the mid-90s, reservations in the selection process have increased from 22 per cent (for SC/ST only) to about 50 per cent (for SC, ST, and BC), as a consequence of the implementation of the Mandal Commission recommendations.

---

[31] The precise rules and mechanisms for promotion into the IAS were evolved in the 50s and 60s. Under these rules all the inducted officers are from within the state (insiders), and all are allotted to their state of origin. The process is much more discretionary than the direct recruitment process: the selection panel has one UPSC member as Chairman, two nominees of the GOI, and five nominees of the state government.

Upper Age Limit for the Civil Service Examination

In recent times there have been a lot of flip-flops on the age of entry. Regular tinkering with this and related provisions of the civil service recruitment process, though on the rise, reached a crescendo during the eighties and nineties. The age limit was increased initially as a one time measure and subsequently repeated and the higher limit has now become the regular limit.[32] Table 7.6 captures the changes in both these elements over time.

Currently, an applicant from the general category is allowed four attempts, and a candidate from the reserved categories, as many as twelve attempts. The large number of attempts that the candidates are allowed inflates the apparent size of the pool of applicants for the civil service.[33]

THE CURRENT STATE

This section attempts a short analysis of the current level of effectiveness of the civil service against the three criteria specified earlier. Three case studies of civil service effectiveness are used to illustrate the main point that is being made in this section.

Criterion I: Effectiveness in Promoting Economic Growth and Reducing Transaction Costs

In marked contrast to the initial design, the IAS today is perceived as having a variety of shortcomings, in so far as our first criterion of institutional effectiveness is concerned, that is, promoting economic growth by reducing transaction costs.[34]

Diminished Independence and Increased Political Interference

There is a widespread perception within and without the IAS, that the average IAS officer's ability to enforce the laws, rule and

---

[32] As per the Annual Report 1999–2000 of the Ministry of Personnel, Public Grievances and Pensions GOI, with effect from the CS examination 1999, the age limit has been raised to 30 years (p. 7).

[33] Das, *Public Office, Private Interest*, p. 97.

[34] The shortcomings pointed out in this section are derived from publicly available information, the authors' own knowledge as members of the IAS, newspaper reports, the authors' structured conversations with other civil servants, and people who interact with civil servants.

TABLE 7.6

Changes in the prescribed age limit and number of attempts permitted in the CS examination over time

Year	Age (in years)	No. of attempts
1947	21–6	No restriction on number of attempts
1948	21–5	No restriction on number of attempts
1949 & 1950	21–4 (except for the IRTS for which 21–5 continued)	No restriction on number of attempts
1951–4	20/21–4 (except for IPS for which it was 20–4)	No restriction on number of attempts
1955–60	20/21–4 (IRTS also follows this age limit now)	No restriction on number of attempts
1961–71	20/21–4	No. of attempts restricted to two for each category
1972–8	20/21–6 (upper age limit raised based on ARC recommendations)	No. of attempts restricted to two for each category
1979–86	21–8 (upper age limit increased)	No. of attempts increased to three
1987–9	21–6	Three attempts continued
1990	21–31 (upper age limit increased)	No. of attempts increased to four
1991	21–8	Four attempts continued
1992	21–33	No. of attempts increased to five
1993–4	21–8	No. of attempts restricted to four again
1995–8	21–8	No. of attempts restricted to four for general category and seven for OBC candidates
1999	21–30	–do–
2000	21–30 (upper age limit of 28 for CISF)	–do–

Source: Department of Personnel and Administrative Reforms, Government of India.

procedures, and to tender policy advice without fear or favour has declined dramatically, to the point where a large number of officers are perceived to routinely act at the behest of political or other interests in the performance of their routine (non-policy) work. The general view is that this decline began in the 70s and has accelerated since. Today, it is quite common for individual executive decisions, expected to be made fairly according to standard procedures—for example, awarding procurement contracts, enforcement of regulations, transfers of personnel, determinations of land tenure issues, etc.,—to be made or seen to be made on the basis of political interference.

It is necessary to be clear about what is meant in this chapter by 'political interference'. The term is used to denote acts of politicians—whether formally part of the executive or not—intended to compel a civil servant, by means of threats or blandishments or both, to follow the course desired by them on decisions which *ought to be taken by the civil servant impartially under government policy*. It does *not* refer to the legitimate role of the political executive (ministers and politically-appointed heads of agencies) in exercising powers duly vested in them—a role which may indeed lead them to legitimately overrule advice tendered by civil servants. The distinction is quite easy to observe in practice; political interference is almost always oral, with the civil servant usually pretending that he took the decision of his own volition.

Political interference is currently perceived to occur at all levels: a local MLA may interfere with a petty official in the issue of a land title document, a state minister may interfere with a district collector in a personnel decision, a central minister may interfere in the award of a contract or in the enforcement of a penal provision of the law, etc. Political interference is also felt to be politically and geographically neutral—members of all political parties are perceived to indulge in it, though there may be variations in degree. Often political interference takes the form of telling a civil servant not to tender advice in the manner the civil servant intended to tender it.

Perception of Increasing Corruption

The IAS, which once had a reputation—like the ICS—for high and near-universal integrity, is today perceived to include a significant number of 'corrupt' officers. Definitions of what is corrupt may vary from observer to observer, but in general it is used in the sense that an officer misuses his official position to secure for himself a pecuniary advantage. The most obvious form of corruption is, of course, bribery.

Ineffectiveness in Law Enforcement

IAS officers were, for a long time, seen to be relatively firm and impartial enforcers of the law of the land, on matters ranging from public order and protection of life and liberty, to enforcing economic regulations. Today, they are often seen as weak and unable to enforce the law against the powerful and the well-connected. This is of course closely related to both political interference and corruption.

Provincialization

There is a feeling that many IAS officers are 'all-India' in name only, as the proportion of officers who genuinely alternate between state and central governments has declined. This reduces the capacity of the civil service (in terms of knowledge and dissemination of good practices) as well as its independence from petty, local considerations.

Decreased Insulation from Communal Considerations

A significant minority of IAS officers are perceived to be 'champions' of their communities (religious or caste-based) in terms of acting as 'protectors' of their group's interests. The political executive has often appeared to sanctify this tendency by seeking a communal 'balance' in key civil service appointments.

These tendencies have clearly affected the performance of the civil service as an institution. Many of the oft-lamented failures of the Indian state in translating vision into action can be laid at the door of the civil service. Enforcing civil rights, preventing communal violence, curbing illegal urban constructions, protecting common property resources, stopping air and water pollution, collecting taxes and other government dues, making sure funds meant for the poor reach them: every one of these is an instance where India has among the most enlightened government policies in the developing world, but a poor record of implementation. Much attention in recent years has focused on changing policy in India as a means of accelerating growth, reducing poverty, and improving the quality of life. *Arguably, there is more 'bang for the buck' in simply implementing existing policy.* The diminished, and diminishing, performance of the civil service is therefore a matter of much more than academic interest.

Criterion II: Preserving the Constitutional Order

The civil service's performance on this criterion must clearly rank higher than on institutional economics criterion. The most obvious proof of this is an indirect one: the fact that India has remained a democracy for more than fifty years and has seen innumerable peaceful transfers of power at both central and state level. While the judiciary has played a key role in preserving Indian democracy, for which it deserves and receives praise, the part played by the civil service is less recognized but arguably as, if not more, important.

Conduct of Elections

Both the polling process and the maintenance of law and order are supervised by the IAS (the latter function in collaboration with the IPS). India's election officials are, in their regular jobs, direct subordinates of the political executive, yet in state after state, incumbency is seen as a disadvantage and incumbent governments lose far more often than they win.

Preserving Continuity, Public Order and/or National Unity at Times of Political Crisis/Internal Strife

To quote one example, the provision for 'President's Rule' under Article 356 , would be practically unenforceable without the AIS (both the IAS and IPS). The abuse of the provision for partisan ends has been justly criticized, but there have admittedly been many situations where the provision prevented or cured genuine constitutional crises in states (in situations of political instability) or prevented the outbreak of civil war (in situations of insurgency). India at the state level has seen political chicanery of the worst Third World variety and yet survived as a democracy partly because President's Rule provides a constitutional substitute for what in other polities of the size of Indian states (for example, Pakistan, Philippines) takes the form of military intervention. The imposition of presidential rule in an Indian state is not accompanied by the movement of tanks in the streets or of people storming the legislature, and the machinery of government functions virtually uninterrupted. The transition problems witnessed, for example, in Mexico after the election of Vicente Fox or in Yugoslavia after the election of Kostunica, are not seen in India. On a different note, it is difficult to see how the Punjab or North East insurgencies could have been handled and brought to successful conclusions without the AIS.

Criterion III: Faithfully Translating the Will of the Political Executive into Action

The perceptions of the civil service's performance on this front are more difficult to judge. Utterances of Indian politicians, especially in recent years, give the impression that the civil service's inability to deliver is a big problem. Clearly, to the extent the civil service fails to perform its law enforcement and policy implementation roles with impartiality, honesty, effectiveness, and efficiency (which as we have noted earlier are widespread problems currently) there is obviously truth in the perception. However what is more difficult to discern is the extent to which the failure is purely a civil service problem versus how far it is the joint responsibility of the political executive. The civil service often lies at the intersection between the political executive's publicly proclaimed lofty intentions and privately expressed specific instructions (usually less lofty). Since civil servants, individually or collectively, do not have the right of reply, it is often difficult to judge.

On the one hand, the civil service clearly was successful (arguably too much so, from a market economist's point of view) in imposing a tight system of controls on the economy in response to the political commitment to the socialistic pattern of society. Indeed the perceived ubiquity and tightness of the licence-permit raj is a testimony to its 'effectiveness' under this criterion. In the 60s and 70s, the relative lack of corruption (compared to most other controlled economies and LDCs) and high capacity of IAS officers to grasp and apply the plethora of rules, and their relative independence from political control, actually made the controls more 'effective' than in those countries where the formal system could more easily be bypassed with bribes or political contacts. In the 60s and 70s, if the civil service was guilty it was on the charge of implementing a flawed policy too well. By that token, the civil service should have been able to respond equally zealously in reversing the controls when the political mandate reversed itself in the 90s. However, by the 80s, other factors affecting the service (discussed elsewhere in this chapter) had led to a more corrupt implementation of the control regime. Once corruption among higher civil servants became more common, the civil service started to acquire a vested interest in the licence-permit raj. This may account for the fact that the service is perceived to have been less effective in rolling back controls in response to the new political commitment to a liberalized regime. Even here, it is difficult to apportion blame between the IAS and the political executive, since, in many instances, politicians have been reluctant to go beyond general statements of intent and surrender controls over the economy.

There is however a lot of evidence to show that where the political executive has a *clear and genuinely-held policy view and expresses it consistently*, the civil service does usually deliver:

Case Study 1
The noon meal programme

In the early 80s, the then Tamil Nadu Chief Minister, M. G. Ramachandran, decided—completely independent of civil service advice—to implement a scheme to provide free hot, cooked, noon meals in every school in the state. Senior civil servants expressed serious reservations on both fiscal and logistical grounds. They were over-ruled and the scheme went forward. The same set of civil servants then proceeded to not only find ways to fund the scheme but to design an implementation system that has stood the test of time. Notwithstanding leakages here and there, even today, a surprise visitor to any government school anywhere in Tamil Nadu (even in the remotest hill villages) can see a hot meal served to every child.

Case Study 2
Refugee relief

India has on several occasions faced major refugee influxes—from Tibet in the late fifties, from East Pakistan in 1971, and from Sri Lanka in the 80s. On each occasion, there was clear political will to help the refugees. The same civil service which is usually accused (rightly) of lethargy and lack of initiative managed a response which was quick and effective.

Each of these situations was handled without any significant contribution from the 'international community' or the UNHCR by a civil service running on a shoe string budget.

Case Study 3
Kumbh Mela

The scale of the logistical arrangements required for the January 2000 Kumbh Mela dwarf almost any other civilian event in the world. The mela takes place in Uttar Pradesh. The political executive is committed to making the event a success. The arrangements, for which IAS and IPS officers are responsible (again on a shoe string budget), are generally acknowledged to be very thorough and well made.

So far, this chapter has dwelt on the initial design of the civil service and its current state. It has assessed the performance of the civil service to be generally poor on the first criterion, good on the second, and fair on the third. Nevertheless it is clear that on the whole, it has not met the expectations placed on it in the initial design. The next step is to assess why the higher civil services—once considered a paragon of integrity and competence, and among the best in the world—have moved so far from the initial design. The analysis of the causes of the declining performance of the service will focus on two aspects:

• Changes in the way the design was implemented;

• Socio-political changes which affected the behaviour of civil servants.

IV. ANALYSIS OF CAUSES OF DECLINING PERFORMANCE

Changes in Implementation

The Power to Punish Arbitrarily

As was pointed out earlier, the initial design put a lot of value on the concept of civil service independence and impartiality and Article 311 was expected to act as a safeguard against arbitrary punishment.

The biggest change that has occurred in the implementation of the All India Service scheme, is the acquisition by governments (at both central and state levels) of the power to demote (and promote) IAS officers at will, without breaching the letter of the law. This has occurred through a series of subtle and gradual changes to the original *spirit* (but not letter) of the All India Services. The direct medium through which this is exercised is the government's unfettered power to *transfer* a civil servant from one post to another, but to understand how this operates as promotion/demotion, one has to grasp the 'micro-structure' of the system, and how it came about.

The first thirty years after Independence saw an almost continuous expansion in the role of the state. As explained earlier in this chapter, this led to an expansion in the size of the service, roughly in proportion to the growth of the government's functions. The IAS branched out from its traditional land-and-public-order-focus into development administration, running public sector industries, creating new agencies and departments. The trend towards nationalization at state and central levels provided IAS officers with ever-expanding vistas.

The original scheme had envisaged that key posts in each state would be 'encadred', that is, reserved for members of the All India Services. It also provided for mechanisms to ensure that only posts which truly merited the services of an AIS officer were encadred; the central government needed to approve the encadrement of new posts. The rules also provided that the number of promotees (from the state civil services) who could be appointed into the cadre would be proportionate to the size of the cadre—which in turn depended on the number of cadre posts.

As the IAS' role expanded, so did the number of cadre posts. A large proportion of the expansion was probably inevitable in the light of the new role of the state. The hierarchical pyramid expanded at most levels, though there could only be one chief secretary or cabinet secretary. This produced expanding opportunities for state civil servants to enter the service. Once within the service, they could of course move laterally to any position in a given grade. Until the nineties, the triennial 'cadre review' almost always ended in a cadre expansion. Officers already in the service (direct recruits very much included) were keen on creating new senior posts, to improve their promotion opportunities. State civil servants were also keen on the expansion—which increased their chances of entering the IAS—and often lobbied the state political executive. The state political executive also liked the expansion because it widened the pool of promotee officers available to man key cadre posts; promotees were felt to be more 'in tune' with the local milieu (at best) or closely allied to the ruling party (at worst). IAS officers were also in charge of the central ministry (currently DOPT, earlier MHA) in charge of approving cadre expansions. The central political executive had nothing to lose. Thus the cadre expansion routine continued over an extended period as Table 7.7 below shows.

TABLE 7.7
Total authorized strength of the Indian Administrative Service

Date	Total authorized strength
1.1.1951	1232
1.1.1961	1862
1.1.1971	3203
1.1.1981	4599
1.1.1991	5334
1.1.2000	5159

Source: Department of Personnel and Administrative Reforms, GOI.

Inevitably, some posts diminished in importance as social and economic conditions changed—but they were rarely de-cadred.[35] These posts continued to be classified as cadre posts, since a zero-base review was not undertaken. Soon, there were multiple posts even at the very senior levels, for example, posts equivalent to chief secretary in pay (but not in job content). Senior officers liked this—more of them could get the pay scale.

The expansion of the service's role into 'autonomous' corporations, not part of the government-proper and not subject to the full rigours of the government's financial rules, had another effect. Officers posted to these corporations often had perquisites not available to their colleagues in the 'main line'—cars, houses, trips abroad on corporate business, ability to stay in expensive hotels instead of dowdy government guest houses. Some of these corporations also had more interesting job content, since there was often a higher degree of autonomy.

[35] In several states, to quote an example, the post of (Land) 'Settlement Officer' is still encadred, decades after the overwhelming majority of land tenure/land revenue settlement work was completed.

The result was that the basic assumptions underlying the cadre rules, namely:

• all posts in a given grade are roughly of equal importance and job content

• all officers in a given grade get the same take-home pay and perquisites were no longer valid. The cadre now consisted of posts *within* each grade which differed widely in importance, job content, and often perquisites[36] as well. State governments also found they could *temporarily upgrade/downgrade* a particular post, and then post a very-differently ranked officer to it.

The stage was now set for transfer to be used as a punishment, and it was just a question of time before politicans discovered (with a lot of help from IAS officers!) that they could, by ordering a simple transfer, effectively execute either demotions or promotions. Once discovered, the instrument spread with rapidity and its use became more frequent.

Case Study 4
From Chief Secretary of a state to Secretary of a local development board

In one celebrated case in 1990, the Chief Secretary of Karnataka, M. Shankaranarayanan, after differences of opinion with the then Chief Minister, was transferred overnight as Secretary Hyderabad Karnataka Development Board in Gulbarga—that post was declared equivalent to the post of Chief Secretary. Shankaranarayanan approached the judiciary for redress but the Central Administrative Tribunal declined to intervene. The Shankaranarayanan case was a landmark in the evolution of the IAS: the signal was clear—a Chief Secretary, no less, could be thrown out without even a pretence of fairness. Matters were not helped by the fact that he was known to be an honest and upright man.

From then on, if an IAS officer wanted to be true to his Conduct Rules by 'always acting according to his own best judgement except

---

[36] In a state that the authors are familiar with, where there are explicit rules prohibiting allotment of government accommodation to officers who have their own houses, most corporations do not have similar prohibitions. The result is clearly an additional income of anywhere between Rs 25,000 to Rs 40,000 per month as rental income (assuming that the house is in a major city). Likewise there are corporations which provide free electricity (an additional income of approximately Rs 2000 per month), etc.

when acting under the written directions of a superior,' he had also to be prepared for a degree of martyrdom. The choice was clear—compromise with principles and succeed, or stay upright and be prepared to stay on the fringes.

The sheer sweep of the IAS' ambit makes penal transfer a very potent threat. It is not difficult to see why. An inconvenient chief engineer of the PWD cannot, for instance, be posted elsewhere very easily. The only resort would be to find him a post of 'Special Chief Engineer,' but that is not too much of a fall. But an IAS officer can be moved from, say, finance secretary managing a $4 billion budget to, say, managing director of the State Sports Corporation with a budget of $200,000, 'in the public interest', with a simple executive order temporarily regrading the latter post as being of equivalent rank *Thus the very diversity and variety of the IAS career has now become its Achilles' heel* . In this respect the IAS is more susceptible to the transfer weapon than the more specialized services including the IPS.

After a few penal transfers, many officers begin to 'adapt' to the situation. Some do what they are told. Others begin to look for protectors. Some form alliances with caste groups or political groups. A penal transfer could then be portrayed as a measure against a particular ethnic group or faction which would then intervene to stop the transfer. This would of course entail future favours to be done in return. Yet others begin to ingratiate themselves with business interests who could likewise intervene on their behalf. Another alternative is to become corrupt, so that comfort of financial gains would make up for the absence of a meaningful career path.

It needs to be emphasized that in spite of all these trends, a great many officers continue to serve with honesty and dedication, oblivious to the career tribulations visited upon them. But their's is a lonely furrow to plough and their motivation has to come from within, and one cannot run a civil service on the premise that every civil servant is an altruist.

Short Average Tenure in a Post

Apart from the deliberate use of transfer as a punishment, the IAS is characterized (particularly in the states) by very short tenures in most assignments (see Table 7.8). Many a time this is not necessarily as punishment and merely reflects poor personnel management. This has taken a heavy toll on efficiency and effectiveness. Officers are often transferred every few months, before they settle into a job. This means that most decisions are taken by what the lower rungs of the bureaucracy want to do—further reducing both honesty and efficiency.

TABLE 7.8
IAS movements (1977–96)

IAS as of 1 January	Number	Length of time in post (% of IAS)			
		Less than 1 year	1–2 years	2–3 years	More than 3 years
1978	3084	58	26	10	6
1979	3236	55	30	10	5
1981	3373	60	22	11	7
1982	3539	52	31	9	8
1983	3734	51	29	13	7
1984	3797	56	26	12	7
1985	3910	51	31	11	7
1986	3970	58	25	12	6
1991	4497	58	25	10	6
1992	3951	56	27	11	6
1993	3991	49	31	13	8
1996	4621	48	28	13	11

Source: Das (1998), p. 163.

The 'Empanelment' Problem

Theoretically, All India Service officers are eligible to serve in the central government. However, the central government has for many years operated an 'empanelment' system as a quality control measure. Under this system, only those officers who have superior career records are put on a 'panel' of names. Only persons on the panel are selected for central government posts. Panels are drawn up separately for deputy secretary, joint secretary, additional secretary, and secretary. An officer not empanelled as joint secretary normally spends the rest of his career entirely in the state, and is usually not empanelled later for additional secretary or secretary.

To an extent, the empanelment system does seem to have the intended effect. The quality of officers in the Government of India is commonly felt to be better than the average in the state governments. However, the empanelment process suffers from several serious defects. First and foremost, the process is completely non-transparent. It is made without either interviewing the candidates or testing them formally. Candidates are officially never informed about their empanelment or otherwise. Obviously therefore candidates not empanelled are not given any reasons and have no right of appeal. Secondly, decisions are made on the basis of officers' written 'Annual Confidential Reports' which are (for senior officers) often written by politicians. This can occasionally produce bizarre results.

Case Study 5
Convicted minister's remarks stop empanelment

In one recent case, a Secretary to Government in a state refused to countenance a corrupt transaction, despite a specific request from his Minister. Instead of writing a lukewarm minute, he wrote a powerfully worded denunciation of the transaction as being *ultra vires* the powers of the executive. He was summarily transferred to a non-descript corporation previously headed by a very junior officer (that post being duly temporarily upgraded). The Minister went through with the transaction anyway and wrote adverse remarks in the officer's Confidential Report to the effect that the officer was not 'responsive to public grievances', which were endorsed by the Chief Minister. These adverse remarks meant the officer, when his file was considered for empanelment, did not have a good record and was not empanelled. In the meanwhile, not only was the transaction declared illegal by a court of law, but the Minister was convicted of corruption, with the officer being a prosecution witness. Yet, despite an outstanding track record of both competence and honesty, he remains debarred from serving the central government.

Thirdly, the process implies that there are 'good' and 'poor' officers; *per se* there is nothing wrong with that if the gradation is done fairly. But it then, by implication, suggests that the 'poor' officers, not considered good enough for the central government, are good enough to continue—and get promotions—in the states. This contradicts the design principle of uniformity in administrative quality.

Politicization of Recruitment by Promotion and Selection

The formal design of the IAS, as pointed out earlier, did envisage promotion from the state services into the IAS, but the provisions were designed to bring in the best officers of the state government. Indeed, the value of this design feature has been established by the number of outstanding IAS officers from the Promotion and Selection categories who have been second to none. However, in practice, the large number of state government representatives in the selection panel has often led to selections being strongly influenced by the state political executive. This has often led to a reduction in the overall calibre of the service and to greater 'provincialization'. The following case study is an example (albeit an extreme one) of the potential negative consequences.

Case Study 6
Politically appointed district magistrate triggers communal violence

A state government officer from a caste which had strong influence over the political executive of a state, and was related to influential state politicians, who did not belong to the state civil service, had little administrative experience in districts and did not have a particularly impressive record, was inducted into the IAS through the 'selection' route. Soon after, using his proximity to the Chief Minister, he secured a posting as District Magistrate of a district where his family and his caste generally had major political interests and where it was in contention with the Scheduled Castes on a variety of social and economic issues. During his tenure, a relatively minor clash between members of his own caste and the Scheduled Castes in a village led to an unduly harsh police response against the latter and Scheduled Castes were subjected to severe beatings and police brutality. Allegations were made (which the authors cannot confirm or deny) that the District Magistrate was present and supervised the police brutality. The whole district and neighbouring districts erupted in waves of communal violence between the two communities which took months to bring under control.

When the promotion/selection system is misused to make politicized appointments, the result is a combination of a US style 'spoils system' with the security of tenure of the mandarin system—a disastrous mix.

Pay Compression
The Indian Civil Service was amongst the best-remunerated in the world. A junior ICS officer in the 30s could buy a car with two months' salary.[37]

[37] Today it takes about 40 months of a junior IAS officer's salary.

The IAS started off with far lower pay scales, but the pay was still good. IAS and Class I Service pay scales enjoyed a high differential over other ranks in the civil service. The 'socialistic pattern of society' meant that there was a deliberate push towards a reduction of differentials. The following table shows the compression ratio between the maximum salary (pre- and post-tax) and minimum salary and the compression ratios.

TABLE 7.9
Compression Ratio (1948–96)

	1948	1949	1960	1965	1970	1973	1986	1996
Maximum salary (pre-tax)	3000	3000	3000	3500	3500	3500	8000	16,580
Maximum salary (post-tax)	2263	2263	2281	2422	2399	2331	5896	12,615
Minimum salary (falls below taxable limit and is thus tax free)	55	65	80	103	141	196	750	2200
Pre-tax compression ratio	54.5	46.2	37.5	34.0	24.8	17.9	10.7	8.0
Post-tax compression ratio	41.0	34.8	28.5	23.5	17.0	11.9	7.9	5.7

Source: Report of the Fifth Pay Commission, vol. I (1997) as quoted in S. K. Das 2001.

Note: Salaries in rupees per month, not adjusted for inflation.

The conscious 'compression' was accompanied, in the 70s and 80s, by a less deliberate but more substantial effect: the use of 'differential DA neutralization'. 'Dearness allowance' (DA) is the periodic increase in salaries granted to compensate for inflation between the decennial pay commissions. For many years between the 60s and the mid-90s, the government decided to economize on dearness allowance by a scheme of 'differential neutralization'—low paid employees were given 100 per cent neutralization (that is, indexation), but this was tapered off to 25 per cent for the highest paid IAS and central service officers.

Inflation rates were high throughout this period and at many junctures (towards the end of the decade leading up to the next Pay

Commission) the amount of DA exceeded basic pay. The differential DA neutralization led to a much greater compression of total numeration than pay commissions had ever intended. When the effects of the progressive income tax were also factored in, there was frequently a situation where IAS officers saw major declines in the real value of their pay, and where promotions could be financially worthless.

The pay compression had several negative effects on the higher civil services. Firstly, it demoralized senior civil servants who found themselves being paid only slightly more than others with far lower responsibilities. Secondly, the 'elitism' which led the Class I direct recruitment officer to see himself as being above the fray (in terms of corruption) was eroded and corruption began to seem somehow less reprehensible.

Socio-Political Trends

In the initial years of the pay compression (the 70s), the effect on morale and on the integrity of the services was limited by two factors operating in the opposite direction. Firstly, socialism was both the prevailing political creed and the intellectual mainstream. (One needs to point out that, for instance, many economists and intellectuals currently spearheading market reforms were at one time advocates of the socialistic pattern.) Private sector pay was regulated. Yes, civil service pay was getting compressed, but there was no great social pressure to consume more or acquire new gadgets. Secondly, the sheer regulatory power of the services was at its zenith. In a controlled economy, the glamour of an (honest) civil service career was at its highest—after all one could sit atop the commanding heights.

The gradual opening up of the Indian economy in the 80s and the overt consumerism that came with it, upset·this balance. Colour TVs, then VCRs, then cable television and so on become *de rigueur* for the urban middle class—but the civil servant suddenly found he could not keep up with the Joneses. At the same time, deregulation under the new economic approach took away the social meaning that had earlier been attributed to regulatory jobs. It is easy to forget that in the mid-70s, the average IAS officer deciding on industrial licensing applications did not see himself as an obstacle to economic progress—on the contrary he was ensuring that the nation's scarce capital was not frittered away on, say, the 6th national brand of toothpaste so that it would be available for, say, a petrochemical plant. And this was not self-delusion—that is what the nation's best and brightest economists of the day wanted him to do. The post-85, and especially post-90, era left officers feeling (perhaps rightly) they were as socially useful as dogs in the manger. If so, then surely they were now foolish, and economically irrational, not to at least make money?

The liberalization policy had a major effect on private sector pay scales, which soon shot through the roof. The IAS officer's social comparators—fellow graduates of, say, IITs or IIMs—suddenly leapt ahead in terms of pay and perquisites. The pride in austerity which marked the period till the early 90s gave way to an open celebration of material success and conspicuous consumption. The gradual increase in the level of venality in the service, when combined with the new view that the bureaucracy was the biggest impediment on the path to India's economic rejuvenation, meant that the services and particularly the IAS became, in the 90s, a favourite target of attack. The political executive, the lower bureaucracy, the press, academics—all of them trained their guns on the IAS. The consequent fall in the image of the service brought about a self-fulfilling prophecy. Civil servants lost the sheen of the social respectability and prestige that had in the past made up for indifferent financial reward. At parties, industrialists and private executives began to exhibit open condescension to civil servants and take every opportunity to lambast the bureaucracy in their presence. The civil servant's élan could not long survive this erosion and he soon gave up the pretence of defending the bureaucracy. The increased public vilification combined with rising private sector pay also began to reduce the attractiveness of the civil services to many bright young graduates. It was not long before a significant number of Class I officers—usually sitting between a corrupt lower bureaucracy and a corrupt political executive—began to 'rationalize' the need to be corrupt. The 'contentment' that Sardar Patel saw as an essential foundation stone of the service, was gone.

An honest IAS officer without wealth of his own, or a well employed or rich spouse, could no longer afford to sustain an upper middle class standard of living, commensurate with his peers at similar levels in other walks of life.

High pay, contentment, social prestige, meaningful job content, a sense of social purpose, a presumption of honesty—every one of these was, by the mid-90s, diminished. The service faced a combination of pay compression, rising private pay scales, diminished social meaning and social relevance, conspicuous consumption, along with the clear signal that corruption would be tolerated. In short, every bulwark that had kept the IAS away from the miasma of petty bureaucratic corruption below and grand political corruption above, had been demolished. Small wonder that many officers began to emulate either their bureaucratic subordinates or political masters, or even both at the same time.

V. THE INCENTIVE STRUCTURE

To understand the current state of the IAS, it is necessary to be aware of the incentives affecting its members. 'Incentives' can be defined as the consequences—positive or negative—which follow, or are expected to follow certain behaviours. Incentives are 'aligned' when civil servants are rewarded for 'good' behaviour and punished for 'bad' behaviour, with 'good' and 'bad' defined (for this analysis) as behaviours which improve/worsen the performance of the institution. When incentives are aligned, what is good for the institution is also good for the individual, and vice versa. Incentive alignment, theoretically and empirically, leads to improved performance.

Before assessing the *alignment* of incentives, it is necessary to first enumerate:

• Which types of behaviours are rewarded;
• Which types of behaviours are punished;
• Which types of behaviours are ignored.

These can then be analysed against the 'desired' state to assess the degree of alignment or misalignment. Rewards (and punishments) are divided, in this study, into three kinds:

• Career rewards and punishments (salary, perquisites, job content, promotion);
• Social rewards and punishments (public or social esteem, ability to contribute to the larger good);
• Rewards and punishments for illegal or illegitimate actions.

Professional Competence and Knowledge

The 'behaviour' which is rewarded at the point of entry into the service of direct recruits is academic competence. Candidates come through a gruelling examination which requires mastery of two subjects (not closely related) plus very good general knowledge and reasonable proficiency in English and one Indian language.[38] In recent years, the increase in the number of attempts allowed may mean that persistence is as important as academic competence, especially for those candidates allowed unlimited attempts.

As probationers in the Academy, 'officer-like qualities' are emphasized—punctuality, deportment, quality of assignments, articulation, etc., and probationers are again assessed for academic competence through the probationer's final exam.

Thereafter, an IAS officer's professional competence is assessed formally entirely through the mechanism of the Annual Confidential Report written by his superior. Promotions are, in practice, predominately seniority-based and are only missed if the officer does something seriously wrong. The government has generous study leave rules, but there is no specific career incentive linked to the acquisition of knowledge or competence either through formal study or through specialization or on-the-job learning. Nor is there any systematic connection between areas of study and the assignments given to an officer. (It is very common for an officer to be sent at public expense for training in, say, hospital management and on return from training find himself posted to the Electricity Board.) The use of the study leave is popular mainly because of the overseas and non-governmental avenues that further study produces. *Officers who take the trouble to learn about their field of work, acquire relevant knowledge, keep themselves abreast of developments in public management or technical fields are usually not rewarded with any tangible career benefits.* However, periodically governments find themselves in need of officers of outstanding competence—usually to tackle a crisis—and at times like this the best officers do get glamorous or high profile assignments. But there is little security of tenure and once the crisis has blown over, the officer is often replaced. The empanelment system, when operated fairly does reward competence.

[38] One feature which changed in 1979 is that IAS candidates are no longer required to show mastery of English.

There is informal reward for competence in the form of social esteem. IAS officers are high profile, especially at the state level, and the local press, citizenry, captains of industry, and fellow officers can usually distinguish officers of good, bad, and indifferent calibre. For many officers, their reputations as 'good' officers are prized. A small, but not negligible, number of 'good' officers leave the service for the private sector, academia, or international organizations. While competence does have some rewards (though not through promotion), incompetence carries few risks. An incompetent officer who follows the rules and makes few mistakes will rise to the top grades, though he is less likely to occupy some of the high profile positions within that grade.

Political Neutrality

Political neutrality is a cardinal tenet of the civil services in India, and one which has survived the rigour of extreme rivalry in the political executive fairly well. While IAS officers are often characterized as 'spineless' or too willing to obey their political masters, relatively few are identified with a particular political party.

Political neutrality is dinned into direct recruits at the Academy and is part of the credo of the new recruit. It is also part of the public's expectations of an IAS officer. One powerful disincentive which operates against political partisanship is that the Centre (since 1977) and the states (since 1967) have seen many changes of government. Getting too closely identified with one party brings short term rewards, but can also bring swift retribution when today's opposition becomes tomorrow's ruling party. For this reason, most officers take pains to avoid being politically identified.

However, beneath the surface, there are several kinds of 'neutrality'. The neutrality which was the objective of the initial design can be termed 'active' neutrality—the officer follows neutrality as an operating principle. This would imply (for example) that when taking decisions on individual matters, he does not favour those belonging to, or recommended by the ruling party, and applies rules and norms impartially. Active neutrality is disliked by most ruling parties most of the time, and (increasingly) by those senior officers who do not themselves subscribe to the credo. Actively neutral officers are often portrayed as 'obstructionist' and transferred. When the government changes, they are usually 'rewarded' with better posts, but this only lasts till they are seen as obstructionist by the new regime. However, these officers usually get their promotions, etc., on time.

The neutrality which is more widespread is that of 'passive' neutrality. This variety is quite different; it simply means total submission to *whoever is in power without any attachment to that party per se*. Here the officer sees it as his duty to carry out the bidding of the ruling party even if it is contrary to established rules or procedures but he makes it clear to the 'losers' that he is simply carrying out 'orders' and is not really 'committed' to the current ruling group. He makes it clear that, should the ruling party change, he would equally happily carry out the bidding of the new group. Most ruling parties 'reward' this class of officer with relatively glamorous or powerful postings. When governments change, this class may suffer an eclipse, but (like all eclipses) it is temporary, and they soon ingratiate themselves with the new dispensation. They generally get their promotions, etc., on time. Officers in this class do face some risk of being 'identified' as having attachment to the current ruling party when in fact their attachment is purely opportunistic.

The third class are the ones with strong and permanent attachments to a particular party or group. When 'their' party is in power, they are handsomely rewarded with powerful positions, but when the opposition is in power they are kept in sinecures, and may face disciplinary action and formal career setbacks like losing promotions. Some among this class, particularly those who combine partisan behaviour with corruption, may even face dismissal or criminal prosecution.

In a sense, the IAS can be divided into three groups[39]—the 'wives' (those officers who are attached to one party), the 'nuns' (officers who remain unattached to any party), and the 'prostitutes'[40] (who attach themselves to whichever party is in power and switch when there is a change of government). Unfortunately, the share of the third group is perceived to be quite high.

---

[39] The contribution of K. Ashok Vardhan Shetty in formulating this analogy is gratefully acknowledged.

[40] These terms are used metaphorically to make an analytical point and should not be misconstrued or misquoted, out of context.

Acting Independently and Fairly in Enforcing the Law and Due Process

IAS officers are often in charge of enforcing laws. They are also often in positions where they (through the advice they give their ministers) can draft delegated legislation. Legally, officers are required to act according to the law and the principles of natural justice. When exercising discretion conferred by law, officers are expected to exercise it in their own best judgement, not on the dictates of a superior.

An officer who exercises his function as expected by law inevitably finds himself in conflict, sooner or later, with a member or supporter of the ruling party. In the last 30 years, the practice of ministers, MLAs, MPs, etc., trying to influence officers in making these decisions has gone from being the exception to being the norm. Those officers (there are still a considerable number) who play by the rules quickly accumulate negative brownie points and they are not 'rewarded' in a career sense, since theoretically that is simply what is expected of every officer. After, or just before, making a crucial decision which the ministers/MLAs/MPs tried to influence, the officer is often punished through a transfer to an obviously inferior post.

Independence in law enforcement is fairly closely linked to the concept of 'active' neutrality. Unlike mere neutrality, however, acting independently does bring a lot of social approbation which is an intangible reward.

Honesty and Integrity

'Honesty and integrity' can be interpreted in several ways. A narrow interpretation is that an officer is one who is not corrupt, in the sense that he does not himself accept bribes or favours in return for performing an official act. This can be called 'passive honesty'. Officers who are 'passively honest' are of course not rewarded, for the simple reason that this is expected of all officers. Since they do not themselves break the rules, their career progression is usually smooth.

A wider interpretation would be that an honest officer is one who is not only free from corruption in a legal sense, but who also follows the Conduct Rules and tenders advice with intellectual honesty (that is, what he advises is what he believes in, not what he thinks his superior wants) and strives to ensure integrity among those he supervises. This can be termed 'active honesty'. An example might make the distinction clear: an officer is required to advise on a matter in which he knows his superior (either political or bureaucratic) has an illicit interest. The officer knows the proposal to be improper. The beneficiary of the decision is willing to pay him a bribe, but the officer declines. Nevertheless the officer refrains from opposing the proposal and instead makes a lukewarm or ambiguous recommendation, so that the superior is not 'inconvenienced' and forced into a possibly embarrassing need to over-rule. This is passive honesty. If the officer in the same situation were to make a clear written recommendation against it, that would be active honesty.

Actively honest behaviour can often result in penal transfers. Indeed a reputation for active honesty may mean the officer is rarely allowed into positions where his behaviour could pose a real 'threat'.

Unlike the related concept of 'independent enforcement of the law', where there is usually a lot of social approbation because it happens in public view, *giving intellectually honest advice brings fewer social rewards*. This behaviour is usually not in public view; the losers from the officer's active integrity are discrete and identifiable parties but the winner is usually 'society at large'. An officer's integrity in such situations is therefore rarely rewarded even intangibly.

Innovation

Innovations in the realm of public administration by civil servants can, for purposes of this incentive analysis, be divided into two types—those which have political consequences (or affect the discretionary powers of the political executive) and those which do not. The former kind of innovation is clearly subject to political control (as it should be), and will of course be subject to the normal political process. There are however a large number of innovations in administration which are apolitical. This section will look at the incentives for such (apolitical) innovation.

Formal career rewards for successful innovation are few, since promotions can only be lost through poor performance, not won by good performance. Those with a reputation for innovation are from time to time, assigned to challenging positions when the political executive needs quick results. Innovation can often bring social rewards in the form of fame and recognition. The eponymous 'Lakhina experiment' in Maharashtra—where an officer (Anil Lakhina) radically altered the work flow in a collectorate to resemble a client-oriented bank teller type system—earned the innovator a place in IAS lore. The successful family planning strategy of Tamil Nadu in the 70s and 80s was spearheaded by an IAS officer (T. V. Antony) who made it a personal crusade. The Ernakulam total literacy campaign in Kerala was likewise an innovation by an IAS officer. The privatization of sewage pumping stations in Madras Metrowater from 1994 onwards was an innovation by two IAS officers (M. S. Srinivasan and Santha Sheela Nair), well before the World Bank or other agencies began pushing private participation in water. There are numerous others. *The political executive rarely blocks, and often encourages, apolitical innovations, and this is one of the abiding attractions of an IAS career.*

In contrast to the neutral, and often supportive, attitude of the political executive, the reaction of the civil service itself as well as of other arms of government is usually ambivalent or negative. The culture of status quo is deeply entrenched. IAS officers who make innovations are often seen by colleagues as publicity-hungry and accused of breaking the long tradition of the 'anonymous' civil servant. Obstacles are often placed in the path of the innovator. Official seniors, bypassed in the process of innovation, may 'strike back' at a later date, by pushing the innovator into an inconsequential post.

Innovation can also bring 'penal' results in other ways. Innovations do not always succeed. The audit approach of the Comptroller and Auditor General in which failed attempts at innovation are often cited as examples of waste, acts as damper. (To be fair to the CAG, *mala fide* or corrupt deals can also be covered up as 'innovation'.) The innovation-curbing effect of the CAG's *ex post* review is probably exaggerated but it does influence officers' thinking.

The Indian judiciary's readiness to grant interim stay orders (often *ex parte*) at the request of an allegedly aggrieved party, stifles many an innovation. These stays, usually at the request of employees or unions who fear a loss of 'rent-seeking' or other powers, are almost always eventually vacated, but by then the innovator has long since been transferred. Occasionally, an officer who attempted an innovation may also find himself at the receiving end of strictures.

Accepting Bribes and Favours

Bribery is a criminal offence and the penalties for proven bribery are high (several years in prison). The Conduct Rules applicable to the Indian civil services are very strict, and prescribe a higher standard of integrity than the criminal law. They contain stringent rules on acceptance of hospitality, on participating in politics, on dealings with persons with whom officers have official dealings, etc. Officers have to file property returns for immovable property and for movable property transactions in excess of a prescribed size. India was a pioneer in using the concept of treating the possession of 'assets disproportionate to known sources of income' as a criminal offence for public servants. Theoretically, it should be fairly easy to catch cases of corruption among senior civil servants, and either prosecute under the criminal law or at least dismiss under service rules.

However, IAS officers also have above average opportunities for corrupt gain. Bribery, as a consensual crime, is difficult to prove beyond reasonable doubt and the only feasible route is through 'disproportionate assets'. In practice, successful prosecutions of IAS officers have been rare.

On the other hand, the pecuniary gains from corruption, especially in posts involving major economic decisions, can be huge, either on a 'few large transactions' or a 'steady flow of moderate sized transactions'. So long as the corrupt officer avoids (i) doing anything blatantly or obviously illegal (ii) engaging in conspicuous consumption, he is fairly safe. And while corruption may bring some negative publicity, it can also produce a certain degree of social rewards among, say, the business classes who may see the officer as 'good for business' since, for a fee, he gets their work done.

Accepting valuable favours—free trips, free hotel accommodation, transportation, etc.,—is also illegal under the conduct rules but violations of these rules are even more frequent. The social stigma attached to corruption among the middle classes has declined and corruption among civil servants is often seen to be as 'normal' as tax evasion among 'respectable' industrialists.

The Risk-Reward Balance

The foregoing section looked at the 'reward' and 'punishments' attracted by various kinds of behaviour. The following table summarizes the incentive effects in terms of a risk-reward balance to see which kinds of behaviour are 'encouraged' or 'discouraged' by the prevailing incentive structure.

Using the analogy of (financial) portfolio theory, the different behaviours can be divided into 'efficient' and 'inefficient' ones in terms of the risk/reward balance. Table 7.10 shows that the following kinds of behaviour are 'efficient' and thus, assuming the conventional 'rational economic man', are encouraged:

- Acquiring/retaining professional competence
- Passive political neutrality
- Political alignment
- Passive honesty
- Bribery

The following types of behaviour are 'inefficient'; and therefore discouraged:

- Active neutrality
- Enforcing the law independently
- Innovation

The preceding analysis assumed each of these types of behaviour can be pursued independently of the others. In practice, there are 'synergies' between some of them—for example between passive neutrality and bribery. An officer who is passively neutral has a better chance of maximizing corrupt opportunities. Likewise, an officer who keeps professionally up to date is more likely to be innovative. Active honesty and active political neutrality go together. There are negative synergies too—a corrupt officer has little to gain from acquiring professional skills.

Going by this analysis, one would assume that an overwhelming majority of IAS officers would tend to be reasonably competent, but politically spineless, incapable of enforcing the law fairly, and corrupt. Yet the actual numbers of principled, neutral, fair, and honest officers is still surprisingly high. One defect of the analysis is that it reflects *today's* situation. An officer's mental outlook is

TABLE 7.10
Risk-reward balance in the IAS

Behaviour	Consequences						Risk/reward balance
	Rewards			Punishments			
	Career	Social	From illegal activity	Career	Social	From illegal activity	
1. Acquiring/retaining professional competence	Low	Low	N/A	Nil	Nil	N/A	Low risk/low reward
2. Political neutrality							
—Active neutrality	Nil	High	N/A	High	Nil	N/A	High risk/moderate reward
—Passive neutrality	Low	Nil	N/A	Low	Nil	N/A	Low risk/low reward
—Political alignment	High	Low	N/A	High	Low	N/A	High risk/high reward
3. Acting independently in enforcing the law & due process	Nil	High	N/A	High	Nil	N/A	High risk/moderate reward
4. Honesty & Integrity							
—Active honesty	Nil	Low	N/A	High	Nil	N/A	High risk/low reward
—Passive honest	Low	Nil	N/A	Nil	Nil	N/A	Low risk/low reward
—Bribery	Nil	Low	High	Mod.	Low	Mod.	Moderate risk/high reward
5. Innovation	Nil	Low	N/A	Mod.	Nil	N/A	Moderate risk/low reward

formed over a period of time and changes in behaviour are not instantaneous. The incentive structure has not always been so misaligned—in particular the lack of social stigma attached to corruption is a fairly recent phenomenon, as also the fact that material wealth is socially more highly valued than, say, adherence to Gandhian norms of 'simple living and high thinking'.

Another defect of the above analysis is that it proceeds purely from the 'economic rationality' perspective and ignores the inner motivations of a non-economic nature—such as the desire to do public service. The IAS offers a means to do genuine public service without starting an NGO.

A third defect is that the effects of incentives to the individual officer can be over-ridden by other factors. For instance though acquiring skills is an 'encouraged' behaviour, it does not necessarily produce commensurate improvement in administrative quality because of the short tenures. Likewise, though active neutrality is normally 'discouraged', during election time the strong disciplinary jurisdiction of the Election Commission leads to much stricter behaviour than normal, which has an important (beneficial) impact.

Despite its defects, what the analysis does show is that *there is a major misalignment between the actual incentives facing IAS officers and the objectives of the service according to the constitutional design.* Unless remedial action is taken, India will eventually get the Service, and the service, its incentive structure deserves.

VI. CONCLUSIONS

Summary of findings

So far this chapter has looked at the formal design of the civil service, changes made to the design during implementation and their effects on performance, as well as the resulting incentive structure facing members of the service. This section will attempt to bring together the analysis of the preceding sections in terms of their implications for the overall effectiveness of the civil service, and then suggest remedial measures.

Most (though not all) of the features of the initial design of the civil service were conducive to the development of a highly effective civil service, on all three of our effectiveness criteria. Not surprisingly, in the early years after Independence, the service did have a reputation for neutrality and effectiveness.

The current state of the service leaves much to be desired, particularly when looked at against the neo-institutionalist criterion of effectiveness, that is, contribution to an efficient and low-transaction cost economic environment. The effectiveness of the service in preserving a democratic polity has been considerably better and it still seems capable of translating clearly articulated and genuine expressions of political will into concrete action. Paradoxically, the service's relative success under the last criterion (carrying out the political will) may have worked against effectiveness in a purely neo-institutionalist sense.

Changes to the design—some explicit, some occurring because of the manner in which the design was implemented—have almost universally militated against institutional effectiveness. In large part this is due to the incentive structure that the changes have generated. The incentives facing individual civil servants are, in most cases, misaligned with the needs of institutional effectiveness.

Remedial Measures

The preceding analysis has shown a number of shortcomings in the effectiveness of the civil service along with some strengths. A full discussion of policy options to remedy the situation would be beyond the scope of this chapter, but this concluding section will outline a few ideas. These recommendations flow from the analysis of the incentive structure and proceed from the premise that effectiveness will improve if incentives facing individual civil servants are aligned with the public interest:[41]

(i) Increase in Average Tenure in a Post and Prevention of Arbitrary Penal Transfers from Sensitive Positions

The government's inherent right to transfer its civil servants needs to be balanced against the need for capacity to do the job (which involves a 'learning curve') and the need for independence in law-enforcing posts. Some practical suggestions:

---

[41] Some of these suggestions, in possibly slightly different form, have been made by others. This is particularly true of items 1 and 6 which were made by the Lal Bahadur Shastri National Academy of Administration in its monograph entitled 'Reforms for the Indian Administrative Service', LBSNAA, Mussoorie, 1996. Suggestions 4 and 5, to the best of the authors' knowledge are new.

(a) Declare a 'normal' tenure for each post; provide that at least 90 per cent of officers in that post should complete the normal tenure (except where they voluntarily agree to, or request, a transfer);

(b) Require the UPSC to monitor postings and place before Parliament a periodic evaluation of average tenures for each post, for each state and for the Centre (what the LBSNAA calls the 'stability index');[42]

(c) Provide that premature transfers in excess of the 10 per cent limit will require clearance from a body independent of the Cabinet, say, the UPSC.

Of these recommendations, the last will involve reducing the powers of the political executive and is thus more difficult to implement. Short of this change, the other recommendations may still have some effect as 'moral suasion' by casting an adverse spotlight on recalcitrant governments.

(ii) Reduction in the Size of the Cadres

The proliferation of inconsequential posts is a proximate cause of both demoralization and the ability to use transfer as a penalty. It is also a drag on the exchequer. As an unscientific rule of thumb, the sizes of most cadres could be cut by a third without adverse effect on administration. The number of posts of Secretary to the Government of India should also be cut by a third. A drastic cut in the size of the IAS will also send the right signal to the rest of the civil service. For a while, as a transition, supernumerary posts should be created to accommodate the excess of officers already in the service. In order to keep the flow of new blood into the service, (a) the promotion quota should be scaled back to the initial design level; and (b) the retirement age for the IAS and IPS should be reduced to 58; and (c) a certain number of officers must be retired compulsorily at the age of 50 using provisions which already exist but are not adequately used.

(iii) Change in the System of Near-automatic
Seniority-based Promotion

The current system is meritocratic at the point of entry but thereafter (other than the arbitrary empanelment process) is largely

[42] LBSNAA Monograph, ibid.

seniority-based. This should be changed so that all officers undergo a rigorous assessment of performance, independent of the political executive, at the 15 years' service and 25 years' service mark, the assessment being conducted by the UPSC based on a combination of:

- panel interviews;
- evaluation of papers to be produced by the officer on practical matters relating to public administration;
- a review of the officer's record and reputation for integrity;
- confidential reports with an opportunity for the officer to discuss all adverse entries; and
- an examination to test general familiarity with developments in selected fields of relevance.

Members of the panel should be distinguished citizens including representatives of academia and the private sector drawn very carefully to exclude all those who could have an interest in the career of an individual officer. All officers who clear the tests should be deemed to be empanelled for Government of India positions at the appropriate level. Officers who do not clear the tests should not be promoted into the next grade and a certain proportion of those not promoted should be retired at the age of 50. A somewhat similar system operates for promotion into the higher ranks of the armed forces.

(iv) Change in Recruitment Procedures and
Cadre Allotment Rules for State Service Promotees

In keeping with the principles of meritocracy, neutrality, and an all India character, the following changes should be made in the promotion of state service officers into the IAS.

(a) The number of state government representatives in the selection panel should be reduced to just one.

(b) All officers promoted into the service should compulsorily be deputed to a different state cadre or to the Centre for 5 years after promotion; given the age of the candidates and linguistic difficulties, officers (other than those deputed to the Centre) should be accommodated in neighbouring states and given a generous allowance to maintain a house in their home state.

These measures will ensure that those promoted into the service are the genuinely meritorious among the state civil servants rather than those who are politically favoured and will go a long way in promoting active political neutrality.

(v) Wider Eligibility for the 'Selection' Category to Bring in Distinguished Non-Government Candidates

At present the 'Selection' category of recruitment is used exclusively to bring in state government staff who do not belong to the state civil service. A change in the rules (by executive order, requiring no legislation) should be made to allow distinguished persons from the private sector, universities, and NGOs to apply for positions under the 'Selection' category. This would bring in valuable new blood.

(vi) Awards for Outstanding Civil Servants

Unlike the British civil service, which receives knighthoods in the annual honours list, civil servants in India normally do not receive civilian awards like the 'Padma Bhushan', etc. which are awarded to distinguished performers in most other walks of life. To improve the self-image of the service and its public image, outstanding civil servants selected by a panel with non-civil servant representation, should receive awards for specific achievements of a tangible nature.[43]

References

Constituent Assembly of India Debates (1949), vol. X, no. 3, 10 October.
Das, S. K. (1998), *Civil Service Reform and Structural Adjustment*, New Delhi: Oxford University Press.
————— (2001), *Public Office, Private Interest: Bureaucracy and Corruption in India*, New Delhi: Oxford University Press.
Hyung-Ki Kim (1996), 'The Civil Service System and Economic Development: The Japanese Experience', EDI learning Resources Series, Washington DC: World Bank.

[43] The LBSNAA has proposed instituting Sardar Patel or Lal Bahadur Shastri Awards for the best three Collectors; in our view it should not be confined to Collectors and indeed should look even more closely at those in less 'glamorous' positions.

Hyung-Ki Kim, Michio Muramatsu, T. J. Pempel, and Kozo Yamamura (eds) (1995), *The Japanese Civil Service and Economic Development: Catalysts of Change*, Oxford: Clarendon Press.

Lal Bahadur Shastri National Academy of Administration (LBSNAA) Mussoorie (1996), 'Reforms for the Indian Administrative Service'.

Lindauer, David and Barbara Nunberg (eds) (1996), 'Rehabilitating Government', *World Bank Regional & Sectoral Studies.*

Ministry of Personnel, Public Grievances and Pensions (1999–2000), *Annual Report*, Government of India.

North, Douglass (1990), *Institutions, Institutional Change and Economic Performance*, Cambridge: Cambridge University Press.

Nunberg, Barbara (1995), 'Managing the Civil Service: Reform lessons from advanced industrialized countries', *World Bank*, February.

Planning Commission (1950), First Five Year Plan Document, Government of India.

Planning Commission (1957), 'Review of the First Five Year Plan', Government of India, May.

Report of the Premiers Conference, October 1946, Government of India.

Singh, Raj (1985), 'Indian Bureaucracy and Development', *Indian Journal of Public Administration*, vol. XXXIV, no. 2.

Sridharan, R. (1999), 'India: Good Governance and Political Culture', Unpublished M.A. Dissertation submitted to the University of Bath.

Subramaniam, V. (1984), 'Some Administrative Aspects of Federalism in the Third World', *International Review of Administrative Sciences* (IRAS 1/1984 47–59).

Tope, T. K. (1992), *Constitutional Law of India*, 2nd edn, Lucknow: Eastern Book Company.

Union Public Service Commission (1998), *Annual Report 1997–98*, New Delhi.

World Bank (1997), 'The State in a Changing World', World Development Report (WDR), Washington, DC.

TABLE A7.1

	Service	Full form of abbreviations
1	IAS	Indian Administrative Service
2	IPS	Indian Police Service
3	IFt.S	Indian Forest Service
4	IA&AS	Indian Audit and Accounts Service
5	ICAS	Indian Civil Accounts Service
6	IDAS	Indian Defence Accounts Service
7	IES	Indian Economic Service
8	IStS	Indian Statistical Service
9	IFS	Indian Foreign Service
10	ICES	Indian Customs and Central Excise Service
11	IITS	Indian Income Tax Service
12	IPoS	Indian Postal Service
13	IIS	Indian Information Service
14	Rly Services	Various Railway Services like the Railway Traffic Service and Engg. Services
15	CPES	Central Power Engineering Services
16	CWES	Central Water Engineering Service
17	CES	Central Engineering Service (Public Works)
18	IDEtS	Indian Defence Estate Service
19	ILS	Indian Labour Service
20	CSS	Central Secretariat Service
21	ISS	Indian Supply Service
22	CCLS	Central Company Law Service
23	IInS	Indian Inspection Service
24	ITeS	Indian Telecommunication Service
25	IOFS	Indian Ordnance Factory Service
26	ICoAS	Indian Cost Accounting Service
27	CTS	Central Trade Service

8

Reserve Bank of India
A Study in the Separation and Attrition of Powers[1]

Deena Khatkhate[2]

In explaining the variance in economic performance among nations, two main reasons are often adduced. The first is the relevance and orientation of economic policy frame and the environment in which it is designed and implemented. The second, closely related to the first, is the adequacy and appropriateness of institutions which impact either directly or indirectly on effectuating economic policies. Economic growth is not merely a function of saving mobilization, or even a high rate of investment; it is crucially dependent on the quality of investment and the efficiency with which savings are utilized. In order to ensure this, a precondition is the elimination of microeconomic distortions and macroeconomic misdirection. One without the other is simply not capable of delivering the results. Removal of micro-distortions may create proper incentive structure, with appropriate prices and markets but without stable macroeconomic policy, the economy would not advance. In recent economic literature as well as in countries pursuing their development strategies, this dual goal of economic polices is well recognized. But what is not yet grasped or inadequately grasped

[1] Perspective of this chapter is situated in a Hicksian theme of separation of powers, as fleshed out by Chandavarkar in his discussion of central banking in developing countries, 1996.

[2] The author would like to thank Anand Chandavarkar and Narendra Jadhav for their perceptive comments on an earlier version of this chapter.

is that even a well articulated, balanced, and incentivated policy framework will not meet its potential because of the failure to recognize the pivotal role of institutions, through which the policy of the state is, in final analysis, implemented. If the institutions are not well-governed or their functions are ill-defined, or the manning of them is ill-matched without the skills required in their management, or their distinctness is left vague, and undefined, no economic, social, judicial, distributive, or monetary policy will function optimally. One can see the evidence of this in several developing countries, which since the middle of 1980s, unshackled their economies from the dirigistic regimes, with open trade, freer markets, and liberalized financial systems. But the actual performance of many of these even with new orientation of their economic policies did not live up to the initial expectations because of the weak institutions, be they central banks charged with maintaining price stability, or regulatory authorities and fiscal agencies aiming at judicious use of public resources, or judicial system responsible for ensuring property rights, and prevention of arbitrary use of power. Nor was there a constructive, healthy, and mutually reinforcing interactive relationship among the various institutions.[3]

There is a common thread running through a policy framework and institutions, which is represented by an ideology. An economic policy laden with incentive rather than force, prices rather than physical allocation, freedom of choice rather than command demands different kind of institutions both in regard to administrative structure, and the mindsets of those who manage them because both economic policy and institutions are the product of the political process dominated by ideology. A liberal economic policy, for instance, requires that every institution has its own sphere of activity well-delineated and its relationship with other state institutions so defined that a separation of power becomes a credo guiding the functioning of each institution.[4]

---

[3] The extreme examples of these are found in African countries and the transition economies like Russia. The policies initiated were, on paper, irreproachable, but these countries far from recording progress in economic performance actually faltered and some like Russia, failed dismally. The main reason for this was that there were either no institutions or institutions were not commensurable with new policy environment.

[4] This view is not, however, universally shared. Citing the experiences of East Germany and Poland after they dismantled the communist regimes, it is

The approach taken in this chapter is that the Reserve Bank of India (RBI) is one of the principal organs of governance in a democratic Indian state with a well-defined sphere of activity, distinct and differentiated from other areas of state functioning and its power needs to be separate from the powers of the executive, judiciary, and the legislature. The underlying assumption is that the RBI is not and cannot be totally independent of the state nor can it be an indistinguishable part of the state, so that its deliberations or decisions are dictated by the executive. This approach is inspired by Professor Hicks's casual but profound insight into the exercise of monetary policy. While commenting on the central importance of bank rate in Hawtrey's work on central banking, Hicks wrote,

...that the issue with which we have been concerned is political—even constitutional—as well as economic. There is the technical economic problem of the Instrument, but it is tied up with the political problem which Keynesian economics, so it seems to me, has refused to face, while the monetarist, who have seen it, have not faced the political implications. For myself, I would face it. I think I should say that monetary regulation is a major function of government, but we should emphasize that if it is to be exercised decisively, it needs to be separated, in what is in fact the constitutional sense, from other functions. We need to remember the ancient doctrine of the separation of powers. The judicial function, in well-ordered states is recognized to be a function of government, but a function is better separated. So it is with the monetary function. It is far too responsible a function... (Hicks 1977: 132-3).

Chandavarkar, however, would prefer to call it 'a separation of authority rather than a separation of power because the monetary function is a shared function of the executive and the central bank' (Chandavarkar 1996: 220). But the central question is whether there could be an authority without a power and if it is not, then a separate monetary authority is invariably equivalent to a separate power.

---

argued, that Poland succeeded in achieving economic growth and efficiency even without changing institutions in contrast to East Germany, which mimicked West Germany in adopting wholesale its policies and institutions but with poor consequences (B. Eichengreen, Personal View, *Financial Times* of 6 September 2000). However, this example does not necessarily disprove that the institutions do not matter. The unfavourable performance of the eastern part of Germany was more due to the inconsistency between newly adopted institutions and flawed new economic policy which equalized wages in East and West Germany without regard to productivity.

Following this basic premise, the chapter will start with the original design of the RBI, intended by its progenitors and then proceed to trace how far the founding conditions had any enduring influence on its evolution over time. It will be argued that the shape and functions of the RBI as a central bank in a classical meaning of the term were strongly conditioned by the ideology which changed radically the structure and nature of the economy in which the RBI was originally expected to operate. In the process, the very concept of monetary policy, which is a defining function of the RBI changed both in its connotation and operating procedures, thereby erasing the separateness of its power or even threatening its existence as a monetary authority. A break came in 1991, with the radical departure of the economic policy of the Government of India from its previous interventionist mould, creating a little more space for the RBI, to capture a semblance of its power. Even under a new liberalized environment however the RBI remained a prisoner of its past, hobbled by the bureaucracy with its ingrained habits of thought and the intensity of the political pressure groups. As an economic institution which can impart a powerful thrust to the country's economy through maintenance of price stability and management of the external sector of the country, it has still many miles to traverse.

The Reserve Bank at the Time of its Creation

The RBI, as a monetary authority was shaped by two different political cultures. Since it was set up in 1935 during British rule, the dominant view then was that it should be independent of government not for any economic or philosophical reasons, but on the ground that it should not be a handmaiden of the foreign government. Surprisingly enough, the then rulers, being under the spell of monetary orthodoxy associated with the central bank in their own country, held similar views on the autonomy of the RBI. The congruence of views for diametrically opposite reasons permeated through the speech of the then Finance Member of the Government of India, when he introduced the Bill in the Indian legislature. 'It has generally been agreed in all the constitutional discussions and the experience of all other countries' he said,

bears this out, that when the direction of public finance is in the hands of a ministry responsible to a popularly elected legislature, a ministry which would for that reason be liable to frequent change with the changing political situation, it is desirable that the control of currency and credit in the country should be in the hands of an independent authority which can act with continuity. Further the experience of all countries is again united in leading to the conclusion that the best and indeed the only practical device for securing this independence and continuity is to set up a central bank, independent of political influence' (Reserve Bank of India 1970: 508–10).

Though this was a political argument for keeping the RBI as a distinct entity, the Finance Member buttressed his case with a simple but a telling economic rationale based on the power to create money and power to spend money by pointing out that 'in modern life and in modern economic organization, there are two important functions: they are the functions of those who have to raise and use money and there are the functions of those who are responsible for producing the actual tokens of money, the money in circulation. The basis of the whole proposal for setting up an independent central bank is to keep those two functions separate (Ibid.: 510–14).

With all these laudable sentiments, the Act establishing the RBI was so drafted that it left several grey areas for interpreting the relationship of the Bank with the government. The ambiguity of the Act allowed scope for the executive to twist and turn the Act to its advantage by practice and precedents. Right from the beginning, the executive started encroaching on the domain of the Bank. The Finance Member P. J. Grigg, exploiting the fuzzy sections of the Act, involved himself in selecting members of the RBI board, on political grounds rather than their suitability for discharging the functions of the monetary authority (Chandavarkar 2000). The first Governor of the RBI Sir Osborne Smith, was virtually dismissed on the ostensible ground of serious disagreement on the issues of monetary policy like changes in the bank rate and the management of the bank's investments (Deshmukh 1948 and Chandavarkar 2000).[5]

The vision of the founders of the RBI soon came into conflict with the exigencies of war finance. The resource mobilization to finance war effort, being the paramount objective, the RBI had to submit to what the then Government of India desired in order to keep the cost of financing war low. This effectively ruled out use

[5] Policy differences were of course the reason publicly given for the forced resignation of Smith. However, there was a multiplicity of factors involved in Smith's resignation including financial malfeasance. For this tragic and intriguing saga see Chandavarkar (2000).

of one of the most potent instruments of monetary policy, that is, the bank rate. Even more important was the manner in which the war was financed. India was a net exporter of goods and services as imports were severely controlled. But the unrequited exports were paid for in sterling, India being on the gold exchange standard and this meant an automatic issue of rupee currency which in a shortage ridden war economy fuelled high inflationary pressures.[6] Thus almost from the very inception, the RBI was made to abdicate two important instruments of monetary policy, defined as control of cost and availability of credit. The first was manifested in cheap money policy and the latter in the relentless monetary expansion.

The Morphology of the RBI in the Context of Planning

The RBI and its policy had a brief interlude immediately after 1947, of relative autonomy when its Board of Directors and the governor could give vent to their views on stabilization and fiscal policies. However, ideology soon dominated the economic policy and the monetary policy came to be a minor part of it. Since 1951 India's policy makers, aimed at an economy with an admixture of public and private sectors but with more weight given to the former as the 'commanding heights' of the economy. The economic policy and the instruments of its implementation were influenced by a strong perception that there was a pervasive market failure in the Indian system and the salvation lay in frequent and decisive government intervention. This led to a drastic shrivelling of the area of monetary policy of the RBI with serious consequences for its functioning, organization, and the use of its policy instruments. Industrial licensing was used as the main instrument to determine the output—both quality and pattern, quality and composition of

[6] The RBI's helplessness is well reflected in the secret telegram sent by the Secretary of State from England to the Finance Member of the Government of India, which is referred to in an autobiography of a well-known Indian civil servant, 'At one stage, the Board of the Reserve Bank, which consisted of most of the prominent industrialists and bankers of India, passed a resolution that a limit should be placed on the credit to be allowed to the Bank of England.... I recall a secret telegram from the Secretary of State on this issue.... It was in strong language and made clear that if the Board continued to misbehave in this fashion, the Secretary of State would have no hesitation in ordering the dismissal of the whole lot. The Board piped down' (B. K. Nehru 1997), p. 197.

imports; foreign exchange was allotted according to what the government considered as of high priority; bank credit was channelled to what were considered to be essential sectors; the terms of credit were governed by category of users; the exchange rate was predetermined by what the government thought to be the right size of the planned investment; prices were controlled, depending upon what the consumers should pay rather than what the producers should receive from their production. The availability of finance to the government and the public sector investment was not constrained as credit from the RBI was counted as a resource, like tax receipts, or the borrowing from the public. What all this meant was that the very ground on which the RBI as a monetary authority rested was knocked down. If the overall bank credit was deemed to be excessive, the first casualty was the private sector credit which was curtailed through various devices so that the pernicious effects of credit to government could be neutralized. Since allocation of credit was done on what sectors should be financed according to the plan priorities, interest rates were required to be capped, thereby taking away another instrument of the monetary policy from the arsenal of the RBI. Price controls eliminated the link between monetary expansion and prices. In short, the RBI was reduced to the role of a helpless spectator (Khatkhate 1991). This is well captured in the RBI history:

Faced with the growing gulf between every day practice and the cannons of orthodox central banking...the practical necessities of decision-making under multiple constraints often led to the adoption, sometimes against the better judgment of its officers if not always of the Bank, of measures which created bigger problems in the longer term than the more immediate ones they helped to resolve. As the logic of decision-making became endogenized in the form of precedents and institutional evolution, the course was set for departures which however small or partial in the beginning exercised over a period of time a tangible influence on the overall effectiveness of the Bank's monetary policy (Balachandran 1998: 10).

The upshot of all this was that the RBI almost ceased to be a power in the economic and monetary affairs of the country, not to speak of its lack of separation from other powers of the state.

Handmaiden of Government

So with the change in the identity of the RBI, the nature of the instruments also changed. The main instruments—the so-called open market operations, cash reserve ratio, and the liquid assets ratio were merely the penumbra of the fiscal instruments of raising resources for the government. It was a misnomer to describe the RBI's purchase and sale of government securities as open market operations, as will be clear from a forthright statement in the official document.

Open market operations are conducted by a central bank mainly with a view to directly or indirectly affect the reserves of banks and thereby the extent of monetary expansion and in the process to create and maintain a desired pattern of yields on government securities and generally to help the government raise resources from the capital market. Thus this policy instrument has two aspects viz. the monetary aspect and the fiscal aspect. For the conduct of open market operations as a monetary instrument, the market for government securities should be well organized, broad-based and deep, so that the central bank is in a position to sell/buy securities to the extent it considers desirable. A prerequisite for the emergence of such market is that the rate of interest offered on government securities is competitive. Since these conditions are not met by the Indian capital market, open market operations are of minor importance as a monetary instrument *though they serve as an adjunct of fiscal policy in India to some extent* (Reserve Bank of India 1985: 262–3) (emphasis added).

The cash reserve ratio (CRR) was both a monetary policy instrument as well as fiscal instrument. It was also used as a safety valve to protect the depositor's interest. However, when the CRRs were maintained at a very high level continuously, it imposed a tax both on the banks and the depositors. To the extent, the part of deposits was impounded by the cash ratio, the government could increase the inflation tax through monetary expansion. And this was what the RBI did during most of the period well through 1991, when it maintained a CRR at 15 per cent of net bank deposit liabilities.

The third instrument used by the RBI was the statutory liquid assets ratio (SLR), which compelled banks to hold government securities as a certain proportion of their deposits. This had been yet another way to raise the resources for the government and other public sector entities. The RBI was very explicit on why the SLR was used more for fiscal needs rather than for monetary policy purposes. 'The objectives to be achieved by the statutory liquid assets ratio are: (a) to create or support a market for government securities in economies which do not have a diversified capital market, and (b) to allocate resources to government for augmenting the resources of the public sector'. The SLR was at 38.5 per cent until 1991 (Ibid.: 265).

With the use of these instruments, the RBI could at least maintain a pretense that it was doing its job of containing monetary expansion and thus the inflationary pressures, whenever it raised the CRR or SLR (which it often did, but not without stifling the credit demand from the private sector). But there was no fig leaf left when it opened the spigot of finance to the government without much restraint, which came to be known as monetization of government deficit. There is a chequered history of deficit financing, beginning with the Second Five Year Plan, which left a yawning gap in resources required for financing the size of the planned investments. The Managing Director of the International Monetary Fund, forewarned the RBI management as early as 1958 that the policy of deficit financing would give the government a substantial command over additional real resources for investment (Balachandran 1998: 14–15) and that deficit financing of such magnitude would not only generate high inflation but also would precipitate a sharp decline in India's accumulated sterling balances. But the RBI management's misplaced optimism and wishful thinking led it to argue that the planned foreign exchange reserve losses (which were grossly underestimated in the Plan document) and the projected income velocity of money would provide a safeguard against deficit financing leading to monetary expansion. In the end, it proved to be a false dawn and the RBI wittingly or unwittingly became a party to its authority being undermined by the government. Even more ominously it opened the flood gates to 'automatic monetization and in the longer run to the inflationary financing of budgetary deficits by the Reserve Bank' (Ibid.: 28).

Though in theory the RBI could not have resisted the government's manic proclivity to indulge in deficit financing, the RBI did not raise any objection to the clandestine manner in which the government made it easier to access credit from the RBI almost without limit. The Government of India could acquire short-term credit from the RBI by issuing to the Bank non-marketable ad hoc treasury bills bearing very low interest rate. The idea behind the latter was that it was merely a short-term expedient of bridge-finance to tide over the temporary needs and as soon as the government could raise resources through market borrowing, it would be liquidated so that there would not be any expansionary impact on money supply. But the short-term prolonged into long-term, as the government's ambitious plans fell short of resources so much so that deficit financing became in fact a source of financing for planned expenditure. This was made possible by the RBI's naivety when the Government of India's requested the RBI to create ad hoc treasury bills, whenever the Government of India's cash balances held with the RBI fell below Rs 50 crores. As time passed, the ad hoc treasury bills spiralled to a very high figure and though the government converted, from time to time, a part of it into funded debt, it remained unsustainably high, denting the RBI's authority as an independent monetary authority. As the RBI history of the period 1951–67 puts it,

the RBI Act merely enabled the Bank to make short-term advances to central government. It did not require the Bank to make such advances. But in January 1955, the Bank agreed rather somnolently and without much serious thought, to a suggestion of the Finance Ministry to create ad hoc treasury bills in such manner as to ensure that the central government cash balances did not fall below Rs 50 crores at the end of each week. The availability of soft credit in unlimited quantities from the central bank through the creation of ad hocs helped undermine the financial discipline at the centre (Ibid.: 29).[7]

What this history failed to point out was that the RBI did not make any attempt to resist the government's encroachment on its territory.[8]

[7] The unlimited monetary expansion through deficit financing was made possible by abandoning the proportional reserve system under which two-fifths of the assets of the Bank's Issue Department were required to be held in the form of gold coin, bullion, and foreign securities. Under the new system, the currency could be increased so long as it was backed by government securities.

[8] It is doubtful though whether the Government of India or its finance minister could have tolerated any governor to defy its instructions. In fact, then Governor Rama Rau protested against the impost levied by government on transactions which had the effect of raising the interest rate in 1958. But the irate Minister hauled the Governor over the coals in such an undignified brawl that the proud Rama Rau quickly submitted his resignation. Since then there was not even a pretense that the RBI is a separate power. Remembering this sorry episode an illustrious civil servant B. K. Nehru, when offered the governorship of the RBI turned it down, as he 'did not cherish the idea of junior functionaries in the Finance Ministry to issue orders to the Reserve Bank' (B. K. Nehru 1997, p. 340).

Perils of Deficit Financing

With the acute foreign exchange shortages and ballooning of deficit financing, it was felt that some sort of a limit on deficit financing, at least notional, should be considered. From this arose a concept of a safe level of deficit financing which together with the credit to the private sector would ensure money supply expansion commensurably with relative price stability. In a formal sense, since the beginning of the Third Five Year Plan, the RBI was associated through a staff level committee with the Government of India in projecting a safe level of net RBI credit to government for a five-year period on certain assumptions relating to GDP growth, tolerable level of prices, and the income velocity of money. But this safe level of deficit financing remained safe only in moniker (Khatkhate 1993). The safe level was never respected in the annual budgets and invariably, the actual net RBI credit far exceeded the level that was projected initially. All that happened after the Chakravarty Committee recommendation (Reserve Bank of India, 1985) was that the budget document was embellished by adding one more definition of 'net RBI credit to government' as a memorandum item to its bewildering array of definitions of budget deficit. Though a formality of consultation with the RBI was maintained, the agreement was observed more in breach than in its compliance.

There were two important consequences of unbridled deficit financing both of which diminished the credibility of the monetary policy of the RBI. For one thing, the safe level of net RBI credit to government initially agreed to was derived from the monetary aggregate target the RBI set for itself (only in 1980s). Since the actual net RBI credit was most of the time above that level and that too by a wide margin, the RBI could maintain the monetary target to the extent possible only through contracting credit to the private sector of the economy. Thus the monetary target setting by the RBI became an exercise in futility. For another, an excessive preoccupation with monetary impact of the fiscal deficit, forced the RBI to abdicate its wider responsibility. A fiscal deficit was financed not only by borrowing from the RBI but also from other banks and non-bank public, and in this sense, had far wider ramifications for the economy. First, the private sector investment which should be the main domain for the exercise of monetary policy as in any other country was crowded out. Second, ever growing public debt other than that absorbed by the RBI tended to increase the budget deficit over time, which was one of the most significant destabilizing factors in the Indian economy since the mid-1980s (Khatkhate 1993).

Exchange Rate Management

The erosion of the RBI's power was equally evident in the discharge of two other defining functions of any central bank. These were the exchange rate management and the supervision and prudent control of the banking system. In the literature on central banking, there is no unanimity of views about whether these functions should be wholly vested in the central bank. But there is no gainsaying that these should be the shared functions between the central bank and the executive. However, even on this liberal construct of the jurisdiction of these two functions, the RBI did not acquit itself creditably not because of its own volition, but more due to—apart from the ill-defined provisions of the Reserve Bank of India and the Banking Compliance Acts—the ideological dispensation of the government of the day. Except during the initial period of the Bank's working, when it played a proactive role in exchange rate management and bank supervision, it was denied the space for exercising its power befitting its stature as a monetary authority. Since 1951 but particularly from 1956, when planning held sway over the Indian economy, with all that it conveyed for policy making, the RBI was left with no choice other than to play second fiddle to the government. The Five Year Plans were based on the premise that prices would be constant and exchange rate being one of the myriad prices, had of necessity, to remain fixed. This was the rationale that underlay the government's aversion to change the fixed exchange rate, even though the conditions had vastly changed. Adherence to the fixed exchange rate was perfectly understandable because any change in its level would have automatically thrown the whole plan out of kilter as it actually happened in 1966, when the government had to devalue the rupee by force majeure. But it was a political decision, to which the contribution of the RBI was purely technical and in a nature of a follow-up in adjusting monetary policy to post-devaluation developments.

However, the RBI's involvement both direct and indirect in exchange rate management improved, restoring some power to it in 1976, when, following delinking of dollar with gold and a subsequent realignment of major currencies in the wake of the Smithsonian agreement in 1971, the single-currency peg regime was replaced by a multi-currency basket link arrangement. Under this arrangement, the rupee exchange rate was determined with reference to the daily exchange rate movement of a select number of currencies that were India's trading partners (Joshi and Little 1994; Kohli 1990). The Government of India, of course, was involved in the background discussion surrounding the exchange rate policy but it gave more voice to the RBI than before, on the basis of its close involvement in observing changes in weights in the basket of currencies required to determine the appropriate exchange rate. With hindsight, it seems that the RBI used this freedom to its advantage in convincing the public that it was not any more a by-stander in this important area of monetary policy. Going by the results too, this was a salutary development as during 1983–90, the RBI's exchange rate management produced a real exchange rate depreciation which heavily contributed to India's export growth (Joshi and Little 1994: 277).

Supervision Role

In the area of supervision of the banking system, the RBI's record was marred by government diktats. The RBI was empowered by the Banking Companies Act to supervise the working of banks, to spot deficiencies in their functioning, and to issue licenses to them, if found to be complying with its norms of soundness. This is a function of vital importance, from the point of view of exercising an effective monetary policy. The banking system is the primary conduit for the transmission of monetary policy signals. Effective implementation of monetary policy requires that the banking system is able to expand and contract its aggregate balance sheet in response to policy initiatives without adversely affecting the efficiency of intermediation or depositors' confidence. This makes it imperative to maintain a sound banking system; otherwise it would render the instruments ineffective and distort the results of monetary policy actions as well as impair the authorities' ability to formulate and conduct monetary policy. Bearing in mind this central tenet, the RBI, in the initial stages, organized its supervision apparatus quite well and was prompt enough in locating problems of banks and also in identifying the mechanism for conflict resolution. However, once the interventionist regime gathered strength, with its wide reach to all the sectors of the economy, it introduced a political element in the RBI's supervision policy and eventually destroyed its raison d'etre. First of all, the Government of India, as the final arbiter in deciding action to be taken about banks, often overruled the RBI's recommendations if found to be unsound. This was dramatized in the case of Palai Central Bank in the erstwhile Travancore Cochin state (now a part of Kerala). As far as back as 1956, the RBI's inspection reports found it to be vulnerable, and suggested drastic action. But the Government of India headed by the Congress party was dilatory, prompted by the fear that it would compromise its political interests as the owners of the bank were its partisans. This deferred the action by many years until the financial position of Palai Central Bank threatened a banking crisis (Balachandran 1998: 767–93).

The second reason for downgrading the RBI's supervision responsibilities was the nationalization of the commercial banking system in 1969 (the largest bank, Imperial Bank of India was nationalized in 1955), which entitled the government to own as many as 27 large banks, accounting for as much as 85 per cent of the total bank assets. As a result, a dichotomy arose between the RBI as owners by proxy and the RBI as the regulator. It was virtually impossible, under these circumstances, for the RBI to avoid conflict of interests and to be objective in its assessment of the financial position of the supervised banks. Nor was it made easy by the government directors, who as owners defended the policies of banks, regardless of their financial conditions. As a consequence, all norms of prudent banking, like capital adequacy, income recognition, the minimum rate of return on assets, and the size of provision against non-performing assets were thrown to the wind, leaving the banking system in shambles. Thus at the end of 1991, seven out of 27 public sector banks had a ratio of non-performing assets to total assets in a range of 25 to 45 per cent, and 17 banks had a ratio between 15 and 25 per cent (Khatkhate 1993).

Perhaps the worst feature of the RBI's supervision policy was that it degenerated into economic regulation rather than prudential control which was its principal objective. And this was not surprising in an atmosphere of pervasive government intervention. The banking system operated within a regulatory thrust arguably characterized as parametric with the RBI stipulating an array of prices and guarantees which banks were required to adhere to rather than prudential with the RBI demanding adequate capital adequacy with rigorous accounting standards, while providing greater microeconomic freedom. Thus, the RBI imposed a maturity specific interest rate structure for deposits. Lending rates were likewise regulated with a plethora of rates depending upon the end use and the maturity of the loans. Furthermore, there were high levels of pre-emption of bank liabilities, partly to finance the borrowing needs of the government, not to speak of micro-management through credit authorization scheme of every loan or advance, to a large universe of big firms. This naturally changed the very perspective of the supervision function of the RBI. The attention was focused not on how the banks managed their balance sheets or the risks involved but on whether they complied with the various economic regulations which themselves were major factors in the financial vulnerability of banks in the first place.

The RBI's whole identity was jeopardized by the establishment of the Banking Department (now Division) in the Ministry of Finance in 1969 on the specious grounds that its proprietary interest in the government-owned banks needed special attention. Its inevitable consequence was that the regulation of the banking system ceased to be the exclusive preserve of the RBI, thereby undermining its authority both in the conduct of monetary policy as well as the management of the banking system. The RBI's subordination to government was complete when it was asked to stipulate a predetermined quantum of credit to the social sectors of the economy regardless of its monetary consequences. A former deputy governor, both during the early part of nationalization and national Emergency of 1975, trenchantly remarked that

nationalization only accelerated the politicization and emasculation of the RBI—there is no clear understanding as to where and in what measure its (RBI) authority should generally be respected by the government and it is this deliberate fudging of jurisdiction that has adversely affected the capacity and moral authority of the RBI and hence its effectiveness.... The Emergency settled once for all the issue in favour of the government by force majeure and the long process of requiring the RBI to seek formally or informally the approval of the Government of India on matters of banking administration and policies, including internal administration was complete (K. S. Krishnaswamy as quoted in Chandavarkar 1996: 239)

With such a denouement, it is easy to agree with Chandavarkar's strictures that 'India presents the curious contradiction of a political separation of powers without a corresponding separation of economic powers between the government and the central bank' (Chandavarkar 1996: 230).

Post 1991: Back to Basics?

The economic context in which the RBI functioned was radically transformed in 1991, when economic rationale and efficiency were given precedence over ideology and politics. This time the economic reform focused on the removal of microeconomic distortions deeply embedded in the economy for almost four decades and aimed at transforming the structure of the economy in such a way that the role of the public sector tended to diminish *pari passu* with the enlarging space for the private sector and a new incentive framework was substituted for the earlier command approach. This time, 'reform by storm has supplanted the reform by stealth of Indira Gandhi's time and the reform with reluctance under Rajiv Gandhi' (Bhagwati 1993: 3). The industrial licensing which straitjacketed the private sector was dismantled, trade barriers were lowered if not eliminated, the foreign exchange control regime was gradually transformed into market-oriented foreign exchange management system and, most importantly from the view point of the RBI, the financial sector was substantially liberalized, contrasting it with the earlier severely intervened one which tended to erase the distinction between the monetary policy of the RBI and the fiscal policy of the Government of India.

Deregulation of Interest Rates

The most significant aspects of the financial sector liberalization pertained to deregulation of interest rates both on bank loans and deposits. Thus capping of interest rates on loans above Rs 200,000 was eliminated and the banks were given freedom to announce maximum spread over prime lending rates on all loans barring consumer credit. The ceiling on rates on deposits of over 30 days were dropped and the maximum rate on deposits of less than 30 days was linked to the bank rate of the RBI, thereby giving the latter a prime role in the interest rate policies. Along with this, the policy instruments of the RBI such as the CRR and the SLR, which were mainly aimed at safeguarding government finance, were deprived of their flexibility. Though not to the full extent desirable, their levels were lowered so that they should be increasingly seen to be protective devices rather than monetary policy instruments. Conditions were created to facilitate open market operations, more as an instrument to manage reserve money and sterilize foreign exchange inflows than as a mechanism to manage government debt. For the first time in the history of banking in post-Independent India, the banking system's soundness and efficiency were given a pride of place to pave way for the use of monetary policy of the RBI in true classical fashion.

From the point of view of the RBI, what the financial reforms accomplished—not fully but in a substantial measure—was to give primacy to the markets, incentives, prices superceding central direction of economic activity, the exact preconditions essential for the unbiased and unhitched exercise of monetary regulation power that intrinsically belonged to the RBI. However, as will be argued below, the RBI's freedom to manouevre remained constrained, because the old remnants of ideology continued to permeate the psyche of the politicians and the obstreperous bureaucrats both in the government and in the RBI stalled change in the way the Bank ought to function.

The RBI in a new milieu of a liberalized financial system began to enjoy a relatively greater freedom to deploy its monetary policy instruments on its own without too much interference from the government. This occurred because of two important developments. First, India liberalized its current account of the balance of payments almost wholly in 1995 accepting obligations under Article VIII of the Articles of Agreement of the IMF and followed it up, by selectively eliminating some restrictions on the capital account. As a result, there was a large amount of private capital flows into India. In 1994 alone, capital inflows consisting of portfolio investment, banking capital, and foreign direct investment all combined exceeded the corresponding cumulative figure during 1981-90. This meant that the RBI had to be sensitive to both the exchange rate and interest movements, since both of them importantly affected them. If the exchange rate depreciates or the domestic interest rate declines, there would be a reversal of capital inflows. And vice versa, if the changes in these two variables are in the opposite direction. Under the flexible exchange rate regime that India adopted since 1993, the nexus between the domestic interest rate and the exchange rate was made stronger. If the exchange rate changed for some reason, it had automatic repercussions on the domestic interest rates and the money stock. The second development was the removal of regulation on domestic interest rates, giving greater leverage to the RBI to influence them through its various monetary policy instruments.

The RBI influences both the availability and cost of money, by changing the reserve money, that is, the currency in circulation and the reserves held with it by the commercial banks. It can do so, if it can control its determinants, which are: net bank credit to the government, net foreign assets, and net claims on the banking system. The effectiveness of its power and its autonomy depend on how much it can vary each of these variables affecting reserve money.

Liberalization and Autonomy

As seen earlier, the most important of these determinants of reserve money which should legitimately fall within the control area of the RBI is the net bank credit to the government and yet, the RBI had been powerless to do anything about it. The question to ask, therefore, is whether the financial liberalization has created an environment more conducive to regaining control over government borrowing from the RBI. This was the issue that assailed the minds of the policy makers both of the RBI and the Government of India, but precious little was achieved since the fiscal deficit remained stubbornly high and other resources of the government fell far short of its total expenditures. A determined effort was made in 1994 to tackle this issue headlong not only to rein in automatic monetization of fiscal deficit but also to restore the autonomy to the RBI. A concordat was entered into, between the RBI and the Government of India under which limits would be placed on net issue of ad hoc treasury bills absorbed by the RBI at the end of every financial year and also within the year. Initially the year-end limit of Rs 6000 crores was stipulated for 1994–5 and Rs 5000 crores each for two succeeding years, the within year limit during the year was kept at Rs 9000 crores. After April 1997, ad hocs would be replaced by ways and means advances (WMA). Furthermore, the ad hocs in the book of the RBI would be funded gradually in the form of marketable dated securities. Since April 1997–8, the RBI provided WMA within specified limits to meet temporary mismatches between government receipts and payments. Dated securities are issued automatically whenever 75 per cent of WMA limit is transgressed. Any credit beyond the limits is treated as an overdraft, permissible for not more than ten consecutive working days on which interest rate charged is the bank rate plus 2 percentage points. This agreement was hailed particularly by the RBI management as 'a watershed in the monetary history of India'.

The real issue is whether the new agreement of placing a ceiling on ways and means advances made any difference either to the government's access to open spigot or the autonomy of the RBI. It is true that if temporary advances are cleared at the end of the period, it would certainly reduce monetized deficit financing. If on the other hand, dated securities are issued whenever the upper limits are breached, the new system would differ from the old as the tweedledum from tweedledee, as the monetary consequences will be the same. To be sure under the new system, dated securities unlike the ad hocs would bear a market approximating interest rate agreed to between the RBI and the government. This, however, is a misleading measure since what the government would lose on the swing of higher interest rate would be offset by its gain on the roundabout, when the RBI profits are transferred to the government budget.

As it turned out, all claims of RBI autonomy were soon falsified. The government got round this limit by placing a large amount of dated securities with the RBI, whenever it floated public debt, under an innocuous sounding rubric of 'devolvement'. This was justified on the ground that though the RBI absorbed debt initially, it would subsequently be palmed off to the market through open market operations. This was plausible but the reality check reveals that it happened but rarely. For instance, during two years—1997–8 and 1998–9—the net open market sales were less than the so-called 'devolved debt' by almost 50 per cent and 33 per cent respectively. Only in 1999–2000 the net open market sales exceeded the initial subscription to the loan by the RBI. Looking at it differently, the ratio of monetized fiscal deficit to GDP was on average 0.56 per cent during 1994-5 as compared to 0.64 per cent between 1990-1 to 1998-9 (Reserve Bank of India 2000: 40, 214, see also *Economic Survey* 1998-9 and 1999-2000). Thus, the 'new system' of short-term RBI credit to government far from being the 'watershed' proved to be no more than a watered down version of the old system.

Foreign Exchange Regulation

The next major determinant of the reserve money is the changes in the net foreign exchange assets of the RBI. And here, the Bank played a very important role befitting a central bank. It had two principal objectives—to maintain a reasonably stable exchange rate, and monetary stability. These two objectives could and did conflict occasionally. When the RBI intervened in the foreign exchange market either to prevent the exchange rate from appreciating or to reduce its volatility, it had impact on the domestic money stock different from what it targeted on the basis of domestic consider-ations. On the whole, the RBI conducted open market operations—an indirect monetary policy instrument suited to new monetary and financial environment, but not without combining it with direct regulations and the use of reserve requirements. As the Indian economy gradually opened out, India's links with the global finan-cial markets were forged by growing inflow of foreign direct invest-ment (FDI), private portfolio investment, and deposits from Non-Resident Indians (NRIs). Between 1992-3 and 1998-9, there was a net inflow of private capital consisting of FDI and portfolio invest-ment to the tune of Rs 29 billion in contrast to a minuscule amount prior to 1991. Naturally, these inflows put heavy pressure on the exchange rate and since the objective of the RBI was to prevent the rupee exchange rate—indirectly the real exchange rate too—from appreciating so that export competitiveness should not be adversely affected, it was a net buyer of foreign exchange. However, since the expansionary impact on money stock, resulting from foreign ex-change purchases tended to conflict with a restrictive monetary policy during most of this period, the RBI's policy was one of sterilized intervention, which meant that it neutralized the expan-sionary effects of its purchases of foreign exchange by sale of government securities as a part of open market operations. During most of the years since 1993 when private foreign capital flowed in on a large scale by historic standards, the RBI was a net purchaser of foreign exchange, particularly during 1993–4 to the middle of 2000. This was matched by net sales of government securities during the same period (Reserve Bank of India 2000: 82; Khatkhate and Nayak 1996). A point to note, however, is that open market operations were conducted more as a counterpart of the exchange rate management than as a monetary policy instrument per se. There were, however, a couple of short intervals when the RBI sold foreign exchange when the pressure on rupee rate sharply increased. Though nominal exchange rate devaluation was generally warranted in the Indian conditions, the RBI's policy objective was to moderate the exchange rate volatility for confidence reasons (Kohli 2000). On the whole, the exchange rate management by the RBI reflected a better judgement on its part and was more effective than in the past.

Pursuing Contradictory Policies

Still, however, the RBI could not shove off completely the dead weight of history on its back. This was well-illustrated by the episode in May–June 2000, when the RBI pursued contradictory monetary and exchange rate policies more to accommodate the politics of the Government of India than to respond appropriately to the developments in the economy. Under the current flexible exchange rate system, the RBI is well placed to carry out an independent monetary policy, tailored to the cyclical turns in the domestic economy. If its monetary policy has any consequences for external balance, they will be reflected in the exchange rate variation, one way or another. In judging that the economy needed a monetary policy relaxation, the RBI reduced bank rate and an array of its other lending rates across the board and also scaled down its cash reserve ratio. The signal was clear that more bank credit should flow to the real sector. There were sceptics who believed that a relaxation of credit policy was not warranted particularly when the fiscal policy was loose with ever enlarging budget deficit and the inflationary pressures, dormant in the previous two years were resurging. Despite that the RBI persisted, if for no other reason than to pacify the government which wanted to borrow in the financial market at a low interest rate to finance its deficit. Soon after, the pressures on the rupee mounted firstly because the interest differential between India and the industrial countries widened due to the restrictive monetary policies in the latter, particularly the US and the European Union. This naturally induced an outflow of short-term portfolio capital from India leading to a slide in the rupee/dollar rate. There was no doubt that some element of speculation was there but it was, far from being an initiating cause, a rational response to the arbitrage possibilities arising from policy inconsistencies and regulatory shortcomings. If the domestic imperative was an expansionary monetary policy in the RBI's view, it should have ignored what happened to the exchange rate. But here again, the RBI became a hostage to politics. Indian politicians have not been able to shed their obsession that the stability of the exchange rate is something sacrosanct, despite what transpired since 1991, and the RBI did a somersault by reversing its monetary policy in June–August which it had relaxed only two months before for the ostensible reason of minimizing the volatility of the rupee rate. The RBI thus threw away the baby—of an independent monetary policy—with the bath water under political compulsions.

Credit to Commercial Banks

The third factor influencing the reserve money which the RBI targets for managing short-term liquidity is its credit to commercial banks. The RBI influences this by changes in cost of banks' access to its refinancing facilities. Since 1991, with the onset of financial reforms, the RBI dispensed with the sector-specific refinance facilities and replaced them with a General Refinancing Facility (GRF) for banks to avail of for meeting temporary liquidity shortages at interest rates linked to the bank rate. The GRF, which underwent metamorphosis first as a Collateralized Lending Facility (CLF) and then as Liquidity Adjustment Facility (LAF) revived the bank rate as a reference rate as in many other central banks and as the main tool of short-term liquidity management. Whenever the money market rates rise beyond what the RBI considers to be too high, the RBI reduces these rates and vice versa. Through the variation in these rates, the RBI controls the access of banks to its credit and the reserve money. This is essentially a market-oriented instrument, that unlike in the past acts as a signal to the market rates of interest. While the new system is certainly a vast improvement on the previous arrangements which entailed greater element of regulation by quantity than price, it is cumbersome in form and is burdened with several discretionary devices—somewhat in pre-1991 tradition. Even with these changes, the bank rate does not act as a signal for the RBI's policy stance. Interest rates charged by banks on their lending and deposits do not respond to changes in the bank rate. This reflects that banks have limited access to RBI credit and further that the banks have surfeit of liquidity. Aside from this, the banks' large non-performing assets and high CRR have raised loan-deposit spreads, making it difficult for them to react to changes in the bank rate. More importantly, the government's policy of offering high statutory rates on government-sponsored provident funds and small savings which compete with bank deposits have weakened the banks' response to the bank rate changes.

In addition to the refinancing rate, the CRR was used on many occasions during 1991–2000, more as a supplement to the bank rate and open market operations. But in a liberalized financial system, it is considered to be a step backward since this ratio along with SLR were symbols of the repressed banking system.

In sum, the RBI has gone quite a distance in liberating itself from the stranglehold of the executive. It has acquired greater leeway to exercise its power within the confines of the economic policy. And yet organizationally and functionally, it is still not as separate from the Finance Ministry as it should be. The Banking Division constantly looks over its shoulders and the public ownership of a major segment of the banking system does not permit it to assert its authority.

THE RESERVE BANK—A NORMATIVE IMAGE

There is some recognition now, though still vague and not fully thought through, that the monetary regulation needs to be separated from the other functions of the state, if it is to 'be exercised decisively' as Hicks put it. But movement toward it will have to be speeded up in the new economic and financial environment. As economic intervention recedes and the regulatory responsibilities multiply, the RBI, being in a vantage position, has to guide the process of financial system restructuring and liberalization with skill, knowledge, and a certain objectivity in its capacity as the bankers' bank, guardian of price stability, a steering controler of the payments system, and the banker and adviser to the government. In coming years, the RBI will have to concern itself with a wider definition of fiscal deficit to articulate its relationship with the government. Financial liberalization policy will succeed only if the Government of India reduces the level of its domestic liabilities. If not, the RBI will not be able to reduce significantly the SLR or CRR, even if it wants to or to withdraw its role in directly influencing the market interest rates. Furthermore, the government's annual sale of debt to the non-bank public, and its timing (when the interest rate on it will be allowed to be determined wholly by market forces) will be a matter of close interest to the RBI, since it will not have any influence on the interest rates resulting from that sale. Also, in a freely operating financial system, with the possibility of rupee convertibility sooner or later, the government's fiscal stance will importantly affect the exchange rate expectations. Since there is a link between the interest rate and the exchange rate, the RBI's monetary policy, unshackled from the monetization possibilities of the fiscal deficit has to play a kind of role, which is different from that in the past and would demand new skills.

With the developmental role emanating from interventionist policies being replaced by a concern with issues of market management as the economy is deregulated, the RBI will be required to cope with situations which are uncertain but unavoidable. Organizationally as well as managerially, the RBI will have to move from a risk-averting environment to a risk-taking one in most of the areas of its operation. These are:

(i) managing a 'demand-led' banking system;

(ii) reacting to the globalization of money and finance;

(iii) acting as a market watchdog.

Each of these will be discussed in broad details below:

Managing a 'Demand-led' Banking System

With the financial reforms gathering speed, and the emergence of new private banks together with the privatization of government-owned banks, the banking system will have to run on its own steam, influenced more by market forces than by the central control from the RBI. If the experience of open and market-oriented economies both in the developed and developing countries is any guide, the banking system will move often in ways, that have to be anticipated to the extent possible by the monetary authorities. New financial products would come in the market, new innovative practices will be introduced and the RBI should be ready to comprehend their significance and act on their regulation taken in the prudential sense. These innovations will change the concept of monetary aggregates, which is the primary concern of the RBI for stabilization purpose and for that reason, it will have to be alert enough to devise new instruments.

Reacting to the Globalization of Money and Finance

The globalization process has to be treated as given with liberalization of the financial system and the eventual convertibility of rupee on capital account. The RBI, like central banks elsewhere, has to be equipped to cope with the risks and opportunities that flow from it. Substitutability between domestic saving and foreign saving will considerably increase which will have costs and benefits. The RBI's monetary policy will have to come to grips with this phenomenon.

Acting as a Market Watchdog

Until now, the RBI was transmitting information from the top—the government to the market. This process will have to be reversed. It will have to be all eyes and ears of the government at the market place, to read the signals of developments in the markets—financial, commodity, foreign exchange and the private real economy, to discipline them, whenever necessary, and to form the judgement as an input into the formulation of the broader economic policy of the government.

In order to have a handle on all these issues which are radically different from what the RBI faced in a regulated economy, it will have to transform itself, as a part of the financial system reform, specially because, being a banker's bank, it has to provide a firm, purposive, and intellectual leadership to the financial system. The shape and nature of the reform of the RBI can be viewed from two angles. First, it is essential to determine whether a formal independence of a central bank is critical for it to confront and resolve the new issues arising in the liberalized economy. Second, the RBI will have to undergo transformation from being an institution which exercised authority on the banking system with rules-bound procedures and theological respect for the manual to one which has quick responses to events in the domestic and foreign markets. The staff managing it, too, will have to have a different mindset to come up with positive action.

There is no settled wisdom about whether legal provisions to ensure a central bank's independence are necessary to undertake these new functions. Some central banks in developing countries like Chile, Mexico, and the Philippines have followed that route. The jury, however, is still out on these issues as far as these countries are concerned. Amongst the developed countries, the US and Germany boast the independence of central banks, both in fact and law. On the other hand, France and Japan, even without formal legal sanction, acted as de facto independent central banks and quite successfully so. This judgement is supported by the empirical study covering 72 countries for two decades, which found that in developing countries legal independence particularly is not a statistically significant determinant of price stability if that is the main objective of central bank policy.[9] Thus legal provisions are neither necessary nor sufficient for ensuring the central bank's independence. On the other hand, a genuine commitment on the part of the political authority is enough to preserve a central bank's independence. The higher the rate of turnover of governors, the weaker the central bank's autonomy, and vice versa.

[9] Alex Cukierman, Steven B. Webb, and Bilin Neyapti, 'Measuring the independence of Central Banks and its Effects on Policy outcomes'. *The World Bank Economic Review*. The authors gave a plausible explanation for why the legal safeguards to ensure autonomy fail to serve their purpose through employing an amusing metaphor. Some of the developing countries in their sample, which included India, have elaborately locked cookie boxes, which are broken or locked when the politicians are hungry. This means that unless political authority has a respect for the central bank charter and management, the law formally providing for autonomy will remain a toothless tiger. There are many other studies as for example by M. Fry, C. A. E. Goodhart, and A. Almeida (1995) and B. J. Sikken and J. de Haan (1998). But nothing definitive has emerged.

The Government of India and the RBI can come to some institutional arrangements about appointment of the governor and the Board of Directors. A healthy convention can be established by appointing the RBI governor for a period of five years and not removing him before he completes his full term. The legal provision in the RBI Act is vague under which the government can appoint the governor for a period not exceeding five years. This has been used often to suit the political convenience of the existing government or a new one. In the period prior to 1969 there was a healthy convention to appoint the governor for five years. Since then only four governors have completed their full term of five years, but one of them did it only through extensions of his initial term of two years. Two of them were appointed for a period of two years. This practice of shoving and shuffling governors has created an impression in the public mind that they are appointed or removed on the ground of political expediency and thus has contributed to the deflation of the stature of the governor and the institution he heads. For the RBI to be effective as an apex institution, the Government of India will have to revert to its earlier sound practice of appointing governors for the full five years and adhere to it in all situations unless they are involved in some financial malfeasance.[10] The same holds true about the constitution of the Central Board of the RBI. The Board should have a four year term and when the term ends, the new Board members' appointment should not be prolonged as has been happening too often in recent years. In addition, the Government of India may consider retiring at a regular interval, say every three years, a third of the Board members in order to insulate the Board from frequent changes in the government. These conventions may help to restore to some extent the prestige of the RBI and refurbish its image. Apart from this, the RBI Board needs to be vested with greater power than it has today in order to make it a more effective deliberative body

[10] An exercise of power, even within the restrictive legal framework depends on the personality of the Governor. In 1966, Governor P. C. Bhattacharya raised serious objection to the size of the Plan in his letter to the Finance Minister on the ground that it was unrealistic and would generate serious inflationary pressures. As a result, the Plan was pruned drastically. Another example was that of Governor I. G. Patel, who sacked in 1989 a dozen members of the RBI staff for organizing illegal strike, despite the opposition from the Government of India and politicians from the ruling Congress party.

rather than a passive one to rubber stamp what the governor together with the Government of India decides. This will imply that the members of the Board possess requisite expertise and knowledge in the monetary and banking areas.

In the ultimate analysis, a central bank's independence can have meaning if it can be demonstrated that it is capable of being accountable to the executive or the legislative wing of the government. The effective execution of the delegated authority and accountability may be impaired if there are no arrangements in existence which facilitate public understanding and monitoring of monetary policy, reveal the central bank's expertise and organizational efficiency, and establish the information channel system necessary for formulation and implementation of monetary policy.

The RBI has to revamp itself organizationally and professionally to deserve autonomy. The RBI, like other public sector banks, offers a wide scope for the application of the Parkinson Law and the Peter principle. Over the years, though some of the major departments such as the Industrial Finance Department and the Agricultural Credit Department were hived off from the RBI, its staff has continued to grow in geometric progression; with 34,000 employees the RBI has entered the Guinness Book of Records as the largest employer among the world's banks.[11] Instead of making any attempt to downsize the staff, the management of the RBI being blessed with a permissive soft budget constraint extended retirement age of employees to 60 years some time ago. Strangely, when the security scam exposed the inadequacy of the RBI's Supervision Department, there was no shake-up of personnel in the higher echelons, which would have occurred in any institution that is serious about its accountability. There is no promotion policy that can throw up persons of ability and merit. In terms of management, organization, staff skills, and modern management tools, it is at the same level of inefficiency as the public sector banks to which it is supposed to provide guidance and advice. The RBI thus has become an institution without *gravitas*. All this suggests that the RBI should have a clear cut plan for its reorganization.

---

[11] *The Economist* (London) noted that there is an inverse correlation between economic performance of a country and the number of employees of the central bank, which may be one of the reasons for India's low growth rate! (see 'A Glut of Central Bankers?', *The Economist*, 1 May 1993.

The RBI does not seem, however, to have awakened to the imperative of a thorough overhaul of its organization. Despite the freeing of current account of the balance of payments and consequent transfer of most of the foreign exchange functions to the commercial banks, the Exchange Control Department is still retained. No dramatic measures have been taken to modernize the department of currency management—which with its largest employee contingent of coin-note examiners—is working in its good old ways. But the most egregious example of the RBI's insensitivity to the emerging needs was the reorganization of its Supervision Department. The financial liberalization heightened the awareness of the prudential control in which the RBI was weak and outdated. But instead of concentrating on the essentials of training its staff, the RBI set up a Board for Financial Supervision (BFS) consisting of the RBI governor as chairman, the deputy governors, other high officials of the Bank, and some members of its Board of Directors. The new arrangements superimposed on the existing Supervision Department, far from improving the RBI's supervisory and prudential functions have made it too cumbersome with additional layers of bureaucracy to permit transmission of information from downstream of the department to its upstream. This again was reflective of the empire-building ethos of the past, which was underpinned by a commonly followed creed that solution to every problem lay in setting up a new department. One is tempted to compare the RBI with the Bank of England whose model the RBI followed, which drastically reorganized itself a few years back when the financial markets in the UK were deregulated.[12]

The RBI will have to introduce a transparent personnel policy with proper performance evaluation and incentive framework. With computerization and modernization of work practices, it will have to have a forward-looking plan. However, it should try to avoid a Bonapartitst recipe of inflating the ranks of generals in order to deflate their importance. In the end, the RBI will do well in

[12] Some of these ideas were presented in a wider context of financial sector reform by the author in his 1993 report, 'Indian Banking System: Restitution and Reform Sequencing', prepared at the request of the then Finance Minister of the Government of India, Manmohan Singh and on the explicit understanding that it would be issued for public discussion. As it transpired, it never saw the light of day because of strong opposition from the then management of the RBI.

remaining a lean and efficient organization with staff equipped with different mix of skills and charged with intense motivation. It had a full scale management audit done a few years ago by an outside consultancy firm and its report contained contours of a strategic plan action. The report was thorough-going and well articulated and would have assisted the RBI's efforts to achieve its reorganization and reform goals. There was also another committee report on human resources development but no action was taken on either of them. What is needed is a time bound action plan ready to be implemented. It is only with such bold organizational, managerial, and human resources reform initiatives that the RBI can raise its stature as an effective central bank and enhance the credibility of its policies thereby qualifying itself for an eventual autonomy. Chandavarkar has aptly summed up what a central bank ought to be in a modern world, 'Central banking, more than any other branch of economics is a uniquely complex amalgam of ideas, traditions, institutions, techniques, and operations, which does not yield a corpus of settled unambiguous conclusions. Nevertheless, it points to a decisive shift in the paradigm from independent to effective central banking, based on the highest professionalism and integrity, lest central banks fail in their appointed role of Platonic bastions of the economy and become the Potemkin Villages of the financial system' (Chandavarkar 1996: 240). This could well be a mantra for the RBI in a new millennium.

References

Annual Report (1999–2000), Bombay: Reserve Bank of India.

Balachandran, G. (1998), *The Reserve Bank of India*, New Delhi: Oxford University Press.

Bhagwati, J. (1993), *India in Transition: Freeing the Economy*, Delhi: Oxford University Press.

Chandavarkar, Anand (1996), *Central Banking in Developing Countries*, London: Macmillan.

——— (2000), 'Was Keynes Anti-Semitic?' *Economic and Political Weekly*, 6 May.

Cukierman, Alex, Steven B. Webb, and Bilin Neyapti (1992), 'Measuring the Independence of Central Banks and its Effects on Policy Outcomes,' in *The World Bank Economic Review*.

Deshmukh, C. D. (1948), 'Central Banking India—A Retrospect', Pune: Gokhale Institute of Politics and Economics.

Economic Survey 1998-9, Government of India: Ministry of Finance.
———— *1999-2000*, Government of India: Ministry of Finance.
Eichengreen, B. (2000), Personal View, *Financial Times*, 6 September.
Fry, M., C. A. E. Goodhart, and A. Almeida (1995), *Central Banking in Developing Countries: Objectives, Activities, and Independence*, London: Routledge.
Hicks, John R. (1977), *Economic Perspectives: Further Essays on Money and Growth*, Oxford: Clarendon Press.
History of the Reserve Bank of India, 1953-1951 (1970), Bombay: Reserve Bank of India.
Joshi, V. and I. M. D. Little (1994), *India: Macroeconomics and Political Economy, 1964-1991*, New Delhi: Oxford University Press.
Khatkhate, Deena (1991), 'National Economic Policies in India', in Dominic Salvatore (ed.), *National Economic Policies: Handbook of Comparative Economic Policies*, vol. I, New York: Greenwood Press.
———— (1993), 'Indian Banking System: Restitution and Reform Sequencing', mimeograph.
Khatkhate, Deena and Jayendra Nayak (1996), 'Private Capital Flows and Financial Integration in India', DEC, Washington DC: World Bank.
Kohli, R. (2000), 'Real Exchange Rate Stabilization and Managed Floating: Exchange Rate Policy in India, 1993-99,' ICRIER Working Paper No. 59.
Nehru, B. K. (1997), *Nice Guys Finish Second*, New Delhi: Viking.
Report of the Committee to Review the Working of the Monetary System (1985), Bombay: Reserve Bank of India.
Sikken, B. J. and J. de Haan (1998), 'Budget Deficits, Monetization and Central Bank Independence in Developing Countries,' Oxford Economic Papers.
The Economist (1993), 'A Glut of Central Bankers.'

9

India's Federal Institutions and Economic Reform

M. GOVINDA RAO and NIRVIKAR SINGH

INTRODUCTION

This chapter provides a broad overview and analysis of India's federal institutions in the context of economic reform. Our main theme is that a careful consideration of the incentives that affect government decision-making in a federal system is the key to improving India's fiscal position, as well as the effectiveness of its government at all levels. The chapter is structured as follows.

In Section II, we review the different institutions of governance in India, paying particular attention to their interaction with federal structures. We examine the federal structures of India's political parties, as well as of the judiciary, police, and bureaucracy. In Section III, we describe the tax and expenditure assignments that form the basis of India's fiscal federal institutions, including their theoretical underpinnings. We examine the rationale for inter-governmental transfers in a federation. We also consider the system of Centre-State transfers that results from, and complements the assignment of fiscal authorities in India.

Section IV provides a conceptual framework within which to consider institutional reform in government. We examine the ideas of transparency and accountability, and discuss various mechanisms of accountability, including voice, exit, hierarchy, and checks and balances. We discuss the role of monitoring, and the institutions that provide it. We analyse the relative incentive efficiency of different accountability mechanisms in a federal system. We extend this conceptual discussion by relating it to the broader context of economic reform in India. Issues such as decentralization are often viewed as independent of or orthogonal to issues of economic reform. Instead, we argue that the two are quite complementary, and that some of the key bottlenecks to obtaining further benefits from market-oriented reform can be overcome by improving the functioning of government through decentralization and forms of delegation.

In Section V, we examine the nature of ongoing local government reform in India, and we evaluate some of its strengths and weaknesses in the light of our conceptual framework and in the last section we make a few concluding remarks.

II. INDIA'S FEDERAL SYSTEM OF GOVERNANCE

In this section, we briefly review the different institutions of governance from a federal perspective. Many of these institutions are examined in more detail in companion papers for the volume (Das, Krishnan and Somanathan, Manor, Mehta, Verma 2001), but here we focus particularly on federal aspects. The basics of India's federal structure are well known: directly elected parliamentary-style governments at the national and state level, as well as nascent directly elected government bodies at various local levels. We focus on the federal structures of India's political parties, the judiciary, police, and bureaucracy. Understanding these governance structures helps to understand the actual workings of India's institutions of fiscal federalism.

Political Parties

To the extent that the essence of federalism is based on democratic politics, the role of political parties in the interactions between central and state level politics, is a crucial aspect of federal structures. To illustrate, consider the extreme case where government powers are notionally decentralized, with residuary powers residing at the state level, but the national and all state governments are all controlled by a single, rigidly hierarchical political party. Here the outcome will effectively be the same as in a centralized, unitary system. For example, during the Nehru era, the Prime Minister's personal authority and prestige were combined with almost complete legislative control of the Centre and the states. In such circumstances, issues of Centre-state relations were often played out within the ranks of the Congress party.[1]

Riker (1975) has noted the increasing decentralization of Indian federalism, measured according to an index of concordance between which party is in power at the Centre, and which parties are in power at the various constituents of the subnational, or state level, after the Nehru era. An additional factor in this period was, of course, the lack of a central figure with Nehru's personal authority. Events after 1975 represented a period where the decentralizing trend was resisted by the Centre, in the increased use of Article 356 of the Constitution to remove elected state governments and impose direct central rule, and, in an extreme manifestation, in the 1975–7 Emergency. However, the last decade has seen a resumption of the decentralizing trend, with regional parties becoming more significant, and diversity in the composition of governments at the Centre and in the various states becoming an ordinary situation.

Even as the Bharatiya Janata Party (BJP) has built up a national constituency to rival that of the Congress, the importance of regional parties has not diminished. The days when regional groups operated only within national parties seem to be over, and most states have significant parties whose bases are *only* regional. This situation will clearly persist. Hence Centre-state political competition will remain very much out in the open, rather than take place within party organizations. Manor (1995) provides a recent analysis of the role of regional parties in India's federal system. He points out that the Congress has always tended to encompass

[1] One of the most striking examples of the substitution of personal relations and party hierarchy for constitutionally mediated federal relations was the 'Kamaraj plan' of the early 1960s. N. Kamaraj, chief minister of Tamil Nadu (then Madras) and a significant Congress party leader, proposed that all central and state ministers of the party should resign, so that some of the party's leaders could be released for organizational work to revitalize the party. This was accepted by the party high command, with the exception that Prime Minister Nehru's offer to resign was not accepted. Instead, Nehru was given full discretion by the party to decide on the reconstitution of state as well as central ministries—all others 'resigned' en masse.

regional alliances, and has therefore had a federal structure within the party organization, and that the BJP itself, as it strives to become more of a national party, and not just based in the Hindi heartland, has had to become more decentralized in nature, if not quite federal.

Manor (1995) makes another significant observation with respect to state level politics based on recognition of the various dimensions of heterogeneity in identities (language, religion, different forms of tribal allegiance, caste, and so on) that there is not obviously a single fault line along which conflict can become concentrated and persist. As a consequence, states with boundaries based on language have not become the basis for secession because of the heterogeneity of identities that exist within each state. Exceptions to Manor's observation exist, of course. In those cases different dimensions of identity coincide enough to lead to concentrated, persistent conflict, exacerbated by inappropriate central government responses. In fact, one might argue that unfettered electoral political competition at the state level is likely to ameliorate such conflicts *whatever* the fault lines that exist.[2]

With some caveats, therefore, Manor's analysis also has favourable implications for extending party politics more firmly down to the local level, as is envisaged in the recent legislative changes to strengthen local governments. It must also be noted that federal political structures allow the provision of a greater diversity in local (or, more generally, subnational) public goods, by improving accountability and incentives. They also allow an unbundling of this provision from that of national public goods, and to that extent make complete separation to enjoy the benefits of local diversity unnecessary. Thus Tamil Nadu, where a regional party has been continuously in power for long periods of time can enjoy considerable autonomy in many spheres, without having to give up the benefits of defence being provided at the national level. This argument assumes, of course, that a regional party provides certain

---

[2] There are clearly many subtleties to be considered here. The statement made implicitly assumes that something like a median voter model, where the median voter does not benefit from secession. It is also possible that, given a set of central policies, the median voter would prefer secession. This still might be resolved by central-state bargaining within the realm of normal politics, rather than violent conflict, if bargaining is permitted to proceed within the appropriate institutional framework for achieving durable agreements.

benefits that cannot be delivered by the state-level organization of a national party.[3]

In conclusion, national political parties in India have incentives to be federal in the nature of their organizations, following the federal structure of Indian government itself. At the same time, purely regional parties may have certain advantages over state-level units of national parties, when regional identities are strong. Issues of commitment and control may arise in political party structures, just as they do in the case of different levels of government. The question of how to manage breakdowns in state-level party politics raises issues of checks and balances among different branches of government. We turn from political parties to a discussion of the component of government that actually implements politicians' will, namely, the bureaucracy.

The Bureaucracy

If elected politicians act as agents of constituents or voters, bureaucrats in turn act as the agents of elected officials. Bureaucrats are partly insulated from political whims and pressures, but ultimately in a democracy, they must be subordinate to the elected representatives. This means that a unitary, hierarchical bureaucracy cannot by itself negate a federal political structure in the same way that a powerful, centralized, national political party might. However, a centralized bureaucracy can act as the agent of such a political party, in acting against the requirements of a federal system. There are elements of such action in the workings of Indian bureaucracy, but the story is also a more complicated one.

The bureaucracy in India has played a crucial role in the country's governance since Independence, and this role has been an important aspect of the conflicts over the degree of centralization or federalism. What is particularly noteworthy in understanding Indian bureaucracy is that it is provided constitutional recognition. The central and state level tiers of the 'public services' are given shape through the provisions of part XIV of the Constitution. Of course any bureaucracy in a federation will have a federal character in the sense that each layer of government requires its

---

[3] In practice, an independent regional party is better able to credibly commit to certain policies—the state wing of a national party might, in the minds of voters, and in practice be subject to national level control.

own administrative apparatus to accompany the political structures. In particular, state governments must be able to appoint (and dismiss) bureaucrats to implement state-level policies: this would seem to be an essential consequence of a federal structure of government. This is certainly the case in India, where there is a central bureaucracy as well as an independent bureaucracy in each state, as indicated by the Constitution.

The federal structures of Indian bureaucracy are complicated by the dual allegiance of a key component, the Indian Administrative Service (IAS). The IAS is an all-India bureaucratic hierarchy: its members are chosen by a central process, and trained together in a National Academy.[4] However, they are then assigned to particular states, and become, technically as well as in most practical matters, members of a state-level bureaucratic hierarchy as well. While an IAS member's entire early career is spent within the home state, and senior level appointments at the state level carry considerable power and prestige, the most prestige and power, and resulting attraction typically lie with appointments within the central government.

Thus, while the structure of the IAS was designed as a compromise between, on the one hand, the desire to have an effective administrative apparatus at the governmental level to which most of the tasks of day-to-day administration, development, and law and order were assigned by the Constitution (that is, the state level), and on the other hand the fear of promoting regional loyalties over national ones (with the further fear of disintegration of the nation), this compromise has been inherently problematic. A lack of clear lines of authority creates difficulties for incentives. To some extent, the incomplete decentralization of the IAS parallels the ambiguities inherent in the political structures of Indian federalism. However, the last decade has seen federalism in the operation of electoral politics, as discussed in the previous subsection, outstrip the more rigid structures of the bureaucracy.

Of course, greater decentralization of the bureaucracy will not remove all problems. There are hierarchies and levels within each

---

[4] A more recent complication has been the induction into the IAS of members of the state level civil services. Such inductions often bring none of the neutrality benefits of the centrally selected members, while compounding dual loyalty issues.

state. The differing incentives of bureaucrats and elected politicians will always lead to conflicts and the question of the limits of political control is a thorny one. In India there are many examples of the distortion of impartial administrative decision-making caused by political pressures and the widespread use of transfers of administrators as a means of exercising political control. As long as the issues of incentives and accountability of politicians are not addressed, there is not much that can be done about providing appropriate incentives to the bureaucracy.

The Judiciary

The judiciary is a specialized bureaucracy, but is conceptually more separate, constituting a distinct branch of government at its higher levels. Much judicial activity involves judging whether the law was broken and who broke the law in particular cases, in which capacity the judiciary acts as a specialized agent of elected officials who frame laws. The higher levels of the judiciary also act as judges of the laws themselves, within the context of the overarching legal and constitutional framework. Furthermore, the judiciary in theory can check the actions of politicians in ways that may be difficult for bureaucrats: 'no one is above the law'. Practice diverges from ideals, of course, and the how and why of this divergence make up the following discussion.

The Indian Supreme Court stands at the top of the judicial hierarchy. Its powers include broad original and appellate jurisdiction and the right to pass on the constitutionality of laws passed by Parliament. In practice, there has been conflict between the Supreme Court and the legislature/executive over the scope of these powers, and their boundaries remain subject to bargaining. The president, in consultation with the prime minister appoints Justices of the Court.

At the state level, below the Supreme Court, are the high courts. Each high court's justices are appointed by the president in consultation with the chief justice of the Supreme Court and the state's governor. Paralleling the situation at the Centre, the state's chief minister is in a position to strongly influence the governor's advice. High courts also have both original and appellate jurisdiction. In addition, they superintend the work of all courts within the state, including district courts, as well as various courts subordinate to the district courts. These subordinate courts are specialized, with smaller civil matters being separated out from criminal cases, for example. Criminal cases are dealt with in magistrates' courts where IAS bureaucrats may fulfil magisterial roles.

The formal judiciary, therefore, is a well-defined hierarchy, with a relatively clear assignment of tasks. This assignment and hierarchy are overly centralized, in the sense that not enough matters are disposed of at lower level courts. This partly reflects a lack of resources devoted to lower level courts (though, the resource problem exists at all levels), but also a centralized assignment of scope of jurisdictions. The problem is compounded by the nature of the appeals process, and by the failure of higher level courts to control appeals. Also, judges below the state level are not appointed by local government officials, representing a significant departure from a federal system below the state level.

In many cases in practice, the formal judiciary does not directly control or enter into the legal process. Several examples of alternative enforcement structures exist in India. Members of the bureaucracy serve as judicial decision-makers, particularly in rural areas. Also in rural areas, traditional local councils (panchayats) have had effective judicial authority over a range of matters. The judicial role of panchayats has been given some policy attention in the past. Since Article 50 of the Constitution requires separation of the judiciary and the executive, an attempt was made, especially after 1959, to create *nyaya* or *adalati* panchayats (NPs) to handle local judicial matters, separating this traditional activity from the panchayats that had performed it in the past. This arrangement was also meant to parallel the decentralization of developmental functions to panchayats, while avoiding overburdening them. However, delays and arrears, ultimately attributable to a lack of adequate funding of the NPs, led to the failure of the system. The decentralization of government structures, through recent constitutional changes strengthening local government in other dimensions, has raised these issues again, and they are revisited in Section V.

One of the most striking features of the state of India's judiciary is the degree of delay. One cause (Mookherjee 1993) is the failure of the number of judges to grow sufficiently quickly over this period. The rate of disposal also matters for delay. Mookherjee notes factors such as effective management of caseloads, antiquated judicial procedures, short workdays, and lax codes of conduct for lawyers.

Reductions in delays could also be achieved by reducing the number of cases that have to be considered at this level. Measures to do this include reassigning jurisdictions between lower level and high courts, better scrutiny of appeal petitions, and the development of alternative dispute resolution mechanisms. There is a strong argument for having many kinds of routine local legal disputes at the lowest level consistent with fairness and efficiency. The second of these, if it results in fewer appeals being heard, also constitutes effective decentralization. The third suggestion is an example of delegation. The microeconomic inefficiencies of the judicial system in India, partly reflect inadequate deconcentration and devolution within the judiciary itself, but ultimately are a consequence of inadequate delegation of powers by the legislative/executive branch. In turn, this is a constitutional problem, because this delegation is absent in some of the particulars of the Constitution.

While a weak central legislature may allow the national judiciary, particularly the Supreme Court, to play a more effective checking role, it does not solve the resource allocation problems that must ultimately be corrected, for smoother working of day-to-day judicial functions. The pressure might come from competition among subnational jurisdictions pursuing commercial motives: this may lead to a correction of some of the worst inefficiencies in legal processes. In other words, as states and localities try to attract investment and commercial activity, they will be under pressure to provide judicial systems that support commercial activity. It should be noted that this argument applies in particular to areas such as contract enforcement, or property rights enforcement more broadly, rather than the criminal justice system.

The Police

The police have a special role, involving both the bureaucracy and the judicial system. Ideally, the police are impartial investigators and monitors, preventing violations of law where possible. Their role complements that of the judiciary in enforcement. However, the police are also organized as a bureaucracy that is under the control of politicians, like other branches of administration, but unlike the judiciary, which has a notional independence. The actual functioning of the police therefore becomes subject to the kinds of influences discussed above in the context of relations between bureaucrats and politicians. One important aspect of this politicization has been the encroachment of the central government into law and order, constitutionally a state subject.

The Indian Police Service (IPS), which is the superior officer cadre for the police in India, is organized on similar dual lines to the IAS, that is, centralized recruitment and bureaucracy, but without the same key role in the central government that belongs to the IAS. This latter difference reflects the fundamental difference between the generalist IAS and the functional specialization of the IPS. However, the fact that the IPS is a central bureaucracy puts its members on a different footing than members of state police forces recruited directly by state governments, even when IPS officers are assigned to particular states. The central government possesses several other police forces also. The Central Reserve Police Force, the Central Bureau of Investigation, the Border Security Force, and the Railway Protection Force. All these together give the central government considerable power over policing, well beyond what might be suggested by the constitutional assignment of powers.

While there are jurisdictional conflicts between the Centre and the states in policing, conflicts also exist between the IAS and the IPS. The lack of clear lines of accountability and control tends to adversely affect incentives and efficiency. Though it is argued that the check of civilian administration, at as many levels as possible, on a police force that is distrusted or inefficient, is a necessary safeguard, it is not clear that the present arrangement is the best possible institutional structure. Ultimately, both the police and the IAS are subject to political control, and this is where the key to restructuring lies. One of the problems perceived in the Indian case is the great degree of improper political influence. The solution to the resultant problems of enforcement—inconsistency, corruption, uncertainty, delays—may be to strengthen the organizational independence of the police vis-à-vis politicians, and possibly other bureaucrats, but allow greater control by a stronger judiciary. This line of reasoning may seem naïve—after all, why should the judiciary provide an effective monitor of the police, especially since judges do not have to be responsive to electorates?

One answer might be that a strengthened judiciary, at least at the local level, might be made subject to election, somewhat along the lines of the United States model. Another possibility is that power and prestige may lead to the opposite of short-term self-interested behaviour. The persistence of the Indian armed forces as an institution with relatively high integrity and efficiency, without obvious abuses of power, yet without direct control by the electorate, is worth considering in this respect. Of course, the interests of the armed forces may be less in conflict with those of politicians than would be the interests of a strengthened judiciary.

An alternative is suggested by trends in countries such as the United States and Britain: a greater role for citizens' organizations, in the form of police review commissions, as a direct democratic check on police behaviour. However, this may be more effective in dealing with sins of commission, rather than of omission. In the United States in particular, much policing is handled at the local level, and local elected officials provide a fairly direct check on the operation of police, ensuring some measure of responsibility and accountability. Some of the pitfalls in local policing in India are similar to those of decentralization in general: lack of resources, training, and equity. These pitfalls are illustrated by the workings of the traditional village police, as described in Bayley (1969: ch. 15), where all three are in short supply. In addition, capture by local elites remains an issue (see Section V). However, a carefully planned and executed decentralization can overcome some of the current problems created by divergence between the interests of citizens and of individuals engaged in law enforcement. Such decentralization would have to include atten-tion to the organizational structures within which the police operate. In particular, the assignment of tasks to different levels of police would have to be done carefully: economies of scale and scope are likely to be quite important, and overlapping of assignments may create confusion.

Conclusions

Thus, neither economic nor political aspects of federalism can be looked at in isolation, if one wishes to gain a proper understanding of the workings of a federal system. In this section, we have tried to unpack the political side of federalism by discussing the various dimensions of government and governance. Governance involves a complex of tasks, and government has different components to handle different aspects, just as would any large organization. Elected officials in theory act directly as agents of constituents to decide policies, and bureaucrats in turn act as the agents of elected representatives, advising on and implementing these policies. The judiciary and police are, in the abstract, special bureaucracies assigned the fundamental task of monitoring and enforcing law and order in general, and the protection of corporate and individual property rights as well as other individual rights.

The existence of different dimensions of governance implies that a federal political system cannot exist simply through a constitutional assignment of responsibilities to different layers of government. Each level of government in a federal system must not only have authority to raise revenues, but it also has to have the authority to carry out decisions made at that level. In India, the bureaucracy, the police, and the judiciary are all perhaps more centralized than they need to be, given the current federal political system. While independent India began with a relatively circumscribed federal model, independent political competition at the state government level has thrived. This decentralization has not necessarily been matched in the other dimensions of government, but may need to be for a more effective federal system to operate.

III. FISCAL FEDERALISM IN INDIA

In this section, we describe the tax and expenditure assignments that form the basis of India's fiscal federal institutions as well as providing some theoretical underpinnings. Then we examine the rationale for intergovernmental transfers in a federation. Finally, we consider the system of Centre-state transfers that results from, and complements the assignment of fiscal authorities in India.

Tax and Expenditure Assignments

We briefly discuss theoretical underpinnings, followed by a summary of tax and expenditure assignments in India. Economic theories of government provide justification for government intervention in the provision of public goods and services. However, public goods can have regional dimensions. Similarly the degree of 'publicness' may vary across goods as well as regions. Once the possibility of subnational public goods is admitted, one should consider the possibility of provision of these goods by governments whose constituencies match the locus of beneficiaries. In a world of perfect information and benevolent governments, however, the issue of hierarchical structure of government becomes irrelevant: one encompassing government can do it all perfectly.

If, more realistically, the information available to governments is not perfect and they are not intrinsically benevolent, subnational governments will be better able to judge the desired levels of some public goods, and can be given more powerful or refined incentives to do so. Comparative advantage in information is an important factor in the assignment of expenditure functions to decentralized governments. Wherever economies of scale, access to resources, and externalities or spillovers do not indicate otherwise, the expenditure assignment should match the locus of beneficiaries. In other words, if the benefits of a public good are local, then local government should have the responsibility for provision.

Turning to the issue of government revenues, what ultimately matters is taxation, since the interest on borrowing must come out of taxes. We put aside issues of collection efficiency. Our focus, therefore, is on the allocational efficiency of different tax assignments. These may be quite significant, because the incentive effects are quite different across levels of government. In particular, mobility across jurisdictions within a federation is greater than mobility across nations. A tax base that is mobile may shrink dramatically in response to a tax. Therefore, it is harder for subnational jurisdictions to raise revenue from taxes than it is for the central government. One can think of the problem as being one of tax 'capacity': this being lower for the subnational jurisdictions. If this factor implies that more taxes should be collected by the center, there will be a tendency for there to be a mismatch between revenues and expenditures for subnational jurisdictions, to the extent that subnational governments are relatively better able to respond to diversity of preferences, as noted above.

At any level, if the government is both benevolent and omniscient, government decision makers know the preferences of constituents, in particular their marginal benefits from the provision of any public good, or from an increase in its level. Therefore, it is easy to assign cost shares, in the form of taxes or user charges, to individuals in a manner such that every individual's marginal cost equals her or his marginal benefit. If information and incentives are imperfect, however, the connection between costs and benefits is harder to establish, and voting schemes provide a limited incentive mechanism. The assignment of taxes to a jurisdiction to cover its costs of public goods provision is desirable, but may be counteracted by the dictates of tax base mobility. A further push towards more centralized assignment of taxes may come from redistribution motives. These principles place a distinct advantage to the central government in levying taxes on broad-based and mobile bases. Hence, they can result in a 'vertical fiscal imbalance'. While the central government is better equipped to raise revenues, the state and local governments are better placed to provide public services. This becomes a reason for the vertical transfer of resources, in addition to the goal of promoting greater equity of jurisdictions.

However, the divergence of revenue and expenditure decisions at the margin can have adverse consequences for incentives, and in the ultimate analysis, the assignment of both revenue and expenditure authorities must take these consequences into account. In particular, tax and expenditure assignments cannot be entirely independent, particularly at lower levels of government, which predominantly provide public or near-public goods and services. Linking expenditures on public services with prices (user charges or tax payments) in fact supports the provision of appropriate incentives and accountability. Therefore one cannot consider expenditure and revenue assignments and the structure of incentives and institutions independently.

The Indian Case

The Indian Constitution, in its Seventh Schedule, assigns the powers and functions of the Centre and the states. The Schedule specifies the exclusive powers of the Centre in the Union List; exclusive powers of the states in the State List; and those falling under the joint jurisdiction are placed in the Concurrent List. All residuary powers are assigned to the Centre. The functions of the central government are those required to maintain macroeconomic stability, international trade and relations, and those having implications for more than one state. The major subjects assigned to the states comprise public order, police, public health, agriculture, irrigation, land rights, fisheries and industries, and minor minerals. Subjects like public health, agriculture, and irrigation involve considerable governmental expenditures. The states, being closer to constituents, also assume a significant role for subjects in the Concurrent List like education and transportation, social security and social insurance.

The assignment of tax powers, however, is based on the principle of separation, that is, tax categories are exclusively assigned either to the Centre or to the states. Most broad-based taxes have been assigned to the Centre, including taxes on income and wealth from non-agricultural sources, corporation tax, taxes on production (excluding those on alcoholic liquors) and customs duty. A long list of taxes is assigned to the states. However, only the tax on the sale and purchase of goods has been significant for state revenues. The Centre has also been assigned all residual powers, which implies that the taxes not mentioned in any of the lists automatically fall into its domain.

In 2000–1, the states on average raised about 38 per cent of total revenues, but incurred about 57 per cent of total expenditures. The important central taxes consist of Union excise duties, customs duty, and personal and corporate income taxes. Among the state taxes, the revenue from sales tax is the most important. While the share of the states in raising revenues has shown a marginal increase from 35 per cent in 1990–1 to 38 per cent in 2000–1, their expenditure share during the period has increased much faster from 52 per cent to 57 per cent. The principal reason for this has to be found in the salary revision of public service employees.

Intergovernmental Transfers

Economic arguments for intergovernmental transfers have been made in terms of (a) offsetting fiscal imbalances or closing fiscal gaps; (b) establishing horizontal equity across the federation; and (c) offsetting inter-jurisdictional cost and benefit spillovers. In addition, transfers may also be given to carry out some agency functions for the central government. We focus here on the first of these arguments, in the Indian context.

Vertical fiscal imbalances are a feature common to all multilevel governmental systems. Even when assignments of functional responsibilities and revenue powers are efficient, imbalances can occur. The central government has a comparative advantage in raising revenues whereas sub-central governments are better placed to provide public services efficiently, corresponding to varying preferences of people of different jurisdictions (Breton, 1987, 1996).

Of course, there can be non-economic considerations for assignments and consequently, vertical fiscal imbalances.

The fiscal imbalance argument does not exclude considering the actual fiscal behaviour of the states. Designing transfers to offset fiscal imbalances can adversely affect incentives for own-revenue raising and for spending control (Wilde 1971; Gramlich 1977), and these disincentive effects ideally should be minimized. General-purpose transfers are given to enable the sub-national governments to offset the fiscal disadvantages arising from a lower revenue capacity and a higher unit cost of providing public services. This can be achieved by giving unconditional transfers in a variety of ways, but the least distorting way is to give transfers equivalent to the recipient's 'need-revenue' gap (Bradbury et al. 1984). The need-revenue gap measures the difference between what a state ought to spend to provide specified levels of public services and the revenue it can raise at a given standard level of tax effort.

In addition to avoiding incentives for fiscal laxity, a formula for intergovernmental transfers should be equitable, simple, transparent, and perceived to be objective. However, such ideal transfer systems do not exist in practice. In the actual design of transfers, historical, political, cultural factors can play important roles, so that simple normative criteria, even if agreed upon, may not easily translate into transfer systems that achieve the objectives.

The Indian Constitution recognized that its assignment of tax powers and expenditure functions would create imbalances between expenditure needs and abilities to raise revenue. Therefore, the Constitution provides for the sharing of the proceeds of central taxes with the states, and making grants to the states from the Consolidated Fund of India.[5] The shares of the Centre and the states and their allocation among different states of both the taxes are determined by the Finance Commission (see below) appointed by the president of India every five years, or earlier as needed. In addition to tax devolution, the Finance Commission is also required to recommend grants to the states in need of assistance under Article 275.

[5] Accepting the recommendation of the Tenth Finance Commission, the 80th amendment to the Constitution in 2000 included all central taxes in the divisible pool as against the previous arrangement of compulsory sharing of personal income taxes (Article 270) and optional sharing of Union excise duties (Article 272).

A notable feature of India's federal fiscal arrangements is the existence of multiple channels of transfers from the Centre to the states. First, as noted, the Finance Commission decides on tax shares and makes grants. Second, the Planning Commission makes grants and loans for implementing development plans. Finally, various ministries give grants to their counterparts in the states for specified projects either wholly funded by the Centre (central sector projects) or requiring the states to share a proportion of the cost (centrally sponsored schemes): these were alluded to earlier.

Historically, as development planning gained emphasis, the Planning Commission became a major dispenser of funds to the states. As there is no specific provision in the Constitution for plan transfers, the central government channelled them under the miscellaneous and ostensibly limited provisions of Article 282.[6] Before 1969, plan transfers were project-based. Since then, the distribution has been done on the basis of a consensus formula decided by the National Development Council (NDC).[7] However, various central ministries still felt the need to influence states' outlays on selected items of expenditure through specific purpose transfers with or without varying matching requirements: these are monitored by the Planning Commission.

Transfers from the central government contribute significantly to state finances. In per capita terms at constant (1993-4) prices, central transfers to the states increased by over 2.5 times from Rs 198 in 1975-6 to Rs 486 in 1996-7 and increased further to Rs 633 in 2001-2. Also, until 1997-8, growth of transfers was faster than both Centre's and states' own revenues. In fact, during the period since the mid-seventies, while the states' own revenues grew at 15.3 per cent and central revenues grew at 14.8 per cent, the growth of central transfers to states was 16.4 per cent. In the latter half of the 1990s, however, the transfers have decelerated. Thus, the share of transfers in central revenues increased from 32 per cent

[6] The legitimacy of these transfers has been seriously questioned. K. K. Venugopal argues that devolving funds to the states under Article 282 is unconstitutional. Others consider that though this is permissible, channelling large amounts under this article is not in keeping with the spirit of the Constitution (See NIPFP 1993).

[7] The NDC is chaired by the Prime Minister and its members include all cabinet ministers at the Center, Chief Ministers of the states, and members of the Planning Commission.

in 1975–6 to 44 per cent in 1997–8 and declined thereafter to 33 per cent in 1999–2000. Similarly, share in state revenues increased from 39 per cent in 1975–6 to 45 per cent in 1997–8 and declined to 36 per cent in 1999–2000. Of course, state expenditures increased at a much faster rate during this period and therefore, the share of transfers in state expenditures declined steadily and yet, they finance almost a third of state expenditures. The relative shares of the three channels of central transfers to states since the Fourth Plan (1969–74) bring out two important features. First, there has been an increase in the *discretionary component* of transfers. Second, within statutory transfers, the proportion of tax devolution, which had already been high, has increased, while that of grants has declined.

Finance Commission Transfers

So far, eleven finance commissions have made recommendations and, barring a few exceptions, these have been accepted by the central government. However, the working of these commissions, their design of the transfer system, and the approach and methodology adopted by them have come in for criticism. The main criticisms are (i) those relating to attempts to restrict the scope of the finance commissions through the presidential terms of reference; and (ii) those on the approach and methodology employed by the commissions and the equity and incentive consequences of the transfer scheme evolved by them.

India's adoption of a planned development strategy with a pronounced socialist bias concentrated economic power in the hands of the Centre and, within the central government, the Planning Commission. The increased dominance of the Planning Commission in allocative decisions, and its empowerment to dispense assistance to the states to finance their developmental activities, curtailed the Finance Commission's role in making intergovernmental transfers. Although the Constitution made no distinction between Plan and non-Plan sides of the budget, presidential terms of reference have confined the finance commissions to making transfers only to meet the non-Plan requirements of the states. The restriction of the finance commissions to the non-Plan side of the budget has led to a number of problems. First, larger transfers through the Planning Commission have significantly reduced the ability of the Finance Commission to achieve redistribution.

Second, it has prevented a holistic review of state finances. Third, conceptually, the Plan and non-Plan distinction is unsound. Besides poor coordination, the separate treatment of Plan and non-Plan expenditure needs, and the emphasis on having large plans have led to inadequate provision for, and maintenance of, assets created under previous plans. From the states' point of view, separate Plan and non-Plan assessments gave them the opportunity to submit different projections to the two commissions—an overestimated non-Plan budgetary gap to the Finance Commission and overestimated saving in the non-Plan account to the Planning Commission.

The Finance Commission's approach consists of (i) assessing overall budgetary requirements of the Centre and states to determine the volume of resources available to the Centre for transfer, and required by individual states; (ii) projecting states' own revenues and non-Plan current expenditures; (iii) determining the distribution of net proceeds of aggregate central taxes (excluding cess and surcharges) with the states and the shares of individual states; and (iv) making up the deficit between projected expenditures and revenues after tax devolution with grants. This is popularly known as the 'gap-filling' approach.

In the evolution of the system of tax devolution over the years, some important features are notable. First, states have preferred tax devolution to grants, due to its inherent responsiveness to price and income increases. Second, the finance commissions, in response to criticism that their transfers promoted laxity in the states' fiscal management, have preferred to increase tax devolution rather than 'gap-filling' grants. As tax devolution is made mainly on the basis of general economic indicators like population, per capita SDP, other indicators of backwardness, collection, and tax effort and not on the basis of fiscal disadvantages *per se*, the overall objective of the transfer system is not met.

In the final step, Article 275 grants fill 'fiscal gaps'. Such grants are determined on the basis of projected gaps between non-Plan current expenditures and post-tax devolution revenues. Some of the commissions moderated the 'gaps' by taking account of normative growth rates of revenues and expenditures in projections, and taking the returns from public undertakings on a normative basis. The Ninth Finance Commission was the first to comprehensively adopt a normative approach and determine the gaps between revenue capacities and expenditure needs, but since the bulk of the transfers was given through tax devolution based on general economic indicators, the effectiveness of this approach was dissipated. The Tenth Finance Commission, however, reverted to the old methodology.

The 'gap-filling' approach suffers from a number of shortcomings. First, finance commissions have made judgements about tax shares without evolving objective criteria for evaluating the Centre's needs. Second, as noted earlier, the separate workings of the Planning and finance commissions have prevented an integrated view of the states' fiscal needs, and distorted their behaviour. A third weakness of Finance Commission transfer schemes is their lack of clear purpose. They have not been designed to meet the major theoretical objective of unconditional transfers, offsetting fiscal disadvantages of the states. Tax devolution was decided on different considerations from those of grants-in-aid, and the criteria for distributing the income tax were different from those for excise duties. Fourth, the gap-filling approach adopted by the finance commissions has had adverse effects on incentives for tax effort, as well as spending.

There has been considerable concern about the Finance Commissions following the 'gap-filling' approach, and its possible disincentives on fiscal management in th states. This was the reason for modifying the terms of reference of the Ninth Finance Commission to follow a 'normative approach'. However, the Commission did not fully make use of the estimate of fiscal capacities and needs of the states in formulating its recommendations. The tenth Finance Commission simply abandoned the approach. The 11th Finance Commission in the additional terms of reference given to it just before the finalization of its recommendations was asked to '…draw a monitorable fiscal reforms programme aimed at reduction of revenue deficit of the state and recommended the manner in which the grants to the states to cover the assessed deficit in their non-plan revenue account may be linked to progress in implementing the programme.'

The Commission worked out a scheme by pooling 15 per cent of revenue deficit grants and adding an equal amount to it to create an incentive fund to be allocated among the based on fulfillment targets of growth of tax and non-tax revenues and expenditures on salaries, interest payments, and subsidies set in the fiscal restructuring plan detailed by the Commission. It gave equal weight to monitorable measures on the revenue and expenditure sides and specified weights to each of the monitorable measures. The incentive fund has been allocated to the states according to their population shares. A state gets the full amount if it fulfils the targets and the amount will vary depending on the degree of achievement of monitorable targets. If a state does not get the full amount during the first four years it will continue to be available in subsequent years, but if by the fifth year the targets are not achieved, the funds will lapse. To implement the scheme a monitoring agency has been set up by the Government of India. The states have signed the memorandum of understanding to implement the Medium Term Fiscal Reform Programme with the Centre, which is monitored by a committee comprising of representatives of Finance Ministry, Planning Commission, Power Ministry, and independent experts.

There are a number of problems with the proposed scheme. Some of them have been pointed out in the Note of Dissent presented by one of the Members of the Commission (Government of India 2000: 9–13). The problems include both with the monitorable measure and implementation mechanism. The measures can vary not only due to factors within the states' control but also beyond. Again, while determining the grants these measures have been taken into account, but a portion of the grants thus determined is withheld for distribution according to the achievement of these measures. There are also problems of fiscal autonomy of the states when its actions are supervised by a monitoring agency. Finally, while the scheme tries to monitor the fiscal performance of the states, there is no mechanism to monitor the performance of the Centre.[8]

Plan Transfers

Plan transfers from the Centre to the states consist of grants and loans. Since 1969, plan assistance has been distributed on the basis of the 'Gadgil formula' approved by the National Development Council and modified from time to time. According to this latest formula, 30 per cent of the funds available for distribution is kept

[8] Also, the Centre still has the incentive to raise non-tax revenues as against tax revenues, and raise administered prices of public monopolies instead of raising excise duties. Further liberalization (e.g., privatization and market borrowing) can ameliorate these problems.

apart for the special category states. Assistance to them is given on the basis of plan projects formulated by them and 90 per cent of the transfer is given as grants, with the remainder as loans. The 70 per cent of the funds available to the major states is distributed based on population, per capita SDP, fiscal management, and special factors. For the major states, assistance is given through grants and loans in the ratio of 30:70.

The Planning Commission works out Five-Year Plan investments for each sector of the economy and each state. With this as background, the states work out their respective annual plans for each year, based on the estimated resource availability, which includes the balance from current revenue, contributions of public enterprises, additional resource mobilization, plan grants and loans, market borrowings, and other miscellaneous capital receipts. The Planning Commission then approves the states plan. Thus, given the amount of central transfers to the states as determined by the Gadgil formula, at the margin it is mainly the states' own resource position that determines their plan sizes.

Plan transfers are not directly related to any shortfall in states' resources, given the required amount of plan investments and own resources reckoned at a standard level of effort. Plan transfers to the states, as well as their grant-loan components, are determined independently of the required plan investments, their sectoral composition, resources available with the states or their fiscal performance. In fact, the grant component of central plan assistance has been kept at 30 per cent because when the Gadgil formula was introduced, the current component of plan outlay was approximately 30 per cent.

Hence, while there were considerable variations in the ratio of current plan expenditures among individual states, the grant-loan mix for plan assistance for the major states has been kept constant. The constancy does not take account of the differing repayment abilities of the states. Also, it involves a bias against states with a strategy for development through human capital formation (for example, education), as against those with an emphasis on physical capital formation. In the former, the current expenditure component, according to prevailing budgeting practices, is higher. Since returns on expenditure initially accrue to the individual rather than the government, states with a larger current component of Plan expenditures would have as much of an interest liability as states with a larger share of capital expenditures, but with much lower levels of revenue-yielding assets.

Assistance for Central Sector and Centrally Sponsored Schemes

Assistance given to states through central sector and centrally sponsored schemes, constituting about 15 per cent of total transfers, is in some respects the most controversial form of transfers, being wholly discretionary. Central government ministries initiate a number of 'National Programmes', either by themselves, or at the request of the relevant ministries at the state level. Central sector schemes are assisted entirely by way of central grants and the states merely have the agency function of executing these programmes. Centrally sponsored schemes are cost sharing programmes, and the share of central assistance is through grants or loans decided for each individual programme. The ostensible rationale for these programmes is financing activities with a high degree of inter-state spillovers, or which are merit goods (for example, poverty alleviation and family planning).

Although the major programmes on family planning and rural development may be well designed, bureaucratic and political discretion play an important role in determining the amount of transfers and the pattern of their distribution. There have also been instances where the prime minister has announced programmes in public meetings, leaving the Planning Commission and the relevant ministries to work out details subsequently. If even a few of the programmes are determined in an arbitrary and non-transparent manner, well formulated programmes under central sector and centrally sponsored schemes also can come under suspicion. Implementation in general remains problematic: we discuss this in Section IV.

These programmes have provided the central government with an instrument to actively influence states' spending. Until 1969, the volume and pattern of assistance to state plan schemes were decided for each project. Once plan assistance was given according to the Gadgil formula, these specific purpose transfers proliferated. At present, there are over 200 centrally sponsored schemes with detailed conditionalities, such as requirements on staffing patterns, tend to distort the states' own spending. Also, the proliferation of schemes seemingly has increased the bureaucracy considerably.

Therefore, the NDC appointed an investigative committee, which recommended scaling down centrally sponsored schemes. This recommendation, however, has not been seriously acted upon. There is a case for consolidating a number of schemes into specific purpose transfers under broad headings, with greater flexibility given to the states in the use of funds.

A Case for Institutional Reform

Normative criteria for a successful intergovernmental transfer system are that, besides being equitable and incentive efficient, it should be simple, objective, and transparent. These criteria, in turn, require a proper institutional mechanism. In India, the Constitution attempted to create this through the Finance Commission. The Commission was to be appointed every five years, to take account of the changing needs of the Centre and the states. The Finance Commission (Miscellaneous) Act also lays down qualifications of the chairman and members of the Commission and the presence of a judicial member/chairman in the Commission is supposed to give it an independent, semi-judicial status.

Despite the provision of an independent agency, the system of transfers evolved over the years in India has not fulfilled its intended objectives. The design of general and specific purpose transfers falls short of the intention of offsetting the fiscal disabilities of poorer states, and of ensuring minimum standards of services in aided activities. Further, transfers formulae are not simple and transparent; the incentives generated by the system do not promote good fiscal management; and transfers are not well targeted to meet the objective of fiscal equalization. There are a number of institutional reasons for this outcome. First, multiple agencies giving transfers in an uncoordinated manner cannot implement singular economic objectives. Second, each of the channels has not only failed to design the transfers to offset fiscal disabilities but also have created disincentives for fiscal management. Third, while the Finance Commission is at least expected to be non-political, the Planning Commission is not. The Gadgil formula used for distributing Plan assistance is determined by consensus in the NDC. Finally, the centrally sponsored schemes are discretionary, where many non-economic considerations enter into the distribution mechanism.

Nor have the finance commissions functioned well in evolving the transfer system. Lack of permanency in their tenure has impeded the development of a satisfactory methodology for dispensing transfers. Although a small research cell has been created in the Finance Ministry, it is ill-equipped to improve the methodology of making projections, estimating fiscal capacities and needs of the states, undertaking analysis of their indebtedness; or maintaining and updating the data required for the analysis by the subsequent Commission. Each Commission has to start afresh and, given its time constraints, finds it difficult to conduct the analysis necessary for making recommendations consistent with overall objectives. Thus, there has been very little improvement in methodology or databases.

The fact that the central government (through the Ministry of Finance) determines the chairman and members of the Commission, and specifies its terms of reference, raises questions about objectivity and fairness, particularly when political personalities are appointed to the Commission. Also, the member-secretary is always a senior bureaucrat belonging to the Indian Administrative Service, appointed not because of expertise or interest in the subject, but because he or she qualifies to be appointed as a secretary.[9] Sometimes, mid-way through the Commission's tenure, the member-secretary secures a transfer to a more prestigious post as a secretary in an important administrative department, and is replaced by another such bureaucrat. The Commission's staff also comes chiefly on deputation from various central ministries: many are unfamiliar with the technical details of state finances, intergovernmental transfers, and research methods.

Lack of coordination between the Planning and Finance commissions further adds to the shortcomings of the current institutional arrangement. There have been cases where the Planning Commission sets about filling the non-Plan gaps of the states in their current accounts, resulting from their non-compliance with the norms set by the finance commissions. The states, as noted earlier, submit different projections of revenues and expenditures to the two commissions. We will return to these issues in the concluding section.

IV. FEDERALISM, INCENTIVES, AND REFORM

The essential problem of designing institutions of governance is one of designing incentives. Democratic governance requires delegating

[9] This designation is the highest rung of the civil service.

decision-making, for a range of tasks, from the people to those who will govern. Hence, government decision-makers are the agents of their constituents and must be given incentives to act in the interests of constituents. Note that this view of governance is in contrast to a traditional paternalistic (and maternalistic) model, where the government is the *mai-baap* of those whom it governs. This is a fundamental difference that must be understood at this basic level as one goes into the reform of federal governance structures in India.

Incentive Mechanisms

Our approach is based on analysing the structure of incentives as embodied in institutions of governance. Two of the most common words used in recent writings on government reform are 'transparency' and 'accountability'. These ideas are central components of our framework as well. Transparency refers to the public availability of information that allows performance (means as well as ends) of government decision-makers to be measured. Attention to means is particularly relevant when corruption is a commonplace problem, but even in general, the ends may not always justify the means.

Measured performance, along with a system of rewards and punishments, constitutes accountability. In other words, accountability is built on transparency, as indicated by the left-hand horizontal arrow in Figure 9.1. We may characterize the combined system of information availability and rewards and punishments as the essence of the 'institutional structure', as indicated in the figure. Hence transparency and accountability are descriptors of a desirable institutional structure, creating appropriate incentives for action by government decision-makers, as shown by the right-hand horizontal arrow. The term that is often used in the context of delivery of public goods is 'responsiveness' to constituents.

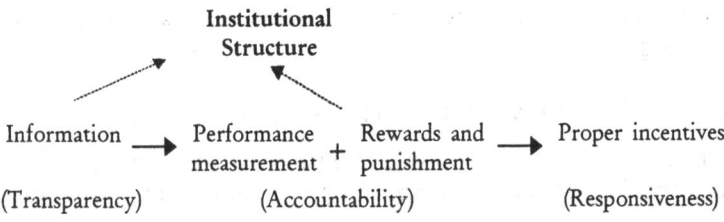

FIGURE 9.1: **Institutional structure and incentives**

While Figure 9.1 provides an overview of the terms that describe the essence of the institutional structure, we must also distinguish between external and internal incentives. External incentives are mainly created by the ability of constituents to change their government—through the ballot box in a democratic system. Thus external incentives apply chiefly to elected officials, or politicians. However, elected officials make up only a small proportion of the government. Appointed officials or bureaucrats perform much of the actual work, particularly the delivery of public goods.[10] Bureaucrats typically cannot be directly removed, or otherwise punished or rewarded, by constituents. To some extent, the power of politicians over bureaucrats is also circumscribed. However, in any democratic system, bureaucrats must be subordinate to elected officials, and therefore the incentives of bureaucrats, internal to government organization, are driven by the external incentives. Internal incentives are determined inside government, by politicians and higher level bureaucrats, and include conventional organizational devices such as bonuses, promotions, attractive assignments, and termination threats.

To clarify these points, consider an example. A bureaucrat is given a task of delivery of a public good. If he (or she) does not perform, there is little that constituents can do directly to affect his situation. His performance is judged internally by his bureaucratic superiors, with input from elected officials. Elected officials, if lobbied by constituents, can bring pressure to bear on the bureaucrat or his superiors. Their own incentive is externally determined, since if they are not responsive to their constituents, they run the risk of being voted out of power. Note that we are not saying here that these are the only incentive mechanisms, or that they work perfectly. For example, lobbying by constituents against bureaucrats may be by narrow interest groups, at the expense of the broader population.

[10] Not every government employee can be elected. The issue is the relative efficiency of different incentive mechanisms: it is very costly for voters to assess the performance of each member in a government organization, especially when the organization's performance is a product of joint efforts. Appropriate electoral incentives for key personnel should lead them to provide incentives in turn for their subordinates. However, a comparison with the United States, where many more government officials are elected, suggests that electoral incentives for 'non-politicians' may be used more effectively in India.

We now look in more detail at the mechanisms and avenues of incentive provision for government. We depart in two ways from the framework illustrated in Figure 9.1. First, whereas the above discussion was applicable to any level of government, we now focus on the case where there exists a higher level government, above the one being analysed. The lower level can thus be state or local government: we will focus on the local for concreteness. In India, there are two tiers above local government, but in other countries, only the national government may be above the local one. Second, we incorporate the existence of alternative avenues of incentive provision in addition to the electoral mechanism ('voice'): 'exit' (the ability to move to a different jurisdiction or constituency, or to a private provider), 'hierarchy' (the administrative and political hierarchies of government) and 'checks and balances' (the existence of different branches of government with their own powers).[11]

Figure 9.2 provides a schematic representation of our framework. In addition to the four accountability mechanisms, it also

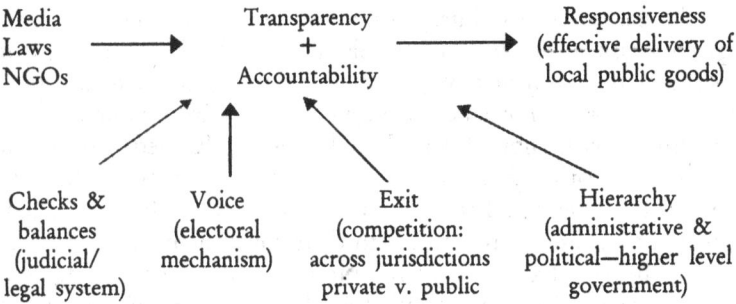

FIGURE 9.2: **Incentives mechanisms and organizations**

[11] 'Exit' and 'voice' are, of course, well known formulations due to Hirschman (1970). 'Hierarchy' is an avenue highlighted by Litvack et al. (1998) in the context of discussing decentralization and local government, and added by them to Hirschman's duo. 'Checks and balances' goes back to debates on the United States' Constitution. While checks and balances are a horizontal division of powers typically discussed in the context of a national government, the concept is clearly relevant for any level of government, so we add it to the Litvack et al. trio. We can briefly relate these mechanisms to the two types of incentives postulated earlier: 'hierarchy' and 'checks and balances' are internal, while 'voice' and 'exit' are external.

displays avenues for enhancing transparency. The role of non-governmental organizations (NGOs) is worth remarking in this figure. NGOs are becoming more and more popular and well looked upon, but their multiple roles are often not delineated. Our framework allows a clearer understanding of the role of NGOs. NGOs are voluntary, non-profit groups. Voluntariness distinguishes them from governments, in that they lack the coercive power that constituents must perforce delegate to government decision-makers. They may serve as information intermediaries, directly enhancing transparency. They may also enhance accountability in several ways: facilitating 'voice' through monitoring electoral processes, 'exit' through providing alternative delivery mechanisms for public goods, and 'checks and balances' and 'hierarchy' by serving as pressure groups or as representatives of constituents who need to make a case to a branch of government. This framework displayed will be helpful in understanding the nature of local government reform in India, and the areas where further attention may be required. Those reforms shift some of the reliance for incentive provision, which ensures accountability, from hierarchy to voice. We discuss the pluses and minuses of this in Section V, as well as the roles of the other two avenues of incentive provision. We also discuss the changing role of the institutions that affect transparency in local government.

Economic Reform and Federalism

The programme of economic reform in India that began in 1991 (though elements were in place earlier) does not, with one exception, include much on the role of government. The exception has been the issue of the government's fiscal deficits, and the need to reduce them. Here, we briefly argue that the reform agenda for India must include a broader consideration of the role of government, and India's federal structures in particular. The essence of our argument is that liberalization, the shifting of economic activity, and decision-making from the government to the market through removal of controls, privatization, and so on, is just one aspect of a more general redefinition of the role of government in the economy. Two other dimensions are also significant. The first of these is 'unbundling' government through the creation of independent or quasi-independent regulatory bodies. Key examples of this approach are the creation of the Securities and Exchange Board of India (SEBI), and the ongoing attempt to create a viable Telecom Regulatory Authority of India (TRAI). One can term these kinds of actions 'delegating sideways'.[12]

Delegating sideways affects another conceptual dimension that guides us in considering governance (in addition to transparency and accountability): the ability to make credible commitments. This can be a knotty problem, because governments are sovereign— they are delegated by an electorate to make and implement laws for a particular term of office, and they can therefore unmake laws as well as make them. Constitutions exist to partially solve this problem: creating hard-to-change frameworks within which everyday governance must take place. But they do not solve the commitment problem for everyday governance, and many issues of governing the market, whether for stocks of wheat or stocks of firms, fall in this realm.

Infact, commitment, transparency, and accountability can all be aided by unbundling government. Where regulation of markets or of private provision of goods and services is required of government, unbundling through creating separate regulatory agencies that are not under the thumb of ministries is critical. Of course this does not guarantee that regulation will automatically be more efficient: even SEBI, while relatively successful, is still feeling its way, and has had missteps. Other examples of existing and potential specialized regulatory institutions include the Reserve Bank of India, and bodies to deal with anti-competitive practices, consumer protection, and specific industries such as energy and telecommunications. It may seem that removing such tasks from the direct control of ministries reduces accountability. It does make the link indirect, but by increasing the ability to commit to policies, and increasing transparency in the sense that there is a well-identified individual with whom the relevant buck stops and cannot be passed on, accountability is potentially enhanced. The potential for rent seeking is also reduced by the transparency of specialization. This kind of sideways delegation will require granting some genuine independence if decision-making incentives are to be improved.

---

[12] Lewis (1995) is the source of this term, though he uses it much more broadly, to include the delegation of authority to private agencies outside the official hierarchy.

A second kind of unbundling is similar in spirit but broader. It requires revitalization of an existing set of institutions, rather than the creation of new, specialized institutions. In particular, the Indian judicial system, which was discussed in Section II, needs resources and reorganization to play its various enforcement roles. The judicial system also provides examples of possibilities for the first kind of unbundling, specialized delegation. For example, inter-state water disputes in India might be better handled by tribunals that are more independent of the legislative and executive branches (Richards and Singh 2002). Other kinds of specialized arbitration might also be handled by permanent, dedicated courts, rather than in the general judicial morass, or by ad hoc, but independent and binding commissions or tribunals.

The third dimension of economic reform is decentralization. Liberalization has brought with it some kinds of decentralization, where state governments rather than the central government can negotiate over and decide on certain matters, such as investment in power generation. The Centre may still have a role in coordi-nation, but its main role in such circumstances should perhaps be toward providing carrots and not vetoes. The Indian Constitution's assignment of responsibilities gave the states much notional power, attenuated in practice by the Centre's political compulsions and by the paraphernalia of planning, as discussed in Section III. A major factor in this attenuation has been the vertical fiscal imbalance created by the mismatch between expenditure responsibilities and revenue authority: Indian states raise much less in revenue than they spend, relying on central assistance (grants and loans) for the rest. In practice, this has led to inefficient influence activities in the determination of transfers (Kletzer and Singh 1997), as well as conflicting objectives.

Part of the solution is a strengthening of the sideways delegation that already exists through the Finance Commission, giving it more scope, simplifying the transfer formulas, and reducing the role of the Planning Commission in determining transfers—replacing dis-cretion with more rule-based transfers. This effectively decentral-izes control over resources. It might be argued that the states are profligate, and our recommendation is a bad idea, one that would worsen the problem of fiscal deficits. However, this problem is one of incentives rather than of structure. More transparent, rule-based transfers will be less subject to the soft budget constraints that now plague federal finance in India. Moving towards market borrowing for the states will also aid this goal, replacing discretionary, non-transparent intergovernmental loans that are made without credible commitments to recover them.

The above three dimensions of economic reform are schematically represented in Figure 9.3 below. While much has been accomplished through simple liberalization, future productivity gains will come about only through the removal of bottlenecks in the development and provision of 'public' capital. This includes not only physical infrastructure such as roads, ports, and power, but also broad-based human capital (which also has a strong public component), as well as public institutional capital that encompasses the various dimensions of governance discussed above. The way to improve public capital use lies precisely in modifying the incentive structures within and across levels of government in ways that enhance efficiency in the operation of government at all levels. Improving India's federal institutions must therefore be a key aspect of future economic and political reform. We have already outlined some features of possible reform in Section III. In the next section, we examine an important ongoing development: local government reforms in India.

V. LOCAL GOVERNMENT REFORM

In this section, we discuss local government reforms to illustrate a major theme of the chapter, that some of the key issues in economic reform are with respect to the design of appropriate

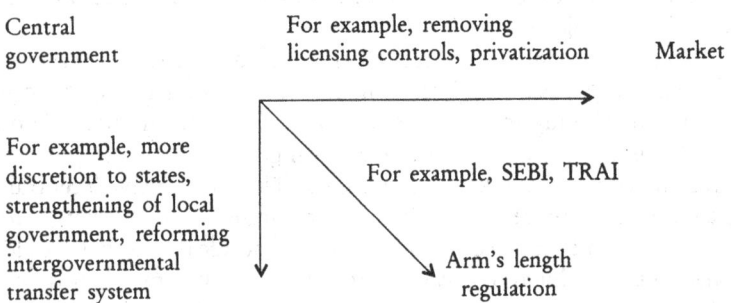

FIGURE 9.3: Dimensions of economic reform

incentives for government decision-makers.[13] After a long history of debate on decentralization, a central government committee recommended that local bodies should be given constitutional status. Two separate amendment bills were introduced, covering panchayats and municipalities respectively, passed by Parliament in 1992, ratified by more than half the state assemblies, and brought into force as the 73rd and 74th amendments to the Constitution of India in 1993. These amendments required individual states to pass appropriate legislation, since local government remained a state subject under the Constitution, and individual states have done so. These legislative changes are the beginning of a process of local government reform in India.

We begin with some basic description. Table 9.1 gives a state-by-state summary of the 'span of control' of rural local governments in India. The population per village government is extremely small, with the median across the state averages being only 2700. There is considerable variation among the states, but the only two obvious outliers are Kerala and West Bengal. These are also the most densely populated states, but the difference is more a reflection of a different institutional arrangement in these states. The small jurisdiction of village governments raises questions of economic efficiency. Populations per block council are considerably larger, with a median across these 16 states of 114,000. The block level is important in approximating the constituencies of the lower houses of the state legislatures (Legislative Assemblies). Populations per district council, the highest rural level, are quite large, with a median across the states of close to 1.5 million. The district is approximately the size of the constituency of the member of the Lok Sabha, the lower house of the national Parliament. The block and district levels—particularly the latter—have been important components of the central administrative and plan implementation apparatus.

Since the lowest level is so small in population size, the intermediate level may be more important for rural local government reform than has been emphasized in previous discussions, both to internalize externalities, and to take advantage of economies of scale and scope. These arguments extend to the highest level, the district, but are counterbalanced by its size, in absolute terms (affecting the

---

[13] Useful evaluations of this issue in a comparative perspective are by Crook and Manor (1998) and Manor (1999).

TABLE 9.1
Rural local governments: span of control

	Population per village government	Population per block council	Population per district council
Andhra Pradesh	2500	45,000	2,210,000
Assam	8000	102,000	463,000
Bihar	6400	127,000	1,443,000
Gujarat	2000	149,000	1,424,000
Haryana	2100	114,000	776,000
Himachal Pradesh	1800	68,000	393,000
Karnataka	5500	NA	1,554,000
Kerala	21,600	141,000	1,530,000
Madhya Pradesh	1600	111,000	1,130,000
Maharashtra	1800	164,000	1,669,000
Orissa	5200	87,000	914,000
Punjab	1200	105,000	1,021,000
Rajasthan	3700	143,000	1,095,000
Tamil Nadu	2900	95,000	1,672,000
Uttar Pradesh	1500	124,000	1,770,000
West Bengal	14,800	145,000	3,086,000
Median population per government	2700	114,000	1,433,500

Source: Compiled from Mathew (1994).

Notes: Population per village government is rounded to the nearest hundred, for the other two levels to the nearest thousand.

span of control), as well as relative to the state level (affecting the ability of state governments to maintain hard budget constraints for the lower level). The highest level of rural local government might not even be characterized as 'local' in this respect: basic public services will typically have smaller constituencies.[14]

Until the recent legislative changes, the ability to exercise local suffrage was very limited: at any given time since Independence, 40–50 per cent of local government bodies in India have been under state supersession (Dillinger 1994). Also, there was previously a

[14] Here one is implicitly appealing to Olson's principle of fiscal equivalence, see Olson (1986).

structural limitation on this exercise, since in most states only the lowest level of rural local government had directly elected local government officials. States such as Madhya Pradesh and Uttar Pradesh did not have even indirect elections at the higher two levels of rural local government, those bodies being nominated by state governments.

There is no tier system for urban governments unlike for rural governments. Government types ranged from corporations (which do have smaller units such as wards within them) to municipalities, and then town and notified area committees. Corporations have more autonomy and wider responsibilities than municipalities, with town and notified area committees being most restricted. A major difference between notified or town area committees on the one hand, and municipalities and corporations on the other, is that the former category had not involved any elected governing body: the committees were appointed by state governments. However, to the extent that elected municipalities and corporations were superseded, the distinction was less important. Even in cases where municipalities and corporations had functioning elected governing bodies, state governments typically retained considerable discretion and bureaucratic control over even the largest urban local governments, for example through municipal commissioners (who would typically be IAS members).

Institutional Reform

Key changes brought about by the 73rd and 74th amendments included the reduction of state government discretion concerning elections to rural local government bodies. Under the 73rd Amendment, direct elections to panchayats must be held every five years. Elections to constitute new bodies must be completed before the term expires. If a panchayat is dissolved prematurely, elections must be compulsorily held within six months, the new body to serve out the remainder of the five-year term. With regard to urban local governments, there is a similar strengthening of the electoral requirements, preventing lengthy supersessions of local powers by the state government, and replacing appointed posts with elected ones. Various aspects of the elections are also specified. State level election commissions are to be created to supervise and manage the electoral processes. At the intermediate and district levels, chairpersons of bodies one level below can be members, as can MPs (Members of Parliament) and MLAs (Members of Legislative Assemblies).

The 74th Amendment provides a parallel set of reforms for urban and transitional areas. For areas in transition from rural to urban, *nagar* panchayats are to be constituted, and, for most provisions of the Act, are treated equally with municipalities. The composition of municipalities remains under the guidelines of the states, subject to population categories outlined in the Amendment. Within larger municipalities, wards and zones, with their own committees, become new tiers of urban government. As is the case for rural local governments, a key feature is the strengthening of local election procedures, with members at the ward and municipal level being chosen by direct elections. The zonal committees are more of an intermediate level, their composition being the chairpersons of the ward committees in the zone.

'Voice' and Accountability

In terms of Figure 9.2, the main thrust of the institutional reforms in Indian local government is the strengthening of 'voice' as a mechanism for promoting accountability. This has been done at the expense of 'hierarchy', which had been the main or only mechanism for Indian local government until the recent reforms. If 'voice' provides appropriate incentives to elected officials, and they have the flexibility to act, they will seek to influence non-elected personnel to act in constituents' interests also. Two fundamental departures from this model in the Indian local government context have been the lack of flexibility in designing incentives within local organizations, and the lack of direct electoral incentives for chief decision-makers at the local government level. Both these departures reflect the intrusion of higher level governments into the details of local action. Of course political influence may not always be benign. The question is to whom the elected official is responsive.[15]

In general, the lack of regular, direct local government elections in India, either because of the absence of legislative provisions, or

---

[15] See Bardhan and Mookherjee (2000) on the problem of 'local capture,' and Banerjee and Somanathan (2001) on the effects of local heterogeneity on delivery of public services.

because of the 'overawing' (Riker 1975) of local elective institutions by state governments, has meant that state or central non-elected officials have often been key local government decision-makers. In such a situation, 'voice' can only work indirectly: constituents, rather than being able to vote out a city government with which they are unhappy, have to register their dissatisfaction about a non-elected agent of the state government who is running the city. They complain to the lowest-level elected official available, their MLA, who then pressurizes the bureaucrat as a way of being responsive to constituents. Such a process loses transparency and certainty, as compared to direct, open elections.

A further problem is that 'voice' is applied at the higher level of government. The state-level politician represents a local constituency, but not just on local matters: she will also participate in state-level policy making. This means that voters are not permitted to discriminate as finely as they can when they can separately vote for local and for state-level elected officials, possibly weakening the responsiveness of government overall. This effect is compounded if the local government is smaller than the smallest state government constituency.[16] This is certainly true in India, where legislative constituencies in state government (the constituencies of MLAs) correspond very roughly with the block or other intermediate level of rural local government. But this is much larger than the smallest rural or urban local governments, so MLAs' constituencies do not coincide with single local jurisdictions, and incentives through 'voice' are weakened.

Regular direct elections at the local level therefore have the potential to increase the accountability of local government by providing more direct and refined incentives to please constituents. While state governments may continue to try and postpone local elections when it suits them (and this has been happening) they will no longer have the law on their side. The counter argument (footnote 14) is that interest groups or powerful individuals will instead have more influence at the local level. However, there is no reason for this problem to always be worse at the local than at the state level.

[16] A nice formalization of related ideas is in Seabright (1996), which also allows for uncertainty in outcomes that affects the ability of voters to discriminate. In that paper, there is a trade-off, since centralization may provide coordination benefits.

'Hierarchy' and Accountability

'Hierarchy', is a less direct accountability mechanism. In smaller countries, the national government lies directly above local governments. In India, the state governments are the main influence on local governments. However, as noted in Section II, the dual role played by the central bureaucracy, with state cadres but also a centralized ethos, complicates matters. The central government's planning process and the vertical fiscal imbalance between the Centre and the states add further complexity. Putting aside these institutional complications, we can say that, in practice, the state government in India has been the main body for monitoring local government performance: 'hierarchy' has been the main accountability mechanism. This was for two reasons: the state government is where expertise has resided, and it is where true ownership or control of resources has been allocated by law (the assignment of revenue authority). The latter reason in turn is traceable to concerns about elite domination of elected rural local bodies. These concerns have existed since Independence.

Yet examples of misuse of funds through incompetence, malfeasance, or both were common even before reform. Focusing on selected examples may give a misleadingly gloomy picture, but one cannot excuse failures to follow basic accounting procedures, or outright misappropriation. 'Hierarchy' has not been very effective in supporting accountability. Two linked explanations, related to the implementation of administrative and higher-level government control, can be adduced. First, the level of auditing, both quantitatively and qualitatively, has been inadequate. This seems to be borne out by case studies, as well as the surveys by Datta (1984) and N. Rao (1986), and applies not just to the identification of irregularities, but also to the enforcement of minimum accounting standards.

Second, more effort seems to have been devoted to other kinds of monitoring rather than to auditing or performance monitoring. We can broadly distinguish between input and output monitoring. There is no general case for preferring one type to the other in the provision of incentives, but local government in India has been marked by excessive control of inputs and process, to the detriment of attention to performance and outcomes.[17] Examples

[17] The choice between input and output monitoring is a complicated one, since certain means may be undesirable in themselves, if they involve

were common of detailed approval required from higher level governments for relatively small projects or expenditures, sometimes as part of a top-down national and state planning exercise in which local governments had little input. At the same time, performance could often be neglected, with overdue and abandoned projects being commonly cited. It is useful to characterize this situation as an imbalance in the types of monitoring used. In other words, the implementation of accountability through 'hierarchy' has been flawed.

More broadly, however, both explanations can be traced to the weakness of the accountability of state governments for local government performance, as discussed earlier. 'Hierarchy' as a mechanism for accountability just pushes a greater burden on to 'voice' at a higher government level. This conceptual point does not seem to have been explicitly recognized in the evolving literature on decentralization.[18] Another important conceptual point that emerges from our framework is that 'hierarchy' as an accountability mechanism has an inherent tendency to undermine assignments. This is the fundamental problem of the higher level government in a federal system overawing lower level governments.

Information and Transparency

We have emphasized that accountability is built on transparency, which refers to the public availability of information that allows performance and processes[19] to be measured and evaluated. Information may be self-disclosed, or obtained by monitoring and investigation. Often, though, disclosure of information must be a legal requirement, since the incentive to disclose problems will not exist, and gathering information may be impossible or very costly without legal backing.

---

corruption or illegality, even though the ends are thus achieved. Mookherjee (1997) analyses these and other issues in a model of tax administration. See also the references in that piece.

[18] See, for example, World Bank (1997), Litvack et al. (1998), and Litvack and Seddon (1999). Such analyses tend to appeal to lack of institutional 'capacity', rather than the fundamental problems with 'hierarchy' as an accountability mechanism.

[19] Thus transparency helps act as a check on corruption. New technologies permit more transparency at all levels of government. See, for example, Halan (2000).

Bajaj and Sharma (1995) note the problems that can arise, in terms of the information required to assess elected officials:

> When village pradhans were entrusted JRY funds for construction of community assets, the village community at large did not have knowledge about the total funds received and the annual expenditure incurred on various projects. The pradhan and the village panchayat officer, who jointly operated the panchayat account, kept the details a closely guarded secret. (p. M-79)

They go on to describe the resolution of the monitoring problem in their example:

> [The higher level] government made it mandatory for information to be posted publicly about the works executed, estimated and actual expenditure and savings if any. The displaying of relevant information on bulletin boards in public places and community halls resulted in community pressure on pradhans to account for public funds, and had the effect of many unfinished projects being rapidly completed.

While all cases may not admit such easy fixes, there is no reason why complete information on a broad range of government activities should not be available to all citizens.

Emphasizing 'voice' as an accountability mechanism highlights the importance of transparency in supporting accountability. On the other hand, the previous emphasis in India on 'hierarchy' as the primary accountability mechanism also led to an inadequate emphasis on transparency.[20] In fact, higher-level government decision-makers have no general incentive to impose transparency on the lower level when 'hierarchy' is the primary mechanism. On the other hand, a shift to 'voice' at the lower level gives the higher level some incentive to impose transparency at the lower level, or at least not to oppose it, though they may not want it for themselves. Our central point is that a positive feedback exists from accountability mechanisms to transparency, if 'voice' is given an appropriate role to play.

Even with a legal framework that supports transparency, or, more generally, the need to be able to monitor performance, there are issues of implementation. In the case of 'voice', the beneficiaries, the monitors, and the implementers of (electoral) rewards and punishments are all citizens. On the one hand, having these tasks

---

[20] Manor (1999) is extremely cautious about the benefits of transparency, but his reasoning (pp. 73–4) is based on short run misperceptions of constituents.

performed by the same individuals avoids the need to provide incentives to delegated monitors with different preferences. However, there are diseconomies associated with large numbers of principals and with lack of specialization. These factors create a role for more specialized monitoring and regulation, through NGOs acting as watchdog groups, the media, and—where poor performance is connected to illegality—the police and the judiciary (see the left hand trio in Figure 9.2).

Exit, and Checks and Balances

We now turn to the other two of the four accountability mechanisms in Figure 9.2. 'Exit' in one sense has been of minimal importance in India. Mobility is low, and is driven by factors that dominate the quality of provision of local public goods. Villagers migrate to cities not because they are following Tiebout-type (1956) logic, seeking the optimal combination of public goods among those offered by competing local governments, but because they are looking for remunerative work. In fact, living in urban slums is a cost that has to be borne by such migrants.

'Exit' can also refer to the option of private provision. Some goods are only quasi-public in nature, involving large fixed costs of provision that create a situation close to non-rivalry, but with excludability possible. Other goods are simply provided by the government for distributional reasons, rather than because of any market failure. If private provision is an option, people may exit the public system. Individually, higher income urban residents in India sink backyard wells and install generators for electricity. Collectively, neighbourhood groups arrange for private garbage disposal services. Unfortunately, such instances do not really represent a major use of 'exit', and they have not created much competition, nor enhanced accountability.

For 'exit' to work as an accountability mechanism in this way, entire constituencies have to be able to switch to private provision. Waste disposal and transportation are two examples where this is not difficult to achieve, though here again, transparency is important, and private provision is not a panacea. Transparency in bidding and allocation of private contracts is obviously required to prevent corruption. Careful contract design is required to avoid inappropriate incentives, such as occurred with disregard for driving safety among competing private bus operators in Delhi. At the same time, explicit private provision is attractive since inefficient[21] de facto privatization is occurring in any case. Private provision therefore has a role independent of its being an avenue of 'exit'. In this case, 'voice' and 'hierarchy' remain as the primary mechanisms for accountability.

We may note the role of the judiciary in the context of assignment of expenditure and revenue authority to local governments. The power to enforce was an important complement to traditional fiscal assignments, one that had not received enough recent attention. The idea of 'checks and balances' as an accountability mechanism raises a different role for the judiciary. The basic concept of checks and balances, or separation of powers, was clearly articulated over two hundred years ago by James Madison (see Persson et al., 1997). In India, the lack of separation of powers between the legislative and executive branches has made the role of the judiciary in providing checks and balances even more important. This role has been exercised differently at different times in independent India, though more prominently only recently.

While there is no easy answer to the question of the optimal structure of checks and balances,[22] federalism raises a further set of issues. Ideally, one would postulate a local judiciary that is both strong enough to enforce the proper authority of the newly strengthened legislative branch of local government, and to place limits on improper exercise of local government powers. Perhaps the state governments are rightly cautious about devolving law and order machinery to the local level, given the well-known vertical and horizontal divisions in India's society. However, there is clearly also a measure of self-interest in state governments' reluctance: bureaucrats and politicians, for example, seem much less satisfied with judicial activism than are ordinary citizens. A major problem in the past has been lack of resources for the judicial system, not just at the local level. This has been worsened by inefficient procedures for litigation, trial, and judgement (Section II). Therefore, an effective local judiciary and legal system may be a long way off.

---

[21] The inefficiencies include both the failure to capture scale economies, and negative externalities. Household level water and electric power production exhibit both these problems.

[22] Persson et al. (1997) have recently begun the task of formalizing the analysis of the problem in the context of legislative and executive separation of powers.

Our framework, however, helps to focus and clarify the conceptual issues with respect to the legal system at the local level.

Responsiveness

A major concern with respect to 'voice' is that the accountability created is not of the appropriate kind. Responsiveness may still be limited, or may not have positive outcomes. For example, Dash (1988: 223) gives examples of the Puri Municipal Council in Orissa providing reductions in, or exemptions from octroi taxes to specific commercial products, benefiting local interest groups. Many case studies mention or imply the reluctance of local governments to impose taxes, being responsive to their constituents in this respect. Aziz (1998) expresses similar worries for Karnataka panchayats even after the local government reform (though in some respects, the 1993 Karnataka Act represented a retreat from earlier reform).

In analysing these issues, it is important to separate two distinct problems. First, 'voice' may be an imperfect accountability mechanism at any level of government. One part of this is that interest groups can have a negative influence in any democratic system. The solution is to design institutions that minimize the negative consequences of interest group operations, or to level the playing field. For example, NGOs also are interest groups: they are viewed as positive influences because they typically represent those whose 'voice' is otherwise unheard. Supporting such NGOs can push responsiveness in a positive direction. Another part of this is that voters may rationally choose not to tax themselves. This aspect is actually one that has not been adequately understood by observers of Indian local government. The solution is not to move away from 'voice', but to make it work better. Voters who reject local taxes are being rational, because they either expect the money to flow from higher level government—the underlying problem in the Karnataka case discussed by Aziz (1998)—or they do not think that the benefits will justify the costs. We return to both these factors later in this section.

A second potential problem is that 'voice' might be a weaker mechanism at the local level than at higher levels. This argument must rest on the assumption of lower institutional capacity at the local level, less transparency, greater inequality, or some combination of these factors. The theoretical argument is actually not straightforward, since, even with all these factors operating, direct and refined incentives at the local level might outweigh them. To a large extent, the question is then an empirical one, and positive evidence can be provided as well as the negative instances given. For example, with respect to elite domination, as long ago as 1965, Béteille observed, in his study of a rural area of Tamil Nadu, 'Adult franchise and Panchayati Raj have introduced new processes into village society' (p. 221), and 'political and legislative changes have altered the bargaining positions of the old economic classes' (p. 223). Béteille argues that local elections increased the power of those who were worse off but were in greater numbers, rather than perpetuating or increasing domination by the traditional rural elite. This is not surprising: democracy rewards numerical superiority. Another example is urban. While the Shiv Sena is better known for other aspects of its ideology, its success as a political organization has also been built on its attention to ward and municipal constituencies in Mumbai: it has striven for and achieved electoral rewards by being responsive to those near the bottom of the economic ladder (Naipaul 1975).

Capacity

Much of the argument for hierarchical control of local government, or simply assignment of tasks and authority to the higher level of government, rests on the idea of low local capacity.[23] While this argument may have some force in rural areas, and smaller towns, it can hardly apply to larger urban bodies. To some extent, these have had more autonomy, but hardly commensurate with their situation. State level functional departments have often exercised rigid control of municipalities, and even corporations. Bhattacharya (1972), in case studies, traces the reasons for this control to the role of these functional departments as providers of technical assistance. This, in turn, has been motivated by concerns for efficiency, driven by a perceived lack of expertise at the local government level. In practice, this has translated into direct control of decision-making, rather than technical assistance coupled with performance monitoring. The lack of well-designed systems

[23] Manor (1999, and in Crook and Manor, 1998) emphasizes the importance of a lively civil society, which mainly seems to boil down to capacity, though monitoring may also be a benefit.

of state-local transfers has reinforced this tendency, since, in the absence of appropriate incentive grants, direct control becomes relatively more appealing.

While Bhattacharya discusses only urban cases, the problems are similar for rural local governments. The solution to the problem of lack of capacity in both cases is not to centralize or rely on hierarchical control, as has been done in the past. Since local governments will certainly continue to require outside expertise, the answer is to make sure that their new status gives them control in contracting for technical help, including going to the private sector, NGOs, the national government, or even other state and local governments, as alternatives to their own state government. This can be combined with a transfer system that does not provide perverse incentives to the receiving government. It must also be recognized that, to some extent, the lack of capacity in India's local government has been a self-fulfilling expectation, since decision-makers at that level have not been given the opportunity to learn by doing.

Monitoring and auditing can be treated in the same way as technical assistance, from the perspective of capacity. Monitoring is often performed by another organization, rather than by constituents: essentially, one agent (for example, the financial auditor) monitors another (the local government). There is no conceptual reason why such auditing or monitoring has to be done by the state government. Some functions of this nature can be and are performed by internal auditors or by private companies. Even if monitoring is to be performed by a higher level government, it could conceivably be done by the next tier up, for each of the two lower rural tiers. The state government's role can be to set and monitor standards, rather than to attempt case-by-case monitoring.

Efficiency and Revenue Authority

Accountability, transparency, and responsiveness matter to the extent that they improve efficiency in the provision of public services. We can explicitly examine the connection between accountability and efficiency. A simple model (Rao and Singh 1999) of government-citizen decision-making can be used to capture the repeated observation for Indian local governments that their decision-makers are reluctant to impose higher taxes, or to collect existing taxes because they fear voters' displeasure. At the same time, the level of local public services is often perceived as too low. The model displays this type of equilibrium. It also shows that increasing efficiency, perhaps even slightly, may lead to a very different equilibrium, with higher levels of provision and higher welfare. The relevance to our discussion is that, if local government reforms provide an environment where the efficiency of provision increases through better regulatory structures,[24] there may be perceptible improvement in the performance of local government in India.

The above points may be related to the assignment of revenue authority. Often there are sufficient tax instruments already assigned by statutes. The problems are in (i) exercising statutory authority, (ii) administering the tax, and (iii) establishing a clear tax assignment. The first problem arises because of inefficiencies in provision, which therefore needs prior improvement. This will also set the stage for more effective use of fees and user charges (see below). The third problem arises because the more significant sources of tax revenue are typically also assigned to state governments. Hence clearer rules for tax sharing are essential, including options such as complete assignment of taxes like land revenue to the local level.[25]

Expenditure Assignments and Incentives

Examination of India's experience suggests two categories of problems with respect to the assignment of expenditure responsibilities: (1) excessive narrowness, and (2) lack of clarity. The recent reforms provide some improvement with respect to the first, but not with respect to the second. Put simply, expanding assignments at the local level without reducing them at the state level is problematic in terms of incentives. Concurrency in assignments is a pervasive feature of Indian federalism, and has created problems at higher levels as well as the local level.

We can think in terms of ownership or property rights, measured by residual control. Local governments in India have had a very restricted locus of control or ownership. While the statutory assignment of responsibilities and authority has been ambitious, it

[24] The model does not endogenize this link between regulation and efficiency, but this can be done along the lines of the approach taken in Mookherjee (1997) and the references therein.

[25] See also the excellent discussion in Rajaraman (1999).

has often overlapped substantially with state government functions and revenue authority. Local decisions have often been made by state or central bureaucrats. Requirements for approval of specific expenditures have further circumscribed the authority of local governments. Personnel practices and assignments have also been heavily state-controlled. Control of local land use is also often in the hands of state governments. A key issue in the development of local government will be whether these loci of control change to any substantial degree, despite the absence of these issues from recent legislation.

The provision for regular local elections may still help, if 'voice' develops as an effective accountability mechanism. For example, an elected city mayor may have stronger incentives to better implement infrastructure projects, to please constituents, than would a state government bureaucrat. To attract capital for such projects, there are incentives to be more efficient in accounting and internal control. At the same time, external agencies may have an easier time dealing with elected governments that will be in office for a predictable amount of time, making specialized state functional departments or specialized state-level agencies (such as housing or water supply boards) relatively less attractive as channels for investment.

On the other hand, there will always be projects where economies of scale or spillover benefits indicate that greater efficiency will be attained by action at a higher government level. For the rural sector, this does not have to be the state: the block and district levels may prove suitable for many larger scale actions, since they will have an independent existence and electoral support hitherto absent in almost every case. While the block and district levels have been the focus for plan implementation in rural areas, they have typically acted as state agencies in this role, with effective control remaining at the state government (or even national) level. The key change will be whether local governments at any level can exercise freedom of decision and action. This requires certainty and transparency in transfers, and standard setting and performance monitoring by state governments, rather than the old system of case-by-case discretion. New legislative assignments can only be effective in the context of a redesign of institutional structures. In this con-text, the presence of MLAs and MPs in local government is also a negative feature of the legislative reform.

Local Government Reform and Indian Economic Reform

How do local government reforms relate to the country's broader set of economic policy changes? This question may seem surprising, since local government reform in India is often associated with ideologies and groups that are critical of economic 'liberalization'. Reform of local government in India certainly had a very different impetus and history than the national economic reforms propelled by the 1991 balance of payments crisis. However, the two reforms are closely connected by the issue of reducing fiscal deficits, and of overall management of government finances, including tax reform. National financial sector reform also has implications for the thorny problems of infrastructure at the local level. More broadly, the contrasting views of government as agent rather than *mai-baap* represent a common thread in a wide variety of reforms in national, state, and in local governance.

With regard to fiscal deficits, one can make the case that the structure of fiscal federalism in India has contributed to the overall problem of government deficits. The states were used to operating with soft budget constraints, and their finances have deteriorated in the post-reform squeeze, negatively affecting their spending in areas such as education and health. Will local government reform make the fiscal situation worse? For example, the World Bank (1995) country study, in discussing tax reform, tax sharing, and the disincentives for lower level resource mobilization, offered the following caution:

The 73rd Amendment...is an important and welcome change, aimed at increasing the autonomy of local governments. However, it may accentuate fiscal indiscipline by establishing between states and local governments a system of transfers similar to the one in place between the central and state governments.

Related concerns, that the Centre will ultimately have to channel resources to local governments, directly and through the states, were expressed in the Tenth Finance Commission report (Finance Commission 1994: chs 10, 15).

However, there are countervailing positive factors. First, the decentralization is down to the local level, where smaller constituencies make it easier to impose hard budget constraints (Wildasin 1997). Second, the above quote neglects the fact that the central finance commissions have done a relatively good job, within their constraints (but see our criticisms in Section III): greater problems have arisen with more discretionary transfers, including categorical grants and various loans. Furthermore discretion has been the *only* system operating between the state and local levels. State Finance Commissions (SFCs) can reduce such discretionary transfers from the states to local governments, and increase the transparency, certainty and, ultimately, efficiency of such transfers. The SFCs can also learn from the past, including the experience of the central Finance Commissions, and avoid grant schemes with perverse incentives, such as those that pay for marginal personnel costs, or 'gap-filling' transfer schemes in general.

While making intergovernmental transfers more efficient will help, raising local resources more effectively is crucial. Here, broader economic reforms are complementary to the reform of local government. The underlying goal of economic reforms in India can be characterized as the achievement of a more efficient use of resources (and capital in particular), to support higher growth. Reforms of trade, industry, and financial markets are all, in some way, driven by this basic objective. Relying on smoothly functioning, well-regulated financial markets to allocate capital, in this view, is crucial for government as well as for the private sector. Since many municipal service projects involve long-lasting capital and equipment, the building up of local capital has been hindered. The creation of urban local governments with independent status, legal authority, and regularly elected officials raises the possibility that these governments may *eventually* be able to regularly borrow money in the financial markets for local sanitation, roads, and schools. Again, for this to work, hard budget constraints must exist. Clearly, the development of market borrowing will take time, but cities such as Ahmedabad have already taken the first steps.

Improving the effectiveness of the tax system is another avenue for revenue enhancement, and is necessary for local government borrowing as well, since borrowing for non-remunerative public projects requires future tax revenues to fund loan repayment. A national tax reform agenda predates the 1991 shift in economic policy, and represents an opportunity for local governments as well, for example through local surcharges on redesigned state level taxes. Effective tax sharing can be an important part of the state finance commissions' role, as it has been at the Centre. True representative government at the local level is more likely to be able to raise revenue through taxes, if the citizens thereby are able to more closely connect benefits received with taxes paid. A third route for increasing local governments' revenues to meet their new functional responsibilities is user charges. For many local government goods, user charges and fees can be quite close to taxes in practical application, and both these sources of revenue have been constrained partly by the inefficient delivery of public services. Local governments with limited accountability, and typically little freedom of action with respect to expenditures, have tended not to risk upsetting constituents by raising resources through these means, preferring to rely on whatever funding they could obtain from higher-level governments. Constituents have been unwilling to pay more for an inefficient provision of services. Ultimately, as we have stressed the issue is whether decentralization will permit the more efficient use of government funds. Increasing efficiency of provision can be the basis for more effective use of taxes and fees.

Finally, there is a clear conceptual and empirical connection between the nature of past regulation of local governments in India and the overall top-down approach to economic policy, relying on the case-by-case discretion of government decision-makers, in areas such as industrial location and expansion, and in the allocation of capital generally. The main point is that the ideas that are guiding changes in how the national government interacts with the private sector are also important for how state governments interact with local governments. The expanded assignments legislated for local governments, and the increased role for local 'voice', together require the state governments to fundamentally change their regulation of local governments underneath them.

VI. CONCLUSION

This chapter has taken a sweeping look at India's federal institutions in the context of economic reform. Despite its broad scope, the basic theme that runs through the chapter is the use of the modern approach to institutional design as a problem of incentives. Examining institutional incentives enables us to go beyond relatively mechanistic normative approaches embodied in setting of macroeconomic targets. In Section II, we provided an outline and evaluation of various components of India's federal institutions, ranging from political parties and the bureaucracy to the judiciary and the police. We argued for some decentralization in these institutional components, as well as improvements in the incentives that are created by the structure of relationships among some of these components. In Section III, we reviewed India's institutions intergovernmental fiscal governance, and provided a critique of some of these institutions, including the structure of assignments of tax and expenditure authority, but more particularly the structure and implementation of the system of Centre-state fiscal transfers.

Section IV provided a conceptual framework within which to think about incentives in a federal system, particularly with respect to common ideas such as transparency and accountability. We discussed the roles of monitoring, and four different accountability mechanisms, namely voice, exit, hierarchy, and checks and balances. We related this conceptual framework to more general issues of federalism and economic reform, arguing in particular that decentralization is one prong of a three-part approach to economic reform that includes shifting the boundaries between state and market, as well as changing the nature of government regulation of the market given those boundaries.

The conceptual framework of Section IV is particularly valuable for our 'case study', an examination in Section V of India's local government reform. We summarized the nature of this reform, and evaluated it in terms of a shift from hierarchy to voice as an accountability mechanism. We also discussed the role of transparency, capacity and efficiency, as well as the connections to the assignments of tax and expenditure authority. In addition to this normative examination, local government reform in India provides an illustration of how reform may proceed from a positive perspective. It can be argued that the ultimate impetus for and success of constitutional change to implement this reform came from considerations of *realpolitik*, the desire of the central government to outflank the growing power of states in the federal system (see Section II). This interest was allied with others who supported decentralization for ideological reasons that had nothing to do with economic motives (and indeed were hostile to many aspects of economic liberalization). Nevertheless, the result is a shift in institutional structures that has the potential to improve the delivery of local public services to a large number of India's people, a goal that is certainly part of the basic objectives of economic reform.

In this chapter, we also touched on the report of the Eleventh Finance Commission. The central finance commissions, as we argued in Section III, have been circumscribed in their operation, and have not always maximized their effectiveness within those limits. Nevertheless, this advisory body has gradually made improvements in India's institutions of fiscal federalism. A major example of this was the Tenth Finance Commission's recommendation for a drastically simpler arrangement for sharing of central tax revenues between the Centre and the States. This recommendation was motivated by academic writing and practical experience. State government representatives discussed it, bargained, and agreed to the change, and the Centre introduced the requisite legislation, again a constitutional amendment. The motivation and coalition of interests were quite different from the case of local government reform. The lesson is similar in the abstract, however: successful reform requires a winning coalition among interest groups and their representatives at the bargaining table. In both cases, tax sharing and decentralization we may also note the virtue of simplicity of the basic idea, in enhancing its appeal. Whether conceptual appeal and winning coalitions can carry the day for further federal fiscal reform items remains to be seen.

References

Aziz, A. (1998), 'Income Structure of Rural Local Governments: The Karnataka Experience', in Konrad Adenauer Foundation, *Local Government Finances in India*, New Delhi: Manohar.

Bajaj, J. L. and Rita Sharma (1995), 'Improving Government Delivery Systems: Some Issues and Prospects', *Economic and Political Weekly*, 27 May, M73–M80.

Banerjee, Abhjit and Rohini Somanathan (2001), 'Caste, Community, and Collective Action: The Political Economy of Public Good Provision in India,' Working Paper, MIIT, September.

Bardhan, Pranab and Dilip Mookherjee (2000), 'Relative Capture of Local and Central Governments: An Essay in the Political Economy of Decentralization,' Working Paper, Boston University.

Bayley, David H. (1969), *The Police and Political Development in India*, Princeton, NJ: Princeton University Press.

Béteille, André (1965), *Caste, Class, and Power: Changing Patterns of Stratification in a Tanjore Village*, Berkeley: University of California Press.

Bhattacharya, Mohit (1972), *State Municipal Relations*, New Delhi: Indian Institute of Public Administration.

Bradbury, K. L., H. F. Ladd, M. Perrault, A. Reschovsky, and J. Yinger (1984), 'State Aid to Offset Fiscal Disparities among Counties', *National Tax Journal*, vol. 37, pp. 151–70.

Breton, Albert (1987), 'Towards the Theory of Competitive Federalism', *European Journal of Political Economy*, Special Issue, vol. 3, no. 1+2, pp. 263–328.

———— (1996), *Competitive Governments: An Economic Theory of Politics and Public Finance*, New York: Cambridge University Press.

Crook, Richard, and James Manor (1998), *Democracy and Decentralization in South Asia and West Africa*, Cambridge, UK: Cambridge University Press.

Das, S. K. (2001), 'Institutions of Internal Accountability,' this volume.

Dash, Gokulananda (1988), *Municipal Finance in India: Based on Orissa*, New Delhi: Concept Publishing.

Datta, Abhijit (1984), *Municipal Finances in India*, New Delhi: Indian Institute of Public Administration.

Dillinger, William (1994), *Decentralization and Its Implications for Urban Service Delivery*, UNDP/UNCHS/World Bank Urban Management Programme Discussion Paper, UMP 16.

Finance Commission (1994), *Report for 1995–2000*, Government of India: New Delhi.

Galanter, Marc (1989), *Law and Society in Modern India*, Delhi: Oxford University Press.

Government of Kerala (1986), *Report of the Panchayat Finance Commission*, Trivandrum: Government of Kerala.

Gramlich, Edward, (1977), 'Intergovernmental Grants: A Review of Empirical Literature' in W. E. Oates (ed.), *The Political Economy of Fiscal Federalism*, Lexington Mass: Lexington Books, pp. 219–40.

Halan, Monika (2000), 'Ungreasing Palms in India: An anticorruption crusader discovers the Internet cuts bureaucracy and bribes', www.thestandard.com/article/display/0,1151,15851,00html, 12 June.

Hirschman, Albert O. (1970), *Exit, Voice, and Loyalty; Responses to Decline in Firms, Organizations, and States*, Cambridge, MA: Harvard University Press.

Kletzer, Kenneth, and Nirvikar Singh (1997), 'The Political Economy of Indian Fiscal Federalism', in *Fiscal Policy in India*, ed., Sudipto Mundle, New Delhi: Oxford University Press.

Krishnan, K. P. and T. V. Somanathan (2001), 'Civil Service: An Institutional Perspective', this volume.

Lewis, John P. (1995), *India's Political Economy: Governance of Reform*, Delhi: Oxford University Press.

Litvack, Jennie, Junaid Ahmed, and Richard Bird (1998), 'Rethinking Decentralization at the World Bank', PRMPS Discussion Paper, World Bank.

Litvack, Jennie and Jessica Seddon (eds) (1999), 'Decentralization Briefing Notes', World Bank Institute Working Paper, World Bank.

Mehta, Pratap Bhanu (2001), 'India's Judiciary', this volume.

Manor, James (1995), 'Regional Parties in Federal Systems,' in *Multiple Identities in a Single State*, ed. Balveer Arora and Douglas Verney, New Delhi: Konark Publishers.

————— (1999), *The Political Economy of Democratic Decentralization*, Washington, DC: The World Bank.

————— (2001), 'The Presidency', this volume.

Mathew George (1994), ed., *Status of Panchayati Raj in the States of India*, Institute of Social Sciences, New Delhi: Concept Publishing Company.

Mookherjee, Dilip (1993), 'Redefining the Economic Role of the State: The Role cf "Positive" and "Negative" Institutional Reforms in India', paper presented at conference on Economic Liberalization in South Asia, University of California, Berkeley, April.

————— (1997), 'Incentive Reforms in Developing Country Bureaucracies: Lessons from Tax Administration', paper presented at Annual World Bank Conference on Development Economics, Washington, DC, 30 April and 1 May.

Naipaul, V. S. (1975), *India: A Wounded Civilization*, New York: Alfred Knopf.

Olson, M. (1986), 'Toward a More General Theory of Governmental Structure', *American Economic Review*, May.

Persson, Torsten, Gerald Roland, and Guido Tabellini (1997), 'Separation of Powers and Political Accountability', *Quarterly Journal of Economics*, vol. 102, no. 4, 1163–202.

Rajaraman, Indira (1999), 'Fiscal Features of Rural Local Government in India', in Jean-Jacques Dethier (ed.), *Governance in India, China and Russia*, Berlin: Springer-Verlag.

Rao, M. Govinda, and Nirvikar Singh (1999), 'Local Government Reform in India: Assignments, Institutions and Incentives', Working Paper, Center for Economic Development and Policy Reform, Stanford University.

Rao, N. Rajagopala (1986), *Municipal Finances in India (Theory and Practice)*, New Delhi: Inter-India Publications.

Richards, A. and N. Singh (2002), 'Inter-state Water Disputes in India: Institutions and Policies, *International Journal of Water Resources Development*, vol. 18, no. 4, pp. 611–25.

Riker, William (1975), 'Federalism,' in *Handbook of Political Science*, vol. 5, Fred I. Grenstein and Nelson W. Polsby (eds.), *Reading*, MA: Addison-Wesley.

Seabright, Paul (1996), 'Accountability and Decentralization in Government: An Incomplete Contracts Model', *European Economic Review*, 40, 61–89.

Tiebout, Charles (1956), 'A Pure Theory of Local Government Expenditures', *Journal of Political Economy*, vol. 64.

Verma, Arvind (2001), 'Design, Performance, and Adaptability: The Police in India,' this volume.

Wildasin, David (1997), 'Externalities and Bailouts: Hard and Soft Budget Constraints in Intergovernmental Fiscal Relations,' Working Paper no. 1843, Washington, DC: World Bank.

Wilde, James E. (1971), 'Grants-in-aid: Analytics of Design and Response', *National Tax Journal*.

World Bank (1995), *India: Recent Economic Developments and Prospects*, Washington, DC: The World Bank.

—— (1997), *World Development Report: The State in a Changing World*, Washington, DC: Oxford University Press for World Bank.

10

New Regulatory Institutions in India*
White Knights or Trojan Horses?

Saugata Bhattacharya and Urjit R. Patel

I. INTRODUCTION

The onset of liberalization in India in the early nineties was the result of the internal fiscal and balance of payments crises, as much as the ongoing process is of international experiences and global competition. The increasing reliance on market forces and price signals has altered the risk profile of economic activity and heightened the prospects of market failures. Independent economic regulators were gradually established to deal with the anticipated abuse of market power by private producers in inherently monopolistic sectors, and to contain the increasingly decentralized and complex transactions in the capital markets leading to risks which lead to a systemic collapse.

The objective of this chapter is to analytically assess the design, performance, and adaptability of independent regulatory institutions in India. It aims to isolate the factors that have determined the effectiveness of these institutions as well as examine the relation of the regulators with other institutions, mainly the government, in terms of the role of their interactions in fulfilling their objectives. Appropriate institutional design will crucially hinge on a correct

* The views expressed in this paper are the authors' and not necessarily those of the institution to which they are affiliated.

identification of flaws in the current establishment. In keeping with the study's ambit, the chapter mostly confines itself to federal regulatory institutions, although state level regulators in India are critical in sectors like electricity, where responsibility for appropriate market structures lies mainly with the state governments.

Evidently, the canvas of the subject is vast. Although the chapter's focus is more on the conduct of regulation in India rather than its theory, it reflects an economist's (as opposed to a political economist's) bias towards institutional issues. In other words, the chapter uses a theoretical underpinning to isolate the key explanatory factors in assessing the performance of regulatory institutions and then assesses the performance of the more important and active regulators in India in terms of these theoretical principles.

In this chapter, we have presented only very broad pointers to the problem of design. The chapter provides mostly anecdotal cases of the ambiguities and asymmetries that were built into the legislation to preserve the suzerainty of the public sector. There are many issues—for example, the relationship of the regulator to the government, the issue of government versus market failures, etc. The lessons of global experience can provide valuable pointers to regulatory effectiveness. We focus on regulation in two sectors—infrastructure and securities—due to the fortuitous coincidence of the presence of regulatory institutions in precisely these areas that are the most critical to future economic growth.

The structure of the chapter is organized as follows. Section II provides a rationale for independent regulation in mitigating market failures and inefficiencies arising from incomplete markets and information asymmetry using simple Principal–Agent models. Section III first provides a brief history of economic institutions in India since Independence, an overview of the process of liberalization and restructuring in the Indian economy since the early nineties, and the current market structures in selected utility industries and the securities markets. It then traces the developments in utilities sectors and securities markets that led to the establishment and evolution of selected regulatory bodies in India, while outlining some design characteristics of these institutions that would likely help or hinder their respective functioning. Section IV, the core of the chapter, is an assessment of the effectiveness of these institutions in terms of the objectives that were set out for them in their respective legislations, as well as some comments on the effectiveness of the instruments that were provided to them for performing their functions. Section V concludes by summarizing some of the causes of the varied effectiveness of regulatory institutions in India.

II. RATIONALE FOR REGULATION

The yardsticks for evaluating the performance of the independent regulatory institutions in India vary—each institution has its own scope and ambit of operations. One approach is to analyse each independently, and draw segmented inferences. The other, which we adopt, is to recognize that regulation, as opposed to individual regulatory institutions, is a response to a problem—market failures and inefficiency—and then use a 'two-step' analysis to evaluate the effectiveness of the institutions in dealing with the problem. This methodology divides the evaluation procedure into two distinct, but inter-connected parts: (a) a primarily theoretical analysis to provide a unified framework for examining market structures and the causes of market failure and (b) a predominantly descriptive analysis of the actual design of regulatory institutions in terms of the congruence of the design with the analytical framework. A theoretical framework serves to highlight those factors that explain the variance in the effectiveness of these institutions—isolating the ones that are unique and those that are common across the institutions, as well as the degrees of commonality. The heuristic part, more explicitly, consists of two distinct sub-elements: (i) the success of the individual institutions in terms of its own objectives and (ii) the initial design of the institutions themselves.

Why regulate? A fundamental theorem of welfare economics postulates that when an economy satisfies certain conditions,[1] if every individual maximizes his own selfish utility, then society automatically attains Pareto optimality (Debreu 1959). Traditional economic analysis provides many reasons for the failure of competitive markets. The most common economic argument for regulatory intervention is the redressal of market failures and inefficiencies.

Why regulate at all? Regulation is meant to correct or mitigate failures of competitive markets that may arise due to economies of scale, technological or network characteristics, to ensure a level

---

[1] For example, no externalities, full convexity, etc.

playing field in those activities that are susceptible to abuse of the resulting monopoly power and to introduce competition where none existed before. Even in markets not amenable to multiple service providers or free entry, appropriate contract structures can introduce competition for these markets. These issues are explored in a unified theoretical framework in terms of special cases of Principal–Agent models with information asymmetry.

The next question is when and how to regulate. This relates to the design of the regulatory institutions, their legal and institutional relation with other institutions, especially the policy making bodies, and the existing market structure. The history of independent economic regulation is a relatively short one, and the inferences that may be drawn from their functioning are only indicative. How effective have these regulators been? This has to be evaluated by two metrics. One, in terms of objectives by which these institutions were established. Second, and more important, is an assessment of these objectives themselves as the philosophical building blocks of regulation.

Economic Efficiency and Market Failure

Economies of Scale and Scope

The failure of such markets to form in the first place may arise from an inherently monopolistic nature of the market caused by economies of scale or scope. Economies of scale are created by indivisible factors of production and lumpy costs. Economies of scale arise when the incremental (marginal) cost of producing successful units of output is lower than the incremental cost of prior units. Hence, the marginal cost of a specific unit of output depends upon the existing scale—how many total units are being produced. Economies of scope are created by complementarities in the production of multiple products by the same firm.[2] A particular form of such economies is especially evident in many infrastructure utilities as network externalities.

Network economies arise when the value to one consumer from a given product increases with the number of other consumers who

---

[2] For a multi-product firm, the incremental cost of producing one product, A, depends *negatively* upon the amount of another (all the other) product(s), B, that is (are) being produced. As more B is produced, the incremental cost of producing A declines (does not rise).

buy a compatible/complementary product or service. Telephone networks are the archetypal example. Some capital market services are other prime illustrations.[3] The value of network access to an individual depends positively upon the number of other individuals who access the same network. The analyses of industry-wide standards, software platforms, telecommunications, and language itself have all been shaped by the notion of 'network effects' or 'network externalities'.[4]

Traditionally, the need to regulate a firm's prices—the widely known 'public utility' examples of surface transportation, electric power, telecommunications—has been based on the premise that such firms possess significant amounts of market power. However, there is no reason to regulate unless competitive markets do not exist or private contracting around the sources of market power is not feasible.

Much of the regulatory practices that we shall be concerned with in this chapter are assessed in terms of their effect on competition. Competition is a critical ingredient in a successful market economy. Even in the limited activities where competition is not currently viable—the so-called natural monopolies which have historically been highly regulated, like electricity transmission or water pipelines—the extent and form of actual and potential barriers to entry are constantly diminishing.

Information Asymmetry

Severe information asymmetries can cause existing competitive markets to unravel.[5] The most severe manifestations of such events

[3] For example, Automated Teller Machines (ATM) networks of third party providers have set interconnection standards for bank ATMs. The network of VISA and Mastercard is another example and have been extensively investigated by the US competition authorities.

[4] Lord Keynes described stock selection as an odd form of beauty contest: the wise investor did not pick stocks because she thought they were beautiful but because she thought others believed they were. Networks have a reverse Yogi Berra effect. Berra allegedly remarked about a restaurant: 'Nobody goes there anymore because it's too crowded.' With networks, individuals select networks that are 'crowded' (but not congested)—they go where they expect to find others with whom to transact.

[5] In India, of course, the pervasiveness of a socialistic ideology with vague implicit notions of social and redistributive justice drove the nationalization programme rather than an explicit recognition of any of these factors.

occur in the financial markets. Investors typically have imperfect information about the quality of the financial services they purchase or about the seller of these services.[6] The complex matrix of transactions spanning different segments of the securities markets creates a risk of systemic economy-wide collapse. Prevention of such occurrences requires contracts to be formulated and enforced to reduce systemic risk.

The Agency Problem

Agency theory addresses incentive and information problems within firms and between them. In agency theory, one party, the Principal, attempts to induce another, the Agent, to take an action that the Agent might not want, in the face of very different attitudes to risk. In an uncertain environment, this task is complicated since the Agent has hidden information or may take hidden actions because it is hard or expensive for the Principal to monitor the agent.

In a Principal–Agent (PA) model, either (i) a regulator can be viewed as an agent of consumers who is appointed to protect the consumers' interests and maintain market integrity by ensuring adequate information and risk disclosure (financial markets) or (ii) the regulated industry as the agent whose performance is overseen by the regulator principal (infrastructure utilities). Information asymmetry is the key common constraint in effective regulation in both these contexts.[7] Moving as much of activity as is feasible to the markets, monitoring stock market reactions in relatively well developed capital markets, and (possibly) allowing mergers and acquisitions are key strategies in the effective monitoring of the regulated economic activity.

There are three basic classes of Principal–Agent models.

(i) *Adverse selection*: The Agent has hidden information about his characteristics and the Principal moves first in the formal model.

---

[6] This is what is referred to as 'Adverse Selection' and the theoretical underpinnings are explained in Section II.

[7] The UK electricity regulator was criticized after its first periodic review of Regional Electricity Companies (RECs) in England and Wales, after the huge increases in share values of these RECs. A similar criticism was also directed at the UK Office of the Rail Regulator after the Train Operating Companies made enormous profits.

The Principal's problem is to offer a contract that induces the Agent to reveal his true type with appropriate incentives or penalty structures. Most applications of such models are in the arena of financial markets, with mandated information disclosures as solutions.

(ii) *Signalling*: The Agent has hidden information regarding his type and moves first. The Agent's problem is to take some visible action that the Principal will correctly (or more often incorrectly) interpret as revealing the Agent's type. The situation is likely to produce gaming situations where each player tries to influence the outcome to their own advantage. Over a period of time, a fruitful way of interpreting regulatory outcomes in this scenario may be through a dynamic repeated 'prisoner's dilemma' game, where the credibility of actions and threats in each period induce appropriate behaviour in subsequent periods. Credibility (and penalties) are the cornerstones of optimal behaviour in this scenario.

(iii) *Moral hazard*: The Agent moves first and takes some action that the Principal cannot observe. The Principal's problem is to establish a contract that induces the Agent to take actions that the Agent does not want to take, but that the Principal values. There is an extensive literature on moral hazard problems in the banking sector and financial securities.[8]

Contracts and Incentives

Principals base their choice of mechanisms for solving adverse selection and moral hazard problems (the contracts) on the costs and benefits of the alternative approaches. There are two basic types of mechanisms—behaviour-based contracts (command and control or the so-called 'cost-based' regulation, the US model) and incentive contracts (or what are called 'performance-based'

---

[8] The government bail-out of the largest mutual fund in India, Unit Trust of India's (UTI) US-64, represents a typical case. Investors did not desert the fund in droves in 1999, as initially expected after the erosion of the Fund's Net Asset Value, since the investors implicitly believed that the government would not allow the scheme to fail. There have been a lot of changes in the functioning of the scheme, thereafter, though, following the ongoing implementation of the recommendations of the Deepak Parekh Committee Report. The periodic recapitalization of the worst performing Indian banks is another example of the disincentive for serious restructuring.

regulation, the UK model). Greater Principal information, greater outcome uncertainty, greater Agent risk-aversion, high costs of measuring outcomes, and length of relationship are positively related with behaviour-based contracts and negatively related with incentive contracts. Greater Principal risk aversion, high costs of measuring behaviour, and goal conflicts are negatively related with behaviour-based contracts and positively related with incentive contracts.

Incentive contracts can have numerous features, most of which have their basis in economic rent-seeking behaviour (Laffont and Tirole 1994). The first feature is the rationality (or participation) constraint, which says that the Principal and the Agent must each receive utility that exceeds their individual reservation utilities in order to be willing to produce. The second feature, incentive compatibility (or truth telling), requires that the Agent be better off expending effort rather than shirking, or truthfully revealing his type rather than lying. This works by making the Agent at least a partial residual claimant of the benefits of the relationship. Incentive compatibility implies that the performance measure must be something the Agent can affect. It also implies that, because incentive contracts shift risk to agents, agents need to be either risk averse or compensated for their risk.

There are other contract features that are useful in particular situations. Credible commitment by the Principal is important, especially in a rapidly evolving industry. This implies either third-party enforcement or sub-game perfection. The Principal's commitment is sub-game perfect if, once the Agent has truthfully revealed his information or type, it is in the Principal's best interest to keep his commitment.[9] A menu of contracts can improve performance if the Agent's post-contractual knowledge is better than pre-contractual knowledge. Any monitoring, even the slight use of imperfect monitoring, improves outcomes. When there are

---

[9] The concession for transmission in Buenos Aires in Argentina is a good example. The incumbent concessionaire was given a 95-year contract, re-biddable first at the end of 15 years and then each 10 years thereafter. To provide incentives for the incumbent to maintain investment levels, especially around the end of each sub-period of the concession, it was stipulated that the incumbent would get the highest bid at the auction, even if it was not itself the highest bidder.

multiple agents and limited ability to commit, principals can obtain improved performance by using competition to reward agents for both actual and relative results.[10] In ongoing relationships, basing compensation on both past and future performance improves outcomes, but using past results to set future goals reduces performance.

Contracts are crucial to the relationship of a regulator (the Principal) with the government in general and India, in particular, where the government is reluctant to let go its control. In conceptual terms and in the framework of the models of the previous section, the government is both a 'super-Principal' (in the role of licensor and policy-maker) as well as the Agent (in the role of publicly-owned utilities). The behaviour of the Principal will be modified by the constant threat of radical action by the super-Principal in the face of inimical action. There are other complications—the chain of appeals is often muddied by not having independent appellate bodies. Appeals against the Securities and Exchange Board of India's (SEBI) decisions are to the ministry of Finance of the Government of India, a process which is likely to lead to very complicated set of optimization behaviour for the securities market regulator.

Characteristics of Utilities and Securities Markets

At first sight, the nature of regulation of financial services and those of infrastructure utilities seem very different. The former is patently more about enforcing fiduciary responsibilities on financial intermediaries and the latter about protecting consumers from the market power exercised by monopoly providers. Securities markets regulation is designed to prevent the abuse of investors' lifetime savings by unscrupulous market operators. It is also about minimizing the systemic risk underlying financial market operations.[11]

[10] Loser-bear-all tournaments can induce better performance than winner-take-all tournaments when relatively little effort is desired.

[11] Despite many existing flaws in our financial markets, it is a matter of justifiable pride for financial markets regulators that India escaped some of the worst excesses of the Asian speculative build-up of the mid-nineties. Of course, external controls served to further isolate the impact of the global turmoil, but in our view, this was a secondary effect. Fortunately, a large part of the

Underlying these apparent differences, however, is a lot of commonality. A competitive market is underpinned by a set of contracts between a buyer and seller and their failure, and the consequent sub-optimal output and price levels, arise essentially due to improper or truncated signals of demand and supply to the various players. A mechanism for proper incentives (and penalties) built into the contracts imposes large costs for deviating from the terms of the contract and thereby provides a credible set of actions for the various players. Information asymmetries make such credible commitments difficult. The purpose of a regulator is to enforce the costs of deviation from a prescribed set of rules of the game.

A significant holdout to competitive pressures are many activities of what are called infrastructure sectors, which due to historical reasons, political and economic ideology, and technological constraints were considered to be the virtually exclusive domain of government ownership and operations, not just in India, but in many other countries. It was believed that economies of scale and network externalities made multiple providers of service unfeasible, and redistributive and social equity concerns associated with these so-called 'essential' services made the government the best monopoly provider. In the last decade, this view has been transformed worldwide, and a change in mentality is evident even in India. Technological advances have made it possible to look at a sector as comprised of separate activities, many of which are amenable to competition. Almost all markets have become more competitive in the nineties, with the entry of new players and service providers. However, multiple providers of service in some activities, especially those dealing with networks, will still be inefficient and costly. Moreover, the residual asymmetry in market shares of the public organizations impart to them market power which often serves to deter the entry of more efficient new players in the market. It is simultaneously recognized that private sector participation serves to incentivize the provision of efficient service, to a greater extent than the public sector, even in the monopoly segments. The question then is of a balancing mechanism between the efficiencies of a private monopoly and the potential of its abuse

---

weaknesses of Indian financial intermediaries has also been in the public domain since the early nineties and have been discounted by global markets.

of its market power. A regulator is, therefore, deemed necessary for overseeing the operation of these private monopolies.[12]

Regulation in Securities Markets

We have deliberately titled this section as 'Regulation in Securities Markets', not 'Regulation of Securities Markets'. This is to emphasize the qualitative difference between securities markets regulation and those of other 'monopolistic' industries with the former best thought of as a natural feature, not an external action imposed by a government. Financial instruments such as stocks, bonds, bank loans, and derivatives are legal contracts that are subject to a particular legal environment. These contracts have evolved to deal with the conflicts of interest between the parties to these instruments. Industry groups, legislatures, government agencies, and the courts create regulations in response to perceived defects in the market.

The liberalization of the capital markets[13] has advanced the farthest in the process of reform, and led to a whole set of issues, some of which are unique to this sector. Effective regulation of these markets is a continual Occam's Razor between increasing efficiency through competition and moderating operating practices to reduce systemic risk. Both the speed and complexity of transactions have pushed the risks of market failure progressively higher. The capital markets also serve to allocate scarce resources efficiently. Poorly regulated banks and the absence of developed capital markets are now attributed to have been a major cause of the Asian crisis of 1997. *Information disclosure is the key for both investor protection and market discipline.* Lack of strict accounting norms, coupled with lax compliance, fosters unsavoury practices

---

[12] This chapter is not about privatization, but about market failures and market inefficiency, be the operator public or private. However, it is important to note that incentive structures make it easier for a regulator to curb monopoly power abuse by private operators than public entities, partly due to the more transparent accounting of commercial service provision and the presence of hard budget constraints.

[13] Capital (or securities) markets are a part of the financial sector, the other main component of which are banks. The securities markets comprises mutual funds, merchant banks, stock exchanges and markets, brokers, depositories, trustees, etc. Globally, the distinction between the two is being progressively eroded with an integration of the functions of the two previously (statutorily mandated) separate set of intermediaries.

like front-running and self-dealing, leading to a further erosion of investor confidence.

Some stylized facts may be helpful in analysing securities markets regulation. First, securities markets and their regulatory systems, worldwide, are evolving rapidly, driven by advances in information technology and the global integration of capital markets, and vice versa. Second, there is no single market structure and regulatory system that is best for all economies or jurisdictions. Inter alia, legal histories, political orientations, technologies, demographics, and economic profiles bear on market structures and regulatory systems. Third, market structure of securities markets is important but there are other qualitative aspects that are as important. One of the main goals of financial regulation is the minimization of systemic risk. Fourth, there may be an ever increasing need to harmonize regulations across countries, and to coordinate or integrate regulatory agencies within jurisdictions.

The transition to a more market-centric financial system is an inevitable consequence of fundamental forces rooted in technology, financial innovation, and the growing inter-connectivity of the global economy. This transition, however, can be a hazardous process for individual economies and for the global financial system. Both half-way, unbalanced deregulation (as in the United States in the early 1980s) and 'Big Bang' approaches (as in transition economies in the 1990s) have resulted in significant systemic problems.

According to the International Organization of Securities Commissions (IOSCO), the three core objectives of securities regulation are:

1. The protection of investors from misleading, manipulative, or fraudulent practices, including insider trading, front-running or trading ahead of customers and the misuse of client assets. Full disclosure of information and accounting standards are key.

2. The establishment of fair, efficient, and transparent markets to ensure that investors are given fair access to market facilities and market or price information.[14]

---

[14] The prevalence of information arbitrage (a polite expression, in many instances, for practices like insider trading and front-running) as also the manipulation of market sentiment is one of the prime regulatory concerns in most capital markets.

3. The reduction of systemic risk (including through capital and internal control requirements) even though regulators cannot be expected to prevent the financial failure of market intermediaries.

Globally, one important lesson of the late 1990s is that the lack of disciplined, market-driven financial institutions can become a dangerous weakness for otherwise dynamic economies. For most countries, the rewards of moving towards a market-centric financial system greatly outweigh the risks, and the financial technology exists to mitigate or control much of the risk. The best incentive regulators can offer is to allow institutions to position themselves to reap the rewards of that investment.

Changes in Regulatory Philosophy

The raison d'etre of the independent sector regulator is to correct market failures and ensure a level playing field. As we have seen earlier, the government chose to internalize the requirement of regulatory supervision of private monopolies by assuming ownership of infrastructure utilities and much of capital intermediation. Globally, though, in the decades of the eighties and nineties, there was a growing conviction that the practice of regulation, either through public control or through cost-based regulation of private utilities, was inherently flawed. Two phenomena gave rise to this changed outlook of regulation—the first was a realization of the failure of government to provide services efficiently and the second was the ongoing technological change.

Compared to the traditionally vertically integrated operations in various sectors, the structure of transactions has become decentralized and enormously complex. From an organization based on internal (public sector) hierarchies, the mode of functioning has now shifted to a contractual-based one within the discipline of markets. Decision-making and contracting in the decentralized environment of the market place needs a subdivision of the (hitherto monolithic) organization into discrete pieces which can communicate with each other through standardized interfaces and architectures. Information flows are critical, especially given the asymmetry faced by different segments of players vis-à-vis the regulated industries. At the same time, information is the key to competitive advantage in the modern market, as is obvious from the amount of research that has gone into the area of Intellectual Property Rights.

Recognition of Government Failure

In retrospect, the most important underlying cause of the problems of natural monopolies was recognized not to be a choice between unfettered market competition and a government monopoly, but between a flawed government ownership and private ownership operating underneath a potentially flawed regulatory structure.

The fact that markets face certain problems does not in itself justify government intervention; it only identifies the potential areas for it...the government is likely to face similar [imperfect information] problems if it intervenes [Stiglitz 1987].

It is exactly this reason—the absence of incentives for efficiency dissipating the advantages of economies of scale from monolithic public ownership—that privatization has become a key ingredient in restructuring industries. With changing technologies and international economic experiences, there has been a progressive recognition of the failures of government vis-à-vis market failures (Datta Chaudhury 1990). Ironically, the inefficiencies first presented themselves through the massive fiscal crisis of the early nineties, which led to the permission for entry of the private sector in India as a means of bridging the resource gap, not considerations of efficiency. These effects were a secondary outcome. Inadequate revenues and prodigal expenditures, increasingly on current heads, resulted in huge deficits and low returns on public sector investments.

Besides these standard objectives of restructuring, a surprising one turns traditional analyses on their heads. It used to be argued that government ownership was necessary in order that public objectives (like universal service or safety) could be effectively pursued. Throughout the world, however, government enterprises were 'captured' by their workers and managers, and they tended to pursue a very narrow set of objectives. The lesson to be drawn from these problems is that organizations most often function better when they have a certain clarity of purpose. Mixing objectives not only causes confusion, but in the process of delegation, those responsible for implementation typically have enough discretion to impose their preferences. Separation of functions often promotes transparency, ensuring that same standards are applied everywhere, which is necessary for economic efficiency.

Technological Change

Competition in industries that were previously thought of as monopolistic was increasingly recognized to be feasible. Small scale units were turning out to be as efficient as large plants, thereby negating the basic premise of the existence of vertically integrated monoliths designed to extract presumed economies of scale. The increasing permeation of information technology not just in securities markets, but also electricity and obviously telecom, merely served to hasten the adoption of these technologies. It was also recognized that subsectors of an industry were very different kinds of businesses—for example, the generation, transmission, and supply activities of power were very different in nature.

III. ECONOMIC REFORM AND REGULATORY INSTITUTIONS IN INDIA

After independence in 1947, India inherited an economy that was largely in private hands. Not that its existing industrial and commercial infrastructure was much to speak of, but what there was—steel mills, jute industries, its major airline, its banks—were all owned and operated by private corporations. India's share of world trade was then about 2.5 per cent.[15] The adoption of a social philosophy of development and creation of new assets was given concrete form through planning models, starting from the Second Five Year Plan in 1956. A gradual process of acquisition of existing assets and resources by the state led to a steadily increasing role for public institutions and enterprises—airlines in the fifties, mines in 1964, banks in 1969 and so on. By the end of the sixties, almost all vestiges of institutional economic activity in India had been transferred under public control.

Due to reasons of history, ideology, and the underlying economic rationale discussed earlier, public sector firms in India were, and still are, large and dominant in almost all sectors of the economy. In the heydays of the government's involvement in economic activity in India, they functioned in the capacities of operator, manager, and regulator—judge, jury, and executioner rolled into one. Quite often, entire sectors were moved into the domain of

[15] This is China's current share of world trade. India's share now is around 0.6 per cent.

state ownership—insurance, energy (oil and gas, coal, etc.). Industrial licensing was used ruthlessly to establish and preserve the monopoly of not just public sector enterprises, but also of the private sector in the (mistaken) belief of economies of scale conferring efficiency advantages—automobiles, steel, cement are a few notable examples. In addition to the problems caused by government patronage, public ownership often distorts the dynamics of competition in the sector in which they operate because of their size, inefficiency, soft budget constraints, and ill-defined objective functions.

The economic philosophy that led to the initial rise to eminence of the public sector in India—desire to direct the growth of the 'commanding heights' of the economy—was gradually transformed into a mechanism to perpetuate its control over the sector.

The Drivers of Change

Economic and financial reforms in India progressed in fits and starts since the mid-eighties. 'Radical' reforms, with a significant role for the private sector, were only instituted after 1991 after the deep fiscal and balance of payments crises. To a large extent, the drivers for this break were fiscal, not structural. Considerations of efficiency in operations and quality of service provision were initially given only second billing, but this is increasingly being recognized as a crucial driver of change.

The rationale normally used for this creeping public acquisition, apart from strategic considerations, was the perceived failure of the private sector to fulfil its obligation to serve. The Indian Banks Nationalization Act of 1969 brought much of the existing banking institutions under government control in one fell swoop. The justification was typical—private banks were not diversifying adequately into areas other than dense urban conglomerates.[16] The Bombay Stock Exchange, of course, had a long history, but its operations were mostly controlled by a cartel of broker-owners who reportedly manipulated stock prices at will. The timing, price, and volume of primary equity issues were determined by the

---

[16] There was even then a system of small savings schemes that were mostly operated through post offices that was designed specifically to mop up such savings.

Controller of Capital Issues (CCI) and have very little link to market supply and demand. In a number of infrastructure industries such as transport, communications, and power, state monopolies persist. The railways in India continue to be a state-owned monopoly with (predominantly) administered prices and a very limited response to competition from other modes of transport. In certain cases, changes in technology have made competition possible in areas that were hitherto considered natural monopolies and limited privatization has taken place, but a suitable regulatory framework is still evolving. In civil aviation, some competition has been allowed but restrictions on entry continue—the airport infrastructure is still almost entirely in the public sector.[17] Most states have publicly-owned road transport corporations with an administered fare structure and competition from private operators has made virtually all of these loss-making.

With a few exceptions, the generation, transmission, and distribution of power continue to be through state-owned (central and state governments) monopolies. Prices are administered, costs are high, and quality is generally poor and unreliable. Although a fair degree of competition has now been permitted in telecommunications, especially mobile telephony, a lot more needs to be done.

In India, a process of gradual de-regulation of the financial sector was started in 1988–9 and entry of domestic and private foreign banks has been permitted. Further rationalization and mergers in this segment will help provide more effective competition to the public sector banks. Liberalization of regulatory controls on Non-Banking Financial Companies (NBFCs) will now enable these to provide some competition to traditional banks. Domestic Financial Institutions have also entered into more conventional banking activities (short term lending) providing some competition to the conventional banking sector. Conversely, the commercial banks have also increased their term lending activities, thus reducing the oligopolistic position of the Domestic Financial Institutions.

The office of the Controller of Capital Issues was abolished in 1992 leading to freer pricing of issues. Private sector mutual funds and Foreign Institutional Investors (FIIs) were permitted to trade in equities, increasing competition on the buyer side of the equities market and reducing the importance of publicly owned FIIs.

---

[17] Except for Kochi airport.

Competition amongst exchanges was introduced with the setting up of the world-class and path-breaking National Stock Exchange, actually ahead of the New York Stock Exchange and London Stock Exchange, in many of its rules and practices.

Regulatory institutions have to be understood and evaluated in the context of the market structures prevalent in the industry at the time of their constitution. This section is, therefore, an extension of the previous one. Each segment describes the evolution of markets since the late eighties and their current state.

There are two segments in India now that have active independent regulators—the financial sector and infrastructure utilities. Prominent among the former are SEBI and the Insurance Regulatory and Development Authority (IRDA).[18] There are ongoing discussions about an Indian Pensions Authority. A number of regulators now oversee infrastructure sectors—Central Electricity Regulatory Commission (CERC), various State Electricity Regulatory Commissions (SERCs), Telecom Regulatory Authority of India (TRAI), and Tariff Authority for Major Ports (TAMP). Other sector regulators, like a proposed Civil Aviation Authority of India (CAAI) and an oil and gas regulator are on the anvil. These institutions have been effective in varying degrees and have transformed the landscape of the sectors under their respective ambits, by activist actions or sustained chipping away of the current logjam of institutional barriers and market power of (public sector) incumbents.

The new regulatory commissions are different from those appointed in the past, like the Tariff Commission, Forwards Markets Commission, even the Disinvestment Commission. These were mostly advisory in nature, or restrictive in nature, implementing centrally planned outcomes. There were other statutory bodies like the Company Law Board, Board of Industrial and Financial Reconstruction (BIFR), Debt Recovery Tribunal, and Income Tax Appellate Tribunal, which are quasi-judicial in nature and have the power to enforce their decisions.

The first statutory independent regulatory commission was SEBI, established in January 1992. The first regulator for infrastructure

---

[18] There are also other regulators, like Reserve Bank of India (RBI) and, (in a more indirect manner), the Department of Company Affairs (DCA) and Ministry of Finance (MoF). These, however, are institutions that are part of the executive branch of government, and are not considered independent regulators.

utilities was the Orissa ERC, established in 1996. This was followed by TRAI in 1997 and TAMP. CERC was established in 1998, and, at last count, there are fourteen states with their own ERCs. Before this, publicly owned monopolies operating infrastructure utilities were 'regulated' either by themselves or some other arm of government. The Ministry of Finance, the Department of Company Affairs (DCA), and the RBI, besides the individual stock exchanges, were the regulators in the financial sector. The Department of Telecom (DoT) was the regulator in the telecom sector under the Indian Telegraphic Act (1885) and the India Wireless Telegraphic Act (1933). The State Electricity Boards (SEBs) and the Central Electricity Authority (CEA) were the electricity regulators under the Electricity Supply Act (1948) and the India Electricity Act (1910). The Directorate General (Shipping) at the centre and respective state governments were the port regulators under the Indian Ports Act (1908) and the Major Ports Trusts Act (1963).

Most regulators came into existence after the reform process was underway. SEBI is the only regulator (apart from the fledgling IRDA) that was set up co-terminously with the restructuring of the market. The scope and functions of the regulators also differ widely across sectors. Independent regulators do not make policy—that is the domain of government—but they do formulate the rules of the game and the conditions for a level playing field for the players in their respective sectors. TRAI has been mandated to regulate the sector as a whole. The CERC has licensing powers for inter-state transmission of electricity.[19] Table 10.1 and the next section summarize the institutional features of selected regulators.

Selected Regulatory Institutions in India

Telecom Regulatory Authority of India (TRAI)

The most controversial and visible of all infrastructure regulators in India, the current TRAI is the second *avatar*, the first having been disbanded in January 2000. The TRAI (Amendment) Ordinance came into force on 24 January 2000, ironically the last day of the third year of the first TRAI, splitting the erstwhile institution into a regulator and an adjudicator. The Department of Telecom (DoT)

---

[19] Albeit with the concurrence of the Central Transmission Utility, Power Grid Corporation of India Ltd (PGCIL).

TABLE 10.1
A comparative profile of selected regulatory agencies in India

	First TRAI (1997–2000)	Reconstituted TRAI (2000)	CERC (1998)	TAMP (1997)	SEBI (1992)
Objectives	Regulate telecommunications services.	Regulate telecommunications services, adjudicate disputes, dispose of appeals and protect interests of service providers and consumers and promote and ensure orderly growth of telecom sector.	Rationalization of electricity tariff, transparent subsidy policy, promotion of efficient, and environmentally friendly policies.	Not specified.	Protection of interests of investors in securities and promotion, development and regulation of securities markets.
Functions	Notify tariffs for all telecom services. Regulate revenue sharing and inter-connection 'arrangements' between service providers. Recommend need, timing and terms,	Same as for old TRAI. Additionally, DoT is required to seek recommendation for licensing and policy decision from TRAI.	Tariff setting for central-sector owned generation plants or IPPs selling inter-state power as well as inter-state transmission. License interstate transmission entities, with concurrence of Central Transmission Utility.	Frame scales of rates and conditions under which services can be provided by Port Authority. Rates of lease of port property. Fix fees for pilotage and other services.	Regulating business in stock exchanges and other securities markets, the workings of securities agents and intermediaries, including mutual funds, prohibiting fraudulent and unfair trade practices, including insider trad-

TABLE 10.1 contd

TABLE 10.1 *contd*

	First TRAI (1997–2000)	Reconstituted TRAI (2000)	CERC (1998)	TAMP (1997)	SEBI (1992)
	and conditions of new service providers.				ing, share acquisition and takeover activities, issues of securities and calling for information for the conduct thereof and disclosure requirements.
Dispute redressal powers	Between service providers, and service providers and consumers, but not between licensor (also the public service provider) and private service providers.	Telecom Disputes Settlement and Appellate Tribunal (TDSAT) to adjudicate on disputes between licensor and services providers.	Between central generators and transmission companies. However, central government can issue policy directives and decide whether an issue constitutes policy.	No provisions in Act. Central government has right to require TAMP to charge certain rates.	Provision for establishment of Securities Appellate Tribunal, consisting of one person to be appointed by central govt. This authority is currently with ministry of finance.
Adjudication/ Appellate authority	High courts.		High courts. Central government can decide if an issue constitutes policy.	Indian courts, level not specified.	Civil courts have no jurisdiction. Appeals only to high court.

TABLE 10.1 *contd*

TABLE 10.1 *contd*

	First TRAI (1997–2000)	Reconstituted TRAI (2000)	CERC (1998)	TAMP (1997)	SEBI (1992)
Funding	Currently through Consolidated Fund of India; provision to charge fees and portion of revenue shares of DoT.	Consolidated Fund of India.	Consolidated Fund of India.	Central Budget, through Ministry of Surface Transport.	Constitution of SEBI General Fund, from grants of central government, fees and charges of SEBI and sums realized from penalties under Act.
Composition	Chairman and six members.	TRAI: Chairman, two full-time members, two part-time members. TDSAT: Chairman and two members.	Chairman and four members.	Chairman and two members.	Chairman and five members.
Appointment of Commissioners	By central government.	By Selection Committee established by central government.	By central government.	By central government.	By central government and RBI.
Removal of Commissioners	By central government following recommendation by Supreme Court.	By president of India, following recommendation by Supreme Court.	By central government, which can suspend Authority by Gazette Notification.	By central government.	By central government, with summary dismissal of professional members.

in its erstwhile combined policy maker-operator-licensor role had created the (previous) independent TRAI in March 1997, when the TRAI Bill was passed, only after its earlier intention to have an administrative-authority regulatory office within the DoT itself was frustrated by the Indian Parliament in 1995-6. The DoT took an adversarial stand. Almost every order of the TRAI was questioned and taken to the courts. The TRAI was finally terminated in late 1999 and reconstituted in 2000.

The TRAI Amendment Ordinance 2000 reconstituted the erstwhile regulatory body into two—the regulator TRAI, and a dispute redressal and adjudicatory body, the Telecom Dispute Settlement and Appellate Tribunal (TDSAT). The Amendment separated the functions of the new TRAI into three operationally distinct areas: (i) a set of recommendatory roles, (ii) a set of binding roles and (iii) tariff setting functions. Table 10.2 is a summary classification of functions of the (erstwhile and reconstituted) TRAI and the DoT.

Electricity Regulatory Commissions (ERCs)

There are now fourteen State Electricity Regulatory Commissions (SERCs) besides the Central ERC. The Orissa ERC is the oldest, established in 1996, and the CERC was created in 1998, through the ERC Act. The Central Commission regulates bulk electricity tariffs upto the boundaries of states and inter-state transmission tariffs. The CERC also has powers to license private investment in transmission, with the consent of the public sector Power Grid Corporation of India Ltd (PGCIL), which is a state monopoly. Tariffs for generation, transmission, distribution within a state, as well as purchase and supply, are regulated by the respective SERC. It is also a mandate for CERC to develop a competitive market for bulk electricity.

Tariff Authority for Major Ports (TAMP)

As in the other sectors, an anticipated shortage of capacity in ports and a paucity of public funds was expected to result in severe bottlenecks in an area deemed in the nineties to be critical to India's growth—exports. Private participation and investment was therefore considered essential.

To address the concerns of private operators of discriminatory treatment and charges by the incumbent Port Trusts, a port regulator—TAMP—was established in 1997. With the Port Laws

TABLE 10.2
Allocation of powers between TRAI and DoT
March 1997–January 2000

TRAI			DoT
Binding	Recommendatory	Absent	
Tariff setting.	Timing and need for new service providers.	Adjudication.	Licensing.
Arbitration between private service providers.	Terms and conditions of licensing.	Interconnection regimes. Revenue shares.	Adjudication.
Appeals may be to courts lower than high courts.			Service provision.
Quality of service regulation.			

January 2000 onwards

TRAI	TDSAT	DoT
Tariff setting.	Adjudication.	Licensing.
Mandatory recommendation requirement for government from TRAI.	Dispute resolution between DoT and private operators.	Policy on entry of players into telecom.
Authority to determine and change interconnection terms contained in agreements between two service providers.	Appeals directly only to Supreme Court.	

(Amendment) Act in April 1997, which repealed significant portions of the Major Port Trusts Act (1963), TAMP was vested with powers of fixing tariffs. There are now terminals, jetties, and other services being provided by major international port operators in many of the major ports. In the meantime, many private and public industrial enterprises, sensing the difficulty of ensuring timely movement of their freight cargoes through the major ports, decided to set up their own ports and specialized terminals. Intra- and inter-port competition is expected to increase rapidly (Patel and Bhattacharya 2000).

TAMP's purview is the most limited amongst the infrastructure regulators in India—it only has a tariff setting role and is not a sector regulator in any sense of the term. Its functions include framing scales of rates and conditions under which services can be provided by the individual port authorities, determine rates of lease of port property, and fix fees for pilotage and other services. It has no jurisdiction over the minor and private ports. TAMP, moreover, has no provision for enforcement of its orders, including powers to summon data or persons and to prescribe time limits for compliance of orders, as well as penal powers. The government (the Ministry of Surface Transport) is the appellate body for TAMP's decisions.

In an environment of increasing competition and market-based pricing, there is a real danger that TAMP's functioning is self-perpetuating, and actually becomes an obstacle to competitive pressures. Tariff fixation, moreover, still continues to be cost-based with an assured rate of return. Recommendations for a statutory levy of fees to be collected from major ports to make TAMP financially autonomous will only serve to increase port charges. An expansion of its role in coordinating the activities of various port related organizations like the Port Trusts, Customs, Container Corporation of India (CONCOR), and Central Warehousing Corporation (CWC) with a view to reduce charges is redundant and can be achieved more efficiently through market forces.

Securities and Exchange Board of India (SEBI)

One of the earliest legislations for the securities market in India was the Capital Issues (Control) Act of 1947. The Government of India formulated a draft Bill for Stock Exchanges in 1951, which was submitted to the A. D. Gorwala Committee for further discussions and sharpening. It submitted the Securities Contracts (Regulation) (SC(R)) Bill in 1954. The SC(R) Act was enacted in 1956, followed by a set of SC(R) Rules. The Companies Act was also enacted in 1956 to administer the setting up and composition of commercial firms. First set up in April 1988 as an advisory body, SEBI did not have statutory status for three years. Its interim functions were:

(i) Collecting information and advising the government on matters relating to stock exchanges and capital markets.

(ii) Licensing and regulation of merchant banks, mutual funds, etc.

(iii) Preparing legal drafts for the regulatory and development role of SEBI.

(iv) Performing any other functions as may be entrusted by the government.

The Pherwani High Level Group on the Establishment of New Stock Exchanges submitted its Report in 1991 and recommended the establishment of a unified regulatory body for the stock exchanges. A Presidential Ordinance promulgated on 31 January 1992 accorded SEBI statutory status as an autonomous body. The SEBI Act[20] was passed by Parliament on 4 April that year, to govern all the stock exchanges and a large part of securities transactions, deemed to come into retrospective effect from 31 January. Almost simultaneously, the 1947 CI(C) Act was repealed in May, and the office of the Controller of Capital Issues (CCI) was abolished. SEBI, as regulator, was set to take over from the CCI, the restrictor.

The SEBI Board is comprised of a chairman, two members from the ministries of the Government of India (GoI) dealing with finance and law, one from the RBI, and two other members, appointed by the GoI, who are professionals and have experience or special knowledge relating to securities markets. The GoI has the right to terminate the services of the chairman or any member of the Board. The decisions of the Board are by majority vote, with the chairman having a tie-breaking second vote.

The Board is bound by the directions given by the central government from time to time on questions of policy and the central government has the right to supersede the Board. The Board is also obliged to submit a report to the central government every year, giving account of its activities, policies, and programmes. Although the Board's decision can be appealed with the courts, given the delays and sloth of the judicial system, the de facto appellate body is the Ministry of Finance.

Section 11 of the SEBI Act provides that '...it shall be the duty of the Board to protect the interest of investors in securities and to promote the development of and to regulate the securities market by such measures, as it thinks fit'. It empowers the Board to regulate

---

[20] A relatively brief one with only 35 sections.

the business in stock exchanges, to register and regulate the working of stock brokers, sub-brokers, share transfer agents, bankers to an issue, trustees of trust deeds, registrars to an issue, merchant bankers, underwriters, portfolio managers, investment advisers, and such other intermediaries as may be associated with the securities market, to register and regulate the working of collective investment schemes including mutual funds, to prohibit fraudulent and unfair trade practices and insider trading,[21] to regulate take-overs, to conduct enquiries and audits of the stock exchanges, etc.

Penalties need to be very strict in the securities market.[22] An efficient and transparent securities market is impossible without the confidence instilled by a regulatory process that can swiftly detect irregularities and mete out deterrent punishment in a relatively short time. Contrast the convictions secured against the main accused in the Indian securities scam of 1992 to those of the traders of Barings Bank or Drexel Burnham Lambert.

Characteristics of Institutional Design for Implementing Effective Regulation

Despite the unique characteristics of each market or sector that a regulator must oversee, there are some unifying principles, congruence with which is likely to determine regulatory effectiveness in enhancing efficiency. Before we proceed to an assessment of regulatory institutions in India, it is worthwhile to tabulate a checklist of these principles that can aid in calibrating the individual assessments.

[21] One of Securities and Exchange Commission's (SEC) biggest tools is its power to reward informants with a bounty of up to 10 per cent of the monetary penalty of an insider trading action which is successful. This is an important incentive for people to speak up against colleagues and senior officials. It also allows the SEC to spread its dragnet wide enough to nab a curious assortment of insiders.

[22] Prudential Insurance Company of America has been convicted in the USA of deliberately training its agents to mislead, misrepresent, and defraud insurance policy holders. It was accused of unjust enrichment to the tune of US$ 2 billion by duping 10.7 million policyholders over 13 years. It also paid up a fine of $ 35 million for misleading policyholders, to return $ 410 million collected unlawfully from them and to pay $ 1 million as a fine for destroying documents.

Despite the relatively short institutional history of most regulators in India (except SEBI), it is still profitable to relate the effectiveness of their early actions and the (perceived) congruence with respective terms of appointment. The primary point of this chapter, one which bears tedious repetition, is that economic regulators, for the most part, are temporary institutions, whose importance should progressively decline with the evolution of competitive markets. The Securities and Exchange Commission of the USA sums it up nicely: 'Ultimately, only fair and vigorous competition can be relied upon to set efficient prices'. A measure of assessment will therefore be the flexibility built into their design that permits them to adapt to changing market structures.

Global experience indicates that a large part of the success of these institutions stems from their effective interaction with various other bodies—legislative, administrative, judicial, civil society, etc. A theory of regulatory institutions has to deal with the difficulty (transactions costs) of writing fully contingent contracts. The structures affecting regulatory outcomes include the distribution of regulatory rights among different levels of the government,[23] the objectives given to agencies and the voting procedures used to elect political principals, all of which influence regulatory decisions. These aspects are not normally discussed in the normative approach of public economics. Moreover, processes are critical to regulatory outcomes—the rules of the game are important, not just isolated specific frameworks. The timing of government intervention, the length and span of control of different regulatory bodies and the design of communications channels within the regulatory hierarchy affect the regulatory outcome.

---

[23] Even in countries with a relatively long history of independent regulation, like the UK, there are often multiple regulators overseeing different aspects of industry. In railways, for instance, besides the Office of the Rail Regulator (ORR), there were the Office of Rail Franchising (OPRAF), the Department of Environment, Transport and the Regions (DETR), the Treasury, the Health and Safety Executive (HSE), to name a few of the more important ones.

The securities markets in India are under the ambit of the RBI (government fixed income securities and Non-banking Finance Companies (NBFCs), SEBI (corporate debt, equity markets and other intermediaries and transactions), the Department of Company Affairs (registration, listing, etc.) and the Ministry of Finance. However, an independent regulator is not supposed to be part of the government—either executive or legislative.

The set of theoretical models in Section II were meant to guide the organizational and functional structure of the regulatory institutions. This segment maps the principles of design to these PA models. Some operational issues in the design of regulatory institutions are as follows:

1. The existing market structure and degree of competition, especially the presence of public sector incumbents.

2. The potential of introducing competition through reform of the market structure, with particular reference to the segments of individual sectors.

3. The degree of market contestability in the industry and barriers to entry, including the allocation of powers to award concessions and franchises in monopolistic segments.

4. Required changes in the existing legal framework, including separation of the licensing and service provision wings of government entities.

5. The time frame required for introducing suitable changes in the market structure.

Given these yardsticks of assessment, the following characteristics of institutional design in India can be used to assess the performance and effectiveness of regulators.

Rules versus Discretion

Regulatory uncertainty has become a deterrent in attracting private investment in many infrastructure segments. Electricity distribution is a notable example. Telecom, before the mid-course correction with the NTP 99 and the reconstitution of the TRAI, was another. The experience of the first TRAI is illustrative of the necessity of well-designated delineation of functional responsibility. Publication of tariff philosophies are in themselves inadequate to abate this uncertainty. Indian experience has been that, given the limited track record of electricity regulation, investors prefer to wait for an actual tariff order before participating in the competitive bidding for the award of a distribution zone. The experience of the Orissa ERC over the course of its first three Tariff Orders provides an interesting insight into the dynamics of interaction between the regulator, private distribution companies, the government of Orissa, and consumers.

Compatibility of Rules with Incentives

Most regulatory institutions cannot have rules to cover all cases: this constrains the evaluation of their performance solely in terms of their objectives at the time of their constitution. Moreover, rapid technology changes in many segments may make any fixed set of objectives other than the broad overall ones relating to principles of market structure actually a hindrance to further development of the sector. There is also the possibility of an inherent conflict between the institution and an individual in case of a flexible structure.[24]

Anti-trust and regulatory policy, as they evolved during the 1970s and 1980s, have come to reflect a pro-consumer orientation. Business activities that make life difficult for rivals typically only violate the anti-trust laws if they result in higher prices to final consumers, a reduction in product quality, or reduced innovation designed to lead to lower prices or better quality.

Decision-Making Process

Transparency in decision-making was mandated in the constitution of the first TRAI, and may have aggravated its conflicts with the DoT. Decision-making processes, with public hearings, inputs from concerned stakeholders, and detailed and well-reasoned decisions and orders are distinguishing characteristics of most of the new (utility) regulators from their administrative ancestors. The nature of securities market regulation being different, the procedures adopted by SEBI for implementing recommendations of committees, whose reports are made publicly available, is in consonance with practices of foreign securities regulators.[25]

Functional Independence of Regulators

In a country like India, with the extreme reluctance of the government to divest its control over important sectors, the independence of regulators attains an importance far beyond that necessary with

---

[24] The experience of rail regulation in the UK was a particularly striking example of this. The reported conflicts of personalities and regulatory philosophies of the Rail Regulator and the Chief of the Strategic Rail Authority, with their divergent views on the functioning of a privatized entity by itself and in the context of the UK's Integrated Transport Policy.

[25] The Financial Services Authority (FSA) of the UK has started to publish reasoned judgements on its website. The SEC's decisions are also reasoned, but mostly through background and discussion papers rather than in the judgements themselves.

436 • *Public Institutions in India*

a government with a market-oriented outlook. The essential question becomes: can the regulator control the government? The pattern of appointments to regulatory bodies enhances this perception with the bulk of chairmen and members being from a pool of persons having 'special knowledge of...administration'. Even when administrative experience is not a qualification, the default choices seem overwhelmingly from (retired) civil servants.[26] The drafting of regulatory legislations seem to make appointment qualifications more of an enabling clause for this pool.

Transfer of Functional Responsibilities from Government

A cursory reading of the legislative frameworks for regulatory institutions the world over makes one point quite clear—the effectiveness of regulation depends on the economic environment and government philosophy more than the jurisdictional ambit of the regulator. The key is the ability and willingness of the governments to institute appropriate market structures that are compatible with competition and incentives. In most countries, policy making functions are retained by the governments. The powers and penal recourse of regulators to the justice systems are also broadly similar.

One major shortcoming that is evident in the statutory composition of the members of the regulatory commissions in India, however, is the latitude allowed in their prescribed qualifications. The legislation almost uniformly can be seen to include an enabling provision for persons with experience in administration. The composition of current regulatory bodies reflects the exercise of the government's discretion with a majority of regulators being either retired or even serving civil servants. This, in conjunction with the dominant presence of public sector incumbents, is likely to skew the incentive structures of regulators to prevent the abuse of market power by incumbents.

Scope and Role of Regulators

The regulatory and development roles of the regulator are (often) conflicting objectives. The development role of regulation is one

---

[26] It can, of course, be argued that this practice is similarly followed even in developed countries like the US Public Utility Commissions and among UK regulators. The difference is in the ownership of infrastructure utilities in those countries by the private sector and the much higher standards of civil service accountability.

of the most argued and controversial issues of modern regulation. Regulation of utilities in mature economies and sectors may be very different from those in developing and shortage-ridden sectors, where the natural inclination of the regulator to promote investments will be tempered by concern with increasing user charges for consumers. As was evident most recently in the experience of the Kanpur zone privatization exercise in Uttar Pradesh, an inequitable and non-commercial distribution of current risks between the private supplier and the conceding authority served as a disincentive to attract bidders for the exercise.

The provision of universal access and subsidies to consumers unable to afford the full cost of service is another development function. Although subsidies should be from the general budget of the government, the regulator needs to make the needs for subsidy transfers explicit in its tariff setting process. It is important to stress that these are transition steps. The same network externalities that confer market power can be used to make an activity previously considered to be commercially unviable, a profitable proposition.

Self-Restraint and Exit

Regulation is widely recognized as 'at best...a pallid substitute for competition'. If regulation is required, the principle used to guide the regulatory approach should be one that seeks to mimic competition.[27] Simple, traditional fully allocated cost methodologies while engaging the regulator in lengthy accounting exercises—including the need to establish a consistent cost-accounting methodology for each of the regulated activities—need not result in either efficient or 'fair' prices.

It has to be emphasized again that regulation has costs, sometimes significant costs.[28] India's public institutional history shows

---

[27] An inept regulation strategy may seek to put too much of the cost-burden on services with more elastic, rather than less elastic, demand and result in a non-viable supplier. According to this 'Ramsey approach' to regulation, rates reflect both cost and value (demand) for the services being offered. When economies of scale and scope, the basis for a need to regulate, are present, setting rates based either on the direct (incremental, marginal) cost of each service separately ensures that the regulated firm(s) will not be viable.

[28] There are diverse estimates of the costs of regulation in the USA. The Cato Institute's estimate, obviously to be considered cautiously, is of the order of $ 45 billion annually.

that it is difficult to shut down these institutions once their task is done. There is a danger that this might also happen with regulatory institutions by arrogating to themselves an ever-increasing scope of functions, responsibility, and authority. The structure of the sectors under the ambit of regulators is changing rapidly, both securities and utilities. Although there will probably be a perpetual need for financial sector regulators, in view of the special risk characteristic of this sector in aiding a systemic collapse, increasing competition in most other sectors is likely to obviate the need for a regulator/watchdog body. Indeed, the design of the regulatory agency itself should encourage it to introduce competition wherever feasible, or to introduce procedures (like auctions) that mimic the results of competition.

There is also the potential of regulators trying to entrench themselves and their offices (Lal 1999). Given the composition of many of the regulatory agencies in India, with a bias towards staffing these bodies with retired or serving members of the administrative services, and the persisting reluctance of the government to relinquish its control over large segments of the economy, there is a real danger in increasing regulatory jurisdiction.

TAMP is an example of a regulatory institution which should be programmed to cease existing with the ongoing process of inter- and intra-port competition. A look at TAMP's tariff orders shows rates for thousands of diverse commodities, services, and port facilities. The process of corporatization of major ports, concessioning port activities and terminal facilities, and the emergence of many privately owned and operated minor ports, even as of date, serves to make most of TAMP's activities irrelevant, at best, and a hurdle to competition, at worst.

Regulatory Jurisdiction

The increasing convergence and seamlessness of service provision amongst different sectors of communications—telecom, cable, broadcasting, media—has given rise to debate on the need for a single regulator for these activities. The Group of Ministers has recently cleared a bill for setting up a Commissioner for Communications. It had earlier been proposed that the (new) TRAI would evolve into the Carriage Commissioner (as part of this Commission) and there would be an additional Content Commissioner.

There is similar debate on the need for a single regulator for the financial sector, patterned on the lines of the UK's Financial Services Authority (FSA), given the increasing integration of financial services, banking, and capital markets the world over.

IV. EXPERIENCE AND ASSESSMENT OF REGULATION IN INDIA

Traditional regulatory perspectives, with their broad categorization of regulation v. deregulation, competition v. monopoly, etc., are not very helpful guides to an assessment of regulation in India. The power of the government and public sector incumbents to influence policies and the course of development of the sector is of an order of magnitude that is rarely found in most other countries of the world. Analysis of regulation in India has to account for these specific ownership and licensing structures.

Congruence of Design Principles with Economic Theory

Table 10.3 below summarizes the effectiveness of regulators in mitigating specific sector inefficiencies in terms of a mapping between the broad categories of market failures presented in Section II and design features of Section III. We have split the manifestations of each category of economic problems into the infrastructure sectors and the securities markets, given that the nature of the two markets are very different. Underlying both, however, is the premise that inefficiencies arise, in one sense or the other, due to improper (and inadequate) information flows.

It needs to be pointed out that individual failures may arise out of a combination of the specific models. The one-to-one mapping is merely a stylistic device to enhance clarity by assigning to specific instances of problems or market practices a preponderant form of failure.

The manifestations of information failures in securities markets are the scandals and scams that have abounded not just in India, but globally. In developed country markets, most of regulatory attention is devoted either to prospective insider trading and mergers and takeovers. While insider trading is a quintessential moral hazard problem, in that some actions of players are not revealed to markets, manipulation can be an active signalling game as well. The widespread use of Information Technology has made markets more

TABLE 10.3

Assessment of the effectiveness of Indian regulators mapping
the economic need for regulation to the design of regulatory institutions

Sectors	Outcome of market failure	Objectives of regulation	Instruments available to regulators	Were instruments used to the limits permitted?
Economies of Scale and Scope				
Electricity	Natural monopolies in transmission and distribution.	Mitigate monopoly pricing.	Price/revenue caps. Competitive bidding for transmission concessions.	Transmission Tariff Order in 1999.
Telecom	Pre-specified standards (GSM) for cellular service provision has the potential to lock in inefficient technologies due to network externalities.	Enabling the provision of the most efficient technologies to the consumer.	A single license for spectrum usage with choice of technology left to operator.	To a large extent now.
Adverse Selection				
Electricity	Wrong generating plant location leads to sub-optimal investment decisions (for example, locating a thermal plant far away from a coal pit-head or gas head), inappropriate transmission lines (for example, Low Tension instead of High Tension).	Promoting investment efficiency.	Single-part unified tariffs for regulated monopolies. Appropriate price cap levels.	Initiated moves for competition in generation through Availability Based Tariff. Opted for two-part tariff over a unified one.

TABLE 10.3 *contd*

TABLE 10.3 *contd*

Sectors	Outcome of market failure	Objectives of regulation	Instruments available to regulators	Were instruments used to the limits permitted?
Telecom	Forbidding use of certain technologies (for example, Wireless in Local Loop (WLL) in favour of land lines in basic telephony), restricting delivery mechanisms (for example, Voice over Internet Protocol (VOIP)).	Promoting investment efficiency by cost-effective technology choice.	Recommendations to government (licensor) on the need for a unified technology-neutral telecom license.	Current TRAI has been encouraging this in Discussion Papers, and the concept of technology neutrality has been accepted by the DoT.
	Auction of licenses individually for separate telecom circles.	Allowing the most efficient aggregation of licenses.	Use multiple unit auctions to allow aggregation over geographic areas (circles).	TRAI has recommended the use of multiple unit ascending auctions for spectrum allocations.
Securities markets	*Primary stock markets.* Fraudulent Initial Public Offerings, vanishing companies, other securities fraud create a loss of investor (especially retail) confidence, and a consequent inability of good companies to raise resources from capital markets through primary issues.	Investor protection, coordination, and mitigation of systemic failure risks.	Enforcing entry conditions, net worth norms. Information disclosure. Penalties, civil (fines, de-licensing) and criminal.	Yes. To a large extent. To a very limited extent.

TABLE 10.3 *contd*

TABLE 10.3 *contd*

Sectors	Outcome of market failure	Objectives of regulation	Instruments available to regulators	Were instruments used to the limits permitted?
Signalling and Gaming				
Electricity	Attempts to preserve monopoly profits by stalling enhanced efficiency requirements (for example, NTPC's appeal against CERC's thermal station operation norms).	Promoting operational efficiency.	Tougher operational norms.	Promulgated operational norms, litigation to end soon.
	Non-responsiveness to incentives and penalties for grid indiscipline (for example, the responses of PGCIL, Uttar Pradesh Power Corporation Limited, NTPC, etc., to the apportioning of responsibility for the collapse of the Northern Grid in early 2001).	Promoting operational efficiency and systemic failures.	Penalties for deviating from grid code.	CERC threatened to levy stiff penalties for any future dereliction of operations code and lack of maintenance.
	Project cost enhancement (for example, padding of capital costs) following mandated rate of return (for example, a mandated 16 per cent rate of return on equity in generation plants).	Promoting investment efficiency.	Use of performance based (incentive) regulation.	CERC uses a mixed cost-performance approach to tariff setting, with larger emphasis on costs.

TABLE 10.3 *contd*

TABLE 10.3 *contd*

Sectors	Outcome of market failure	Objectives of regulation	Instruments available to regulators	Were instruments used to the limits permitted?
	Desire for revenue maximization of the government leads to unrealistic valuations of existing assets (for example, Orissa distribution companies privatization).	Ensuring a detailed and credible due diligence exercise by bidders.	Enunciating a comprehensive regulatory philosophy of cost and capital accounting in tariff setting.	CERC has issued two concept papers on depreciation and calculation of rates of return. Orissa ERC has issued four tariff orders, incorporating its philosophy for distribution companies.
	Wrong zoning choices in distribution privatization (for example, carving out mixed agricultural and urban zones instead of segregating urban areas, with an implicit intention of concealing distribution losses).	Rapid and transparent privatization procedures to minimize losses.	Appropriate tariff and incentive structures to attract private investors. Impose metering requirements.	Use of mixed cost-plus and performance rules, but emphasis on former.
	Preventing market contestability (for example, PGCIL's right to refuse entry of private utilities (PTUs) into transmission).	Encourage competition for the market.	Allow PTUs to compete for transmission concessions.	This is a policy issue, but the CERC has been advocating this change in the Draft Electricity Bill 2000.

TABLE 10.3 *contd*

TABLE 10.3 contd

Sectors	Outcome of market failure	Objectives of regulation	Instruments available to regulators	Were instruments used to the limits permitted?
Telecom	Demand for preferential treatment by public sector incumbent citing social obligations (for example, DoT's request for concessions and levy of Universal Service surcharges for providing access to remote areas).	Least-cost service to uneconomic areas.	Minimum subsidy bidding for rural and remote areas.	TRAI has suggested the use of minimum subsidy bidding as a possibility for Universal Service, but it needs to be more assertive.
	Preventing market contestability (for example, MTNL's granting of very limited Points of Interconnection over land lines to cellular operators in Delhi, or the attempts by cellular operators to restrict limited mobility (WLL) basic services).	Reducing market power of incumbent utilities and public sector companies.	Grant of open access rights and uniform pricing for third parties as for own services.	TRAI has started the process of determining access and interconnection and call termination in various telecom segments (local, long distance, basic, and cellular).
	Unfair competition (for example, using incumbent profits to cross-subsidize other activities, as is being claimed for MTNL's cellular service pricing decisions).	Non-discriminatory pricing of access to services.	Separation and ring-fencing accounts for individual services.	TRAI has mandated account separation for MTNL's entry into cellular services.

TABLE 10.3 contd

TABLE 10.3 *contd*

Sectors	Outcome of market failure	Objectives of regulation	Instruments available to regulators	Were instruments used to the limits permitted?
	Collusion among bidders and cartelization among service providers (for example, very similar and high rates of the restricted numbers of cellular providers).	Prevention of oligopolistic rent extraction.	Well-designed auctions to divest public assets and award licenses and concessions.	The use of auctions is being proposed for a range of concessions and sales.
Securities Markets	*Secondary stock markets.* Market manipulation and fraudulent practices (for example, price rigging in equities markets, front running and insider dealing in mutual funds).	Coordination, non-price discrimination.	Automated trading, rolling settlements, dematerialized (electronic) share transfers, futures and forwards markets.	Although many measures towards transparent share operations have been instituted, a more aggressive inclusion of stocks is needed.
	Non-transparent takeovers and mergers and acquisitions proceedings.	Ensuring non-discriminatory practices for shareholders.	Notification procedures, clear open offer rules.	Although rules are in place, there are a lot of opacity in operations of promoters and majority stakeholders.

TABLE 10.3 *contd*

TABLE 10.3 *contd*

Sectors	Outcome of market failure	Objectives of regulation	Instruments available to regulators	Were instruments used to the limits permitted?
Moral Hazard and Hidden Actions				
Electricity	Low maintenance investment (for example, non-replacement of faulty governors and frequency relays by various transmission entities was a key contributory factor of the Northern Grid collapse, in contravention of CERC guidelines under its grid Code).	Promoting operational efficiency.	Long-term concessions with periodic re-bidding and incumbent getting full value even if it loses to entrant.	No, partly because of dominant public sector transmission utility making penalties ineffective.
	Long-term administratively determined PPAs (inexperience of public sector buyers in negotiating commercial terms with IPPs leads to locking in expensive power for long periods, when new technologies can deliver cheaper power, for example, Dabhol Power Company in Maharashtra).	Promoting operational efficiency.	Migrate to competition, use auctions to assess stranded costs, imposition of Competitive Transition Charges.	Maharashtra ERC ordered its Electricity Board to strictly follow merit order scheduling of its electricity supplies, taking power from cheap sources first.
Transport	Accidents (airlines, railways) (for example, non-accountability of railways to passengers leads to under-investment in safety systems).	Promote safety.	Inspection and surveillance, delicensing.	The proposed Civil Aviation Authority of India is tasked with enforcing safety standards.

TABLE 10.3 *contd*

TABLE 10.3 *contd*

Sectors	Outcome of market failure	Objectives of regulation	Instruments available to regulators	Were instruments used to the limits permitted?
Securities Markets	Insider trading (personal profiteering and information arbitrage lowers investor confidence in markets, and leads to problems of governance, for example, SEBI's prosecution of a top Indian FMCG company's executives and directors of trading on inside information).	Market integrity and robustness.	Recommend criminal proceedings and levy civil penalties.	Market surveillance still weak and enforcement not adequate.
	Conflicts of interest (multiple activity firms can use non-price discriminatory practices to develop business of high net worth individuals or favoured corporates. For example, the recent decision of the SEC to force accountancy firms to separate their consulting activities from audit. Credit ratings agencies and investment banks face similar conflicts of interest).	Transparency in business practices and good governance.	Discourage non-price discrimination. Separation of AMC from holding company for mutual funds. Disclosure of interests in ancillary activity. Mark to market accounting practices.	Many measures are formally in place, but poor enforcement often creates lax adherence to mandated practices.

transparent and frauds easier to track down, and therefore, in developed markets, active manipulation of markets is a relatively rare phenomenon.

Manipulation of securities is much more widespread in markets that have inadequate penalties or disclosure requirements, primarily the former. Price manipulations are even more widespread in thin markets—this is one area where policy can aid in adding depth and liquidity. Applications of the models to infrastructure utility inefficiencies is more novel. An example of a moral hazard problem recently created headlines in India after the collapse of the Northern Regional Grid due to the 'islanding' and frequency mismatches created by the snapping of a transmission link in a segment with overproduction of electricity in one zone of the grid and overconsumption in another. Each player was pursuing his own agenda (objective function) but the outcome for the system was very suboptimal. The actions of the DoT in the face of the erstwhile TRAI's decisions, or of NTPC vis-à-vis CERC, are illustrative of this class of signalling and gaming models.

Assessment of Regulatory Institutions in India: Effectiveness and Design

Independent regulatory institutions have now become part of India's language of economic reform. However, in our national enthusiasm for things, there is a danger of overemphasis on regulation, to the detriment of the development of competitive markets. Such markets are now possible in the overwhelming majority of economic activity, thanks both to new technology and information systems and our understanding of the theory of contracts and incentives. The absence of an overt price discovery activity need no longer be a constraint on discovery of value—there are contract mechanisms now available that can extract or mimic this discovery.

There are two sets of issues that will need to be addressed in any such assessment:

(i) The performance of the institutions relative to the objectives set out for them.

(ii) The design of these institutions themselves.

Our focus in this chapter is an assessment of the functioning of the regulators. An assessment of their design is a much more ambitious task, a formal treatment of which will predominantly be delegated to later development of the chapter. This chapter contains isolated remarks on the design of the institutions, mainly due to the complex interactions of market structures and the terms of reference of the regulatory institutions.

Telecom

The process of restructuring and opening the telecom sector to competition began early in the nineties, and its flawed premises delayed meaningful progress in the sector for almost half a decade. The National Telecom Policy 1994 (NTP 94) expressed the government's intention of introducing competition in various telecom services and increasing the availability of telephones in India. A flawed understanding of telecom markets and a consequently poor sequencing of reforms resulted in a conspicuous lack of any progress of its objectives. Its most damaging impact was in its ignoring trends that were even then becoming quite evident that many telecom services were amenable to competition. The decision to award basic (fixed land-line) licenses through auctions failed to foresee the number of potential providers of telephony that would have entered the markets. The government's decision to auction cellular mobile licenses in 1995 was a radical departure from its practice hitherto of awarding the rights to service provision through administrative and negotiated routes.[29] The trouble was a totally wrong choice of the auction method that led to interminable litigation and defaults of the license fees, as well as an inappropriate pricing of the use of (the scarce public property) radio-frequency spectrum (Bhattacharya 2000).

Defaults on the license fees started right after the completion of auctions. While cellular service providers remained on track on their subscriber targets, revenues were much below expectations. Given the nature of fees imposed on the cellular providers, on the basis of handsets and cellular antennae, there was a built-in disincentive for increasing subscriber base, and concentrating on per-subscriber revenues. Roll out of basic services were also delayed by an inability to arrange for the substantial investments required after the payment of license fees.

The first TRAI's actions have been one of the most transparent in India. It set the standards (along with the OERC) of following a

[29] Memoranda of Understanding (MoUs) as they are called.

systematic procedure of decision-making with detailed consultation papers on issues and tariff philosophies, a series of public consultations and hearings and, finally, reasoned and documented orders. The experience of the telecom sector bolsters the need for a clear division of jurisdictions of the regulator and the government. The ambiguities in the TRAI Act were compounded by the fact that TRAI had been constituted much after the entry of private players in the telecom sector and the subsequent contracts. Its troubles started with the DoT adopting an aggressive stance against what it presumed was an arrogation of its powers of policy making by TRAI. The TRAI's interpretation of the Act deemed it to have a wide range of powers. There were two issues that permeated these differences—interconnection and revenue sharing. The DoT took the position that the TRAI had no jurisdiction over the existing contracts and arrangements which it held were in the domain of policy making and hence under its own ambit.

Four cases were filed against TRAI's decisions in the high courts over 1997 through 1999—the stay on DoT's grant of a license to MTNL for metro cellular operations, disputes regarding licenses for Internet Service Providers (ISPs), TRAI's jurisdiction over interconnection regimes, and over revenue sharing 'arrangements'. TRAI's proposal to shift to a Calling Party Pays (CPP) regime for calls from fixed phones to cellular subscribers had been opposed both by DoT and cellular providers, albeit for different reasons. This followed a significant amount of resistance from consumer groups to its tariff order of 1999 where it increased its fixed rental charges while lowering call tariffs and another NGO challenged the CPP order as well.

There was also the question of the TRAI's role in dispute redressal. After the New Telecom Policy 1999 (NTP 99), the government issued a Gazette Notification specifying that the TRAI was assigned the role of an 'arbitrator' in disputes between the licensor (DoT) and any licensee (service provider). These proceedings, however, would be governed by the Indian Arbitration and Conciliation Act 1996. The TRAI felt that this was inconsistent with the provisions of the TRAI Act which (in their view) empowered TRAI with a range of powers (to adjudicate) that include summons, examination of documents, receipt of evidence, etc., which arbitration powers do not confer. It insisted that the Notification required an amendment of the TRAI Act itself.

The final straw was the decision of the Delhi High Court in January 2000 striking down two TRAI orders—issued in May and September 1999, respectively—on an interconnection regulation overriding existing license agreements between the government and service providers and then on the revenue sharing regime between fixed and cellular operators. The Group on Convergence had already begun drafting the re-constitution of TRAI and an Ordinance based on the recommendations of the Group was promulgated in January 2000.

Recognizing the shortcomings of the NTP 94, both in terms of the slow pace of investments in the sector and the ongoing tussle with TRAI, the government formulated the NTP 99. At the same time, the first steps to corporatizing DoT were initiated, and the Department of Telecom Services (DTS) was made a separate entity from the parent (policy making and licensing) DoT.

Assessing the success of TRAI's actions is difficult. Its very public disagreement and litigation with the DoT might well have served to hasten a major reform of a sector in complete disarray, with the formulation of the NTP 99. Media publicity of the differences led to increasing public awareness of the failings of the DoT, and its service arms. The NTP 99 acknowledged failure of the process of awards of fixed and cellular licenses, and migrated private sector service providers from up-front license fees to revenue sharing with the government. There is a fairly widespread opinion that the TRAI may have been able to leverage its weaker position vis-à-vis the DoT with an aggressive enforcement of quality of service, rather than persisting in defending its rights of regulating interconnection and revenue shares.

Electricity

One of the remarkable features of the investigations following the collapse of the Northern Grid on 2 January 2001 was the notable absence of the Central Electricity Regulatory Commission in the proceedings. This was symptomatic of the lack of importance attached to the CERC by the public sector enterprises in the electricity business.

Amongst the utilities, the generation segment of electricity was one of the first to be opened to private sector participation, with an Amendment to the 1948 Electricity Supply Act in 1991. A decade after an initial rush of Memoranda of Understanding (MoUs) between Independent Power Producers (IPPs) with the government failed to translate into any significant investments, the realization has sunk in that augmentation of generation capacity would not occur without reforms in the distribution and supply segments of the industry. The CERC and the various SERCs have complementary roles in increasing the viability of the sectors.

Realizing the unsustainability of the situation arising from the recurring and huge losses of the State Electricity Boards (SEBs), and the political unwillingness to either increase tariffs or reform the existing SEBs, the governments, central and state, hit upon the idea of establishing independent Electricity Regulatory Commissions. An underlying motive was the desire to distance the political executive from the inevitable and unpopular hikes in tariffs, as one of the means of increasing revenue generation.

One of the biggest disappointments about the role of the CERC has been its failure to develop a competitive market for bulk electricity. Bulk (or wholesale) electricity refers to the matching of big suppliers of electricity, like the National Thermal Power Corporation (NTPC), National Hydroelectric Power Corporation (NHPC), etc., to the bulk buyers of electricity, mostly SEBs or their successor entities. The admonition above, undoubtedly, should be amply qualified. The CERC has started the process: its Availability Based Tariff (ABT)[30] Order and Indian Electricity Grid Code is meant to instil a degree of grid discipline in the rampant flouting of norms. A system of merit order despatch, whereby the cheapest producer of electricity is despatched to the grid, was designed to induce SEBs to schedule and dispatch power in a rational manner. High Unscheduled Interchange (UI) charges, imposed on deviations from contracted demand and supply, were meant to reinforce this discipline.

While evidently constrained by the state of the sector, it is likely that it could have adopted a more activist role in influencing policy positions. What are the constraints in the development of bulk markets? A stated power shortage scenario, especially peaking power shortage, is one.[31] Consistent under-investments in transmission

---

[30] The ABT is a two-part tariff that consists of a capacity charge and an energy charge. The SEB plants are considered as sunk costs and electricity scheduling was purely on the basis of costs of generation, which led to inefficient plants being dispatched first.

[31] The strong caveat, of course, is that there are no firm commercial estimates of power demand, given the excessively skewed tariffs for different segments of power purchasers.

systems, and lack of linkages between different grids, rampant grid indiscipline, lack of hard budget constraints on different public sector entities that make them unresponsive to incentives and penalties,[32] and the complete absence of a commercial approach to transactions are formidable hurdles for any regulator. Buyers, too, have no incentives to source the cheapest available power.

Had the CERC been more successful in establishing bulk power markets, its scope of functions would have been significantly reduced although it would still be tasked with regulating inter-state transmission tariff. Many of these changes in the structure of the electricity market had been mandated or enabled in the draft Electricity Bill 2000, which has been passed.

A feature of the ERC Orders that deserves praise is the universal adoption of the public hearings route to decision-making despite this not having been mandated in the ERC Act.

Capital Market

The technology used in India's capital markets today is some of the best in the world. The establishment over time of the NSE, the National Securities Clearing Corporation of India (NSCCL), the National Securities Depository Ltd (NSDL), the Central Securities Depository Ltd (CDSL), Stock Holding Corporation of India Ltd (SHCIL), etc., has put in place high quality institutions as well. Although the credit for these institutions must mainly be given to market intermediaries, SEBI played a part in providing the motivation for their establishment by progressively instituting market best practices in trading, delivery, and settlement. The fortuitous development of the National Stock Exchange as a competitor to the Bombay Stock Exchange, Mumbai, aided SEBI immensely in these objectives.

SEBI has moved on a large number of fronts. Its primary concern has, rightly, been the equity markets as this is the operational ambit of a large section of capital market intermediaries. Electronic screen-based trading, dematerialization of securities, and rolling settlements have made the equities markets more safe and transparent and dramatically reduced the amount of speculative trading and

---

[32] The public ownership of both generators and buyers of power make penalties meaningless and merely transfers between various organs of government.

price rigging. Has SEBI been aggressive enough? A chorus of protests from brokers following the drop in turnover in those securities with mandated rolling settlement cycles forced SEBI into delaying the inclusion of other stocks into this format.

SEBI has also progressively increased the requirements of various market intermediaries to disclose information. It has to be noted that proprietary information in the intensely competitive segments of capital markets is what drives innovation and confers an advantage on efficient players. Forcing these institutions to divulge such information may be inimical to the growth of these markets. Balancing disclosure of information with ensuring proprietary ownership of information then becomes the basic challenge of securities regulation. On the whole, market perception is that the availability of the currently disclosed information needs to be disseminated more widely amongst investors.

There are also, quite often, mixed signals that emanate from the regulator and other branches of government. The recent conflicting decisions from SEBI and the Central Board of Direct Taxes (CBDT) of the Ministry of Finance on the tax incentives for Venture Capital companies was one such instance.

One critical aspect where SEBI has displayed unwarranted timidness is in a more rapid institution of derivatives markets. Part of the hesitation is understandable—prudence in the handling of instruments that involve significant leveraging.

Despite the institution of best practices, SEBI is widely perceived to be a relatively toothless regulator. The nature of securities transactions makes credible deterrence a key weapon against fraud. The number and magnitudes of the SEC's fines, as well as its active coordination with the US Department of Justice, is a pointer to the need for such punitive action even in a mature and (more) transparent market. The securities scandal in India in 1991–2 was an example. The gravity of its effect is still being felt with retail investors not having regained their confidence in the securities markets despite the strengthening of the regulator, SEBI, in the intervening period and the framework of prudential safeguards and information disclosure requirements now in place. Not a single major perpetrator has been punished. Relatively trivial fines let several involved institutions off the hook. More such fraudulent schemes have emerged since, and none has attracted harsh deterrent penalties. The unwillingness of retail investors to subscribe to securities issues is a major impediment for companies in raising capital.

CONCLUSION

Have independent regulators in India been white knights that came to the rescue of sectors that were being mismanaged by public sector monopolies? Or have they functioned as insidious de facto agents of government, perpetuating public sector control under a veneer of competitive forces?

It is difficult to pass a sweeping judgement on their effectiveness. Overall, they have not been fully effective—their performance has been varied. While this is due in part to the faulty design of these institutions, where they have not been conferred the required powers and given the appropriate instruments to enable them to fulfil their objectives, the primary failure has been the lack of attention to the reform of the market structure and an inadequate understanding of the nature of interaction between the market structure and the effectiveness of the regulatory process.

There was inadequate appreciation of the technological changes that were already driving changes in other countries and a lack of understanding of the possibility of competition inherent in these changes. The design of regulation was mostly conceived in terms of intrusive, cost-based behavioural models rather than incentive based. The costs of regulation were not appreciated. The regulators are not likely to attain their objectives of efficient delivery of services given their current resources.

Even in terms of their own (limited) objectives, the performance of regulators has been mixed. An important barrier for effective regulation has been the pervasive presence of public institutions which have used their incumbent advantages to delay the progress of competition in many sectors. They have nudged, at varying rates, their respective sectors towards greater competition. The legislations that set up the individual regulatory institutions have also provided variable leeway in fulfilling this objective.

It is obvious that the government has been reluctant to let go and relinquish its control. It has also drafted most of the legislations establishing the regulators with sufficient ambiguity to enable reversal or contest of regulatory decisions that it deems inimical to its interests. The qualifications prescribed for membership of the regulatory commissions almost uniformly include an administrative background, and this has been taken full advantage of, given the numbers of retired and serving civil servants in these commissions. Moreover, there is some evidence that a lack of suitable aggressiveness in their approach might prolong their existence more than is warranted by advances in competition.

The Securities and Exchange Board of India has been a notable success, partially due to its supervision of a sector where the government recognized the correct structure and devised, more or less, the right policies to foster competition and efficiency. Securities markets in India have been transformed beyond recognition. However, much more could have been achieved by more stringent punitive action. In its third year of existence, the Central Electricity Regulatory Commission has still not been able to make substantive progress on the establishment of a competitive bulk electricity supply market. The continued existence of the Tariff Authority for Major Ports is the least justifiable, given the current state of inter- and intra-port competition.

References

Armstrong, M., S. Cowan, and J. Vickers (1994), *Regulatory Reform: A Economic Analysis and British Experience*, Cambridge: MIT Press.

Berra, Yogi with Tom Horton (1989), *Yogi...It Ain't Over*, New York: McGraw Hill.

Bhattacharya, S. (2000), 'Competitive Bidding for Infrastructure Services', Mimeograph, Infrastructure Development Finance Company Limited, Mumbai.

Bhattacharya, S. and U. R. Patel (2000), 'Transport Pricing and Financing: Issues and Lessons for India', in Proceedings of UNESCAP-AITD Conference on *Transport Pricing and Charges for Promoting Sustainable Development*, New Delhi.

Datta-Chaudhury, M. (1990), 'Market Failures and Government Failures', *Journal of Economic Perspectives*.

Debreu, G. (1959), *Theory of Value*, New Haven: Yale University Press.

Laffont, J. J. and J. Tirole (1994), *A Theory of Incentives in Procurement and Regulation*, Cambridge: MIT Press.

Lal, Deepak (1999), 'From Planning to Regulation: The New Dirigisme', in *Unfinished Business: India in the World Economy*, New Delhi: Oxford University Press.

Stiglitz, J. (1987), 'Some Theoretical Aspects of Agency Policies', *World Bank Research Observer*, vol. 2.

11

A Rising Tide of Demands
*India's Public Institutions and the
Democratic Revolution*

SANJAY G. REDDY

I. INTRODUCTION

This is a volume on India's public institutions. However, public
institutions take shape in the context of social relations and political
economy. States are embedded in societies. This chapter argues that
India's public institutions function in the context of a shifting
pattern of social demands caused by its experience of a 'long
democratic revolution'. A factual and theoretical account of changes
in India's political economy is needed to illuminate this shift and
its implications.

The problem will be approached here by way of a 'macro-
history' of India's post-Independence political economy. This
'macro-history' will first offer an account of the glacial but
fundamental shift in India's political regime, originating in
widespread changes in social relations, which is called here
India's 'long democratic revolution'. Second, it will explore the
implications of this 'democratic revolution' for the nature and
scale of the economic and social demands on the Indian state,
and on its capacity to meet these demands. Third, it will
examine the future of India's public institutions in light of this
transformation.

458 • *Public Institutions in India*

II. A LONG DEMOCRATIC REVOLUTION?

From Mediated to Direct Appeal

India at its Independence established an electoral democracy in conditions of relative social 'backwardness', accentuating the extent of its apparent 'democratic exceptionalism'. However, India's democratic exceptionalism was in fact accounted for in part precisely by its backwardness, which led to a form of electoral politics that limited challenges from below. By most accounts, low levels of urbanization combined with the continued salience of dense ascriptive ties, interlocking social obligations, and widespread patron-client relations in rural areas, to define a political culture in which electoral power derived pre-eminently from the ability of local notables to mobilize votes on the basis of such ties.[1] The presence of this regime, which we will refer to as *mediated mobilization* was exemplified by a variety of features of Indian electoral politics in the first two decades after Independence. One such feature was the high proportion of rural landowners and members of dominant castes active in formal politics.[2] Another such feature was the dominance of the Congress party and the high prevalence of intra-party factionalism within it.[3] This reflected the relative homogeneity of interests among the political elite, embodied in a cooperative consensus within the Congress party over key elements of development strategy, combined with an element of conflict over rights to participate in the governing coalition.

By all accounts, the regime of mediated mobilization began to unravel beginning in the mid-1960s. In particular, a mounting although still nascent rural social transformation caused the undermining of the hold of the rural dominant castes over the electoral process, and created the social basis for challenges to Congress dominance.[4] This unravelling gained force through the 1960s,

[1] For example, 'Congress under Nehru relied on the personalized and caste-based networks of local bosses to deliver the support of the lower social orders in the rural areas' [Jalal (1995), p. 41].

[2] For evidence in this regard see for example Frankel and Rao (1990).

[3] See for instance Brass (1997), Manor (1997), Morris-Jones (1978), and Weiner (1967).

[4] Thus, for example, Kothari (1995) writes '...1962 revealed that new social formations had emerged as a result of shifts and mobility in the caste basis of politics. Both the rise of the Swatantra party—ideologically right wing but

leading to the loss of power in six states by the Congress in 1967. That this was more than simply a shift in the coalitional basis of existing patron-client politics is testified to by the ideological orientation of some of the new alternatives to the Congress (in particular the United Front government in West Bengal and the DMK government in Tamil Nadu, as well as arguably Charan Singh's Bharatiya Kranti Dal). These ascendant alternatives to the Congress provided a more direct appeal to new classes of voters who exercised a higher level of autonomous political agency than in the past.

Other evidence of the social foundations of the challenge to Congress dominance is offered by the mounting rates of electoral participation throughout India—most markedly in the states in which non-Congress governments came to power (see Table 11.1).[5] It is telling that the first state to elect a non-Congress government, Kerala, had by far the highest rate of electoral participation in the first four general elections (and fully twenty-five per cent higher than the all-India level in the first). Other states that mounted challenges to Congress governance in 1967 (in particular West Bengal and Tamil Nadu) also had sharply rising electoral participation rates in the preceding years (see Table 11.1). These facts lend credence to the view that greater autonomous political decision-making led voters increasingly to challenge existing dominant coalitions.

Underlying factors in the demise of the regime of mediated mobilization were the economic empowerment of a class of middle peasants in certain rural areas as a result of the Green Revolution, and arguably, increasing urbanization.[6] Congress support fell precipitously in urban areas between the general elections of 1952 and

socially drawing on rural awakening, particularly of lower-middle caste peasant groups that had been excluded by the dominant castes—and the considerably increased sway of the socialists, who had lately acquired a rural base among the Backward Classes, posed a new challenge to Congress hegemony.'

[5] On the role of the breakdown of the influence of rural notables and of mounting electoral participation in making possible the victory of non-Congress governments in West Bengal and Tamil Nadu respectively see Kohli (1997) and Washbrook (1989).

[6] On the role of the former in the rise of Charan Singh's Bharatiya Kranti Dal see 'Party Politics and Electoral Behavior: From Independence to the 1980s' in Weiner (1989).

TABLE 11.1
Rising electoral participation

Year	1952	1957	1962	1967	1971	1977	1980	1984	1989	1991	1996	1998
All India	45.7	47.7	55.4	61.3	55.3	60.5	57.0	64.1	62.0	56.7	57.9	61.9
Andhra Pradesh	44.7	43.9	64.7	68.7	59.1	62.5	56.9	69.0	70.4	61.4		
Arunachal Pradesh						56.3	68.6	75.5	59.2	51.3		
Assam	47.7	46.6	52.8	59.3	50.7	54.9	53.4	79.7		75.3	78.6	62.1
Bihar	40.5	42.9	47.0	51.5	49.0	60.8	51.9	58.8	60.2	60.4	59.5	64.8
Goa				68.4	55.9	62.8	69.5	71.8	58.2	42.4		
Gujarat			58.0	63.8	55.5	59.2	55.4	57.9	54.6	44.0	36.5	60.7
Haryana				72.6	64.4	73.3	64.8	66.8	64.4	65.8	70.8	69.2
Himachal Pradesh	25.3	37.6	35.6	51.2	41.2	59.2	58.7	61.5	63.9	57.4	57.6	66.5
Jammu and Kashmir				55.2	58.1	57.9	58.7	61.5	63.9	57.4	57.6	66.5
Karnataka	51.9	52.8	59.3	63.0	57.4	63.2	57.7	65.7	67.5	54.8	60.5	65.3
Kerala	71.0	66.6	70.6	75.6	64.5	79.2	62.2	77.1	79.3	73.3	71.2	70,7
Madhya Pradesh	45.0	38.0	44.8	53.5	48.0	54.9	51.9	57.5	55.2	44.4	54.5	62.8
Maharashtra	52.4	55.7	60.4	64.8	59.9	60.3	56.8	61.7	59.9	48.8	53.7	58.4
Manipur	51.0	52.7	65.3	67.2	48.9	60.1	81.7	85.7	71.8	69.7		
Meghalaya						49.9	51.2	54.5	51.9	53.6		

TABLE 11.1 contd

TABLE 11.1 *contd*

Year	1952	1957	1962	1967	1971	1977	1980	1984	1989	1991	1996	1998
Mizoram									58.3	58.6		
Nagaland								66.5	74.7	77.1		
Orissa	35.4	36.1	23.6	43.7	43.2	44.3	46.3	56.3	59.3	53.8	59.2	58.0
Punjab	55.3	55.0	65.4	71.7	59.9	70.1	62.7	67.6	62.7	24.0	62.3	61.6
Rajasthan	38.4	40.6	52.4	58.3	54.0	56.9	54.7	57.0	56.5	47.2	43.3	60.2
Sikkim							44.7	57.6	72.0	71.6		
Tamil Nadu	56.4	49.1	68.8	76.6	71.8	67.1	66.8	73.0	66.9	63.9	67.3	58.6
Tripura	47.7	64.7	68.0	74.8	60.8	70.1	80.0	77.3	83.9	67.3		
Uttar Pradesh	38.4	47.8	51.0	54.5	46.0	56.4	50.0	55.8	51.3	49.2	46.5	55.7
West Bengal	40.5	48.6	55.8	66.0	61.9	60.2	70.7	78.6	79.7	76.7	82.7	79.3

Source: Butler, Lahiri and Roy (1995), Rao and Balakrishnan (1999).

1967 although the all-India urbanization rate rose only marginally from 17.1 per cent in 1951 to 19.9 per cent in 1971.[7] Diminishing support for the Congress led to a crisis within the party ranks, embodied in the rise of a 'defectors market' among legislators after 1967 and ultimately the dramatic party split of 1969.

The epochal significance of the Congress party split of 1969 and the pursuant general election of 1971 is that it marks the end of the period of the *centrality* of mediated mobilization as a political strategy. Although mediated mobilization continued to be salient in subsequent Indian politics, these developments mark the gradual but determined emergence of a new and ascendant alternative logic of politics. In particular, Indira Gandhi chose to pursue centrally for the first time in India's post-Independence history a strategy of *direct appeal* to voters, unmediated by traditional patron-client relations. Whereas the 'Syndicate' of powerful regional party bosses was losing its ability to deliver votes to the Congress, Indira Gandhi attempted to use the same factors that were undermining its power to her own advantage. In particular, she de-linked the parliamentary from state assembly elections and chose to seek an electoral majority on the strength of her nationally charismatic political identity and a popular political slogan: 'garibi hatao' or 'abolish poverty'. Indira Gandhi's strategy, viewed as risky due to the Congress party's historically essential party machine being primarily in the hands of the Syndicate members' Congress (O), proved an astute reading of India's emerging new social conditions—a reading that rewarded her with a decisive victory.[8]

Indira Gandhi's strategy of mass politics was a pioneering instance on a national scale of the politics of direct appeal, but took place in a context in which mediated mobilization continued still

[7] The Congress share of the all-India urban vote fell from 45.6 to 38.2 per cent between 1952 and 1967 whereas it only fell from 43.2 to 41.6 per cent in rural areas (Weiner 1989).

[8] This first national effort at 'direct appeal' led to a marked rise in the Congress party's share of the vote between 1967 and 1971 from 38.2 per cent to 48.7 per cent in urban areas and from 41.6 per cent to 46.2 per cent in rural areas (Weiner 1989). The urban-rural differential suggests the comparative efficacy of the political strategy of direct appeal in urban conditions as compared to rural ones, in which the slowly changing character of rural society gave a substantial continuing role to mediated mobilization, even as it continued a slow and steady descent.

to be greatly influential. A central hypothesis of this chapter is that the last thirty years of Indian political life have been characterized by the gradual and now near-complete demise of mediated mobilization and its replacement by the strategy of direct appeal in all sections of the Indian polity.[9]

Toward 'Massified Mobilization'

Electoral conditions since 1971 have demonstrated the heightened significance of the politics of direct appeal and the demise of mediated mobilization making use of stable social structures. This is evidenced both in the changed qualitative content of politics (as discussed further subsequently) and in its increased quantitative volatility. One measure of the latter is that the level of 'swing' in Indian elections (defined as the 'increase or decrease in the Congress percentage of the vote between one election and the next') has been steadily increasing. Whereas 'the average swing till 1971 was 3.2 per cent, (in the interval from 1971 to 1995) this has more than doubled to 6.9 per cent' (Butler, Lahiri, and Roy 1995).

The progressive breakdown of traditional patron-client relations and their replacement by new social relations has continued to take place, if at a differential rate throughout the country [For the case of transformed agrarian relations in south Gujarat, see Breman (1985, 1993, 1996). For evidence on the decisively changed character of rural labour contracts in Uttar Pradesh, see Lanjouw and Stern (1991)]. Alongside this process of changing social relations through rural transformation has been that of changing social relations through increasing urbanization (rising from 20 per cent in 1971 to 23 per cent in 1980 and 28 per cent in 1999).

The rising average level of electoral participation rates since 1971 is a testament to the breakdown of mediated mobilization and the rise of direct appeal in Indian politics, as individual voters have come to believe that their votes have significance. Electoral participation rates among women, rural voters, uneducated workers, and lower castes in particular have risen sharply. In a departure from the experience of other democracies, rural voters are now more likely to vote than urban voters and lower caste voters are more

[9] Direct appeal refers here to the effort to gain the allegiance of voters on the basis of both their interests *and* their identities.

likely to vote than upper caste ones.[10] This unusual pattern, and sharp rise in rates of voting among otherwise disprivileged groups suggests an increasing sense among these groups that voting is a politically relevant act, that is suggestive of a shift from the politics of mediated mobilization to the politics of direct appeal.

The glacial but all important shift from the politics of mediated mobilization to that of direct appeal only partially describes the historic transition in the character of the Indian polity. In order to understand more fully the transition it is useful to introduce the concept of *massified mobilization*. Massified mobilization may be defined as the specific form of direct appeal to individuals that proclaims collectively shared interests or identity.

Since 1971, India's political system has increasingly seen the emergence of the politics of massified mobilization. In this form of mass politics, contestatory direct appeals are made to voters on the basis of imagined identities and interests, projected on a large scale. As with the demise of mediated mobilization and the rise of the politics of direct appeal in general, the pace of development of this form of politics has been gradual and uneven, but its rise is highly significant. In particular, its rise marks the supplementation (though not supplantation) of traditional interest-group politics with more broad-based and diffuse demands that emerge from mass politics.

A number of disparate facts concerning India's post-1971 political regime seem to cohere with this observation.

First, the spectacular rise of parties that make reference to collective identities—language, region, religion, and caste—is suggestive of the rise of the contestatory politics of massified mobilization in India. Political parties with an element of identitarian self-definition increasingly contest for the space of the mass polity.

The political trajectories of Tamil Nadu and Andhra Pradesh in the 1980s offer particularly stark examples of this phenomenon, which has been taking place throughout the country. Under M. G. Ramachandran and N. T. Rama Rao respectively, state power was captured symbolically for a linguistic group called 'Self-Respect'. Charismatic politics and cult of personality were amalgamated with a populist redistributive discourse (emblematized by such state programmes as 'mid-day meals' and 'two rupee rice') bespeaking the

---

[10] For substantiation of each of these claims, see Yadav (1999).

charismatic political figure's ostensible identification with the poor.[11] This combination proved a powerful formula for electoral success, in a manner and to an extent that would not have been conceivable in the era of mediated mobilization. In one way or another these figures still overshadow regional politics. In north India, the political regimes of Mayawati in Uttar Pradesh and of Laloo Prasad Yadav in Bihar have shared some of these elements—in particular the symbolic triumph of capturing state power for 'backward' classes—although both their regional and their redistributive dimensions have been comparatively muted.[12] The BJP also struggles to capture the 'symbolic centre' of state power for a shared identity on a national scale, partially so as to defend its comparatively upper caste constituency against strong redistributive claims, especially from lower caste groups, that may emerge from competing political identities.[13] Although the BJP has aspirations of mobilizing voters nationally, it is fair to say that the currently prevalent arena of massified mobilization is the state. This is hardly surprising. For instance, Yadav (1999) notes that

The rise of state politics has been viewed with considerable suspicion...as the beginning of political fragmentation if not balkanization of India. Such a reading fails to note that this development is a function of an aggregative rather than disintegrative process at work in our polity. It is better interpreted as the first step on the Indian path towards the creation of a mass society through the mechanism of competitive politics. In a continental size polity like ours, it is precisely by articulating rather than suppressing the distinctiveness of states that a context for massification is prepared.

III. IMPLICATIONS

The Political Economy of Fiscal Deficits

Through the early 1980s India was fairly successful at maintaining internal and external fiscal discipline. Since the early 1980s, the

[11] See for example Dickey (1993), Pandian (1997), Pinto (1999), Washbrook (1989). Following the classic Weberian postulate, in both instances the charisma of these leaders has proved partially transferrable to their successors.

[12] On the central role of the symbolic objective in backward caste politics see for instance Chandra (2000).

[13] For evidence of the BJP's comparatively upper caste support base see for example Jaffrelot (1998). On the extent to which this is changing see Yadav (1999).

fiscal deficits of the central and state governments together have shifted sharply upward (See Table 11.2), to a point where they are now among the highest in the world.

TABLE 11.2
Consolidated fiscal deficit of central and state governments
1960/61 to 1999/2000
(percentage of GDP at market prices)

1960/61 to 1964/65	1965/66 to 1969/70	1970/71 to 1974/75	1975/76 to 1979/80	1980/81 to 1984/85	1985/86 to 1989/90	1990/91 to 1994/95	1995/96 to 1999/2000
5.7	5.5	4.7	5.4	8.0	10.0	10.4	9.2

Source: Joshi and Little (1994), World Bank (1998), IMF (2001).

A more detailed view leads moreover to the observation that the rise in fiscal deficits is overwhelmingly due to a rise in consumption and interest expenditure. This may be observed in Table 11.3, which represents the changing proportion of the fiscal deficit of the Centre and the states made up by their 'revenue deficits', which are defined as the excess of non-capital expenditure over current receipts (tax and non-tax revenue from all sources including inter-governmental transfers). It may be observed from the table that whereas low revenue deficits or even revenue surpluses has been the norm, beginning in the early 1980s, central and then state revenue deficits have mounted sharply. Moreover, the rising share of the revenue deficit as a percentage of the fiscal deficit implies that capital expenditures have been falling rapidly as a share of expenditure over the period.[14]

It is not entirely easy to identify the budgetary origins of the rising revenue and fiscal deficits. For instance, it is quite clear that rising interest payments (both because of higher interest rates faced by government, and the effect of previously accumulated debts) have been a major component of the increased revenue deficits. The stock of debt of the state governments as a proportion of GDP has risen from 16.4 per cent in 1975-6 to 21.5 per cent in

[14] Lahiri (2000) finds that for the states as a whole, 'Capital expenditure as a proportion of total revenue receipts have progressively declined from 19.6 per cent to 11.5 per cent between 1980-1 and 1996-7'.

TABLE 11.3
Revenue deficit and fiscal deficit

Year	Fiscal deficit as % GDP (states)	Fiscal deficit as % GDP (Centre)	Revenue deficit as % GDP (states)	Revenue deficit as % GDP (Centre)	Revenue deficit as % fiscal deficit (states)	Revenue deficit as % fiscal deficit (Centre)
1970–1	2.01	2.83	0.04	–0.36	1.99	–12.72
1971–2	2.17	3.51	–0.02	0.20	–0.92	5.70
1972–3	2.58	4.66	0.13	–0.03	5.04	–0.64
1973–4	2.23	0.24	0.18	–0.36	8.07	–0.36
1974–5	1.63	2.74	–0.52	–0.98	–31.90	–35.77
1975–6	1.34	3.06	–1.14	–1.06	–85.07	–34.64
1976–7	1.71	4.15	–1.22	–0.31	–71.35	–7.47
1977–8	2.04	3.61	–1.00	–0.42	–49.02	–11.63
1978–9	2.44	4.93	–1.03	–0.26	–42.21	–5.27
1979–80	2.41	5.26	–1.28	0.57	–53.11	10.84
1980–1	3.01	5.85	–0.62	1.18	–20.60	20.17
1981–2	2.53	5.11	–0.77	0.17	–30.43	3.33
1982–3	2.70	6.53	–0.47	0.66	–17.41	10.11
1983–4	2.95	6.11	–0.10	1.09	–3.39	17.84
1984–5	3.37	7.05	0.36	1.42	10.68	20.14
1985–6	2.79	8.38	–0.19	1.99	–6.81	23.75
1986–7	2.99	8.40	–0.01	2.48	–0.33	29.52
1987–8	3.09	7.61	0.29	2.57	9.39	33.77
1988–9	2.68	7.30	0.43	2.48	16.04	33.97
1989–90	3.03	7.31	0.72	2.44	23.76	33.38
1990–1	3.19	7.85	0.90	3.26	28.21	41.53
1991–2	2.82	5.56	0.87	2.49	30.85	44.78
1992–3	2.68	5.38	0.68	2.49	25.37	46.28
1993–4	2.28	7.01	0.40	3.81	17.54	54.35
1994–5	2.64	5.71	0.55	3.07	20.83	53.77
1995–6	2.71	5.10	0.74	2.52	27.31	49.41
1996–7	2.67	4.90	1.18	2.40	44.19	48.98
1997–8	2.86	4.83	1.10	3.06	38.46	63.35
1998–9	4.15	4.54	2.29	3.43	55.18	75.55

Source: Anand et al. (2001), as drawn from GOI documents.
Note: States' include UTs. Minus (–) sign denotes surplus.

1999-2000.[15] Moroever, in this period, the average across states of interest payments as a share of revenue receipts rose from 9.4 per cent to 19.3 per cent.[16] However, the underlying causes of debt accumulation (even in a simple accounting sense) are more cloudy. Rising expenditures under various headings appear responsible although a meaningful assessment is difficult to make without detailed expenditure data that is not readily available. It seems likely, for instance, that a rising public sector wage bill (associated with the implementation of the Fifth Central Pay Commission recommendations) has been a significant contributing factor in the 1990s.[17] Similarly, large subsidies to power, water, and food consumption are likely to have been significant factors, although their respective role is difficult to isolate. Explicitly identified subsidies (which are only a small proportion of total subsidies) have increased significantly and consistently from the early 1970s to the present.[18] Table 11.4 shows the level of different explicit central government subsidies as a share of GDP and in relation to the revenue deficit over this period. Between 1971-2 and 1998-9 explicit central government subsidies rose from a level of 0.29 per cent of GDP to 1.41 per cent of GDP (reaching a peak of 2.15 per cent of GDP in 1989-90). From a negligible impact on the

[15] Anand, Bagchi, and Sen (2001). The authors note that 'The debt figures on which these ratios are based do not include contingent liabilities, like unfounded pensions or the loans of the public sector enterprises guaranteed by state governments'.

[16] Author's calculations based on Anand, Bagchi, and Sen (2001).

[17] Lahiri (2000) reports that 'The government wage bill in the states as a percentage of the respective state GDPs has gone up by 2 to 4 percentage points during the decade' and that 'For example, salaries as a percentage of GDP went up from 7.5 in 1990-1 to 8.9 in 1990-8 in UP, from 5.5 in 1990-1 to 6.7 in 1997-8 and further to 8.4 in 1998-9 in Rajasthan, and from 8.4 in 1993-4 to over 11 in Orissa in 1998-9. The Centre's salary bill went up by 78 per cent from Rs 14,895 crore in 1995-6 to Rs 26, 484 crore in 1998-9.' Moreover 'In some states overstaffing led to a ballooning of the wage bill even before the recent pay revision. In Assam, for example, wages and salaries for state government employees accounted for over 10 per cent of the GSDP in 1994-5, and the wage bill for the government rose by 13 per cent per year between 1986-7 and 1994-5.'

[18] Srivastava and Bhujanga Rao (2001) cite various estimates suggesting that hidden subsidies are double explicit central government subsidies, and on the order of twenty times explicit state government subsidies!

TABLE 11.4

Explicit central government subsidies and revenue

(Rs Crore)

Year	1	2	3	4	5	6	7	8	Total as % GDP	Total as % rev. def.
1971-2	47		54		5		34	140	0.285	142.5
1972-3	117		62		12		14	205	0.378	-126.0
1973-4	251		66		20		24	361	0.548	-152.2
1974-5	295		80		30		14	419	0.538	-54.9
1975-6	250		149		47		24	470	0.562	-53.0
1976-7	506	60	241		66		74	947	1.051	-339.0
1977-8	480	266	324		88		129	1287	1.261	-300.2
1978-9	570	342	375		59		129	1475	1.333	-512.7
1979-80	600	603	361	56	92		109	1821	1.500	263.2
1980-1	650	505	399	69	253		152	2028	1.405	119.1
1981-2	700	381	477	78	102		203	1941	1.145	673.5
1982-3	711	603	477	97	217		157	2262	1.198	181.5
1983-4	835	1042	463	93	118		198	2749	1.251	114.8
1984-5	1101	1928	518	100	135		256	4038	1.636	115.2
1985-6	1650	1924	603	128	271		220	4796	1.711	86.0
1986-7	2000	1898	785	144	229		395	5451	1.738	70.1
1987-8	2000	2164	962	174	393		287	5980	1.683	65.5
1988-9	2200	3201	1386	207	406		332	7732	1.826	73.6
1989-90	2476	4542	2014	233	881		328	10,474	2.147	88.0
1990-1	2450	4389	2742	283	379		1915	12,158	2.138	65.6
1991-2	2850	5185	1758	312	316	1425	407	12,253	1.876	75.3
1992-3	2800	5796	818	353	113	1500	615	11,995	1.605	64.5
1993-4	5537	4562	665	412	113	500	893	12,682	1.476	38.7
1994-5	5100	5769	658	420	76	341	568	12,932	1.281	41.7
1995-6	5377	6735	318	388	34		520	13,372	1.131	44.9
1996-7	6066	7578	397	468	1222		633	16,364	1.202	50.1
1997-8	7900	9918	429	536	78		644	19,505	1.287	42.1
1998-9	9100	11,596	573	602	1452		1463	24,786	1.410	41.1

Source: Srivastava and Bhujanga Rao (2001), Anand, Bagchi, and Sen (2001) and author's calculations.

Note: 1 = Food, 2 = Fertilizer, 3 = Exports, 4 = Railways, 5 = Interest, 6 = Debt Relief for Farmers, 7 = Others, 8 = Total. Negative (-) number indicates that revenue account is in surplus.

central government revenue deficit account (then in surplus) in 1971, explicit central government subsidies rose to account for 88.1 per cent of the substantial revenue deficit in 1989–90, falling to 41.1 per cent of the revenue deficit in 1989–90. The latter figure reflects the impact of rising interest expenditures from a sustained high debt stock as well as of reductions in the level of subsidies. It must be emphasized that implicit subsidies, on electricity, petroleum products, water, and many other factors are likely to be sizeable. When implicit subsidies are taken into account, subsidies are likely to account for the entire revenue deficit of government.[19] Insofar as implicit subsidies have moved conjointly with explicit subsidies, the trend of explicit subsidies is likely to give a strong indication of the trend of subsidies as a whole.

What accounts for this slow but definitive drift? The argument of this chapter is that the shifting nature of politics, and in particular its increasingly popular character, has led to a compounding of the common pool resources problem that potentially besets any public fisc. In an era of increasingly massified politics, it has become progressively more difficult to deny a share of public resources to newly politically active constituencies. At the same time, the political constituencies with traditional influence over the Indian state continue to have substantial influence, which makes it equally difficult to shunt them aside. This quantitative rise in demands occasioned by the structural transformation of the polity is accompanied by a qualitative factor: the contestatory nature of mass politics ensures the accentuation of the common pool problem underlying the drainage of the public fisc. Tax revenues also prove difficult to raise. This is partially because there are a limited number of tax handles available to the state in a developing economy with a small organized sector and a large unorganized sector that is relatively impervious to efforts at taxation. It is also because political demands manifest themselves in part as resistance to taxation. As the base of political demands widens at a more rapid rate than does the revenue base, the net result is an increasing fiscal deficit.

In a similar vein, Lahiri (2000) writes , commenting on the states' deficits, 'Populist policies, such as the supply of free power to farmers and cheap power to households, inadequate water charges, supply of subsidized rice, and the inability of states to mobilize additional resources promised at the time of formulating the

[19] See previous note.

five-year plans have contributed to the worsening of the fiscal position....'

IV. INDIA'S PUBLIC INSTITUTIONS AMIDST THE DEMOCRATIC REVOLUTION

The weakening fiscal position of the Indian central and state gov-- ernments over a lengthy period is only the most obvious manifestation of the impact of the rising demands engendered by the democratic revolution. Other consequences include increasing local struggle to acquire a share of the limited resources that are available to the state to distribute. Much of corruption, in this light, is simply the underbelly of the fiscal imperative of rationing. Increasingly widespread gaps in the provision of certain services (for example, electricity) equally reflect the inescapability of rationing in the simultaneous presence of widespread political demands for free or subsidized resources and severe fiscal constraints. These demands derive from the increasingly broad (though still minoritarian) organized constituencies as well as increasingly from contestatory mass politics.

Fiscal and service gaps can both be eliminated through a series of readily identifiable measures, from increasing cost recovery through increasing the tax take.[20] Properly speaking, these gaps reflect therefore not only the rising tide of demands but also the weakness of the state at carrying out the available compensatory measures. In India's case this weakness derives from two sources. The first is a phenomenon complementary to the rising tide of demands itself. Strong political constituencies resist imposition of taxes and cost-recovery as they believe (correctly) that costs can ultimately be substantially externalized on to others. The primary beneficiaries of subsidies, especially medium-sized and large farmers, public employees, and certain sections of industry, are organized constituencies on a sufficient scale in an otherwise disorganized polity to block corrective fiscal measures, although they are minorities when considered as parts of the larger electorate.

The second source of the weakness of the Indian state at undertaking revenue generation and cost recovery derives from the central structural feature of the Indian economy. This is its fundamental

[20] The exact balance between these will depend, inter alia, on income distribution goals.

and pervasive dualism. A relatively small organized sector supplies the most feasible 'tax handles' and provides the overwhelming majority of tax revenues (in the form of customs duties, excise taxes, corporation taxes, and income taxes). However there is an upper bound on the extent of individual tax burden that can realistically be placed on these sources, for both political and economic reasons. In contrast, it is not possible to generate substantial tax revenues from the vast unorganized and agricultural sectors without raising the level of their income and progressively drawing them into the ambit of formal sector activity. Short of combating the dualistic structure of the economy itself, through effective efforts at raising the incomes and capacities of the relatively excluded, the state cannot overcome this limit to its fiscal capacity.

These observations have significant implications for India's public institutions. In particular, they lead to the conclusion that Indian central and state governments can expect to continue to face a rising tide of potentially unperformable demands, which can threaten fiscal solvency and state capacity. There is no readymade technical or administrative solution to this challenge. Efforts to raise tax revenues and state capacity to meet the challenge of increasing demands must come to terms with the fundamental fact that increasing numbers of people are politically empowered to demand some share of available resources, and will do so, even if at times through less materially focused and more charismatic forms of populist politics. A plausible way to fill the resource gap is therefore to make these demanders themselves contributors, drawing them into fuller participation in a widened and dynamic taxable economy. In this way, the state can hope to generate the resources with which to sustain its promises.

This proposed trajectory has significant implications for public institutions. It requires that they must turn themselves toward providing progressive access for the relatively excluded to the more remunerative forms of economic opportunity, drawing them into an expanding circle of production that can ultimately generate both private incomes and tax revenues for the state. The wager that small islands of remunerative formal sector activity will by themselves provide the resources with which to fulfil the rising tide of demands emanating from a larger public has until now proven unrealistic, and there is no immediate reason to think that it will cease to be so. India's public sector institutions must therefore not only foster the development of such islands, but also become more truly *public*, fostering the productive capabilities of the broadest number. It may be hoped that in this way they can come to terms with the features of India's democracy that threaten to overwhelm them.

References

Anand, M., A. Bagchi, and T. K. Sen (2001), 'Fiscal Discipline at the State Level: Perverse Incentives and Paths to Reform', New Delhi: National Institute of Public Finance and Policy.

Bardhan, P. (1984), *The Political Economy of Development in India*, Oxford: Oxford University Press.

Baxi, U. and B. Parekh (1997), *Crisis and Change in Contemporary India*, New Delhi: Sage.

Béteille, André (1996), 'Caste in Contemporary India', in Fuller (1996), *Caste Today*.

Brass, P. (1997), 'National Power and Local Politics in India: A Twenty Year Perspective', in Chatterjee ed. (1997), *State and Politics in India*.

Breman, J. (1985), *Of Peasants, Migrants, and Paupers: Rural Labour Circulation and Capitalist Production in West India*, Delhi: Oxford University Press.

————— (1993), *Beyond Patronage and Exploitation: Changing Agrarian Relations in South Gujarat*, Delhi: Oxford University Press.

————— (1996), *Footloose Labour: Working in India's Informal Economy*, Cambridge: Cambridge University Press.

Butler, D., A. Lahiri, and P. Roy (1995), *India Decides: Elections 1952–1995*, New Delhi: Books and Things.

Chandra, K. (2000), 'The Transformation of Ethnic Politics in India: The Decline of Congress and Rise of the Bahujan Samaj Party in Hoshiarpur', *Journal of Asian Studies*, vol. 59, no. 2.

Chatterjee, P. (ed.) (1997), *State and Politics in India*, New Delhi: Oxford University Press.

Dickey, S. (1993), *Cinema and the Urban Poor in South India*, Cambridge: Cambridge University Press.

Frankel, F. and M. S. A. Rao (1989, 1990), *Dominance and State Power in Modern India*, two vols, Delhi: Oxford University Press.

Fuller, C. (1996), *Caste Today*, Delhi: Oxford University Press.

Hansen, T. B. and C. Jaffrelot (ed.) (1998), *The BJP and the Compulsions of Politics in India*, New Delhi: Oxford University Press.

International Monetary Fund (2001), 'India: Recent Economic Developments and Selected Issues', IMF Country Report No. 01/181, Washington DC.

474 • *Public Institutions in India*

Jaffrelot, C. (1998) 'The Sangh Parivar Between Sanskritization and Social Engineering', in Hansen and Jaffrelot (eds), *The BJP and Compulsions of Politics in India*.

Jalal, A. (1995), *Democracy and Authoritarianism in South Asia*, Cambridge: Cambridge University Press.

Jha, P. S. (1980), *The Political Economy of Stagnation*, Delhi: Oxford University Press.

Joshi, V. and I. M. D. Little (1994), *India: Macroeconomics and Political Economy, 1964–1991*, New Delhi: Oxford University Press.

Kalecki, M. (1972), 'An Intermediate Regime', in *Essays on the Economic Growth of the Socialist and the Mixed Economy*, London: Unwin.

Kohli, A. (1990), *Democracy and Discontent: India's Growing Crisis of Governability*, Cambridge: Cambridge University Press.

————— (1997), 'From Breakdown to Order: West Bengal', in Chatterjee (ed.), *State and Politics in India*.

Kothari, Rajni (1995), 'Interpreting Indian Politics: A Personal Statement', in Baxi and Parekh (ed.), *Crisis and Change in Contemporary in India*.

Lahiri, A. K. (2000), 'Sub-National Public Finance in India', *Economic and Political Weekly*, 29 April.

Lanjouw, P. and N. Stern (1991), 'Poverty in Palanpur', *World Bank Economic Review*, vol. 5, no. 1.

Manor, J. (1997), 'Parties and the Party System', in Chatterjee (ed.), *State and Politics in India*.

McCartney, M. and B. Harris-White (n.d.), 'The "Intermediate Regime" and "Intermediate Classes" Revisited: A Critical Political Economy of Indian Economic Development from 1980 to Hindutva', Queen Elizabeth House, University of Oxford, Working Paper QEHWPS 34.

Morris-Jones, W. H. (1978), *Politics Mainly Indian*, Madras: Orient Longman.

Namboodiripad, E. M. S. (1973), 'On Intermediate Regimes', *Economic and Political Weekly*, 1 December.

Pandian, M. S. S. (1997), 'Culture and Subaltern Consciousness: An Aspect of the M. G. R. Phenomenon', in Chatterjee (ed.), *State and Politics in India*.

Pinto A. (1999), 'Andhra Pradesh: Politics of Opportunism', *Economic and Political Weekly*, 4 September.

Rao, G. V. L. N. and K. Balakrishnan (1999), *Indian Elections: The Nineties*, New Delhi: Har-Anand Publications Ltd.

Rudolph, L. and S. H. Rudolph (1987), *In Pursuit of Lakshmi*, Chicago: University of Chicago Press.

Srivastava, D. K. and C. Bhujanga Rao (2001), 'Government Subsidies in India: Issues and Approach', New Delhi: National Institute for Public Finance and Policy.

Varshney, A. (1995), *Democracy, Development and the Countryside*, New Delhi: Cambridge University Press.

Washbrook, D. (1989), 'Caste, Class and Dominance in Modern Tamil Nadu', in Frankel and Rao (1989), *Dominance and State Power in Modern India*.

World Bank (1998), 'India 1998 Macro Economic Update', Report No. 18089-IN, Washington DC.

Weiner, M. (1967), *Party Building in a New Nation: Indian National Congress*, Chicago: University of Chicago Press.

——— (1989), *The Indian Paradox: Essays in Indian Politics*, New Delhi: Sage Publications Pvt. Ltd.

Yadav (1999), 'Electoral Politics in the Time of Change', *Economic and Political Weekly*, 21–8 August.

Contributors

ARUN AGRAWAL is Associate Professor at the School of Natural Resources and Environment (SNRE), University of Michigan, Ann Arbor.

SAUGATA BHATTACHARYA is Vice-President, Business and Economic Research, Unit Trust of India (UTI), Mumbai.

S.K. DAS is with the Indian Administrative Service (IAS) and is Member (Finance) Atomic Energy Commission and Space Commission.

DEVESH KAPUR is Director, Center iur the Advanced Study of India, University of Pennsylvania. He also holds Madan Lal Sobti Professorship for the Study of Contemporary India, University of Pennsylvania, and is Associate Professor, Political Science, University of Pennsylvania.

DEENA KHATKHATE is an independent researcher based in Washington.

K.P. KRISHNAN is Joint Secretary (Capital Markets), Ministry of Finance, Government of India.

JAMES MANOR is Emeka Anyaoku Professor at the Institute of Commonwealth Studies, University of London, and the V.K.R.V. Rao Professor at the Institute for Social and Economic Change, Bangalore.

PRATAP BHANU MEHTA is President, Centre for Policy Research, New Delhi.

URJIT R. PATEL is Executive Director, Policy, Infrastructure Development Finance Company Ltd (IDFC), Mumbai.

M. GOVINDA RAO is Director, National Institute of Public Finance and Policy (NIPFP), New Delhi.

SANJAY G. REDDY is Professor, Department of Economics, Barnard College, Columbia University, New York.

NIRVIKAR SINGH is Professor, Department of Economics, University of California, Santa Cruz.

T.V. SOMANATHAN is with the Indian Administrative Service (IAS) and is Secretary to Chief Minister (Monitoring) in the Office of the Chief Minister of Tamil Nadu.

ARVIND VERMA is Associate Professor, Department of Criminal Justice, Indiana University.

Index